The Archaeology of Identities: A Reader

The study of identity is rapidly gaining ground as a focus of archaeological enquiry, and has recently become a component in a variety of new and challenging developments.

The Archaeology of Identities: A Reader brings together 17 seminal articles from this exciting new discipline in one indispensable volume for the first time. Editor Timothy Insoll expertly selects a cross section of contributions by leading authorities to form a comprehensive and balanced representation of approaches and interests. Issues covered include:

- Gender and sexuality
- Ethnicity, nationalism, and caste
- Age
- Ideology and religion
- Disability

Chapters are thematically arranged and are contextualized with lucid summaries and an introductory chapter, providing an accessible introduction to the varied selection of case studies included and archaeological materials considered from global sources.

This volume will prove to be the definitive sourcebook in the archaeology of identities and essential reading for students, lecturers, and researchers in the field.

Timothy Insoll is Professor of Archaeology at the University of Manchester. His research interests include theoretical archaeology and African and Islamic archaeology. Previous publications include *Archaeology, Ritual, Religion* and *The Archaeology of Islam*.

The Archaeology of Identities

A Reader

Edited by Timothy Insoll

 Routledge
Taylor & Francis Group

LONDON AND NEW YORK

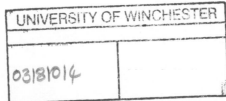

First published 2007
by Routledge
2 Park Square, Milton Park, Abingdon, Oxon OX14 4RN

Simultaneously published in the USA and Canada
by Routledge
270 Madison Avenue, New York, NY 10016

Routledge is an imprint of the Taylor & Francis Group, an informa business

© 2007 Timothy Insoll

Typeset in Sabon by Saxon Graphics Ltd
Printed and bound in Great Britain by The Cromwell Press,
Trowbridge, Wiltshire

British Library Cataloguing in Publication Data
A catalogue record for this book is available from the British Library

Library of Congress Cataloging in Publication Data
A catalog record for this book has been requested

ISBN 10: 0-415-41501-2 (hbk)
ISBN 10: 0-415-41502-0 (pbk)
ISBN 13: 978-0-415-41501-9 (hbk)
ISBN 13: 978-0-415-41502-6 (pbk)
ISBN 13: 978-0-203-96598-6 (ebk)

Contents

Contributors

Benjamin Alberti, Framingham State College, MA, USA.

Susan C. Andrews, AMEC Earth and Environmental Inc., Louisville, KY, USA.

Joanna Brück, University College Dublin, Ireland.

Elizabeth M. Brumfiel, Northwestern University, Evanston, IL, USA.

Robin Coningham, University of Durham, Durham, UK.

Morag Cross, Kirkintilloch, UK.

James P. Fenton, Wilbur Smith Associates, Lexington, Kentucky, USA.

Kelley Hays-Gilpin, Northern Arizona University, Arizona, USA.

Timothy Insoll, University of Manchester, UK.

Siân Jones, University of Manchester, UK.

Rosemary A. Joyce, University of California, Berkeley, CA, USA.

Lynn Meskell, Stanford University, Stanford, CA, USA.

Michael Rowlands, University College London, UK.

Joanna Sofaer, University of Southampton, UK.

Julian Thomas, University of Manchester, UK.

Barbara L. Voss, Stanford University, Stanford, CA, USA.

Tony Waldron, University College London, UK.

Alison Wylie, University of Washington, Seattle, WA, USA.

Ruth Young, University of Leicester, UK.

Acknowledgements

My foremost debt of gratitude goes to Rachel MacLean for typing up the chapters where needed, for completing the index, and for ensuring that all the errors and revisions were corrected as necessary. Though, obviously, the responsibility for any remaining errors or omissions is mine. I would also like to thank Jon Pickup for scanning the chapters and illustrations so efficiently and at long distance! I am also grateful to Richard Stoneman at Routledge for his assistance, and to Sarah Croucher for tracking down various elusive contact details. Otherwise, acknowledgements due the other contributors are appended, where necessary, at the end of their individual contributions; every effort has been made to trace copyright holders. Any omissions brought to our attention will be remedied in future editions.

The chapters in this volume have been reprinted through the kind permission of their authors and publishers, from the following original sources:

Meskell, L. (2001). Archaeologies of Identity. (In) Hodder, I. (ed.). *Archaeological Theory Today*. Cambridge: Polity. pp. 187–213.

Jones, S. (1996). Discourses of Identity in the Interpretation of the Past. (In) Graves-Brown, P., Jones, S., and Gamble, C. (eds). *Cultural Identity and Archaeology*. London: Routledge. pp. 62–80.

Rowlands, M. (1994). The Politics of Identity in Archaeology. (In) Bond, G.C. and Gilliam, A. (eds). *Social Construction of the Past*. London: Routledge. pp. 129–43.

Joyce, R.A. (2000). Girling the Girl and Boying the Boy: The Production of Adulthood in Ancient Mesoamerica. *World Archaeology* 31(3): 473–83.

Sofaer, J. (1997). Engendering Children, Engendering Archaeology. (In) Moore, J. and Scott, E. (eds). *Invisible People and Processes*. Leicester: Leicester University Press. pp. 192–202.

Wylie, A. (2002). The Constitution of Archaeological Evidence: Gender Politics and Science. (In) Wylie, A. *Thinking from Things: Essays in the Philosophy of Archaeology*. Berkeley: University of California Press. pp. 185–99.

Voss, B.L. (2000). Feminisms, Queer Theories, and the Archaeological Study of Past Sexualities. *World Archaeology* 32(2): 180–92.

Alberti, B. (2001). Faience Goddesses and Ivory Bull-Leapers: The Archaeology of Sexual Difference at Late Bronze Age Knossos. *World Archaeology* 33(2): 189–205.

Hays-Gilpin, K. (2000). Beyond Mother Earth and Father Sky: Sex and Gender in Ancient Southwestern Visual Arts. (In) Rautman, A.E. (ed.). *Reading the Body.* Philadelphia: University of Pennsylvania Press. pp. 165–86.

Cross, M. (1999). Accessing the Inaccessible: Disability and Archaeology. *Archaeological Review from Cambridge* 15(2): 7–30.

Waldron, T. (2000). Hidden or Overlooked? Where are the Disadvantaged in the Skeletal Record? (In) Hubert, J. (ed.). *Madness, Disability and Social Exclusion: The Archaeology and Anthropology of 'Difference'.* London: Routledge. pp. 29–45.

Thomas, J. (2002). Archaeology's Humanism and the Materiality of the Body. (In) Hamilakis, Y., Pluciennik, M., and Tarlow, S. (eds). *Thinking through the Body.* New York: Kluwer, Plenum. pp. 29–45.

Andrews, S.C. and Fenton, J.P. (2001). Archaeology and the Invisible Man: The Role of Slavery in the Production of Wealth and Social Class in the Bluegrass Region of Kentucky, 1820 to 1870. *World Archaeology* 33: 115–35.

Coningham, R. and Young, R. (1999). The Archaeological Visibility of Caste: An Introduction. (In) Insoll, T. (ed.). *Case Studies in Archaeology and World Religion.* BAR S755. Oxford: Archaeopress. pp. 84–93.

Brumfiel, E.M. (1998). Huitzilopochtli's Conquest: Aztec Ideology in the Archaeological Record. *Cambridge Archaeological Journal* 8(1): 3–13.

Brück, J. (1999). Ritual and Rationality: Some Problems of Interpretation in European Archaeology. *European Journal of Archaeology* 2: 313–44.

Insoll, T. (2005). Changing Identities in the Arabian Gulf: Archaeology, Religion, and Ethnicity in Context. (In) Conlin Casella, E. and Fowler, C. (eds). *The Archaeology of Plural and Changing Identities.* New York: Kluwer/Plenum, pp. 191–209.

Figures and tables

Chapter 1

Introduction

Configuring identities in archaeology

Timothy Insoll

Frameworks

Identity today is a 'hot' topic even though it might not be defined as such. Open a newspaper, watch or listen to the news and many of the stories are concerned with, essentially, the struggle of identity manifestations for a voice or for power, be they ethnic, religious, sexual, or related to disability, for instance. Equally, within the Western world (the primary but not exclusive focus of this introduction), related concerns centred around equality and diversity figure prominently, which again can predominantly be grouped within the umbrella remit of identities as well. However, archaeological contributions to this debate are rare, which is unfortunate, for 'debate' is not always the best descriptive term for what occurs, 'polemics' perhaps being sometimes more apt. This is regrettable, for archaeologists, through exploring themes such as past identities, their interactions, and the successes and failures of these interactions, could, importantly perhaps provide a new, or at least an alternative perspective. But it is from sociology or anthropology (see for example Barth 1969; Gellner 1983; Jenkins 1994), concerned as they are with current or recent identity groups, that examples are drawn, upon which theories are developed, and approaches to the study of identities formulated.

However, if we as archaeologists seek for a contemporary relevance for our work (see Meskell 2002: 281; Thomas 2004), this would appear to offer one area at least in which this could be found, and this is a subject which is further considered again later. Yet it should also be stated that the archaeology of identities is not some form of esoteric sub-discipline, rather it forms part of the total endeavour of archaeology, which Gosden (1994: 166) has described as 'part of a perilous, but necessary, search for the things that bind and divide human groups locally and globally'. For the issue is really whether one can actually have an archaeology that is *not* concerned with identity.

Hence this volume indicates, through the contributions chosen, that identities in many different manifestations are approachable via archaeology. However, this is a theme the selections herein are left to convince the reader of, and this introduction is instead concerned with assessing both what is meant by the term identity, and how the notion of identities in all their various forms has been used, and, indeed, misused by archaeologists and others. The emphasis is placed here upon assessing, primarily, definition and concept, as opposed to for example considering the history of archaeological approaches to identities, or what archaeologists have done and where. This is possible for these last themes have been adequately covered by others (e.g. Jones 1997; Schmidt and Voss 2000; Conlin Casella and Fowler 2005), and not least by Meskell in this volume (and see Meskell 2002).

Similarly it is also worth noting that the compilation of any Reader obviously reflects the editor's personal choice. There are clearly many other excellent contributions which could have been included if cost and word-length restrictions did not impinge, but these did, and they have had to be omitted. Moreover, it should also be stated that unfortunately it has only proven possible to reproduce contributions published in English, which obviously does not reflect all the relevant scholarship. Nonetheless this was a further restriction which had to be accommodated. Finally it should also be indicated that this introduction does not necessarily reflect the views of the contributors herein. Rather it is a personal reflection on the archaeology of identities.

Definitions and categories

The first subject which perhaps needs considering is that of definition. Can we see differences in how the terms we use today with reference to describing and defining identity in archaeological (and other) contexts have altered in their meaning over time? Obviously, this is a subject which has been considered by others, most notably Raymond Williams (1988) and his analysis of 'keywords' of relevance here; 'ethnic', 'racial', and 'sex'. However, understandably, Williams is not concerned with the archaeological relevance or implications of his keywords, and hence in addressing the question of definition and meaning just posed recourse was made to a few selected dictionaries, these being: *The Oxford Handy Dictionary* (Fowler and Fowler 1986); *The Little Oxford Dictionary of Current English* (Ostler 1931); *An Etymological Dictionary of the English Language* (Skeat 1882); *The Spelling and Explanatory Dictionary of the English Language* (Bentick 1786); and the *Glossographia Anglicana Nova* (Brown *et al.* 1719). While the terms considered were expanded to include 'identity', 'gender', 'queer', 'ethnic', 'race', and 'disability' (for religion see Insoll 2004: 6–8). The entries (slightly edited to remove abbreviations) are as follows –

> 'Identity' – 'absolute sameness, individuality, personality' (1986: 427); 'absolute sameness; individuality' (1931: 248); 'sameness' (1882: 280); 'sameness' (1786: 183); no entry (1719).

> 'Gender' – 'classification (or one of the classes) corresponding roughly to the two sexes and sexlessness (see MASCULINE, FEMININE, NEUTER); (jocular) one's sex' (1986: 358); 'any of the classes (*masculine, feminine, neuter gender*) corresponding to the two sexes and sexlessness' (1931: 214); 'kind, breed, sex' (1882: 230); 'a sex, kind or sort' (1786: 166); '...is the difference of sex or kind' (1719: 248).

> 'Queer' – 'strange, odd, eccentric; of questionable character, shady, suspect, out of sorts, giddy or faint (*feeling queer*); (slang, especially of man) homosexual...' (1986: 729); 'strange, odd, eccentric; of questionable character; out of sorts. (slang) put out of order' (1931: 401); 'strange, odd' (1882: 484); 'odd, fantastical' (1786: 269); 'odd, fantastical, sorry' (1719: 508).

'Ethnic' – 'Pertaining to race; heathen; originating from specified racial, linguistic etc., group' (1986: 291); 'of race; heathen' (1931: 178); 'relating to a nation' (1882: 196); 'heathenish' (1786: 144); 'heathenish, or which of or belongs to the heathens' (1719: 209).

'Race' – 'Group of persons or animals or plants connected by common descent, posterity *of* (person); house, family, tribe, or nation regarded as of common stock; distinct ethnical stock (*the Caucasian race*); genus or species or breed or variety of animals or plants; any great division of living creatures (*the human race*); descent, kindred; class of persons etc. with some common feature (*the race of poets, dandies*, etc.)' (1986: 733); 'group of persons having common ancestor; the posterity of; family; kindred people; a particular breed of animals; genus or species of plants' (1931: 404); 'lineage, family, breed' (1882: 487); 'lineage, stock, family…' (1786: 270); no entry (1719).

'Disability' – 'thing or lack that prevents one's doing something, physical incapacity caused by injury or disease' (1986: 237); 'thing that incapacitates or disqualifies' (1931: 150); (no entry, 1882) 'disable' – 'to make unable, disqualify' (1882: 168); 'unfitness, incapacity' (1786: 122); 'being unable or unfit' (1719: 165).

From the above, though it is a far from comprehensive survey, it can be seen that the definitions which have been considered have generally remained broadly similar over time. They share 'family resemblances' (Wittgenstein 1953; and see Insoll 2004: 144–5). The exceptions would appear to be provided by the slang application of 'queer' to sexual identity, which is a seemingly somewhat recent development, and 'ethnic', which has shifted in meaning from the emphasis placed upon 'heathen' to one denoting racial characteristics (Williams 1988: 119). Similarly the development of the term 'identity' itself, away from 'sameness', and its absence in the earliest dictionary consulted (1719) is of interest. This is because its connection with individuality also seems to be a relatively recent phenomenon. Perhaps this is unsurprising as the very idea of individual identity is something of a recent construct (Williams 1988: 163). As Johnson (1999: 83) has noted, there 'is no excuse for taking the modern Western "cult of the individual" as self-evident, or true for all times and all places'. The 'consciousness of self' (La Fontaine 1985: 124) might be universal, but the 'social concept of the individual' (ibid.) is not. As the studies in Carrithers, Collins, and Lukes (1985) indicate, the notion of the individual varies widely across the world today, and would have done so in the past as well.

These are also issues which have been considered with reference to archaeology by various scholars: Johnson (1999) has already been cited, and Thomas (2004: 147), for instance, has discussed how 'we think of ourselves as unique and unrepeatable, yet possessing a series of attributes that are common to all individuals'. Besides general theorizing, the concept of the individual has, occasionally, been considered with reference to more specific periods or areas of archaeology. Eleanor Scott (1997: 9) provides a case in point for she has posed the question as to whether, for example, a Bronze Age Briton or a Roman would have had a self-identity. This, she answers, is unlikely; they would have possessed an identity, informed by gender, kinship, or class, but not by individual concerns.

Hence we have to be aware that sometimes there is a danger of potentially recognizing past identities along modern lines which might be inapt, and in so doing we risk, as Meskell (2002: 281) has noted, 'an elision of difference, conflating ancient and modern experience in the process'. Certainly, gender (both male and female), children and other age-related identity manifestations, as well as sexual activity, and disabilities, obviously existed. But beyond this the onus is upon the archaeologist to attempt to prove as far as possible that other identity manifestations existed in the past be they ethnic, religious, or sexual, the last here of relevance when used to consciously create identity. We must not assume that in line with a diverse society today, a mirror image must have existed in the past as well, with 'X' per cent of this group, and 'Y' of that present. Arbitrary divisions, perhaps in line with fashionable social theory or policy, or political correctness, are very unlikely to have any validity. We do not want to 'overwrite' the past with the present, and in so doing substitute 'our concerns' for those of the past (Moreland 2001: 116).

Although we cannot assume that any 'norms' existed in past societies as has been cogently emphasized via 'queer' archaeology (Dowson 2000; and see Meskell this volume, and 2002: 283), equally it should be noted that in the pursuit of reconstructing past identities, including sexual ones, it has to be recognized, that our current freedom of expression is not replicated everywhere today, and certainly was not in the past. There is certainly much virtue in 'queer' readings of the past, but it cannot be assumed, conversely, that all the past was queer. The archaeological evidence should be allowed to 'speak' where possible, rather than being interpreted according to a pre-existing blueprint be it either normative or 'queer'.

It should also be remembered that identities are not necessarily chosen by free will but can be ascribed; as the existence of the caste system in India indicates (Hocart 1950; Quigley 1996). The foundational underpinnings of the archaeology of identities, largely secular Western democracy with its accompanying freedom of expression, unfortunately do not accord with the contemporary situation in much of the world, and would not have done for the past either. Hence the same identity categories as those we note today may have existed in the past, including those requiring 'proof' rather than assumption as to their prior existence, but how they may have been manifest could have been covert or hidden, and, moreover, their current identification may not always be welcome (see Insoll 2005). Thus there is a certain ethical dimension which must also be acknowledged within exploring the archaeology of identities. The solution is far from universal, but must be considered on a case-by-case basis rather than by what might be, in the grand hermeneutical scheme of things, more perhaps a fleeting window of social expression, or academic popularity.

Furthermore in pursuing social interpretations we should not forget other facets of the hermeneutical framework. So that, for example, we need to recognize that our bodies are not purely socially constituted – biology obviously plays a major factor as well! As Caldwell (2005: 30) has noted, 'our bodies need to be biological bodies if they are also to be social ones'. Yet there sometimes seems to be within the archaeology of identities an emphasis upon forgetting the prosaic, but equally important foundational rudiments such as biology, in favour of the more popularly perceived social theoretical elements. Moreover the empirical body from which adequate interpretation and theory are generated in pursuing past identities must also not be neglected; otherwise there is a danger that empty shells are created.

Similarly it could also be noted that the current unpopularity of economic interpretations in favour of social ones is not necessarily useful. Both deserve merit, but not to the exclusion of the other; they need not be mutually exclusive. The archaeological recognition of childhood and other age-related identity categories is a relatively recent phenomenon (see Sofaer this volume; and Chamberlain 1997; Kamp 2001), and an admirable one, but we would not want, for example, to forget the economic potential of children in favour of ascribing them an individual worth along the lines of the modern, frequently, but not exclusively, Western concept of the child, i.e. what Giddens and Pierson (1998: 123) have referred to as 'the prized child'. This is a concept, the development of which they describe as reflecting the decline in economic importance of having children and the concomitant rise of a 'semi-mythical status' (ibid.) around the child. Of course, it is slightly reductionist to appear to deny love and emotional bonds to children in pre-modern (Western) conditions, which is of course absurd, but the general premise is noteworthy, namely that the economic element of childhood should not be forgotten entirely in favour of an emotional one; the two can of course be combined.

This point would certainly seem to be of relevance for archaeology. Cooper (2002: 139–40), for instance, in an engaging discussion of the archaeology and history of the Andaman Islands, describes how the contribution of random foraging by children to the diet was 'significant enough to warrant mention'. Similar economic motivations connected with childhood have also recently been discussed by Kamp (2001: 2, 14–18). Such an economic role and the requisite ancillary skills involved could well feature in many areas during prehistory as well, and in recognizing children's identity it should not be forgotten. In other words our identity categories should continually be evaluated so that we do not merely provide mirror images of what we might be used to or what we think should exist in the past.

However, it is undeniable that the identity categories which we as archaeologists discuss have broadened out considerably over the past couple of decades, reflecting, in part, the debate which is occurring. Age, as represented by the archaeology of childhood as just described, is one category, only really recently considered. But age is of great significance, obviously, for we are not born with our identities complete, these can be both created over time and alter as we complete our 'life cycles' (see Gilchrist 2000). Yet this said, equally it would be unwise to attempt to wholly define our identity categories, according to what Cornell (2004: 177) describes as, in 'Sartrean' terms; i.e. that 'identity often lives only for short moments' (ibid.). Obviously, this is based upon the work of Jean-Paul Sartre (1960), the existentialist philosopher, but it can be criticized as regards potential archaeological applications at least, for although the notion that identities are changeable and not always fixed or stable is fully accepted (see Rowlands; Meskell this volume), emphasizing the transient moments of identity could equally be irrelevant in relation to what are frequently more permanent categories, i.e. some of those related to age, and, for example, ethnic, or religious identities.

Age can also be of great significance in dictating what we might know via the agency of experience, or conversely what we might be allowed to know via the operation of age sets or grades, secret societies, initiation groups and suchlike. Admittedly via archaeology our insights into this area of identity are perhaps sometimes limited. Though examples of the possible recognition of initiation rites are discussed by Kamp (2001), including ancient Egyptian circumcision rites, Aztec initiations, and the interpretation of certain caves used during the Neolithic in Abruzzo, Central Italy, as locations for initiation rituals based on the presence of offerings and sub-adult human remains (see also Skeates 1991, cited in Kamp 2001: 5).

Rock art would also appear worthy of investigation in this respect. Whitley *et al.* (2004: 226), for instance, describe how some of the rock art on the Modoc Plateau in far western North America was associated with puberty initiations, with rock structures such as cairns and alignments created at higher elevations and motifs rendered at lower ones. Anthropology and art history also indicate the extent to which age can be a factor in identity construction and how this can be directly linked to aspects of materiality. Allison (1968: 45), for example, describes how the ownership of ivory carvings among the Balega of Eastern Congo was restricted to the most senior grade of the Bwami society.

This idea of restricted knowledge, often in relation to age, as a key variable potentially influencing the manifestation of identities needs acknowledging. However, it can in the modern Western world easily be forgotten as a concept of any importance where, routinely, we frequently believe that knowledge is a commodity easily acquired and discarded, and conversely experience and age are undervalued (see Insoll forthcoming). Yet age can act in restricting what other identity variables can be manifest, as for example with regard to religion, or the exercise of sexuality. Amongst the Tiwi, an Australian Aboriginal group of the Melville and Bathurst Islands off the northern coast of Australia, age is the key variable in dictating access to marriage partners. Hart *et al.* (1988: 33) describe how successful older men could have up to 20 wives each, whereas men under 30 had no wives at all and men under 40 were mostly married to elderly women. Although we cannot, obviously, correlate the absence of marriage with a lack of sex. It is highly likely that the sexual rights of a married man's wives would have been patrolled by the husband. Hence this admittedly unusual system can be seen to be directly related to age, and may in less extreme circumstances be applicable for other contexts outside of the recent Australian past.

A further important point to make is that as well as recognizing the importance of age as a manifestation of identity we have to acknowledge that age categories are, to a degree, cultural constructs (Kamp 2001: 3), as with age grades. Additionally, in assessing categories and definitions, it is sometimes easy to think in terms of the singular. Looking at the dictionary entries considered above, one of their striking features is in fact how they interrelate, blur, and are in fact cross-referenced. Words are not singular but are understood in the context of the sentence, hence we see them in multiple associations which give them meaning (see Schlee 2002a), and identities function similarly. This is vital in considering identities, i.e. that although we obviously have different categories, the overall construction of identity is usually what Kealhofer (1999: 63) has defined as 'multivalent'. In other words it is not defined by the singular but rather by multiple elements even though one might be ascribed precedence, which can alter depending upon context and audience (see Conlin Casella and Fowler 2005). Identities are not static, but rather are actively constructed; they are what Gosselain (2000: 208) has described as, 'complex, dynamic, and profoundly mixed constructions'.

Polemics, politics, and pitfalls

Yet as already alluded to above, it would be naïve to think that the archaeological study of identities is a hermeneutically 'risk-free' enterprise. Perhaps one of the most extreme, though best-known examples is provided by Gustaf Kossinna's use of cultural diffusion models in relation to identifying geographical regions in prehistory with ethnic groups on the basis of material culture. An approach which formed the groundwork for what Arnold (1990: 464) describes as, 'ethnocentric German prehistory', and which ultimately, in identifying former 'Germanic' territories to which a spurious (pre)historic claim was promoted, was used in partially justifying the horrific actions of the Nazi regime (see Arnold 1990). Kossinna's work in relation to the archaeology of ethnicity was overt and he was aware of what he was doing. However, for the unwary, the archaeology of identities, perhaps more than any other area of archaeological endeavour, is also potentially loaded with pitfalls and opportunities for the hijack of what might seem like innocent research for polemical purposes. Territorial land claims on the basis of supposed links with ancestor groups is an obvious possible recurring arena of potential misuse of archaeological data in relation to identities.

Another factor of possible relevance could lie in highlighting potential 'differences' of an ethnic or religious group based on archaeological material, conceivably unconsciously, but which could have implications or even profound consequences for a successor group. Perhaps, in part, this is why the archaeology of ethnicity has remained largely unexplored in the Sudan for example (excluding Hodder's [1982] ethnoarchaeological research on the Nuba), where the archaeological material itself does not preclude such an exploration (see Insoll 2003; Welsby and Anderson 2004). David Edwards (2004: 19) has considered this briefly and suggests that looking for earlier 'histories' of ethnic groups presents problems where these peoples are creations of history and hence have been continually formed and reformed.

To this could be added the factor that the generation of an Arab identity in the Sudan, existing as it does within colonially imposed and inappropriate borders, is seen almost as a mark of conformity. Hence those that differ, including both Muslims, the Fur of Darfur for example (Musa Mohammed 1986), who continue to be the target of murderous attacks by Arab militias, and largely non-Muslim groups such as the Nuba (Faris 1972; Manger 1994), or various ethnic groups of the southern Sudan (Mack 1982), who have equally been the focus of military action by the largely Arab government in the capital, Khartoum, could be further turned into the 'other' via exploring their identities, and their creation and maintenance through archaeological evidence. Alternatively, such a notion of 'otherness' might be welcomed in some circumstances. But the point to emphasize is that potential pitfalls in the archaeological study of identities exist, and their interpretation at academic 'distance' can have profound implications.

Equally the very labels we use in considering the archaeology of identities need consideration. The misuse and misunderstanding of identity labels is also a factor: for example Orientalism – whereby all the diverse identities (ethnic and religious for instance) of a vast geographical area, starting somewhere in the vicinity of Istanbul and stretching as far Japan, were either treated as the exotic 'other', or lumped together as an amorphous 'Oriental' mass. Hence Indians, Arabs, Persians, Chinese, Hindus,

Zoroastrians, Muslims, Christians, Buddhists, etc., and all the myriad subdivisions, and moreover blurred identities therein, were thus subsumed, categorized, and frequently misrepresented. Archaeology may not have been directly implicated in this, but it certainly operated within an Orientalist milieu, as with, for example, aspects of Islamic archaeology (Insoll 1999). However, Orientalism has been well studied and exposed (Lewis 1996; Lockman 2004), since it was initially documented by Edward Said (1978).

Conversely, a more recent but similar phenomenon has been less well considered certainly with regard to its relevance for archaeology. This is the opposite of Orientalism – Occidentalism – which as the name implies is concerned with the West, and provides a stereotypical view of the Occidental world, as was formerly done with the 'Orient'. This is a subject recently considered by Buruma and Margalit (2004), who describe Occidentalism as the mirror image of Orientalism. Post 9/11 and the London bombings of July 2005, Occidentalism has grown, but attempting to unpick its various elements and attribute sources to its growth is impossible, for it is neither an ideology nor hermeneutic with a single origin point. Rather it seems to reflect multiple grievances, some well founded, others not, with the Western world, which are generated in many different ways. However, an element of unity is lent by stereotyping so that all the geographical diversity of Europe, North America, Australia, and New Zealand, for example, is treated as if structured by one uniform Christianized world view, which is presented as rational, and holding a single conception of humanity, and is patently flawed in its reductionist logic, as Orientalism has also been shown to be. As Buruma and Margalit (2004: 10) note, 'to diminish an entire society or civilisation to a mass of soulless, decadent, money-grubbing, rootless, faithless, unfeeling parasites is a form of intellectual destruction'.

Fortunately, within archaeology Occidentalist perspectives would seem rare, if not altogether absent. Though this does not mean that strongly held 'identity'-related views do not exist. Al-Ansary (2002: 4–6), for example, writing in the journal *Adumatu*, provides a case in point with his tirade against the 'World's international organizations', something of a generalization in itself, in what he sees as their biased response to the destruction of the Bamiyan Buddhas in Afghanistan, and accompanying depiction of 'Muslims as antagonistic to other religions' (ibid.: 5), and conversely the absence of opposition relating to the fate of Islamic sites in Israel/Palestine. The last of these, to quote, is described as,

> the mark of 21st century civilization with which the East must be branded; it features the imposition of the Civilization of destruction and usurpation in the wildest sense. It seeks to eradicate the indigenous people so that the 'others' enjoy a land to which they are nothing but strangers. This is surely a replay of the catastrophe of the old 'new world' when the white man arrived in the two Americas.
> (Al-Ansary 2002: 6)

Excluding Al-Ansary's comments, which reflect, as already noted, his strongly held political grievances, which are of direct interest here simply because of their marriage of identity (religion and ethnicity) and archaeology, the important point to make is that, beyond stereotyping, the more insidious element of Occidentalist, Orientalist, and other such views can be in the promotion of hatred. This is an emotion often not far removed from identity if identities are perceived of as being contrary, perhaps, to the dominant one, or if they are seen as threatening or subverting, as already noted. Identities can be fragile constructs which might not, outside of the context of secular Western democracy, necessarily be recognized as existing even today. But though considered by anthropologists (see Schlee 2002b), hatred and its implications have been little considered by archaeologists. Warfare or violence might be (Walker 2001; Roksandic 2004; Guilaine and Zammit 2005), but not necessarily, one and the same: warfare can easily be waged for cold political reasons. Whereas, in contrast, hate is emotion, which can if manipulated and targeted, as history too clearly shows us is the case (witness recent events in the former Yugoslavia), have profound implications for identity groups of all types.

However, a considered approach to identity 'labels' and/or categories is not always evident; the usage of the term 'black', for instance, in contemporary Britain reflects this lack of clarity for it can and has been used to refer to anyone with a non-'white' skin (the latter an equally problematic descriptive classificatory category) (see Reeves 1983: 255–8 for relevant discussion). The use of black in this way, it can be suggested, is something of a gross generalization, for as Cashmore (1994: 69) discusses, albeit in reference to Brazil but nevertheless a generally applicable point, 'nobody is quite sure where whiteness ends and blackness begins'. In essence the point to stress is that 'one size fits all' identity categories are not necessarily that useful, i.e. categories and labels which do not reflect the diversity therein. This is evident, for example, in a recent instance in Britain where a white Jewish college lecturer got himself included as a 'black' member of an equal opportunities committee in a trade union. This was possible as, 'he established that the definition of "black" members was wide enough to include Jews – as an ethnic minority that suffers racism' (Baty 2005: 2).

Moreover the label 'black' as described here does not match with Jones's (1997: 100) definition of ethnicity that it is a 'multi-dimensional phenomenon constituted in different ways in different social domains'. Nor does it match what Ålund (2003: 258) defines as 'a variable social phenomenon; it is created and re-created constantly'. Rather they shift the polarity back to race in a manner which has been criticized for being 'a benign form of discursive racialization' (Reeves 1983, cited in Cashmore 1994: 101). The question can be asked do such unsubtle skin-colour classification schemes (which do not work anyway as the example just cited indicates) really accord with the dynamics and complexity of identity manifestations? Identity categories, be they racial, ethnic (the crossover between the two is obviously acknowledged), religious, or whatever, exist and are often necessary for descriptive purposes but need consideration at a more subtle level (see Meskell 2002: 286–7 for relevant discussion). We also need to keep in mind, as Goldberg and Solomos (2002: 4) note, that categories such as race and ethnicity 'are best conceived as political resources...used by both dominant and subordinate groups for the purposes of legitimizing and furthering their own social identities and interests, claims and powers'.

Related points can be made with regard to the use of the label 'Muslim' today, again using Britain as an example. In Britain 'Muslim', which obviously refers to a religious group composed of different ethnicities, has in fact been used as a racial term for political expediency by both Muslims and non-Muslims alike, so that Muslims become a racial group, which is patently erroneous (see Williams 1988: 250 for other examples of the loose application of the term 'race'). This is not confined to Britain either: Aktan (2005: 4) in a recent editorial in the *Turkish Daily News* similarly describes Muslims as a race and further argues that, 'European racism stems from religious differences rather than skin colour – as can be seen in anti-Semitism'. This is a statement which indicates how identity terminology can be both misunderstood and adapted to suit the commentator's particular viewpoint. In short, identities are complex constructs, not best served by, for example, the division of maps and agenda with quotas or rigid boundaries based upon a spurious misreading of history, 'ancestry', and ideology.

That politics and identity can be intertwined is obvious, and material culture and archaeology is not necessarily divorced from this either. The recent exhibition, *Turks: A Journey of a Thousand Years*, held in a prestigious art gallery, the Royal Academy in London, provides a case in point. The timing of this exhibition can be seen to coincide with Turkey's attempt to gain entry into the European Union, a process supported by Tony Blair, the British Prime Minister, as indeed his opening statement to the accompanying catalogue indicates, 'their long and complex journey [the Turks] through Central Asia, the Middle East and, of course, Europe is something we should understand and reflect upon. It demonstrates that the interaction of different cultures in our world is crucial if we are to survive' (Roxburgh 2005: 9). Similar sentiments are, unsurprisingly, expressed by the Turkish Prime Minister, Tayyip Erdogan: 'cultural diversity is a source of richness for all nations. This exhibition comes at a most propitious time, as Turkey's aspirations towards membership of the European family of nations in the European Union are centre stage' (ibid.).

Besides omitting potential Kurdish and Armenian views on the nature of multicultural society in Turkey, this is of interest as it stands somewhat in contrast to a point made by the Turkish archaeologist Burcu Erciyas (2005: 187) in a recent review of archaeology and ethnicity in Turkey, i.e. that a new concept of nationalism exists in Turkey, 'in which the origins of Turks are not linked to Hittites or any local Anatolian culture, but rather the grandeur of the Turks who arrived from Central Asia is emphasized'. Moreover, the non-European origins of the Turks are something which is immediately apparent even in a quick perusal of the exhibition catalogue, where the material culture on display serves to highlight their Central Asian heritage. Thus an interesting dichotomy is actually produced in terms of identity construction in what the material culture seemingly indicates and the aspirations of politicians.

Finally in considering polemics, politics, and pitfalls in the archaeology of identities, it is also necessary to note that the 'ring-fencing' of identities by interest groups, whatever they might be, is also to be avoided – meaning that, for instance, the archaeology of ethnicities, religions, and sexualities is not somehow controlled by those with a usually, self-defined, vested interest. This is something that has recently been considered by Normark (2004) with reference to Maya archaeology and contemporary Maya identities, whereby the leaders of the contemporary Maya movement have criticized, rightly or wrongly, non-Maya Mayanist archaeology for the labels it ascribes. The Maya movement's reaction to identity discourse is locked into a range of variables (the application of contemporary ethnic labels, the aftermath of the long civil war in Guatemala, which is the focus of Normark's case study), but the main problem between 'most archaeologists and the Maya movement is whether there is cultural continuity or discontinuity' (Normark 2004: 130), and in how 'surviving' elements of Maya culture are used to strengthen the pan-Maya identity.

Although the reasons underpinning this example are obviously complex, and this author is not qualified to comment on Guatemalan politics and identities, the important point to reiterate is that, in general, hermeneutical and empirical 'apartheid' which can be generated by vested-interest identity groups is not at all conducive to either the understanding of identities, past and present, or to the development of relevant theory and methodology in approaching past identities. Yet with the currents of relativism swirling around the edges of archaeology, but not to the degree of anthropology (Eriksen 1995; Geertz 2000), reluctance to engage with the archaeology of other identities, perhaps vocal ones, is partly understandable. Nonetheless, archaeology as a discipline and archaeologists as its proponents should be both mature and confident enough to overcome such hurdles in recognizing difference, but also in emphasizing complexity, and where necessary commonality, or what Gosden (1994: 196) has termed (though not in the context of identities), 'the creation of some common ground without undermining the nature of difference'.

The multicultural society: a new phenomenon?

A core contribution, perhaps, which archaeology can make in considering identities is in assessing the phenomenon of the multicultural society. Which is obviously predicated upon, to put it crudely, the interaction of identity groups, and within the context of this author's life (just short of four decades), multiculturalism has gone from being a term not frequently heard to one at the top of the agenda, at least in Western Europe. This has been an era of massive change, with the decline of colonialism, the collapse of the Soviet bloc, and the growth of globalization with its allied information and people flows (see Schlee 2002a). The opposites of political-economic instability and freedom have meant that people have migrated to an unprecedented extent. New identities are being constructed, but more so the interaction of different 'identity' groups is occurring within the new societies which are being constructed, both virtually and physically.

Yet within the overall debates as to what multiculturalism actually means (Cashmore 1994; May 2002; Brochmann 2003a), very little thought appears to have been given to whether contemporary multicultural societies have any precedents. A historical perspective (and included here is archaeology) beyond the context of 40–50 years, i.e. the beginnings of the current multicultural phenomenon, is neglected (see for example Brochmann 2003b). Furthermore archaeologists have been unusually mute about this subject as well. This is surprising for it is obviously of the greatest relevance for us as archaeologists, for through the entirety of the slabs of time with which we deal the absence of suitable 'multicultural' comparative examples would be astounding. And we can withhold our astonishment for they do exist, with perhaps the best-known example being Imperial Rome, i.e. the city, where both archaeology and history allow us to assess an earlier experiment in multiculturalism.

The parallels between Rome and modern cities/societies have been noted by others; Brian Hayden (2003: 404–5), for instance, makes the point that 'today's Industrial society is much more reminiscent of Imperial Rome, in which all cults were tolerated provided that they abided by the laws of the land and respected the rights of others'. The status of Rome as a 'cosmopolis', a world city, is also discussed by Edwards and Woolf (2004), and they mention how documentary sources describe peoples from the

Danube region – Germans, Arabs, and Ethiopians, among others – as all being inhabitants of Rome.

Yet, unsurprisingly, there were also many differences between Rome and modern multicultural cities represented, say, by London or New York. For example:

- The latter do not claim, as Rome did, according to Edwards and Woolf (2004: 4), 'to rule the world'.
- An active emphasis is not put upon gathering together 'the world's greatest books and greatest scholars', as was also undertaken in Rome (ibid.: 15).
- Disease, a correlate of Rome's world city status in drawing together 'the most noxious germs of the Empire' (ibid.: 10), is obviously not such a factor of importance today.

But the similarities are also surprising. These include:

- as already mentioned, the plurality of religious beliefs found in Rome, described by Edwards and Woolf (2004: 9) as 'a bewildering variety of cults from all over the empire';
- in the process whereby smaller 'colonies' were established within the larger city – which today we might translate into different areas inhabited by different ethnic, religious, or other identity groups;
- or in the angst recorded in Latin historical sources as to the nature of immigration, very resonant in Europe today, and reflected in 'attempts to police, limit and control the influx of people and traditions on which the physical and demographic survival of the city depended' (ibid.: 9);
- or again, in Rome in the immigrant's portrayal 'as opportunistic economic migrants' (Edwards and Woolf 2004: 12).

But making an overall judgement as to whether Rome was a multicultural 'success' or not is problematic, for we have to allow for the filters which serve to obscure our evidence: those associated with archaeology per se, which are well known (Hodder 1986; Insoll forthcoming), but also all those associated with historical sources and their interpretation – bias, propaganda, prior agendas, etc. (Moreland 2001). The task is not easy, but considering the evidence it can be suggested that on face value Rome was seemingly a multicultural success. Though it should be remembered that the routine brutality of the authorities under what sometimes amounted to a dictatorship, as well as the limited notion of what constituted a citizen allied with the existence of a large slave class, means that this is perhaps not the comparative example we should seek. The example of Rome, unsurprisingly, differs from the contemporary era.

This could help in explaining why the term 'multicultural' would appear to be studiously avoided by, for example, Edwards and Woolf (2004), in favour of their notion of 'cosmopolis'. Differences exist, and although Rome was inhabited by people manifesting different identities, the situation in comparison to that of contemporary London or New York was obviously dissimilar. This was perhaps due to factors such as the use of Latin literary culture as an index of Roman identity – English could not be said to play the same role (the focus here is upon Rome itself in relation to multiculturalism, not 'Romanization' in general [for the latter see, Hingley 1996, 2005; Laurence and Berry 1998]); or the use of antiquity to sustain the role and identity of the city. Both factors are mentioned by Edwards and Woolf (2004: 7, 16), but not assessed within the context of multiculturalism.

In other instances, where multiculturalism could be said to have existed and often thrived, archaeology has not been utilized to see if we can learn anything about this via evidence of material culture. Thus, for example, the trade centres of the Arabian/Persian Gulf, Red Sea, and Indian Ocean which flourished variously between the eighth to sixteenth centuries AD (Hodges and Whitehouse 1983; Chaudhuri 1985) have been neglected (see Insoll this volume). Instead these are frequently represented on paper as assemblages of pot sherds, glass fragments, faunal remains (if one is fortunate), and stratigraphic and building plans, as with Kilwa in Tanzania (Chittick 1974), or Manda in Kenya (Chittick 1984), for instance, rather than as communities of peoples from diverse cultural backgrounds manifesting different identities and interacting with each other, often over the course of several centuries (Insoll 2003, 2005).

Yet is the entrepot of several centuries ago also representative of multiculturalism, the interaction of different identities, in the modern age? It is not; Rome might be closer in analogical terms because of its size and complexity, but obviously it is not directly comparable. The screen of time means that we cannot look to the past as the provider of examples of a golden harmonious age of multicultural understanding. It was not, and even if it were, the contemporary globalized era means that the circumstances which exist are quite different, not least in terms of scale, manifest by, for example, the difference in numbers of people alive today and the speed of transport and communication. Past and present are separated by very different circumstances. Moreover, the very notion of multiculturalism would seem not to be universally applicable, at least as defined today, across time and space. Multiculturalism means something quite different in the modern era due to the fact that the Enlightenment effectively argued that all distinct identities should be merged into a single, universal, national society. Multiculturalism arrests that difference, and diversity is acclaimed as positive (J. Thomas pers. comm.). In view of such changes in meaning perhaps archaeologists should shift their attentions to contribute to understanding the potential variability of notions such as multiculturalism cross-temporally.

The value of the archaeology of identities?

Ultimately we are left with the question as to the value of the archaeology of identities if:

- The circumstances separating past and present are so markedly different that the study of past identities allows no inferences to be drawn of relevance for today.
- The archaeological evidence frequently precludes the recognition of past identities in their primary contexts anyway.
- The archaeological study of identities is a luxury only afforded those in certain contexts in the world, and bears little relevance to the majority.
- The study of past identities is often politically difficult, potentially subject to manipulation, and can hold consequences of a profound nature.

The answer to these points is perhaps beyond the limits of this introduction and, more-over, it can be added that the pessimistic view has deliberately just been proposed, and is not necessarily entirely agreed with here, as the discussion thus far has hopefully shown.

Hence on a more positive note, the answer to the question is that the value of the archaeology of identities is various, and in particular that it is more than just the ascription of labels such as male/female to the past. The archaeology of identities is essentially concerned with the complex process of attempting to recover an insight into the generation of self at a variety of levels: as an individual, within a community, and in public and private contexts. Moreover it is not the preserve of social archae-ology alone but crosses categories in so far as the pursuit of interpreting identities at the expense of neglecting other fields of life such as economics or politics is foolhardy. These, which are by no means intended to be the only other interlocking variables, can be interwoven with identities, and the latter can be defined, subverted, sup-pressed, or made overtly manifest by the former. Archaeology should strive for the reconstruction of ontology, the essence of humanity, but reconstructions of ontology which neglect the interrelation of other variables of life, which can be subsumed within the overarching identity category such as religion (see Insoll 2004), or which can sit beside them, such as gender, are only partial.

Moreover, to repeat, the recognition of complexity would seem key to the success of the archaeological study of identities; that is complexity in both the definition and categorization of identities, but also in how we conceive of their interrelation and maintenance. Here the notions of syncretism and bricolage might be of use as inter-pretive and conceptual mechanisms. Usually it is argued that 'syncretism' should be reserved for the blending of religious forms (Shaw and Stewart 1994: 10; Insoll 2004: 131–9), while bricolage applies to the 'formation of new cultural forms from bits and pieces of cultural practice of diverse origins' (ibid.). Based upon this definition the latter would appear to hold no advantages over syncretism as applied to identities, rather it is the notion both incorporate that is useful: blending, reworking, adapta-tion, flexibility, and this should be central within the archaeology of identities, and indeed in the conceptualization of identities in general.

In such concepts the success of multiculturalism also lies, for though archaeology may offer few insights, it is notions such as these which can be seen to be central to its success. For in essence multiculturalism is concerned with flexibility, the requisite compromise between the sometimes competing notions of commonality and differ-ence as reflected in the bonds of 'citizenship', and the maintenance of distinct reli-gious, cultural, or ethnic identities as well. We cannot assume that multiculturalism will succeed just because it is thought to be politically incorrect to think otherwise. It, like any other endeavour, needs to be critiqued, and actively worked towards and maintained in order to be successful, and here archaeologists, concerned as we are (or should be) with the history and materiality of the manifestations of cultures and iden-tities, can and should contribute.

However, something of a conceptual conundrum is offered within the archaeology of identities. For if the reasoning of Geertz (2000: 71) is followed then the past was much more structured by an ethnocentric ethos than the present, something he attributes to the marginal involvement of different groups with each other. This, of course, can be ques-tioned as something of a generalization, but it does raise the issue of the modern interpreter's horizon, in recognizing that, contrary to many of the social and political currents influencing the manifestation of ethnic and national identities at present, the boundaries of identities in the past could have been much more rigidly maintained and patrolled than they are today. Tuan (1974: 30) defines ethnocentrism as 'collective egocentrisms'.

What many archaeologists perhaps unwittingly do is create an egocentric view of the past when in reality much of it probably was ethnocentric, for we (in the sections of Western society from which many archaeologists derive) give prominence to the individual as has already been described. Yet as was also mentioned, the group is very significant, and ethnocentrism rather than being a pejorative term to avoid may actually be a more accurate reflection of past mindsets in relation to identities, for, again as Tuan (1974: 31) notes, 'the illusion of superiority and centrality is probably necessary to the sustenance of culture'. Relativism, which structures much of academic discourse and social policy, rightly or wrongly, is not necessarily relevant in configuring the past. Syncretism and bricolage might be more relevant, but notions of who was 'in' and who was 'out' also have to be recognized as of potential importance. A degree of ethnocentrism has to inform interpretation, as Geertz also notes, otherwise if excluded we get 'a sort of moral entropy' (2000: 71).

The 'collage' that the modern world entails, and to which Geertz (2000: 85) refers, means that we face challenges as Geertz also notes, but it is something which we as archaeologists can also contribute to understanding. The challenges may be more pronounced than ever before, but they are not necessarily unique – we are not forever inventing the wheel, though we might think we are. Equally it must be remembered that not all the world is a collage. Reservoirs of less-affected areas exist, though these too are not immune from globalization. But, nonetheless, not everything everywhere should be benchmarked according to the Western 'globalized' relativistic position. 'Globalization' and 'multiculturalism' are phrases easily used but which mask a variety of interpretations and positions; witness the Arabian/Persian Gulf region today, for a long time multicultural but also protected by 'firewalls', be they religious or ethnic, which would not be used in the West today for fear of being exclusive or racist (see Insoll this volume). We need to acknowledge that different cultures and ethnicities exist, and we must seek not to impose one view upon our data because that is politically correct, but rather allow it to speak to us either for or against the existence of such entities in the past. Complexity in conceptual configuration would again seem key (Insoll forthcoming), but perhaps, equally importantly, the understanding of past identities very much requires a contextual case-by-case approach as opposed to general ascription using checklists.

Finally for the archaeologist of the future, new challenges seemingly await. Material culture is emblematic of identities as the chapters herein indicate, but we do not want to simplify what are undoubtedly complex processes of identity manifestation and interrelations. For perhaps we (some of us at least) live in a unique era where various identities can be masked behind material culture of a global nature – on the surface at least – though what goes on inside this 'shell', admittedly irretrievable by archaeologists, could mean that these 'clear-cut' globalized identity tags can be and are reworked in myriad ways. Understanding identities might sometimes appear deceptively simple today, but they are not; they are still subject to complex manifestation which can be camouflaged via similarities in material culture, and which will hold new challenges for future generations of archaeologists. For the archaeology of identities is not merely a hermeneutic fad or fashion but is here to stay.

Acknowledgements

I am grateful to Julian Thomas, Rachel MacLean, and Siân Jones for reading various drafts of this introduction. Obviously all mistakes, errors of interpretation, omissions, etc. remain my own responsibility. I am also grateful to Richard Hingley for providing references on Rome.

Bibliography

Aktan, G. 2005. A Minimum Amount of Attention. *Turkish Daily News* 10/11/05: 4.
Al-Ansary, A.R. 2002. Editorial. *Adumatu* 6: 4–6.
Allison, P. 1968. *African Stone Sculptures*. London: Lund Humphries.
Ålund, A. 2003. Ethnicity, Social Subordination and Cultural Resistance. In Brochmann, G. (ed.), *The Multicultural Challenge*. Oxford: Elsevier, pp. 245–61.
Arnold, B. 1990. The Past as Propaganda: Totalitarian Archaeology in Nazi Germany. *Antiquity* 64: 464–78.
Barth, F. 1969. Introduction. In Barth, F. (ed.), *Ethnic Groups and Boundaries: The Social Organisation of Cultural Difference*. Bergen: Universitets Forlaget, pp. 9–38.
Baty, P. 2005. White Activist Qualifies as 'Black'. *Times Higher Education Supplement* 13/5/05: 2.
Bentick, J. 1786. *The Spelling and Explanatory Dictionary of the English Language*. London: Thomas Carnan.
Brochmann, G. (ed.). 2003a. *The Multicultural Challenge*. Oxford: Elsevier.
Brochmann, G. 2003b. Citizens of Multicultural States: Power and Legitimacy. In Brochmann, G. (ed.), *The Multicultural Challenge*. Oxford: Elsevier, pp. 1–11.
Brown, D., Goodwin, T., Walthoe, J., Took, B., Midwinter, D., and Ward, T. 1719. *Glossographia Anglicana Nova*. London.
Burcu Erciyas, D. 2005. Ethnic Identity and Archaeology in the Black Sea Region of Turkey. *Antiquity* 79: 179–90.
Buruma, I. and Margalit, A. 2004. *Occidentalism: The West in the Eyes of its Enemies*. New York: Penguin.
Caldwell, R. 2005. Ships on a Collision Course. *Philosophy Now* 50: 28–30.
Carrithers, M., Collins, S., and Lukes, S. (eds). 1985. *The Category of the Person*. Cambridge: Cambridge University Press.
Cashmore, E. 1994. *Dictionary of Race and Ethnic Relations*. London: Routledge.
Chamberlain, A. 1997. Commentary: Missing Stages of Life – Towards the Perception of Children in Archaeology. In Moore, J., and Scott, E. (eds), *Invisible People and Processes*. London: Leicester University Press, pp. 248–50.
Chaudhuri, K.N. 1985. *Trade and Civilisation in the Indian Ocean*. Cambridge: Cambridge University Press.
Chittick, N. 1974. *Kilwa: An Islamic Trading City on the East African Coast*. Nairobi: British Institute in Eastern Africa.
Chittick, N. 1984. *Manda, Excavations at an Island Port on the Kenya Coast*. Nairobi: British Institute in Eastern Africa.
Conlin Casella, E. and Fowler, C. (eds). 2005. *The Archaeology of Plural and Changing Identities*. New York: Kluwer.
Cooper, Z. 2002. *Archaeology and History: Early Settlements in the Andaman Islands*. New Delhi: Oxford University Press.
Cornell, P. 2004. Social Identity, the Body, and Power. In Fahlander, F. and Oestigaard, T. (eds), *Material Culture and Other Things*. Gothenburg: University of Gothenburg, pp. 161–84.

Dowson, T. 2000. Why Queer Archaeology? An Introduction. *World Archaeology* 32: 161–5.

Edwards, C. and Woolf, G. 2004. Cosmopolis: Rome as World City. In Edwards, C. and Woolf, G. (eds), *Rome the Cosmopolis*. Cambridge: Cambridge University Press, pp. 1–20.

Edwards, D. 2004. *The Nubian Past*. London: Routledge.

Eriksen, T.H. 1995. *Small Places, Large Issues: An Introduction to Social and Cultural Anthropology*. London: Pluto Press.

Faris, J.C. 1972. *Nuba Personal Art*. London: Duckworth.

Fowler, F.G. and Fowler, H.W. 1986. *The Oxford Handy Dictionary*. London: Chancellor Press.

Geertz, C. 2000. *Available Light*. Princeton: Princeton University Press.

Gellner, E. 1983. *Nations and Nationalism*. Oxford: Blackwell.

Giddens, A. and Pierson, A. 1998. *Conversations with Anthony Giddens: Making Sense of Modernity*. Oxford: Polity.

Gilchrist, R. 2000. Archaeological Biographies: Realizing Human Lifecycles, -Courses and -Histories. *World Archaeology* 31: 325–8.

Goldberg, D.T. and Solomos, J. 2002. General Introduction. In Goldberg, D.T. and Solomos, J. (eds), *A Companion to Racial and Ethnic Studies*. Oxford: Blackwell, pp. 1–16.

Gosden, C. 1994. *Social Being and Time*. Oxford: Blackwell.

Gosselain, O. 2000. Materializing Identities: An African Perspective. *Journal of Archaeological Method and Theory* 7: 187–217.

Guilaine, J. and Zammit, J. 2005. *The Origins of War: Violence in Prehistory*. Oxford: Blackwell.

Hart, C.W.M., Pilling, A.R., and Goodale, J.C. 1988. *The Tiwi of North Australia*. New York: Holt, Rinehart, and Winston.

Hayden, B. 2003. *Shamans, Sorcerers and Saints*. Washington: Smithsonian Books.

Hingley, R. 1996. The 'Legacy' of Rome: The Rise, Decline and Fall of the Theory of Romanisation. In Webster, J. and Cooper, N. (eds), *Roman Imperialism: Post-Colonial Perspectives*. Leicester: Leicester University Press, pp. 35–48.

Hingley, R. 2005. *Globalizing Roman Culture*. London: Routledge.

Hocart, A. 1950. *Caste: A Comparative Study*. London: Methuen.

Hodder, I. 1982. *Symbols in Action*. Cambridge: Cambridge University Press.

Hodder, I. 1986. *Reading the Past*. Cambridge: Cambridge University Press.

Hodges, R. and Whitehouse, D. 1983. *Mohammed, Charlemagne and the Origins of Europe*. London: Duckworth.

Insoll, T. 1999. *The Archaeology of Islam*. Oxford: Blackwell.

Insoll, T. 2003. *The Archaeology of Islam in Sub-Saharan Africa*. Cambridge: Cambridge University Press.

Insoll, T. 2004. *Archaeology, Ritual, Religion*. London: Routledge.

Insoll, T. 2005. *The Land of Enki in the Islamic Era: Pearls, Palms, and Religious Identity in Bahrain*. London: Kegan Paul.

Insoll, T. Forthcoming. *Archaeology – The Conceptual Challenge*. London: Duckworth.

Jenkins, R. 1994. Rethinking Ethnicity: Identity, Categorization and Power. *Ethnic and Racial Studies* 17: 197–223.

Johnson, M. 1999. *Archaeological Theory: An Introduction*. Oxford: Blackwell.

Jones, S. 1997. *The Archaeology of Ethnicity*. London: Routledge.

Kamp, K.A. 2001. Where Have All the Children Gone? The Archaeology of Childhood. *Journal of Archaeological Method and Theory* 8: 1–34.

Kealhofer, L. 1999. Creating Social Identity in the Landscape: Tideswater, Virginia, 1600–1750. In Ashmore, W. and Knapp, A.B. (eds), *Archaeologies of Landscape*. Oxford: Blackwell, pp. 58–82.

La Fontaine, J.S. 1985. Person and Individual: Some Anthropological Reflections. In Carrithers, M., Collins, S., and Lukes, S. (eds), *The Category of the Person*. Cambridge: Cambridge University Press. pp. 123–40.

Laurence, R. and Berry, J. 1998. *Cultural Identity in the Roman Empire*. London: Routledge.

Lewis, R. 1996. *Gendering Orientalism: Race, Femininity and Representation*. London: Routledge.

Lockman, Z. 2004. *Contending Visions of the Middle East: The History and Politics of Orientalism*. Cambridge: Cambridge University Press.

Mack, J. 1982. Material Culture and Ethnic Identity in Southeastern Sudan. In Mack, J. and Robertshaw, P. (eds), *Culture History in the Southern Sudan*. London: British Institute in Eastern Africa, pp. 111–30.

Manger, L.O. 1994. *From the Mountains to the Plains: The Integration of the Lafofa Nuba into Sudanese Society*. Uppsala: Scandinavian Institute of African Studies.

May, S. 2002. Multiculturalism. In Goldberg, D.T. and Solomos, J. (eds), *A Companion to Racial and Ethnic Studies*. Oxford: Blackwell, pp. 124–44.

Meskell, L. 2002. The Intersections of Identity and Politics in Archaeology. *Annual Review of Anthropology* 31: 279–301.

Moreland, J. 2001. *Archaeology and Text*. London: Duckworth.

Musa Mohammed, I. 1986. *The Archaeology of Central Darfur (Sudan) in the 1st Millennium A.D*. BAR S285. Oxford: British Archaeological Reports.

Normark, J. 2004. Discontinuous Maya Identities – Culture and Ethnicity in Maya Discourse. In Fahlander, F. and Oestigaard, T. (eds), *Material Culture and Other Things*. Gothenburg: University of Gothenburg, pp. 109–60.

Ostler, G. 1931. *The Little Oxford Dictionary of Current English*. Oxford: Clarendon Press.

Quigley, D. 1996. *The Interpretation of Caste*. New Delhi: Oxford University Press.

Reeves, F. 1983. *British Racial Discourse*. Cambridge: Cambridge University Press.

Roksandic, M. (ed.). 2004. *Violent Interactions in the Mesolithic: Evidence and Meaning*. BAR S1237. Oxford: Archaeopress.

Roxburgh, D. (ed.). 2005. *Turks: A Journey of A Thousand Years*. London: Royal Academy.

Said, E. 1978. *Orientalism*. London: Routledge and Kegan Paul.

Sartre, J.P. 1960. *Critique de la Raison Dialectique*. Paris: Gallimard.

Schlee, G. 2002a. Introduction. In Schlee, G. (ed.), *Imagined Differences: Hatred and the Construction of Identity*. Münster: Lit, pp. 3–32.

Schlee, G. (ed.). 2002b. *Imagined Differences: Hatred and the Construction of Identity*. Münster: Lit.

Schmidt, R. and Voss, B. (eds). 2000. *Archaeologies of Sexuality*. London: Routledge.

Scott, E. 1997. Introduction: On the Incompleteness of Archaeological Narratives. In Moore, J. and Scott, E. (eds), *Invisible People and Processes*. London: Leicester University Press, pp. 1–12.

Shaw, R. and Stewart, C. 1994. Introduction: Problematizing Syncretism. In Stewart, C. and Shaw, S. (eds), *Syncretism/Anti-Syncretism: The Politics of Religious Synthesis*. London: Routledge, pp. 1–26.

Skeat, W. 1882. *An Etymological Dictionary of the English Language*. Oxford: Clarendon Press.

Skeates, R. 1991. Caves, Cult and Children in Neolithic Abruzzo, Central Italy. In Garwood, P., Jennings, D., Skeates, R., and Toms, J. (eds), *Sacred and Profane*. Oxford: Oxford Committee for Archaeology, pp. 122–34.

Thomas, J. 2004. *Archaeology and Modernity*. London: Routledge.

Tuan, Y.-F. 1974. *Topophilia*. Englewood Cliffs: Prentice-Hall.

Walker, P.L. 2001. A Bioarchaeological Perspective on the History of Violence. *Annual Review of Anthropology* 30: 573–96.

Welsby, D. and Anderson, J. 2004. *Sudan: Ancient Treasures*. London: British Museum.

Whitley, D.S., Loubser, J., and Hann, D. 2004. Friends in Low Places: Rock-Art and Landscape on the Modoc Plateau. In Chippindale, C., and Nash, G. (eds), *The Figured Landscapes of Rock-Art*. Cambridge: Cambridge University Press, pp. 217–38.

Williams, R. 1988. *Keywords: A Vocabulary of Culture and Society*. London: Fontana Press.

Wittgenstein, L. (G.M. Anscombe, trans.). 1953. *Philosophical Investigations*. Oxford: Blackwell.

Part I

General perspectives, ethnicity, and nationalism

An introduction

Timothy Insoll

As noted in the introduction to this volume, the archaeological study of identities is now firmly fixed as an area of research growing in volume every year. This is reflected in the first three chapters forming Part I of this Reader, which both consider some of the general perspectives involved in exploring identities via archaeological evidence, as well as consider in greater detail archaeological approaches to, specifically, ethnicity and nationalism.

The origins of archaeologists' interest in identities are charted by Meskell in this volume. Meskell, writing from a self-stated feminist perspective, a recurrent theme herein, highlights the often-found emphasis placed upon categories in Western archaeological discourse, and how in fact identities are formed of multiple strands. She also seeks to critique simplistic notions of gender construction and ultimately of the archaeology of identities – hence aiming for a true archaeology of difference, where required. The latter, similarly, is an issue which many of the contributions chosen for inclusion in this Reader explore.

Overall Meskell's chapter is concerned with signalling complexity, what she terms 'multi-dimensional analysis', and in turn demanding this of our interpretations. The mechanism by which this can perhaps be achieved, as she suggests, is considering social lives and social experience – identities, sex, age, ethnicity, class – in terms of the life cycle rather than as lists of social signifiers. Lynn Meskell has been at the forefront of the archaeological study of identities, both in relation to their manifestation in ancient Egypt (Meskell 1999), and in general as the chapter included here indicates, as well as in her more recent publications (Meskell 2002). Her contribution to bringing the inherent complexities of the archaeology of identities to attention, thus making it part of the mainstream of archaeological research, is thus duly acknowledged.

Meskell also touches upon the archaeology of ethnicity and nationalism but this is more fully explored by Siân Jones, who examines the common discourses of identity which have structured notions such as 'peoples' and 'cultures'. She indicates the historical contingency of the concepts used in the archaeological identification of past ethnicities, and, importantly, suggests alternative ways of conceptualizing ethnicity, indicating that it is dynamic and contested rather than necessarily static or homogeneous. The point is well made that archaeology has tended to deal with 'wholes': bounded entities of peoples, ethnic groups, 'tribes', and suchlike. Instead Jones indicates that a more complex view of such phenomena is key to understanding the archaeology of identities. Rather than presume the existence of discrete 'categories', 'entities', or 'wholes', their relevance in fact needs to be proven (Insoll forthcoming).

Jones here introduces her notion, building upon the work of Pierre Bourdieu, of a 'practice theory of ethnicity' (p. 48, this volume), later expanded upon in her influential study, *The Archaeology of Ethnicity* (1997). She argues that the concept of 'habitus' can be used to articulate the way 'in which subjective ethnic classifications can be grounded in the social conditions and cultural practices characterising particular social domains'. In this respect the chapter by Jones and indeed the others in this section can be best described as the second stage of the archaeological study of identities, i.e. in signalling complexity rather than just ticking boxes for the presence of, for example, 'women' or 'tribes'. The latter is admittedly a necessary first stage in what was originally usually a largely identity 'free' archaeology, but also a stage which ultimately needed to be passed as the chapters by Jones, Meskell, and Rowlands indicate.

Hence Michael Rowlands's chapter is similarly broad in perspective and provides a forceful overview of the use of the term 'identity' and how archaeologists have both conceptualized and studied identity primarily with reference to the political implications of nationalism and ethnicity. This he also relates to contemporary philosophical issues revolving around postmodernity and the idea of the 'other'. Of especial relevance here is Rowlands's discussion of the different usages of 'identity' dependent on the perspective involved: whether 'primordialist' with an accompanying deep, permanent, internal view of identities, or, alternatively, an 'interactionist' one involving a more external, contingent, and shallow view of the same. Again, a 'taken for granted' perspective is questioned. Thus the notion of essentialist, primordialist identity is challenged by all the chapters in this part of the book, and indeed, the other chapters in this volume, through invoking, for instance, the idea of complexity.

Bibliography

Insoll, T. forthcoming. *Archaeology – The Conceptual Challenge*. London: Duckworth.

Jones, S. 1997. *The Archaeology of Ethnicity*. London: Routledge.

Meskell, L.M. 1999. *Archaeologies of Social Life: Age, Sex, Class etc. in Ancient Egypt*. Oxford: Blackwell.

Meskell, L. 2002. The Intersections of Identity and Politics in Archaeology. *Annual Review of Anthropology* 31: 279–301.

Chapter 2

Archaeologies of identity

Lynn Meskell

> Do we *truly* need a *true* sex? With a persistence that borders on stubbornness,
> modern Western societies have answered in the affirmative. They have obstinately
> brought into play the question of a 'true sex' in an order of things where one might
> have imagined that all that counted was the reality of the body and the intensity of
> its pleasures.
> Michel Foucault, *Herculine Barbin, Being the Recently Discovered Memoirs of a*
> *Nineteenth Century Hermaphrodite*

With these words Michel Foucault opened his famous study of sexual identity based
on the memoirs of Herculine Barbin (Foucault 1980), also known as Alexina, Camille,
and Abel. It is a brief and compelling account of the life of a hermaphrodite, but also
an exposé of juridico-medical classifications and our cultural fascination with category. In the case of Herculine those pronouncements had disastrous effects resulting in
suicide. Apart from our current preoccupation in all matters sexual, the story of this
Herculine is important for it belies the rigidity of Western taxonomizing, especially
where it concerns identity, be it race, class, gender, or sexual preference. That rigidity
necessitates that all individuals be neatly pigeonholed and categorized according to a
set of predetermined labels. So too in our archaeological investigations we have concentrated on single-issue questions of identity, focusing singularly on gender or ethnicity, and have attempted to locate people from antiquity into a priori Western
taxonomies: heterosexual/homosexual, male/female, elite/non-elite, etc. Archaeologists
tend to concentrate on specific sets of issues that coalesce around topics like gender,
age, or status, without interpolating other axes of identity, be they class, ethnicity, or
sexual orientation for example, because this has been seen as too vast or complex a
project. As Sarah Nelson (1997: 16) recently commented, while feminists have been
discussing other variables such as ethnicity, sexual orientation, age, and the other ways
people are categorized, 'everything cannot be studied at once'. This is where the generations divide. Being feminists it is surely part of our project to open up the debate to
all those vectors of difference by which individuals are named and subjectified.
Following Sawicki (1991: 47), 'theoretical pluralism makes possible the expansion of
social ontology, a redefinition and redescription of experience from the perspectives of
those who are more often simply objects of theory'. Without such sensitivities we run
the risk of doing interpretive violence in representing the people of the past and, by
seamless extension, those imbricated in present-day struggles.

In this chapter I have two aims: the first is to present a third-wave feminist outline of what an archaeology of identity might look like, moving beyond a simple position of identity politics. The second is to break the boundaries of identity categories themselves, blurring the crucial domains of identity formation, be they based on gender, sexuality, kin, politics, religion, or social systems. Only through deconstruction of the domains we see as 'natural' or prediscursive can we truly approach an archaeology of difference – real cultural difference and contextuality.

Identity issues: ethnicity, class, sex, etc.

While examining identity in a holistic manner might represent one of the newest fields represented in this volume, single-issue studies have been of great interest to archaeologists for the past few decades. Most scholars acknowledge that we all have a number of social identities which entail constant negotiation and organize our relationships to other individuals and groups within our social world (Craib 1998: 4–9), yet we often forget the subjective, inner world of the individual. It is not simply a matter of uncovering the top-down implementations of power that have effects on people or the 'technologies of the self' that infer a disembodied force. Here the popular writings of Giddens, Foucault, and even Bourdieu often fall short of an archaeology of identity. Although some aspects of our identity are given to us as a starting point – our sex, class, ethnicity, etc. – this frames the self, it does not rigidly determine the sort of person we might become or our actions in the future. Understanding social identity often requires a metanarrative, just as awareness of individual selves requires that identity and life experience be inserted into that equation (Craib 1998: 28). In fact there are two levels of operation: one is the broader social level in which identities are defined by formal associations or mores; the other is the individual or personal level where a person experiences many aspects of identity within a single subjectivity, fluid over the trajectories of life. The latter is more contingent, immediate, and operates at a greater frequency, whereas society's categories and constraints take longer to reformulate. But as the case of Herculine Barbin illustrates, those typologies of identity can change within the space of a few decades. The two levels operate in a recursive manner, with individuals playing important roles in the mechanisms of change.

Archaeological materials are deeply imbricated in political discourse and objectives (see papers in Meskell 1998b). It is the very materiality of our field – the historical depth of monuments and objects, their visibility in museums, their iconic value – that ultimately has residual potency in the contemporary imaginary. These objects can be mobilized and deployed in identity struggles, whereas anthropological ethnographies and theorizing cannot, despite their influence in scholarly circles. For so long in the shadow of anthropology, this unique aspect of the archaeological project should be of prime importance to a host of other disciplines, providing a rare opportunity to contribute to rather than simply borrow from, the social sciences. The materiality of the past has long-term consequences in the lives of numerous generations, extending beyond a heuristic enterprise. Inequalities get reproduced, be they based on sexuality, religion, ethnicity, or other axes of difference. And it is the very tangibility and longevity of our data that are often at the source of those processes.

One obvious dimension has been the archaeological interest in ethnicity, ethnogenesis, and the related trajectories of politics and nationalism (see Emberling 1997 for a full summary). There has never been any consensus in terminology, and 'ethnicity' has been used to denote the individual versus the group, the contents of an ethnic identity versus its instrumental expression, personal feelings versus the instrumental expression of identity, etc. (Banks 1996: 47). Ethnic identity is only one social determinate which can be cut across by status, occupation, gender, etc. that allows contact between groups. But it involves the social negotiation of difference and sameness, and it often entails larger tensions between individuals, the group, and the state. According to Emberling (1997: 305) ethnic identity is not fundamentally hierarchical like class and status in either a Marxist or Weberian sense. It is a concept aligned to the construct of kinship, albeit larger than the group, clan, or lineage. Archaeologists have shown that ethnicity is not always synonymous with a single language, race, location, or material culture. Some markers are more telling than others, such as styles of food or household arrangements, rather than language or pottery for example. Studies from areas as diverse as Mesoamerica (e.g. Teotihuacan, Chichen Itzá, Kaminaljuyú) and Mesopotamia (e.g. Kultepe Kanesh) have shown the complexities of identifying ethnicity, enclaves, and cultural boundaries due to the processes of cultural assimilation or maintenance of differences (see Emberling 1997: 316–18). Michael Spence's work (1992) on Oaxacan-influenced material culture and social practices at Teotihuacan provides an excellent example of these complex valences.

There has been a flood of volumes and papers which deal with these concepts as articulated in antiquity or as they have been deployed in modern settings (e.g. McGuire 1982; Marcus and Flannery 1983; Auger *et al.* 1987; Trigger 1989; Aldenderfer 1993; Brown 1994; Brumfiel and Fox 1994; Chapman 1994; Pollock and Lutz 1994; Baines 1996; Jones 1996). Nazi uses of archaeological materials to ground claims of ethnic superiority provide a particularly evocative and chilling example (Arnold 1990; Anthony 1995). Volumes on nationalism and the creation and maintenance of ethnic identities have traced developments over the past few centuries and demonstrate how archaeological accounts have been deeply imbricated (Kohl and Fawcett 1995; Trigger 1995; Díaz-Andreu and Champion 1996; Hamilakis 1996; Meskell 1998b). For example, Ataturk's creation of a modern, secular Turkish state drew on imagery and heritage claims from Sumerian Mesopotamia as well as the Hittites in an explicitly political manner to rebuild a nation. Indeed some have claimed there is a positive and empowering aspect to studies of ethnicity (Rowlands 1994; Naccache 1998). In a climate of post-colonialism, indigenous archaeologists have also been called on to produce narratives to counter the hegemonic discourses of Western commentators (papers in Bond and Gilham 1994; Gathercole and Lowenthal 1994; Shennan 1994; Meskell 1998b). The World Archaeology Congress has had a particularly influential role in these developments.

As is clearly seen in sociology, ethnicity and gender may reside at the forefront of interpretive debate. However, archaeology has had a long-standing interest in class and status (e.g. Peebles and Kus 1977; Tainter 1978; J.A. Brown 1981; Chapman *et al.* 1981; Chapman and Randsborg 1981; O'Shea 1984; Morris 1987, 1992; Lesko 1994; Wason 1994; Joyce 1996; Nordström 1996; S. Brown 1997; Meskell 1997). In Weberian terms, class refers to a group of people who have in common a specific causal component of their life chances in so far as this component is represented exclusively by economic interests. He distinguished class from status, since the latter is based on a specific, positive or negative, social estimation of honour and styles of life. However, there is often a strong correlation between the two phenomena. Class Theory in sociology, based on Marx and Weber, has been recently charged with constructing an over-socialized conception of human nature (Crompton 1995). From the 1960s onwards there has been an active critique of the closed system where the social world is perceived as a cohesive totality, resistant to change and structured by a tightly arranged hierarchy of power (Bauman 1995: 77). Comparative studies of civilizations have demonstrated that no human population is confined within a single system, but rather in a multiplicity of only partly coalescing organizations, collectives, and systems. After the 1970s, discussion of these issues fragmented into structure/agency debates. Major players like Althusser, Foucault, and Bourdieu diffused the image of society as an implacable machine that serves to maintain inequality, power, and privilege (Touraine 1995: 85), and this vision has persisted in archaeological theorizing, particularly in mortuary studies (e.g. Kristiansen 1991; DeMarrais *et al.* 1996; Earle 1997).

The growing interest in rank within archaeology emerged out of a broader trend towards a social archaeology, largely stimulated by the work of Childe, Clarke, Renfrew, and the Cambridge school (e.g. Hodder, Miller, Tilley, Shanks). Following the work of Service and Fried, archaeologists in the United States, like Yoffee and Earle, pursued models derived from anthropology (particularly the big man, chiefdom, stratified society, and state typologies) to describe the evolution of complex society. Most of these archaeologists were aiming to identify institutionalized status inequality i.e. any hierarchy of statuses that form part of social structure and extend beyond age, sex, individual characteristics, and inter-familial roles (Wason 1994: 19). Another development stemmed from Marxist notions of class struggle and oppression and found its fullest expression in historical archaeology (e.g. Spriggs 1984; Paynter and McGuire 1991). From the 1980s, many archaeologists have been gripped by Giddensian structuration theory: the notion that modes of economic relationships are translated into non-economic social structures (Giddens 1981: 105). This approach implies that class relationships are actively structured, although Giddens has received serious criticism for undermining agency in his own writing (Craib 1992; Shilling and Mellor 1996). Similarly Bourdieu has been embraced by archaeologists as a social theorist who promises to dissolve the structure/agency dualism and for allowing agents some contribution to their construction in the world (Bourdieu 1977, 1987, 1998). However, many of the same criticisms could be levelled at Bourdieu, who still manages to perpetuate a top-down vision of class structure and identity, delimiting the possibilities for self-fashioning. In archaeology, the ground-breaking paper which re-envisioned class in relation to a host of other signifiers was Elizabeth Brumfiel's American Anthropological Association Distinguished Lecture on gender, class, and faction. Here she argued against the system-based (or ecosystem) approach in favour of an agent-centred one which acknowledges the dynamism of gendered, ethnic, and class interactions (Brumfiel 1992). She imputed that elites were not the only prime movers of change and that subordinate groups could affect the structure of hierarchy. From this position paper we can witness the nascent stirrings of a third-wave feminist position that encompassed a range of identity markers allowing for hierarchies of difference in archaeological interpretation.

Approaches to other dimensions of identity that are burgeoning are those of age, the body, intimate relations (e.g. Gamble 1998; Lyons 1998; Meskell 1998c), and sexuality (see below). To date, studies of ageing have largely referred to a focus upon children, though this is gradually being replaced by more nuanced readings of the life cycle (papers in Gilchrist 2000). A recent study of Egyptian private life employs the life cycle as a more relevant template from which we might apprehend Egyptian experience, rather than traditional, Western, and ultimately teleological categorizations (Meskell 2004). These vectors of enquiry are related to an engendered enterprise but are depicted as often being tangential to it since they do not explicitly target 'women' per se.

Conceptualizing the body has recently provided a salient nexus for reconciling issues such as biological imperatives, cultural markers, personal embodiment and experience, diachronic diversity, and social difference. There has been a vast outpouring of case studies from prehistoric contexts (e.g. Shanks and Tilley 1982; Yates and Nordbladh 1990; Kus 1992; Marcus 1993; Thomas and Tilley 1993; Yates 1993; Shanks 1995; Knapp and Meskell 1997) to historically embedded examples (e.g. Bahrani 1996; Meskell 1996, 1998d, 1999; Robins 1996; Winter 1996; Gilchrist 1997, 1999; Joyce 1998, 2000a, 2001; Montserrat 1998; Osborne 1998a, 1998b). These studies suggest that archaeology as a discipline has much to offer other social sciences in being able to discuss the cultural specificities of corporeality, as well as a long temporal trajectory. Many of the initial studies drew heavily on Foucauldian notions of bodily inscription, that is, the literal marking of society upon the body of the individual. Social constructionism, largely influenced by post-structuralist theorizing, conceives bodies and identities as constructed through various disciplines and discourses. Following Craib (1998: 7), I would argue that in matters of agency and politics, identity is irreducible, it cannot be explained away. Foucauldian archaeology was followed in the 1990s by more contextual readings of embodiment on both cultural and individual levels, influenced by feminist and corporeal philosophies. Identity and experience are now perceived as being deeply implicated and grounded in the materiality of the body. Although there is social malleability, evident in the construction of bodily identity, there is also a material fixity which frames the individual, as there is with most strands of identity. Other related arenas of interest converge around subjectivity, selfhood, agency, emotionality, and the individual (Blake 1999; Meskell 1999; Tarlow 1999).

Explications of the body in all its sexed specificities prompted new discussions of sexuality in archaeology in the late 1990s (e.g. Montserrat 1996; Koloski-Ostrow and Lyons 1997; Robb 1997; McCafferty and McCafferty 1999; Meskell 1999, 2000; Hollimon 2000; Joyce 2000a). Generally the field has been slow to recognize the interpretive potentials of this significant vector of identity. It was only in 1998 that the first session on sexuality was organized for the Society for American Archaeology meetings (Schmidt and Voss 2000). Sexuality is very much a historical construction which brings together a host of different biological and psychical possibilities, such as gender identity, bodily differences, reproductive capacities, needs, desires, and fantasies. These need not be linked together and in other cultures have not been (Weeks 1997: 15). It is variety, not uniformity, that is the norm. Like the other strands of identity discussed, 'sexuality may be thought about, experienced and acted on differently according to age, class, ethnicity, physical ability, sexual orientation and preference, religion, and region' (Vance 1984: 17). For archaeologists it may be possible to pursue the subject of sexuality in a number of ways. Following Weeks (1997: 23) we might ask how is sexuality shaped and articulated by economic, social, and political structures; how and why has this domain come to be so central to Western culture given its various possibilities; what is the relationship between sex and power specifically in terms of class and race divisions? In addition gendered archaeology has taken heterosexuality to be the normative category, although the rise of queer theory, and the enormous popularity of Judith Butler's writings, exposed this position as untenable (Claassen 1992a; Joyce 1996; Meskell 1996). In all our engagements with this volatile topic we have to recentre human agency, volition, and variability.

Archaeology in its current interpretive guise is enjoying a frisson of activity in the arena of identity. Made possible through the plurality of a post-processual archaeology, the debate has been most ardently influenced by the recent outgrowth of gender and feminist archaeologies. It is for this reason that I will briefly chart the developments in this critical area of identity in archaeology.

Gendered identities

In the 1980s gender archaeology emerged within the conceptual space of a post-processual archaeology. It became *de rigueur* to critique the construction of knowledge within the field, especially those studies which claimed scientific objectivity. The first programmatic paper appeared in 1984 (Conkey and Spector 1984), although its real impact was felt in the 1990s when the validity of feminist perspectives gained widespread recognition. Reasons for this initial reluctance have been posited as the earlier positivist, hypothetico-deductive trends in processual archaeology, particularly in its American guise (Wylie 1991, 1992). The first volume devoted to gender and informed by feminist theory appeared as late as 1991 (Gero and Conkey 1991) and was influenced by long-standing feminist contributions in anthropology (see also Conkey and Gero 1997).

Like Wylie (1991) I see the course of gender archaeology as having taken several different turnings in the preceding two decades. She saw a tripartite development beginning with the critique of androcentrism, followed by the search for women, and a fundamental reconceptualization: this was not an unfolding of stages but a parallel structuring (Joyce and Claassen 1997: 2). The first forays are best characterized as 'finding women', which refers not only to those women of prehistory, but also to female archaeologists who had been erased from our own historiographic record (e.g. Gero 1985; Nixon 1994). To remedy this came numerous volumes dedicated to eminent women of the past, many of whom were far from feminist in their own politics (e.g. Kathleen Kenyon, Harriet Boyd Hawes; see Reyman 1992; Parezo 1993; Claassen 1994; Schrire 1995). Extensive studies that highlighted equity issues in both academic and non-academic archaeologies underscored the glaring bias in regard to education, employment, publication, and academic seniority (Nelson *et al.* 1994). The inherent sexism involved in conducting fieldwork, central to both archaeology and anthropology (Gero and Root 1990), was another key issue. Similar concerns have continued into later writings (e.g. Gero 1996).

Feminist contributions then moved towards revisionist histories (Gilchrist 1991), recasting women as active agents, who created their own social realities and resisted domination in the process (e.g. Arnold 1991; Beaudry *et al.* 1991; Gero and Conkey 1991; Hodder 1991; Øvrevik 1991; Spencer-Wood 1991). This was particulary visible in prehistoric scenarios which had tacitly promoted a history of 'mankind', characterized by 'man the hunter' and similar stone age *mentalités*. In the mid-1990s a series of contextual studies emerged, putting into practice theories of gender (e.g. Gibbs 1987; Robins 1993; Gilchrist 1994; Spector 1994; Wall 1994; Yentsch 1994). However, many were to remain implicitly studies of women. These concrete case studies were a marked departure from earlier position papers and critiques of andro-centrism. With them came a flurry of edited books, often conference proceedings (e.g. Bertelsen *et al.* 1987; Walde and Willows 1991; Claassen 1992b; du Cros and Smith 1993; Kokkinidou and Nikolaidou 1993; Balm and Beck 1995; Wright 1996; Casey *et al.* 1998). Many of these 1990s' studies have been firmly locked in the language of second-wave feminism, reiterating the constant oppression of women, and *doing gender* as finding women, looking at women's clothes and hairstyles, and ignoring the complexities of sex, sexuality, ageing, status, ethnicity, thus eliding all possibilities of difference. Gender is only one social determinate in the hierarchy of identity issues. As Conkey and Gero ask:

> Why, despite the many new studies in the archaeology of gender, have most merely added gender as just another variable into an otherwise depersonalized view of the past? into an archaeological account in the passive voice? into a way of framing human life that distances and categorizes more than allowing our own positionalities to inform and generate engagements with the people of the past? We worry that the recent archaeological studies of gender have participated in narrowing the field rather than opening up our studies.
>
> (1997: 425)

At the end of the 1990s archaeologists of gender pursued third-wave agenda, often implicitly, by interpolating factors such as age, sexual orientation, ethnicity (e.g. Claassen and Joyce 1997; Gilchrist 1997; Hollimon 1997; Joyce and Claassen 1997; Lesick 1997; Lesure 1997; Prezzano 1997; Rega 1997; Wilson 1997; Sweely 1999; Woodhouse-Beyer 1999). This was a long-overdue shift from the second-wave femi-nist tenets of finding women, as a homogeneous group, at the cost of all others. Gender identity should be seen as a complex assortment of networks of signifying practices, varying for individuals over time, as it intersects with other networks of sig-nifying practices located in such concepts as class and race. As Alison Wylie (1992: 59) commented over a decade ago, 'feminists can no longer assume substantial com-monalities in the power held, exercised, or suffered by women *as women*; their own critical and empirical explorations make it clear that, even within a single society, the extent and kinds of power women exercise varies dramatically across class, race, and ethnic divisions, and also through the life cycles of individual women'. The corollary of this could be found in contemporary masculinity theory, yet studies of social rela-tions, masculinity (Knapp and Meskell 1997; Knapp 1998), or sexuality have not generally been construed as gender archaeology. There remains a considerable time lag in the recognition of these more nuanced engagements. *Ipso facto* gender remains the domain of women writing predominantly about women.

It is now axiomatic that our identities are fluid and mutable, under negotiation as we experience life, and open to manipulation if we have the opportunity. Life on the Web has demonstrated that people will avidly change their gender and their sexual prefer-ences when confronted with the opportunity afforded by anonymity (Turkle 1996;

Porter 1997). People do not always perform as 'men' or 'women' and identities are not coherent or prior to the interactions through which they are constituted. Individuals are gendered through discursive daily practices: 'gender is thus a process of becoming rather than a state of being' (Harvey and Gow 1994a: 8). This new concept of identity politics does not necessarily entail objective needs or political implications, but challenges the connections between identity and politics and positions identity as a factor in any political analysis. Thus we can say that though gender is not natural, biological, universal, or essential, we can still claim that it is relevant because of its political ramifications. Here gender is defined in positional terms. In the past few decades we have been indelibly influenced, both in political and professional terms, by the sexual revolution, gay liberation, feminism, and race-minority power (di Leonardo and Lancaster 1997). It must come as no surprise then that much work is suffused with those very concepts or that, in the least, contemporary theory has been influenced by those events.

Some would posit distinct problems with the use of contemporary identity terminologies to discuss the ancient past. For example how do we reconceptualize 'sex' in societies that do not conform to Western binary categories and how do we even begin to use the word 'gender', itself founded on the discursive construction of biological sex versus culturally created gender? Additionally in cultures such as Egypt there was no word for heterosexual or homosexual (Parkinson 1995), so how might we apprehend same sex relations in that well-documented context? I would suggest that there are two projects that archaeologists could pursue. First, we can acknowledge that 'homosexuality' is an aspect of identity with enormous contemporary valency and that it is entirely valid to examine similar engagements in the past, while acknowledging that there are cultural specificities which name and label practices and people, in divergent ways (Foucault 1978, 1985, 1986). Second, we can acknowledge that 'same-sex relations' may present a less loaded terminology, and focus predominantly on the salient differences with which people name and construct their lived identities. Archaeologists might focus on the diverse ways people experience their lives without the constraining taxonomies with which modern Westerners have shackled themselves, i.e. that 'homosexuality' did not exist as a typology prior to the late 1800s. But we should not let semantics impede us: language and culture do not necessarily constitute what is talked about. As Craib quips:

> I cannot talk about my liver without language, but it does not make any sense to say that my liver is constructed by language or culture...different societies might have different conceptions of the liver and its function and one might surmise that modern medical science has a very sophisticated concept of the liver – much more sophisticated, for example, than classical Greek society. However, it does not follow that my liver is more sophisticated than was Plato's liver.
>
> (1998: 109)

Unnatural domains

I would like now to argue that it is not enough to provide a list of salient identity markers, we must interrogate the very foundations of our imposed categories and try to understand social domains in their cultural context. I suggest that archaeologists have been reticent in adopting a third-wave feminist approach, whereby they would conduct complex analysis of identity in holistic terms, and this represents the first stumbling block. Without a recognition of the full spectrum of social difference and the specificities of operation, archaeologists cannot move on to further contextual understandings by deconstructing the 'natural' categories we create and project. So I see that archaeology has a double project to fulfil. And the inspiration for this theorization has come from anthropology, specifically from the work by Sylvia Yanagisako and Carol Delaney (1995a), *Naturalizing Power*. Theirs is a provocative thesis which focuses attention on the domains in society that are crucial for the formation of people's identity – family, sexuality, race, nation, religion. They argue that we cannot assume a priori that what *we* consider as natural, no matter how institutionalized, is fundamental. They argue that,

> [t]he verities on which identity – whether gender, sexual orientation, nationality, ethnicity, or religion – has traditionally been based no longer provide the answers, in part because of the contact and conflict between peoples and in part because the explanatory schemes upon which identity was based have been shown to rest not on the bedrock of fact but suspended in narratives of origin.
>
> (1995b: 1)

While the false foundational premises of sex and gender have only recently been challenged in archaeology, this has rarely extended to other vectors of identity – whether it be sexuality or ethnicity. Archaeologists have found it difficult to extricate themselves from 'naturalized power' in the discourses of identity that are fundamental to our own culture: thus we have construed gender in the past, for instance, as simplistically mirroring specific contemporary terms and agendas, or connoted sexuality as existing primarily in a modern European guise. The specificities of the ancient data, when studied contextually, challenge that normativity. Reciprocally, anthropologists and social sociologists might draw upon archaeology's provision of a deep temporal sequence in terms of cultural difference, often as it is mediated through the discursive production of material culture. This rich strata of evidence can only enhance, and contribute to, the complex picture already emerging of identity as having both contextual and embedded entanglements.

Anthropologists Yanagisako and Delaney ask: 'what is more natural than sex?' Yet we can easily go about demonstrating the cultural diversity of approaches in specific contexts: understanding biology/reproduction is not necessarily correspondent with the obvious logical causality that we make. Consider David Schneider's work with the Yap, a group living in the Pacific, who recognize the linkage between sexual organs, intercourse, and reproduction in pigs, yet view human sexuality rather differently. After all, as they wisely point out, pigs are not people (Yanagisako and Delaney 1995b: 7). There are other ways of seeing and deploying similar knowledges. For ourselves,

> [g]ender definition and value have been inherent in the Western theory of procreation, but procreation is not just about the natural; it includes an ontological dimension. Because gender is at the heart of these socio-religious systems it is not surprising that issues of gender and procreation, marriage, family, birth control, abortion, sexuality, homosexuals, new reproductive technologies are at the centre

of contemporary debates in our society, for new beliefs and practices are not just about the private, domestic domain, but challenge the entire etymological order.
(Yanagisako and Delaney 1995b: 9; see also Weeks 1997)

And much the same point could be directed at the ancient Egyptian evidence, specifically the domestic evidence at the New Kingdom site of Deir el Medina (c. 1550–1070 BC: see Meskell 1998a) with its iconography of female sexuality, birth, children, ritual, and religion all existing harmoniously in a settlement context (Meskell 1999, 2000), and usually within the same room, signifying the necessary blurring of category and the linkage between identity and the cosmological order. What we see as natural exists largely within our own temporal and cultural borders, yet we take this as fixed and 'natural' and thus transferable to ancient contexts. The elision of difference results in a predictably normative picture of the past that may bear little relation to ancient realities.

For a fuller explication of these processes of identity formation and social domains, archaeologists might look to anthropological case studies. Lila Abu-Lughod's influential studies of the Egyptian Bedouin suggest that formal institutional domains are not cross-culturally applicable and that coherent systems of meaning can exist in seemingly contradictory ways: the discourse of honour and shame is set beside the poetic discourse of vulnerability and attachment (Abu-Lughod 1991: 162; Abu-Lughod 1993). Although not wanting to infer lineage or stasis, I would posit that similar contradictory themes were interwoven in ancient Egyptian society: female sexuality, desire, and romantic freedoms could be easily juxtaposed with mothering, birth, and domestic ritual, as well as sexual inequality, legal discrimination, and harsh, sometimes misogynist, treatments of women in society (Meskell 1994, 1998a, 1999). Other societies, from the Pacific to Latin America, constellate sexuality and violence in ways Anglo-Americans find difficult to conceptualize or accept (Harvey and Gow 1994b). Love and desire can be predicated on socially sanctioned practices which threaten the physical integrity of the beloved. In essence we should relinquish our own desire for a coherent narrative structure of social identity and life experience.

Archaeologists might also draw on, and contribute to, recent feminist analyses of identity, specifically those which source individual (and gender) identity along multiple lines. The engendered subject occupies the site of multiple differences and thus multiple subjectivities (Moore 1994: 143). Drawing on the work of de Lauretis, Moore refers to this as a post-post-structuralist concept of subjectivity. De Lauretis (1986: 9) cites a body of emergent feminist writing that offers the concept of a multiple, shifting, and often self-contradictory identity – this entails 'an identity made up of heterogeneous and heteronomous representations of gender, race and class, and often indeed across languages and cultures'. Feminist musings on embodied subjectivity and the contradictory positions we assume as part of daily (gendered) negotiations are helpful for archaeologists examining the contradictions presented to us by the ancient data, particularly those related to intimate relations and sexed hierarchies of power and inequality. It is perhaps at this level that archaeologists can finally participate within wider gender debates about issues of representation and reality – offering the potentials of real interdisciplinarity.

The meanings of male and female are not always about natural or prediscursive difference, thus prompting us to explore the ways in which these meanings are connected with other inequalities, supposedly structured by other differences. Feminists have been committed to challenging the gender status quo and feminist anthropologists played a crucial role in situating ideologies of natural identities within structures of inequality. Research on gender already suggests that its construction does not always follow predetermined, 'natural' patterns so that archaeological interpretations 'will have to focus on the particularities of gender constructs, especially their symbolic and ideational dimensions, in specific contexts' (Wylie 1991: 49). We should further recognize that hierarchies of status and power come already embedded in symbolic systems which can only be revealed through contextually specific cultural practices (Yanagisako and Delaney 1995b: 10–11). So instead of structuring identity along single, unilinear lines as Nelson (1997: 16) would argue, we might consider revising the entire ontological basis of our investigations. Might it not be better to consider social lives in terms of the life cycle rather than a list of social signifiers? To date we have followed the latter line of enquiry, reducing social relations to a simple set of separate identity politics. By considering the life cycle we might more closely approximate the realities of social experience, since age and sex, sexuality and life course, ethnicity and class more often coalesce together and in indivisible ways. This is also part of the deconstruction of naturalism, a breaking down of the categories we hold as distinct.

Recent investigations at Deir el Medina, specifically the rich mortuary data (Meskell 1998c, 1999), suggest that sex cannot be singled out as the primary structuring principle since a host of factors were operative and subject to change within a matter of generations. In the poorer cemetery of the early-mid-18th Dynasty, age and marital status seem to be the primary issues for structuring inequality, whereas sex was generally smoothed over. The burial wealth of males and females was basically commensurate at this lower socio-economic level. The spatial layout of this cemetery was based on the life cycle: neonates were buried at the base of the slope, children further up, adolescents were buried mid-slope, and adults were positioned at the top of the slope. In the wealthier cemetery the main distinction structuring tomb wealth was sex and to a lesser degree age. Men were buried with many times the burial wealth of their female counterparts. For the same cemetery in the Ramesside period, some 100 years later, divisions on the basis of sex lessen and tombs begin to include a large number of family members and generations, suggesting a move to lineage-based burials. There is no children's cemetery and all family members tend to be incorporated into these multi-vaulted tombs. Nonetheless, male relatives continue to get the lion's share of funerary wealth and are featured more prominently in mortuary iconography and representations. The 400 tombs at Deir el Medina which span the entire New Kingdom provide a concrete example of the complexities of identity issues, which cannot be reduced to unidimensional analyses but must be made complex, rather than doing interpretive violence to the data – that is, privileging one dimension of difference because of our own political commitments.

This need for multidimensional analysis equally applies to the taxonomies that archaeologists regularly deploy, domains such as the domestic, religious or ritual, social and sexual spheres, etc. In the settlement at Deir el Medina we can also see the breakdown or blurring of categories. I have previously discussed the overlapping of domesticity, sexuality, and ritual life in Egyptian social life. The iconography of these households might strike us as contradictory: in rooms supposedly relating to women's space and birthing we had an example of a nude, female musician replete with several erotic signifiers (Meskell 2000). At first glance the woman depicted has all the visual cues we would associate with a male view of sexuality – possibly even prostitution. The workman Nebamun either painted this image himself or had it commissioned, and it occupied a prominent position, being immediately visible to anyone who entered the house. I remember wondering how the women of the house related to this example of erotica – was it pornographic, offensive, or even desirable for these women? It is easy for us to separate out such images as being sexual or pornographic because of contemporary labels and taxonomies (see Hunt 1993). Yet these initial reactions were gradually replaced by a sense of blurred boundaries and collapsed dichotomies, a sense that sexuality did not exist as a separate sphere; there is no word for 'sexuality' in Egyptian language. One is not designed heterosexual or homosexual either; there were names for practices rather than people (Parkinson 1995: 59). From the archaeological and iconographic data it appeared that what we term 'sexuality' pervaded so many aspects of Egyptian social and ritual life that it was a truly embedded concept, free of many of the moralistic connotations we are familiar with. It proved unproductive to hold to Western categories when Egyptian ones were so culturally different and fundamental to a more contextual understanding of social dynamics. Judaeo-Christian sentiments might radically erase the connections between family and sexuality, the sexualization of children, or the possibilities of sexuality in the next life – but the Egyptians had no such framework. The interstices of all these networks of identity and experience provide the really interesting terrain of ancient life.

Another dimension through which identity is formulated and established is that of what we construe as kin, usually as defined by anthropological theorizing. According to Yanagisako and Delaney, 'any particular kinship system was thought to be a cultural elaboration of the biological facts of human reproduction, and anthropologists recognized that there were significant differences in how far these genealogical maps extended and how relations in them were classified' (1995b: 9–10). As a demonstration of a challenge to this normativity we might return to Egyptian kinship terminology, which extended to those of blood relation as well as unrelated peer groups. The term *sn* for 'brother' is a salient example; it includes the relationship of brother, brother-in-law, brother's son, mother's brother, and sister's son (Robins 1979: 202). Much the same pattern exists for the female equivalent *snt* for 'sister'. Lovers frequently refer to themselves as brother and sister (Robins 1979: 203; McDowell 1999), which read literally has led to much confusion over Egyptian incest.

David Schneider famously critiqued the reduction of kinship to genealogy, arguing that kinship cannot be conflated simply with a biological infrastructure since the cultural dimension, terms, and practices vary widely from society to society (Weston 1995: 88). If we find it difficult to refigure kin outside our own Western terminologies then consider our own deconstruction of kinship as a domain. Our own notions of kinship are now being challenged by two powerful domains: new reproductive technologies and changing gender and sexual relationships (see Dolgin 1995; McKinnon 1995). Today we are effectively rewriting kin relations in social and legal spheres. This predicament underscores that nothing is natural (see Laqueur 1990), since science and sexuality have begun impinging on what many would posit were the most fundamental of human social relationships at the very nexus of individual identity.

In ancient contexts we can never be clear where one cultural domain ends and another begins. Take the example of the ancestor busts in Egypt, revered relatives who had become effective spirits in the next world (Demarée 1983; Friedman 1985, 1994). The boundaries are blurred among kinship, magic, and religion. These arte-facts bridged the classic divide between the functioning objects of this world and the world beyond the grave. Even the concept of the object as a static artefact without agency in and of itself has been rendered suspect (Gell 1998: 134, 223). In a similar study Rosemary Joyce (2000b) has suggested that Mesoamerican heirloom valuables such as jades and costume ornaments were circulated for hundreds of years after their production, thus retaining residual memories and taking on new meanings for Classic Maya nobles. Here again artefacts become repositories of more than single meanings and histories, they become liminal pieces in the worlds of both living and dead. According to Yanagisako and Delaney, only culture makes the boundaries of domains seem natural, gives ideologies power, and makes hegemonies appear seamless. It might be more interesting to enquire how meanings migrate across domain bound-aries and how specific actions are multiply constituted. How do we as archaeologists historicize our domains and trace their effects? We also have to interrogate what we have constructed as the facts of life, calling into question the constricting construc-tions of motherhood, the domain of kinship, the spheres of sexuality and religiosity for example. If the sacred is open to divergent readings then what is supposedly 'natural' must be revisited. Anthropologists, and by extension archaeologists, have happily read across other people's cultural domains. In fact anthropology has shown us the inherent pitfalls of that approach, suggesting to those of us who study the past that we too have been guilty of projecting 'natural' boundaries and categorizations onto unsuitable, very different cultural contexts. We cannot assume that in other soci-eties cultural domains are structured like ours and expect the same analytic constel-lations and results. Contextual archaeology is premised on the recognition of local patterns of meanings in-practice. But I would argue we have not taken it far enough. Archaeologists have been reticent to explore the full spectrum of social identity, either because they are wary of increased complexity in their analyses or due to their privi-leging of specific discourses of difference – predominantly gender-based inequality.

As a feminist I argue we need to democratize our struggles by giving equal respect to the claims of other minorities, resulting in a real theoretical pluralism which is in keeping with both third-wave feminism as well as post-processual or contextual archaeology. Extending this redescription further I have suggested we critique and explore the construction of ancient social domains, those which we have overlain from contemporary culture assuming that they are 'natural' and fundamental due to our own institutionalization. Following Yanagisako and Delaney, these are generally the analytic domains of kinship, gender, politics, religion, and social systems. I have pro-posed that many of these domains are now being refigured in contemporary society and should similarly be interrogated more fully before application to archaeological or historical contexts. If we fail to push these questions further we risk an elision of dif-ference, conflating ancient and modern experience in the process. Identity provides a salient case in point – as one of the most compelling issues of our day it is right that we focus on the social experiences of ancient people, yet what makes these questions so intriguing is how specific societies evoked such different responses prompted by cat-egorical differences in their understandings and constructions of social domains. We should fight the temptation to elide history through the deep-seated conviction that what is 'real' cannot, should not, be subject to change (Weston 1995: 90–1) and acknowledge that as cultural commentators we continually reinvent and romanticize the 'real'.

Acknowledgements

This chapter owes a substantial intellectual debt to the work of Sylvia Yanagisako and Carol Delaney in *Naturalizing Power*. It is not often that a single work impels us to re-envision our ways of seeing culture and category in ontological terms or to reframe the operationalizing of identities in a well-known context such as ancient Egypt. I would also like to thank Victor Buchli, Geoff Emberling, Ian Hodder, Rosemary Joyce, and Chris Gosden for reading and commenting on the piece. A special thanks to Alison Wylie for her close reading of the text and for her many insights.

Bibliography

Abu-Lughod, L. 1991. Writing Against Culture. In Fox, R.G. (ed.), *Recapturing Anthropology: Working in the Present*. Santa Fe: School of American Research Press, pp. 137–62.
Abu-Lughod, L. 1993. Islam and the Gendered Discourse of Death. *International Journal of Middle Eastern Studies* 25: 187–205.
Aldenderfer, M.S. (ed.). 1993. *Domestic Architecture: Ethnicity and Complementarity in the South Central Andes*. Iowa: University of Iowa Press.
Anthony, D. 1995. Nazi and Eco-Feminist Prehistories: Counter Points in Indo-European Archaeology. In Kohl, P. and Fawcett, C. (eds), *Nationalism, Politics and the Practice of Archaeology*. Cambridge: Cambridge University Press, pp. 82–96.
Arnold, B. 1990. The Past as Propaganda: Totalitarian Archaeology in Nazi Germany. *Antiquity* 64: 464–78.
Arnold, B. 1991. The Deposed Princess of Vix: The Need for an Engendered European Prehistory. In Walde, D. and Willows, N. (eds), *The Archaeology of Gender*. Calgary: University of Calgary, pp. 366–74.
Auger, R. *et al.* (eds). 1987. *Ethnicity and Culture*. Calgary: Archaeological Association at the University of Calgary.
Bahrani, Z. 1996. The Hellenization of Ishtar: Nudity, Fetishism, and the Production of Cultural Differentiation in Ancient Art. *Oxford Art Journal* 19(2): 3–16.
Baines, J. 1996. Contextualizing Egyptian Representations of Society and Ethnicity. In Cooper, J.S. and Schwartz, G.M. (eds), *The Study of the Ancient Near East in the 21st Century*. Winona Lake, IN: Eisenbrauns, pp 339–84.
Balm, J. and Beck, W. (eds). 1995. *Gendered Archaeology: The Second Australian Women in Archaeology Conference*. Canberra: ANU Press.
Banks, M. 1996. *Ethnicity: Anthropological Constructions*. London: Routledge.
Bauman, Z. 1995. Sociology and Postmodernity. In P. Joyce (ed.), *Class*. Oxford: Oxford University Press, pp. 4–83.
Beaudry, M.C., Cook, L.J., and Mrozowski, S.A. 1991. Artifacts and Active Voices: Material Culture as Social Discourse. In McGuire, R.H. and Paynter, R. (eds), *The Archaeology of Inequality*. Oxford: Blackwell, pp. 150–91.
Bertelsen, R., Lillehammer, A., and Naess, J.-R. (eds). 1987. *Were They All Men? An Examination of Sex Roles in Prehistoric Society*. Stavanger: Arkeologisk Museum i Stavanger.

Blake, E.C. 1999. Identity Mapping in the Sardinian Bronze Age. *European Journal of Archaeology* 2(1): 55–75.

Bond, G.C. and Gillam, A. (eds). 1994. *Social Construction of the Past: Representation as Power*. London: Routledge.

Bourdieu, P. 1977. *Outline of a Theory of Practice*. Cambridge: Cambridge University Press.

Bourdieu, P. 1987. What Makes a Social Class. *Berkeley Journal of Sociology* 22: 1–18.

Bourdieu, P. 1998. *Practical Reason: On the Theory of Action*. Cambridge: Polity.

Brown, J. A. 1981. The Search for Rank in Prehistoric Burials. In Chapman, R., Kinnes, I., and Randsborg, K. (eds), *The Archaeology of Death*. Cambridge: Cambridge University Press, pp. 25–37.

Brown, K.S. 1994. Seeing Stars: Character and Identity in the Landscapes of Modern Macedonia. *Antiquity* 68(261): 784–96.

Brown, S. 1997. 'Ways of Seeing' Women in Antiquity, an Introduction to Feminism in Classical Archaeology and Art History. In Koloski-Ostrow, A.O. and Lyons, C.L. (eds), *Naked Truths: Women, Sexuality, and Gender in Classical Art and Archaeology*. London: Routledge, pp. 12–42.

Brumfiel, E.M. 1992. Distinguished Lecture in Archaeology: Breaking and Entering the Ecosystem – Gender, Class, and Faction Steal the Show. *American Anthropologist* 94: 551–67.

Brumfiel, E.M. and Fox, J.W. (eds). 1994. *Factional Competition and Political Development in the New World*. Cambridge: Cambridge University Press.

Casey, M. *et al.* (eds). 1998. *Redefining Archaeology: Feminist Perspectives*. Canberra: ANU Press.

Chapman, J. 1994. Destruction of a Common Heritage: The Archaeology of War in Croatia, Bosnia and Hercegovina. *Antiquity* 68(258): 120–6.

Chapman, R. and Randsborg, K. 1981. Approaches to the Archaeology of Death. In Chapman, R., Kinnes, I., and Randsborg, K. (eds), *The Archaeology of Death*. Cambridge: Cambridge University Press, pp. 1–24.

Chapman, R., Kinnes, I., and Randsborg, K. (eds). 1981. *The Archaeology of Death*. Cambridge: Cambridge University Press.

Claassen, C. (ed.). 1992a. *Exploring Gender through Archaeology: Selected Papers from the 1991 Boone Conference*. Madison, WI: Prehistory Press.

Claassen, C. 1992b. Questioning Gender: An Introduction. In Claassen, C. (ed.), *Exploring Gender through Archaeology: Selected Papers from the 1991 Boone Conference*. Madison, WI: Prehistory Press, pp. 1–9.

Claassen, C. (ed.). 1994. *Women in Archaeology*. Philadelphia: University of Pennsylvania Press.

Claassen, C. and Joyce, R.A. (eds). 1997. *Women in Prehistory: North America and Mesoamerica*. Philadelphia: University of Pennsylvania Press.

Conkey, M.W. and Gero, J.M. 1997. Programme to Practice: Gender and Feminism in Archaeology. *Annual Review of Anthropology* 26: 411–37.

Conkey, M.W. and Spector, J.D. 1984. Archaeology and the Study of Gender. *Advances in Archaeological Method and Theory* 7: 1–38.

Craib, I. 1992. *Anthony Giddens*. London: Routledge.

Craib, I. 1998. *Experiencing Identity*. London: Sage.

Crompton, R. 1995. The Development of Classical Inheritance. In Joyce, P. (ed.), *Class*. Oxford: Oxford University Press, pp. 43–55.

de Lauretis, T. (ed.). 1986. *Feminist Studies/Critical Studies*. London: Macmillan.

Demarée, R.J. 1983. The *3ḫ Ikr n Rꜥ*-Stelae: On Ancestor Worship in Ancient Egypt. Leiden: Nederlands Instituut voor het Nabije Oosten te Leiden.

DeMarrais, E., Castillo, L.J., and Earle, T. 1996. Ideology, Materialization, and Power Strategies. *Current Anthropology* 37(1): 15–32.

di Leonardo. M. and Lancaster, R.N. 1997. Embodied Meanings, Carnal Practices. In Lancaster, R.N. and di Leonardo, M. (eds), *The Gender/Sexuality Reader: Culture, History, Political Economy.* New York: Routledge, pp. 1–10.

Díaz-Andreu, M. and Champion, T. 1996. *Nationalism and Archaeology in Europe.* London: University College London Press.

Dolgin, J.L. 1995. Family Law and the Facts of Family. In Yanagisako, S. and Delaney, C. (eds), *Naturalizing Power: Essays in Feminist Cultural Analysis.* New York: Routledge, pp. 47–67.

du Cros, H. and Smith, L.-J. (eds). 1993. *Women in Archaeology: A Feminist Critique.* Canberra: ANU Press.

Earle, T. 1997. *How Chiefs Come to Power.* The Political Economy in Prehistory. Palo Alto: Stanford University Press.

Emberling, G. 1997. Ethnicity in Complex Societies: Archaeological Perspectives. *Journal of Archaeological Research* 5(4): 295–344.

Foucault, M. 1978. *The History of Sexuality.* London: Routledge.

Foucault, M. 1980. *Herculine Barbin: Being the Recently Discovered Memoirs of a Nineteenth Century Hermaphrodite.* New York: Pantheon.

Foucault, M. 1985. *The History of Sexuality: The Use of Pleasure.* Harmondsworth: Penguin.

Foucault, M. 1986. *The History of Sexuality: The Care of the Self.* Harmondsworth: Penguin.

Friedman, F.A. 1985. On the Meaning of Some Anthropoid Busts from Deir el Medina. *Journal of Egyptian Archaeology* 71: 82–9.

Friedman, F.A. 1994. Aspects of Domestic Life and Religion. In Lesko, L.H. (ed.), *Pharaoh's Workers: The Villagers of Deir el Medina.* New York: Cornell University Press, pp. 95–11.

Gamble, C. 1998. Paleolithic Society and the Release from Proximity: A Network Approach to Intimate Relations. *World Archaeology* 95(3): 426–49.

Gathercole, P.W. and Lowenthal, D. (eds). 1994. *The Politics of the Past.* London: Routledge.

Gell, A. 1998. *Art and Agency: An Anthropological Theory.* Oxford: Oxford University Press.

Gero, J. 1985. Socio-Politics and the Woman-at-Home Ideology. *American Antiquity* 50(2): 342–50.

Gero, J. 1996. Archaeological Practice and Gendered Encounters with Field Data. In Wright, R.P. (ed.). *Gender and Archaeology.* Philadelphia: University of Pennsylvania Press, pp. 251–80.

Gero, J.M. and Conkey, M.W. (eds). 1991. *Engendering Archaeology: Women and Prehistory.* Oxford: Blackwell.

Gero, J. and Root, D. 1990. Public Presentation and Private Concerns: Archaeology in the Pages of *National Geographic.* In Gathercole, P. and Lowenthal, D. (eds), *The Politics of the Past.* London: Routledge, pp. 19–37.

Gibbs, L. 1987. Identifying Gender in the Archaeological Record: A Contextual Study. In Hodder, I. (ed.), *The Archaeology of Contextual Meanings.* Cambridge: Cambridge University Press, pp. 79–89.

Giddens, A. 1981. *The Class Structure of the Advanced Societies.* London: Hutchinson.

Giddens, A. 1984. *The Constitution of Society: Outline of a Theory of Structuration.* Cambridge: Polity.

Gilchrist, R. 1991. Women's Archaeology? Political Feminism, Gender Theory and Historical Revision. *Antiquity* 65: 495–501.

Gilchrist, R. 1994. *Gender and Material Culture: The Archaeology of Religious Women.* London: Routledge.

Gilchrist, R. 1997. Ambivalent Bodies: Gender and Medieval Archaeology. In Moore, J. and Scott, E. (eds), *Invisible People and Processes: Writing Gender and Childhood into European Archaeology.* London: Leicester University Press, pp. 42–58.

Gilchrist, R.L. 1999. *Gender and Archaeology: Contesting the Past.* London: Routledge.

Gilchrist. R. (ed.). 2000. Human Lifecycles. *World Archaeology* 31(3).

Hamilakis. Y. 1996. Through the Looking Glass: Nationalism, Archaeology and the Politics of Identity. *Antiquity* 70: 975–8.

Harvey, P. and Gow, P. 1994a. Introduction. In Harvey, P. and Gow, P. (eds), *Sex and Violence: Issues in Representation and Experience*. London: Routledge, pp. 1–17.

Harvey, P. and Gow, P. (eds). 1994b. *Sex and Violence: Issues in Representation and Experience*. London: Routledge.

Hodder. I. 1991. Gender Representation and Social Reality. In Walde, D. and Willows, N.D. (eds), *The Archaeology of Gender: Proceedings of the 22nd Annual Chacmool Conference*. Calgary: University of Calgary Archaeological Association, pp. 11–16.

Hollimon, S.E. 1997. The Third-Gender in Native California: Two-Spirit Undertakers Among the Chumash and their Neighbors. In Claassen, C. and Joyce, R. (eds), *Women in Prehistory*. Philadelphia: University of Pennsylvania Press, pp. 173–88.

Hollimon, S.E. 2000. Gender and Sexuality in Prehistoric Chumash Society. In Schmidt, R. and Voss, B. (eds), *Archaeologies of Sexuality*. London: Routledge, pp. 179–96.

Hunt, L. (eds). 1993. *The Invention of Pornography: Obscenity and the Origins of Modernity 1500–1800*. New York: Zone Books.

Jones, S. 1996. *The Archaeology of Ethnicity: Constructing Identities in the Past and Present*. London: Routledge.

Joyce, R.A. 1996. The Construction of Gender in Classic Maya Monuments. In Wright, R.P. (ed.), *Gender and Archaeology*. Philadelphia: University of Pennsylvania Press, pp. 167–95.

Joyce, R.A. 1998. Performing the Body in Prehispanic Central America. *RES: Anthropology and Aesthetics* 33(Spring): 147–66.

Joyce, R.A. 2000a. A Precolumbian Gaze: Male Sexuality Among the Ancient Maya. In Schmidt, R. and Voss, B. (eds), *Archaeologies of Sexuality*. London: Routledge, pp. 263–83.

Joyce, R.A. 2000b. Heirlooms and Houses: Materiality and Social Memory. In Joyce, R.A. and Gillespie, S. (eds), *Beyond Kinship: Social and Material Reproduction in House Societies*. Philadelphia: University of Pennsylvania Press, pp. 189–202.

Joyce, R.A. 2001. Performance and Inscription: Negotiating Sex and Gender in Classic Maya Society. In Klein, C. (ed.), *Gender in Prehispanic America*. Washington, DC: Dumbarton Oaks, pp. 107–39.

Joyce, R.A. and Claassen, C. 1997. Women in the Ancient Americas: Archaeologists, Gender and the Making of Prehistory. In Claassen, C. and Joyce, R.A. (eds), *Women in Prehistory: North America and Mesoamerica*. Philadephia: University of Pennsylvania Press, pp. 1–14.

Knapp, A.B. 1998. Who's Come a Long Way Baby? Masculinist Approaches to a Gendered Archaeology. *Archaeological Dialogues* 5(2): 91–106.

Knapp, A.B. and Meskell, L.M. 1997. Bodies of Evidence in Prehistoric Cyprus. *Cambridge Archaeological Journals* 7(2): 183–204.

Kohl, P.L. and Fawcett, C. (eds). 1995. *Nationalism, Politics and the Practice of Archaeology*. Cambridge: Cambridge University Press.

Kokkinidou, D, and Nikolaidou, M. (eds). 1993. *Archaeology and Gender Approaches to Aegean Prehistory*. Thessaloniki: Banias.

Koloski-Ostrow, A.O. and Lyons, C.L. (eds). 1997. *Naked Truths: Women, Sexuality, and Gender in Classical Art and Archaeology*. London: Routledge.

Kristiansen, K. 1991. Chiefdoms, States, and Systems of Social Evolution. In Earle, T. (ed.), *Chiefdoms: Power, Economy and Ideology*. Cambridge: Cambridge University Press, pp. 16–43.

Kus, S. 1992. Toward an Archaeology of Body and Soul. In Gardin, J.-C. and Peebles, C. (eds), *Representations in Archaeology*. Bloomington: Indiana University Press, pp. 168–77.

Laqueur, T. 1990. *Making Sex: Body and Gender from the Greeks to Freud*. Cambridge, MA: Harvard University Press.

Lesick, K.S. 1997. Re-Engendering Gender: Some Theoretical and Methodological Concerns on a Burgeoning Archaeological Pursuit. In Moore, J. and Scott, L. (eds), *Invisible People and Processes: Writing Gender and Childhood into European Archaeology*. London: Leicester University Press, pp. 31–41.

Lesko, B.S. 1994. Ranks, Roles and Rights. In Fesko, L.H. (ed.), *Pharaoh's Workers: The Villagers of Deir el Medina*. Ithaca, NY: Cornell University Press, pp. 15–39.

Lesure, R.G. 1997. Figurines and Social Identities in Early Sedentary Societies of Coastal Chiapas, Mexico 1550–800 b.c. In Claassen, C. and Joyce, R.A. (eds), *Women in Prehistory: North America and Mesoamerica*. Philadelphia: University of Pennsylvania Press, pp. 227–48.

Lyons, D. 1998. Witchcraft, Gender, Power and Intimate Relations in Muta Compounds in Dela Northern Cameroon. *World Archaeology* 95(3): 344–62.

Marcus, J. and Flannery, K.V. (eds). 1983. *The Cloud People: Divergent Evolution of the Zapotec and Mixtec Civilizations*. New York: Academic Press.

Marcus, M.I. 1993. Incorporating the Body: Adornment, Gender, and Social Identity in Ancient Iran. *Cambridge Archaeological Journal* 3(2): 157–78.

McCafferty, G.G. and McCafferty, S.D. 1999. The Metamorphosis of Xochi Quetzal. In Sweely, T. (ed.), *Manifesting Power: Gender and the Interpretation of Power in Archaeology*. London: Routledge, pp. 103–25.

McDowell, A.G. 1999. *Village Life in Ancient Egypt: Laundry Lists and Love Songs*. Oxford: Oxford University Press.

McGuire, R.H. 1982. The Study of Ethnicity in Historical Archaeology. *Journal of Anthropological Archaeology* 1: 159–78.

McKinnon, S. 1995. American Kinship/American Incest: Asymmetries in a Scientific Discourse. In Yanagisako, S. and Delaney, C. (eds), *Naturalizing Power: Essays in Feminist Cultural Analysis*. New York: Routledge, pp. 25–46.

Meskell, L.M. 1994. Dying Young: The Experience of Death at Deir el Medina. *Archaeological Review from Cambridge* 13(2): 35–45.

Meskell, L.M. 1996. The Somatisation of Archaeology: Institutions, Discourses, Corporeality. *Norwegian Archaeological Review* 29(1): 1-16.

Meskell, L.M. 1997. Egyptian Social Dynamics: The Evidence of Age, Sex and Class in Domestic and Mortuary Contexts. Ph.D. thesis. Department of Archaeology, Cambridge University.

Meskell, L.M. 1998a. An Archaeology of Social Relations in an Egyptian Village. *Journal of Archaeological Method and Theory* 5(3): 209–43.

Meskell, L.M. (ed.). 1998b. *Archaeology Under Fire: Nationalism, Politics and Heritage in the Eastern Mediterranean and Middle East*. London: Routledge.

Meskell, L.M. 1998c. Intimate Archaeologies: The Case of Kha and Merit. *World Archaeology* 29(3): 363–79.

Meskell, L.M. 1998d. The Irresistible Body and the Seduction of Archaeology. In Montserrat, D. (ed.), *Changing Bodies, Changing Meanings: Studies on the Human Body in Antiquity*. London: Routledge, pp. 139–61.

Meskell, L.M. 1999. *Archaeologies of Social Life: Age, Sex, Class etc. in Ancient Egypt*. Oxford: Blackwell.

Meskell, L.M. 2000. Re-Embedding Sex: Domesticity, Sexuality and Ritual in New Kingdom Egypt. In Schmidt, R. and Voss, B. (eds), *Archaeologies of Sexuality*. London: Routledge, pp. 253–62.

Meskell, L.M. 2004. *Private Life in New Kingdom Egypt*. Princeton, NJ: Princeton University Press.

Montserrat, D. 1996. *Sex and Society in Graeco-Roman Egypt*. London: Kegan Paul International.

Montserrat, D. (ed.). 1998. *Changing Bodies, Changing Meanings: Studies on the Human Body in Antiquity*. London: Routledge.

Moore, H.L. 1994. The Problem of Explaining Violence in the Social Sciences. In Harvey, P. and Gow, P. (eds), *Sex and Violence: Issues in Representation and Experience*. London: Routledge, pp. 138–55.

Morris, I. 1987. *Burial and Ancient Society: The Rise of the Greek City-State*. Cambridge: Cambridge University Press.

Morris, I. 1992. *Death-Ritual and Social Structure in Classical Antiquity*. Cambridge: Cambridge University Press.

Naccache, A.F.H. 1998. Beirut's Memoryside: Hear No Evil, See No Evil. In Meskell, L.M. (ed.), *Archaeology Under Fire: Nationalism, Politics and Heritage in the Eastern Mediterranean and Middle East*. London: Routledge, pp.140–58.

Nelson, M., Nelson, S.M., and Wylie, A. (eds). 1994. *Equity Issues for Women in Archaeology*. Washington: Archaeological Papers of the American Anthropological Association 5.

Nelson. S.M. 1997. *Gender in Archaeology: Analyzing Power and Prestige*. Walnut Creek, CA: AltaMira Press.

Nixon, 1994. Gender Bias in Archaeology. In Archer, L.J., Fischler, S., and Wyke, M. (eds). *Women in Ancient Societies*. London: Macmillan, pp. 1–23.

Nordström, H.-A. 1996. The Nubian A-Group: Ranking Funerary Remains. *Norwegian Archaeological Review* 26(1): 17–39.

O'Shea, J.M. 1984. *Mortuary Variability: An Archaeological Investigation*. Orlando: Academic Press.

Osborne, R. 1998a. Men Without Clothes: Heroic Nakedness and Greek Art. *Gender and History: Gender and Body in the Ancient Mediterranean* 9(3): 80–104.

Osborne, R. 1998b. Sculpted Men of Athens: Masculinity and Power in the Field of Vision. In Foxhall, L. and Salmon, J. (eds), *Thinking Men: Masculinity and its Self-Representation in the Classical Tradition*. London: Routledge, pp. 23–42.

Øvrevik, S. 1991. Engendering Archaeology. Review section. *Antiquity* 65: 738–41.

Parezo, N. (ed.). 1993. *Hidden Scholars: Women Anthropologists and the Native American Southwest*. Albuquerque: University of New Mexico Press.

Parkinson, R.B. 1995. 'Homosexual' Desire and Middle Kingdom Literature. *Journal of Egyptian Archaeology* 81: 57–76.

Paynter, R. and McGuire, R.H. 1991. The Archaeology of Inequality: Material Culture, Domination, and Resistance. In McGuire, R.H. and Paynter, R. (eds), *The Archaeology of Inequality*. Oxford: Blackwell, pp. 1–27.

Peebles, C.S. and Kus, S.M. 1977. Some Archaeological Correlates of Ranked Societies. *American Antiquity* 42(3): 421–48.

Pollock, S. and Lutz, C. 1994. Archaeology Deployed for the Gulf War. *Critique of Anthropology* 14(3): 263–84.

Porter, D. (ed.). 1997. *Internet Culture*. New York: Routledge.

Prezzano, S. 1997. Warfare, Women, and Households: The Development of Iroquois Culture. In Claassen, C. and Joyce, R.A. (eds), *Women in Prehistory: North America and Mesoamerica*. Philadelphia: University of Pennsylvania Press, pp. 88–99.

Rega, E. 1997. Age, Gender and Biological Reality in the Early Bronze Age Cemetery at Morkin. In Moore, J. and Scott, E. (eds), *Invisible People and Processes: Writing Gender and Childhood into European Archaeology*. London: Leicester University Press, pp. 229–47.

Reyman, J. (ed.). 1992. *Rediscovering our Past: Essays on the History of American Archaeology*. Aldershot: Avebury.

Robb, J. 1997. Female Beauty and Male Violence in Early Italian Society. In Koloski-Ostrow, A.O. and Lyons, C.L. (eds), *Naked Truths: Women, Sexuality, and Gender in Classical Art and Archaeology*. London: Routledge, pp. 43–65.

Robins, G. 1979. The Relationships Specified by Egyptian Kinship Terms of the Middle and New Kingdoms. *Chronique D'Egypte* 54(107): 197- 217.

Robins, G. 1993. *Women in Ancient Egypt*. London: British Museum Press.

Robins. G. 1996. Dress, Undress, and the Representation of Fertility and Potency in New Kingdom Egyptian Art. In Bergman, B., Cohen, A., Steh, E., and Boymel Kampen, N. (eds), *Sexuality in Ancient Art*. Cambridge: Cambridge University Press, pp. 27–40.

Rowlands, M. 1994. The Politics of Identity in Archaeology. In Bond, G.C. and Gilliam, A. (eds), *Social Construction of the Past: Representation as Power*. London: Routledge, pp. 129–43.

Sawicki, J. 1991. *Disciplining Foucault: Feminism, Power and the Body*. New York: Routledge.

Schmidt, R. and Voss, B. (eds). 2000. *Archaeologies of Sexuality*. London: Routledge.

Schrire, C. 1995. *Digging through Darkness: Chronicles of an Archaeologist*. Charlottesville: University Press of Virginia.

Shanks, M. 1995. Art and Archaeology of Embodiment: Some Aspects of Archaic Greece. *Cambridge Archaeological Journal* 5(2): 207–44.

Shanks, M. and Tilley, C. 1982. Ideology, Symbolic Power and Ritual Communication: A Reinterpretation of Neolithic Mortuary Practices. In Hodder, I. (ed.), *The Archaeology of Contextual Meanings*. Cambridge: Cambridge University Press, pp. 129–54.

Shennan, S. (ed.) 1994. *Archaeological Approaches to Cultural Identity*. London: Routledge.

Shilling, C. and Mellor, P.A. 1996. Embodiment, Structuration Theory and Modernity: Mind/Body Dualism and the Repression of Sensuality. *Body and Society* 2(4): 1–15.

Spector, J.D. 1994. *What this Awl Means: Feminist Archaeology at a Wahpeton Dakota Village*. St Paul: Minnesota Historical Society Press.

Spence, M.W. 1992. Tlailotlacan, a Zapotec Enclave in Teotihuacan. In Berlo, J.C. (ed.), *Art, Ideology and the City of Teotihuacan*. Washington: Dumbarton Oaks, pp. 59–88.

Spencer-Wood, S.M. 1991. Toward an Historical Archaeology of Materialistic Domestic Reform. In McGuire, R.H. and Paynter, R. (eds), *The Archaeology of Inequality*. Oxford: Blackwell, pp. 231–86.

Spriggs. M. (ed.). 1984. *Marxist Perspectives in Archaeology*. Cambridge: Cambridge University Press.

Sweely, T. 1999. Gender, Space, People and Power at Cerèn, El Salvador. In Sweely, T. (ed.), *Manifesting Power: Gender and the Interpretation of Power in Archaeology*. London: Routledge, pp. 155–71.

Tainter, J.A. 1978. Mortuary Practices and the Study of Prehistoric Social Systems. *Advances in Archaeological Method and Theory* 1: 105–41.

Tarlow, S.A. 1999. *Bereavement and Commemoration: An Archaeology of Mortality*. Oxford: Blackwell.

Thomas, J. and Tilley, C. 1993. The Axe and the Torso: Symbolic Structures. In Tilley, C. (ed.), *Interpretive Archaeology*. Oxford: Berg, pp. 225–324.

Touraine, A. 1995. Sociology and the Study of Society. In Joyce, P. (ed.), *Class*. Oxford: Oxford University Press, pp. 83–9.

Trigger, B.G. 1989. *A History of Archaeological Thought*. Cambridge: Cambridge University Press.

Trigger, B.G. 1995. Romanticism, Nationalism, and Archaeology. In Kohl, P.L. and Fawcett, C. (eds), *Nationalism, Politics and the Practice of Archaeology*. Cambridge: Cambridge University Press, pp. 263–79.

Turkle, S. 1996. *Life on the Screen: Identity in the Age of the Internet*. London: Weidenfeld and Nicolson.

Vance, C.S. (ed.). 1984. *Pleasure and Danger: Exploring Female Sexuality*. Boston: Routledge and Kegan Paul.

Walde, D. and Willows, N.D. (eds). 1991. *The Archaeology of Gender: Proceedings of the 22nd Annual Chacmool Conference*. Calgary: University of Calgary Archaeological Association.

Wall, D. diZerega. 1994. *The Archaeology of Gender: Separating the Spheres in Urban America*. New York: Plenum.

Wason, P.K. 1994. *The Archaeology of Rank*. Cambridge: Cambridge University Press.

Weeks, J. 1997. *Sexuality*. London: Routledge.

Weston, K. 1995. Naturalising Power. In Yanagisako, S. and Delaney, C. (eds), *Naturalizing Power: Essays in Feminist Cultural Analysis*. New York: Routledge, pp. 87–110.

Wilson, D. 1997. Gender, Diet, Health, and Social Status in the Mississippian Powers Phase Turner Cemetery Population. In Claassen, C. and Joyce, R.A. (eds), *Women in Prehistory: North America and Mesoamerica*. Philadelphia: University of Pennsylvania Press, pp. 119–35.

Winter, I.J. 1996. Sex, Rhetoric, and the Public Monument: The Alluring Body of Naram-Sîn of Agade. In Kampen, N.B. (ed.), *Sexuality in Ancient Art: Near East, Egypt, Greece and Italy*. Cambridge: Cambridge University Press, pp. 11–26.

Woodhouse-Beyer, K. 1999. Artels and Identities: Gender, Power, and Russian America. In Sweely, T. (ed.), *Manifesting Power: Gender and the Interpretation of Power in Archaeology*. London: Routledge, pp. 129–54.

Wright, R.A. (ed.). 1996. *Gender and Archaeology*. Philadelphia: University of Pennsylvania Press.

Wylie, A. 1991. Gender Theory and the Archaeological Record: Why is There No Archaeology of Gender? In Gero, J.M. and Conkey, M.W. (eds), *Engendering Archaeology: Women and Prehistory*. Oxford: Blackwell, pp. 31–54.

Wylie, A. 1992. Feminist Theories of Social Power: Implications for a Processual Archaeology. *Norwegian Archaeological Review* 25(1): 51–68.

Yanagisako, S. and Delaney, C. (eds). 1995a. *Naturalizing Power: Essays in Feminist Cultural Analysis*. New York: Routledge.

Yanagisako, S. and Delaney, C. 1995b. Naturalizing Power. In Yanagisako, S. and Delaney, C. (eds), *Naturalizing Power: Essays in Feminist Cultural Analysis*. New York: Routledge, pp. 1–22.

Yates, T. 1993. Frameworks for an Archaeology of the Body. In Tilley, C. (ed.), *Interpretive Archaeology*. Oxford: Berg, pp. 31–72.

Yates, T. and Nordbladh, J. 1990. This Perfect Body, This Virgin Text: Between Sex and Gender in Archaeology. In Bapty, I. and Yates, T. (eds), *Archaeology After Structuralism*. London: Routledge, pp. 222–37.

Yentsch, A.E. 1994. *A Chesapeake Family and their Slaves: A Study in Historical Archaeology*. Cambridge: Cambridge University Press.

Chapter 3

Discourses of identity in the interpretation of the past

Siân Jones

> The uniqueness and unity of European history must be dismantled....If our cultural consciousness has become objectified in a particular historical *genre* (cf. Sahlins 1985: 52) that is *linearised and continuous*, analysis reveals the *non-synchronicity and discontinuity* of social experience.
>
> Hastrup, *Other Histories* (my emphasis)

The mode of European cultural consciousness explored by Hastrup is integral to dominant discourses of cultural identity in Europe, whether they be European, national, or ethnic. Typically group identities are represented as unified, monolithic wholes, with linear and continuous histories which in turn are used in the legitimation of claims to political autonomy and territory within the prevailing ideological climate of ethnic nationalism (see Chapman *et al.* 1989; Just 1989; Danforth 1993; Shore 1993). Thus while competing interpretations of the past arise in the context of political disputes, they tend to share a common mode of representation; a mode which is not restricted to ethnic and national groups, but also extends to supranational entities. For instance despite the emphasis on the coexistence of supranational, national, and regional cultural identities, the symbolic terrain on which the New Europe is being actively produced, 'is precisely that upon which the nation-state has traditionally been constructed' (Shore 1993: 791). That is the 'New Europe' is being constructed as a unified entity with a unilinear continuous history.

Archaeology has undoubtedly played a central role in the construction of such identities, and the details of particular liaisons between archaeology and nationalism have been the subject of a number of recent studies (e.g. Olsen 1986; Kohl 1993; Kristiansen 1993; Ucko 1995). In this chapter I take a more abstract approach and examine the common discourses of identity[1] which have characterized myths of origin and historical continuity during the nineteenth and twentieth centuries. There is always a tension between past and present in archaeological interpretation – between the past meanings and processes which we wish to reconstruct from the material remains, and the meanings which we wish these remains to reveal to us in the present. This tension is nowhere greater than in accounts of past cultural groups. The critical role of the past in the assertion and legitimation of group identities often leads to a problematic slippage between contemporary concepts of group identity and the mapping of past groups in archaeology. Here, I explore the way in which contemporary, historically contingent concepts of culture and identity shape our understanding of the past, and I suggest that we need to adopt a radically different theoretical framework for the analysis of cultural identity in the past. Such a theoretical framework must accommodate the fluid and contextual nature of cultural identity and facilitate the exploration of alternative associations of identity, history, and place.

Peoples and cultures

Archaeology, like anthropology, has tended to deal with 'wholes'; a concern epitomized in the identification of past peoples and cultures, which continues to provide a basic conceptual framework for archaeological analysis today. Throughout the history of archaeology, from its antiquarian origins onwards, the material record has been attributed to particular past peoples (see Daniel 1978 [1950]; Trigger 1989). However, it was with the development of the culture history paradigm in the late nineteenth and early twentieth centuries that a systematic framework for the classification of cultures in space and time was established. Despite the diverse histories of archaeology in different regions and countries, culture history has provided the dominant framework for archaeological analysis throughout most of the world during the twentieth century (see contributions in Ucko 1995). Processual and post-processual archaeologies have rejected culture historical interpretation as an end product in itself. Yet even these archaeological 'schools' are still largely dependent upon material evidence which has been described and classified on the basis of an essentially culture historical epistemology (see Jones 1994: 19–20).

One of the main assumptions underlying the culture historical approach is that bounded uniform cultural entities correlate with particular peoples, ethnic groups, tribes, and/or races. Thus, Kossinna, one of the pioneers of culture history, asserted that 'in all periods, sharply delineated archaeological culture areas coincide with clearly recognisable peoples or tribes' (cited in Malina and Vasicek 1990: 63).[2] This assumption is based on a normative conceptualization of culture: that within a given group, cultural practices and beliefs tend to conform to prescriptive ideational norms or rules of behaviour. It is assumed that culture is made up of a set of shared ideas or beliefs which are maintained by regular interaction within the group, and the transmission of shared cultural norms to subsequent generations through the process of socialization, which, it is assumed, results in a continuous cultural tradition. Childe was explicit about this process, arguing that 'Generation after generation has followed society's prescription and produced and reproduced in thousands of instances the socially approved standard type. An archaeological type is just that' (Childe 1956: 8).

Within such a theoretical framework the transmission of cultural traits/ideas is generally assumed to be a function of the degree of interaction between individuals or groups. A high degree of homogeneity in material culture is regarded as the product of regular contact and interaction (e.g. Gifford 1960: 341–2), whereas discontinuities in the distribution of material culture are assumed to be the result of social and/or physical distance. Gradual change is attributed to internal drift in the prescribed cultural norms of a particular group, whereas more rapid change is explained in terms of external influences, such as diffusion resulting from culture contact, or the succession of one cultural group by another as a result of migration and conquest: 'Distributional changes [in diagnostic types] should reflect displacements of population, the expansions, migrations, colonizations or conquests with which literary history is familiar' (Childe 1956: 135).

It has been argued (Trigger 1978: 86) that the widespread adoption of the culture historical approach in archaeology was a product of the need to establish a system for classifying the spatial and temporal variation in material culture which became evident in the nineteenth century. However, such an argument implies that discrete monolithic cultures constitute a natural and universal mode of socio-cultural differentiation waiting to be discovered by the discipline of archaeology. Certainly, spatial and temporal variation in human ways of life is an unequivocal fact which is manifested in the archaeological record. However, it can be argued that the particular classificatory framework developed in archaeology in order to describe and explain such variation was based on historically contingent assumptions about the nature of cultural diversity; that rather than '*discovering* a general form of universal difference' archaeologists, along with other social scientists, invented it (Fardon 1987: 176, my emphasis).

The expectations of boundedness, homogeneity, and continuity which have been built into ideas concerning culture since the nineteenth century are related to nationalism and the emergence of the nation-state (see Wolf 1982: 387; Handler 1988: 7–8; Spencer 1990: 283). As Handler points out, 'nationalist ideologies and social scientific inquiry [including that of archaeology] developed in the same historical context – that of the post-Renaissance European world – and...the two have reacted upon one another from their beginnings' (1988: 8).

Nations are considered, in the words of Handler, to be 'individuated beings'; endowed with the reality of natural things, they are assumed to be bounded, continuous, and precisely distinguishable from other analogous entities (ibid.: 6, 15). The idea of culture is intricately enmeshed with nationalist discourse; it is culture which distinguishes between nations and which constitutes the content of national identity. Moreover, 'culture symbolises individuated existence: the assertion of cultural particularity is another way of proclaiming the existence of a unique collectivity' (ibid.: 39). The representation of culture in nationalist discourses is strikingly mirrored in the presuppositions which have dominated traditional concepts of 'culture' and 'society' in academic theory and practice. Such categories have been traditionally seen as well integrated, bounded, continuous entities, which occupy exclusive spatio-temporal positions and which are assumed to be the normal and healthy units of social life (see Clifford 1988; Handler 1988).

The concept of an archaeological culture represents a particular variant of this formula. As discussed above, bounded material culture complexes are assumed to be the material manifestation of past peoples, who shared a set of prescriptive learned norms of behaviour. Archaeological cultures came to be regarded as organic, individuated entities, the prehistorian's substitute for the individual agents which make up the historian's repertoire: 'prehistory can recognize peoples and marshal them on the stage to take the place of the personal actors who form the historian's troupe' (Childe 1940: 2; see also Piggott 1965: 7). Moreover, as in the case of contemporary claims concerning the relationship between nations and cultures, the relationship between archaeological cultures and past peoples is based on teleological reasoning in that culture is both representative of, and constitutive of, the nation or people concerned. As Handler points out: 'the almost *a priori* belief in the existence of the culture follows inevitably from the belief that a particular human group...exists. The existence of the group is in turn predicated on the existence of a particular culture' (1988: 39).

Through the concept of an archaeological culture the past is reconstructed in terms of the distribution of homogeneous cultures whose history unfolds in a coherent linear narrative measured in terms of objectified events, such as contacts, migrations, and conquests, with intervals of homogeneous, empty time in between them.[3] Furthermore the understanding of culture which is embodied by the notion of an archaeological culture enables history, place, and people to be tied together in the exclusive and monolithic fashion common to contemporary representations of ethnic, national, and European identity. Yet recent anthropological research (see Fardon 1987: 176; Handler 1988: 291) suggests that the relationship between culture and peoplehood is not so straightforward, and that the idea that ethnic and national groups are fixed, homogeneous bounded entities extending deep into the past is a modern classificatory invention.[4] On the contrary it has been shown that ethnic and national identities are fluid, dynamic, and contested.

Ethnicity and culture

During the 1960s and early 1970s there was a shift in the analysis of cultural differentiation in the context of critiques of existing social scientific concepts.[5] This shift was marked by the proliferation of research into ethnicity, and the use of 'ethnic group' in place of 'tribe' and 'race'. However, it was not merely a terminological sleight of hand, it also represented important changes in the orientation of research and theories of cultural differentiation (see Cohen 1978; Jones 1994). Increasing emphasis was placed on the self-identifications of the social actors concerned, the processes involved in the construction of group boundaries, and the interrelationships between socio-cultural groups. Such approaches contrast sharply with the traditional holistic analysis of supposedly discrete, organic entities.

As early as 1947 Francis had argued that the ethnic group constitutes a community based primarily on a shared subjective 'we-feeling' and that 'we cannot define the ethnic group as a plurality pattern which is characterized by a distinct language, culture, territory, religion and so on' (1947: 397). A number of other authors adopted a similar argument (e.g. Wallerstein 1960: 131; Moerman 1965; Shibutani and Kwan 1965: 40). Yet the real turning point in the definition of ethnic groups seems to have followed Barth's (1969) reiteration of the subjective aspects of ethnic identity within a programmatic theoretical framework (Cohen 1978). He argued that ethnic groups cannot be defined by the cultural similarities and differences enumerated by the analyst, but rather on the basis of 'categories of ascription and identification by the actors themselves' (Barth 1969: 10). In many instances ethnic groups may possess social and cultural commonalities across boundaries and exhibit considerable variation within the group. Yet in the process of social interaction both real and assumed cultural differences are articulated in the maintenance of ethnic boundaries (Barth 1969). Ethnographic research has confirmed that ethnicity involves subjective processes of classification, and in much of the recent literature it has been regarded as a consciousness of real or assumed cultural difference *vis-à-vis* others; a 'we'/'they' opposition (e.g. Cohen 1978; Chapman *et al.* 1989; Ringer and Lawless 1989; Shennan 1989).

This emphasis on the formation and persistence of subjective ethnic categories in the context of embracing social systems also contributed to a concern with the economic and political dimensions of ethnicity. Ethnic identity, it is argued, is 'instrumental' in that it provides a group with the boundary maintenance and organizational dimensions necessary in order to maintain and compete for a particular socio-economic niche (e.g. Barth 1969; Cohen 1974). In this sense, ethnic groups are a product of differential socio-structural and/or environmental conditions. Moreover it is argued that ethnicity is manipulated and mobilized, on an individual and group level, in the pursuit of economic and political interests (e.g. Barth 1969; Patterson 1975). For instance some of the hoe-agricultural Fur of the Sudan have adopted the lifestyle and identity of the nomadic cattle Arabs, the Baggara (see Barth 1969: 25–6; Haaland 1969): a shift in identity which can be explained by the limited opportunities for capital investment in the village economy of the Fur, in contrast to the opportunities presented by the Baggara economy.

Broadly speaking, instrumentalist approaches dominated research on ethnicity in the 1970s and 1980s. The recent literature on ethnicity has further illustrated the dynamic nature of ethnicity, not only historically (see contributions in Tonkin *et al.* 1989), but also in different social contexts according to the interests and positions of the actors (e.g. Cohen 1978; Wallman 1977).

The recognition that ethnic groups are fluid self-defining systems which are embedded in economic and political relations, represents an important contribution to our understanding of the maintenance and transformation of ethnicity. Most significantly in terms of this discussion, such an approach to ethnicity reveals a critical break between culture and ethnicity. While it is still assumed that there is some relation between ethnicity and culture, it is generally accepted that there is rarely a straightforward correlation between cultural similarities and differences and ethnic boundaries. Hence, recent theories of ethnicity mark a significant departure from the notion of ethnic groups as culture-bearing units; a notion which, as discussed above, is central to nationalist discourses as well as traditional social scientific theory. However, while ethnographic research supports a distinction between culture and ethnicity, the precise nature of the relationship between ethnicity and culture has been a neglected area of research. Instrumentalists tend to focus on the organizational aspects of ethnicity and take the cultural differences on which ethnicity is based for granted. Culture is reduced to an epiphenomenal and arbitrary set of symbols (Eriksen 1992: 30) manipulated in the pursuit of changing individual and/or group interests (Bentley 1987: 26, 48; Eriksen 1992: 44).

Towards a practice theory of ethnicity

One important problem which subjective instrumental approaches to ethnicity fail to resolve is the relationship between agents' perceptions of ethnicity, and the cultural contexts and social relations in which they are embedded. Such a question can be addressed by drawing on theories of practice that are concerned with the general relationship between the conditions of social life and agents' subjective constructions of social reality. For instance Bourdieu (1977) argues that social actors possess durable, often subliminal, dispositions towards certain perceptions and practices (such as those relating to the sexual division of labour, morality, tastes, and so on) which he calls 'habitus'. Such dispositions, which are inculcated into an individual's sense of self at an early age (Bourdieu 1977: 78–93), are generated by the conditions constituting a particular social environment, such as modes of production or access to certain resources (Bourdieu 1977: 77–8). However, the practices engendered by such conditions are not constituted by the mechanistic enactment of a system of normative rules which exist outside of individual history (Bourdieu 1977: 72). Rather, structural orientations exist in the form of the embodied knowledge and dispositions of social actors, but these structures depend for their existence on the practices and representations of social actors, which lead to their reproduction or transformation. As Postone *et al.* (1993: 4) point out, the orientations of the habitus 'are at once "structuring structures" and "structured structures"; they shape and are shaped by social practice'.

The concept of the habitus can be used to articulate the way in which subjective ethnic classifications are grounded in the social conditions and cultural practices characterizing particular social domains. Ethnicity is not a passive reflection of the cultural similarities and differences in which people are socialized, as traditional normative approaches assume. Nor is ethnicity, as some instrumental approaches imply, produced entirely in the process of social interaction, whereby epiphenomenal cultural symbols are manipulated in the pursuit of economic and political interests. Rather drawing on Bourdieu's theory of practice, it can be argued that the subjective construction of ethnic identity in the context of social interaction is grounded in the shared subliminal dispositions of the habitus which shape, and are shaped by, commonalities of practice. As Bentley puts it: '[a] shared habitus engenders feelings of identification among people similarly endowed. Those feelings are consciously appropriated and given form through existing symbolic resources' (Bentley 1987: 173).

Moreover these 'symbolic resources' are not essentially arbitrary. The cultural practices and beliefs which become objectified as symbols of ethnicity are derived from and resonate with the habitual practices and experiences of the agents involved, as well as reflect the instrumental contingencies of a particular situation. As Eriksen argues, symbols of ethnicity 'are intrinsically linked with experienced, practical worlds containing specific, relevant meanings which on the one hand contribute to shaping interaction, and on the other hand limit the number of options in the production of ethnic signs' (Eriksen 1992: 45).

Yet within this theoretical approach the habitus and ethnicity are not directly congruent, thereby constituting a similar position to the traditional equation of culture and ethnicity. There is a break between the structured dispositions constituting the habitus as a whole, and the objectified representation of cultural *difference* involved in the production and reproduction of ethnicity. Shared habitual dispositions provide the basis for the recognition of commonalities of sentiment and interest, and the basis for the perception and communication of cultural affinities and differences which ethnicity entails. However, social interaction between actors of differing cultural traditions engenders a reflexive mode of perception contributing to a break with forms of knowledge which, in other contexts, constitute subliminal, taken-for-granted modes of behaviour. Such exposure of the arbitrariness of cultural practices, which had hitherto been taken as self-evident and natural, permits and requires a change 'in the level of discourse, so as to rationalize and systematize' the representation of those cultural practices, and, more generally, the representation of the cultural tradition itself (Bourdieu 1977: 233). It is at such a discursive level that ethnic categories are produced, reproduced, and transformed through the systematic communication of cultural difference with relation to the cultural practices of particular 'ethnic others'.[6]

This process can be further elaborated by reference to a specific example, that of the construction of Tswana ethnicity in the context of European colonialism (see Comaroff and Comaroff 1992: 235–63). In the process of interaction and communication between the Tswana and evangelist missionaries, both groups began to recognize distinctions between them: 'to objectify their world in relation to a novel other, thereby inventing for themselves a self-conscious coherence and distinctness – even while they accommodated to the new relationship which enclosed them' (Comaroff and Comaroff 1992: 245). This objectification is not a fabrication; an entirely instrumental construction. Tswana ethnicity is based on the perception of commonalities of practice and experience in *Setswana* (Tswana ways) in opposition to *Sekgoa* (European ways). Yet the form which Tswana self-consciousness takes in this context is different from the cultural identities which prevailed in pre-colonial times when they were divided into political communities based on totemic affiliations. In both pre- and post-colonial times the construction of identity involves the marking of contrast – the opposition of selves and others – but colonialism provided a new context in which Tswana tradition was objectified as a coherent body of knowledge and practice uniting the Tswana people.

Thus the objectification of cultural difference involves the dialectical opposition of different cultural traditions. The particular forms which such oppositions take is a product of the intersection of people's habitus with the social conditions constituting any particular context. These conditions include the prevailing power relations, and the relative distribution of the material and symbolic means necessary for the imposition of dominant regimes of ethnic categorization. For instance in many colonial contexts ethnic or 'tribal' categories were imposed by colonial regimes (see Colson 1968; Fried 1968), or were a product of large-scale urban migration and associated social and cultural dislocation (see Comaroff and Comaroff 1992). Hence the extent to which ethnicity is embedded in pre-existing cultural realities represented by a shared habitus is highly variable. The extent of contiguity depends upon the cultural transformations brought about by the processes of interaction and the nature of the power relations between the interacting 'groups' (Comaroff and Comaroff 1992: 56). In some instances, for example as in colonial situations, minority ethnic groups may be composed of people of diverse origins, and 'the substance of their identities, as contrived from both within and outside, is inevitably a *bricolage* fashioned in the very historical processes which underwrite their subordination' (Comaroff and Comaroff 1992: 57). However, even when ethnicity is as much a product of the historical relations of inequality between 'groups' as it is a reflection of pre-existing cultural realities, the reproduction of these emergent forms of cultural difference will, over time, lead to their internalization as part of the structured dispositions of the habitus.

Thus manifestations of ethnicity are the product of an ongoing process involving multiple objectifications of cultural difference and the internalization of those differences within the shared dispositions of the habitus. Such processes will lead to fluctuations in the correspondence between constructions of a particular ethnic identity, in terms of objectified cultural difference, and the overall cultural practices and historical experience of the people involved. Furthermore the expression of cultural difference depends upon the particular cultural practices and historical experience activated in any given social context, as well as broader idioms of cultural difference. Consequently the cultural content of ethnicity may vary substantively and qualitatively in different contexts, as may the importance of ethnicity in general (see Eriksen 1991 and 1992).

On the basis of this theoretical approach it can be argued that there is unlikely to be a one-to-one relationship between expressions of a particular ethnic identity and the entire range of cultural practices and social conditions associated with that particular 'group'. Yet this is not because culture is an epiphenomenal resource which is consciously and deliberately manipulated in the pursuit of individual and group interests. While ethnicity always involves active processes of performance and interpretation in the objectification of cultural difference, it is still constituted in the context of specific cultural practices and historical experiences which provide the basis for the perception of similarity and difference.

From a 'bird's-eye view' the construction of ethnicity is likely to be manifested as multiple overlapping boundaries constituted by representations of cultural difference, which are at once transient, but also subject to reproduction and transformation in the ongoing processes of social life. Such a view of ethnicity undermines conventional methodological approaches which telescope various spatially and temporally distinct representations of ethnicity onto a single plane for the purposes of analysis and attempt to force the resulting incongruities and contradictions into an abstract conceptualization of the ethnic group as a discrete, internally homogeneous entity characterized by continuity of tradition. The theoretical approach developed here suggests that such a methodological and conceptual framework obliterates the reality of the dynamic and creative processes involved in the reproduction and transformation of ethnicity.

A reconsideration of archaeological approaches to ethnicity

The traditional assumption that a one-to-one relationship exists between the sum of the cultural similarities and differences and the ethnic group has recently been criticized in archaeology (e.g. Hodder 1982; Shennan 1989), as in other disciplines. It has also been argued that ethnic groups are not the product of social and physical isolation, but rather a consciousness of difference reproduced in the context of ongoing social interaction. Consequently archaeologists cannot continue to regard variation in the archaeological record as a passive measure of physical/social distance between groups (see Hodder 1982). Nor can they assume that close contact between groups or the incorporation of one group by another will lead to gradual and uniform acculturation. However, it is necessary to make more wide-reaching changes to our analytical frameworks in order to analyse the construction of ethnicity in the past. In particular there is a need to discard classificatory and interpretive frameworks based upon the presumed existence of bounded socio-cultural units – frameworks which are still fundamental to much archaeological theory and practice (and see Conkey 1990: 12).

Ethnicity must be distinguished from mere spatial continuity and discontinuity in that it refers to self-conscious identification with a particular group of people (Shennan 1989: 19). I have argued that ethnicity involves the objectification of cultural difference *vis-à-vis* others in the context of social interaction. Such objectifications are based upon the perception of commonalities of practice and experience, as well as the conditions prevailing in particular social and historical contexts. A variety of scenarios may arise. At one extreme there may be a high degree of homology between the structuring principles of the habitus and the signification of ethnicity in both material and non-material culture (as in Hodder's [1982] study of the Baringo District). Whereas at the other end of the spectrum there may be a dislocation of such homologous relationships to the extent that the generation and expression of a common ethnic identity incorporates a *bricolage* of different cultural traditions characterized by heterogeneous structuring principles in many social domains (see Rowlands 1982: 164 for a similar argument).

Yet whatever the degree of homology between the habitus and ethnicity, it must be emphasized that archaeologists may not be able to find a reflection of past 'ethnic entities' in the material record (see also Miller 1985: 202 with relation to caste). It is possible to question the very existence of bounded, homogeneous ethnic entities except at an abstract conceptual level. As Bourdieu (1977) has pointed out, such conceptual categories are based on the methodological reification or objectification of transient cultural practices taking place in different spatial and temporal contexts, and the 'group' exists only in the context of interpretation where it justifies and explains past practices and modes of interaction, and structures future practices.

In contrast the praxis of ethnicity results in multiple transient realizations of ethnic difference in particular contexts. These realizations of ethnicity are both structured and structuring, involving, in many instances, the repeated production and consumption of distinctive styles of material culture. Yet they are a product of the intersection of the perceptual and practical dispositions of social agents and the interests and oppositions engendered in a particular social context, rather than abstract categories of difference.

Hence configurations of ethnicity, and consequently the styles of material culture involved in the signification and structuring of ethnic relations, may vary in different social contexts and with relation to different forms and scales of social interaction. From an archaeological point of view the likely result is a complex pattern of overlapping material culture distributions relating to the repeated realization and transformation of ethnicity in different social contexts, rather than discrete monolithic cultural entities. Patterns in the production and consumption of material culture involved in the communication of the 'same' ethnic identity may vary qualitatively as well as quantitatively in different contexts. Furthermore items of material culture which are widely distributed and used in a variety of social and historical contexts may be curated and consumed in different ways and become implicated in the generation and significance of a variety of extractions of ethnicity.

The analysis of these contextual realizations of ethnicity, and ultimately the manifestation of ethnicity in the past, is not beyond the possibilities of archaeological interpretation. The systematization and rationalization of distinctive cultural styles in the process of the recognition, expression, and negotiation of ethnic identity is likely to result in discontinuous, non-random distributions of material culture of the type suggested by Hodder (1982) and Wiessner (1983). However, in order to analyse such patterns in archaeological material it will be necessary to adopt a radically different framework for both classification and interpretation.

Most archaeological classification is ultimately based on the assumption that stylistic groupings are co-extensive with normative historical entities. Two particular principles are central: (i) that change in material culture is a gradual, regular process which occurs in a uniform manner throughout a spatially homogeneous area; (ii) that the prime cause of variation in design is the date of manufacture. Such an approach to classification presupposes a normative view of culture and produces what is essentially an illusion of bounded uniform cultural entities. Artefacts are extrapolated from their contexts of deposition, grouped together into predetermined classes of material, and classified, spatially and temporally, according to the principles noted above. Such an approach obscures the kind of information which is of interest in the analysis of ethnicity (and arguably past cultural processes in general).

Ethnicity, among other factors, may disrupt regular spatio-temporal stylistic groupings, resulting in boundaries which are discontinuous in space and time. Yet in order to analyse such patterns it is necessary to consider artefact assemblages within a contextual framework, and to date assemblages, where possible, on the basis of independent methods and stratigraphy. Such an approach to the basic classification of material culture will enable the analysis of variation in the deposition and use of material culture in different social domains. Any distinctive non-random distributions of particular styles and forms of material culture in different contexts which emerge from such an analysis may plausibly relate to the expression of ethnicity. Yet a variety of factors may be involved in producing such variation, and it will be necessary to employ independent contextual evidence in the interpretation of ethnicity, as the significance of material culture in terms of ethnicity is culturally and historically specific (Hodder 1982; Shennan 1989: 21; Wiessner 1989: 58).

Thus a broad understanding of past cultural contexts derived from a variety of sources and classes of data is a necessary part of any analysis of ethnicity in archaeology. As ethnicity is a product of the intersection of the habitus with the conditions prevailing in any particular social and historical context, it will be important to have a broad understanding of such conditions, including the distribution of material and symbolic power. An adequate knowledge of past social organization will also be important, as ethnicity is both a transient construct of repeated acts of interaction and communication, and an aspect of social organization which becomes institutionalized to different degrees, and in different forms, in different societies.

Moreover a historical approach will be particularly important given the role of historical context in the generation and expression of ethnicity. A diachronic framework may enable archaeologists to pick up shifts in the expression of ethnicity, and those dimensions of material culture which signify it, over time. Such shifts may involve greater or lesser fixity and institutionalization of expressions of ethnic difference, and changes in the use of particular aspects of material culture in the signification of ethnicity. In short the use of a diachronic contextual framework may reveal something about the contexts in which ethnicity is generated, reproduced, and transformed; to examine 'the mobilisation of group as process' (Conkey 1990: 13).

Conclusions: discourses of history and place in the construction of ethnicity

> Ultimately, in the state-ist conception of the nation, state and nation become one, an 'imagined community' that ignores the various nations/identities' histories it may include. To maintain this conception of the nation-state it is necessary constantly to stress the existence of only one possible cultural model, one history, one language, one social project.
>
> Devalle, *Discourses of Ethnicity*

In this chapter I have argued that the very concepts used in the archaeological identification of past peoples are historically contingent. The concept of 'a culture' which
has been embraced in archaeological epistemology, and its conflation with ethnicity,
is the product of a particular ideology of cultural differentiation which emerged in the
context of post-Enlightenment European nationalism. Cultures are considered to be
bounded, continuous, unified entities that bear witness to the existence of the nations
which are their bearers. This conceptualization of culture contributes to the assertion
of a congruency between territorial contiguity and ethnic unity across a historical
stage – a mosaic of discrete spatially and temporally bounded, monolithic entities.
Such a conflation of social scientific and political ideological concepts serves to
hinder the analysis of the real nature of the processes involved in the construction of
ethnic and national identity (Llobera 1989: 248). Instead the unfortunate implication
is that social scientists (including anthropologists and archaeologists) may have developed paradigms 'to explain that which they have themselves created' (Bond and
Gilliam 1994: 13; see also Handler 1988).

In some spheres of archaeology, culture history, and its equation of cultures with
peoples, has been rejected (for a review see Jones 1994; Shennan 1989). However, a
normative concept of culture still underlies much of archaeological description and
classification (see Jones 1994), and ethnic groups are still considered to be bounded
continuous, if dynamic, entities. The presupposition that an exclusive congruence
exists between ethnic unity, territory, and history remains intact, although more
elastic (e.g. see Blackmore *et al.* 1979; Kimes *et al.* 1982). Drawing upon recent
research, I have argued that ethnicity is a dynamic, contested phenomenon, which is
manifested in different ways in different contexts, with relation to different forms and
scales of interaction. Moreover the representations of cultural difference involved in
the articulation of ethnicity are transient, although subject to reproduction and transformation in the ongoing processes of social life. Such an approach to ethnicity challenges the assumption that bounded, homogeneous ethnic or cultural entities
constitute the natural units of socio-cultural differentiation. Furthermore it explodes
the exclusive association of ethnic entities with a single, discrete, territory and history.
From an archaeological perspective the material manifestation of ethnicity, among
other factors, may disrupt regular spatio-temporal stylistic patterning, resulting in an
untidy and overlapping web of stylistic boundaries in different classes of material
culture and in different contexts – boundaries which may be discontinuous in space
and time.

My aim has been to suggest alternative ways of conceptualizing the relationship
between history, place, and identity in archaeological theory and practice. Returning
to the representation of European identities the argument presented here inevitably
represents a threat to certain understandings of European national and ethnic identity. As Boyarin points out in his analysis of Israeli nationhood:

> It seems almost gratuitous to state that my point is not to dismantle the state of
> Israel. But if the Israeli state, once established, is implicitly understood by its own
> elites as a *static* reality dependent on functional equilibrium, then a threat to any of
> its parts (including its self-generated history) is a threat to its very existence. Related
> to the equilibrium model is the image of the nation as an integral collective.
>
> (1992: 118)

It is necessary to challenge such static functional conceptions of cultural groups (whether they be ethnic, national, or Europe-wide), and their self-generated histories, in order to explore the possibility of a plurality of histories and identities.

Ethnicity is not constituted by the historical legacy of a primordial, essentialist identity; rather, the formation and transformation of ethnicity is contingent upon particular historical structures which impinge on human experience and condition social action. As Devalle (1992: 18) points out, ethnicity is a historical process, as 'time provides the necessary ground on which ethnic styles are maintained (recreated) and collective identities formulated', lending such identities substance and legitimation. However, 'Being firmly grounded in the concrete history of a particular social reality, an ethnic style cannot be simply understood as the immutable and intangible *"essence"* of a given people, or as a fixed sociological idealised type' (Devalle 1992: 19).

Archaeologists have tended to utilize such immutable 'essentialised' (Conkey 1990: 13) categories of ethnicity, leading to the projection of a modern classificatory framework onto all of human history. Instead we need to develop theoretical frameworks that allow us to explore the ways in which ethnicity is manifested in particular historical contexts, and to explore multiple associations between kinds of identity and notions of time and place. These frameworks will facilitate analysis of the multiple, twisted, and discontinuous histories of the 'New Europe', rather than attempt to impose a linear, continuous, and homogeneous past.

Acknowledgements

Many thanks to Andrew Crosby, Clive Gamble, Paul Graves-Brown, Claire Jowitt, Tony Kushner, Yvonne Marshall, Stephan Shennan, Cris Shore, Julian Thomas, and Peter Ucko for their helpful comments on earlier drafts of this chapter. Of course any errors or deficiencies remain my own.

Notes

1. The term discourse is being used here to refer to a clustering of ideas, an ideological configuration, which structures knowledge and experience in a particular domain, in this case in the construction of group identity.
2. Further expressions of this basic principle can be found in Childe (1929: v–vi and 1956: 2), Hawkes (1940: 1), and Piggott (1958: 88).
3. This kind of temporal framework is what Fabian (1983: 23) identifies as 'typological time'.
4. The argument, that the representation of human groups as the bearers of bounded, monolithic cultures is a product of post-Enlightenment discourses of identity (in particular those associated with nationalism), is clearly supported by studies of cultural identity in the context of European colonialism (e.g. see Fardon 1987; Comaroff and Comaroff 1992). However, I do not support the related theory that ethnicity is an entirely modern phenomenon. Instead I suggest that different forms of ethnicity are produced in different socio-historical contexts, and the nationalist conflation of political and cultural units (and the associated concept of culture as homogeneous, bounded, and spatially contiguous) cannot be assumed to be a universal form of

socio-cultural organization. In fact there are many examples to the contrary today (see Eriksen 1993), as there are in medieval Europe (see Greengrass 1991) and other areas of the world prior to European colonization (see Comaroff and Comaroff 1992).

5. Throughout the first half of the twentieth century a number of anthropologists expressed concern about both abstract and pragmatic definitions of the 'cultural' or 'tribal' entities which constituted the objects of their research (for example see Fortes 1945). By the 1950s and 1960s critiques of the concept of tribe had emerged challenging the traditional assumption that social, cultural, and political boundaries are commensurate with the boundaries of the tribe (for example Leach 1954). Others indicated the pejorative connotations of the concept of tribe and suggested that the category, as well as its socio-cultural referents, were constructs of colonial regimes (for example Colson 1968; Fried 1968). Sociologists also became increasingly aware of problems with the conceptual frameworks which dominated their discipline. In particular, the presupposition that continuous cultural contact would lead to acculturation and homogenization was challenged by the persistence of cultural difference and ethnic self-consciousness among minority groups. It is important to note that these critiques were connected in a plurality of ways with processes of colonization and decolonization in the 'Third' World, as well as the increasing political salience of minority voices in 'Western' countries.

6. If this argument is extended to national identity it contradicts Foster's suggestion that national culture and identity is 'doxic' in nature (1991: 240). In fact, Foster's own discussion of the contested and negotiated nature of many national identities and cultures suggests that his use of Bourdieu's concept of 'doxa' is inappropriate, as does Eriksen's (1992: 3) analysis of Mauritian and Trinidadian nationhood, in which he states that in these two cases nationhood belongs to 'the sphere of opinion, not to that of *doxa*'.

Bibliography

Barth, F. 1969. Introduction. In Barth, F. (ed.), *Ethnic Groups and Boundaries*. Boston: Little Brown, pp. 9–38.

Bentley, G.C. 1987. Ethnicity and Practice. *Comparative Studies in Society and History* 29: 24–55.

Blackmore, C., Braithwaite, M., and Hodder, I. 1979. Social and Cultural Patterning in the Late Iron Age in Southern Britain. In Burnham, B.C. and Kingsbury, J. (eds), *Space, Hierarchy and Society: Interdisciplinary Studies in Social Area Analysis*. Oxford: BAR, pp. 93–112.

Bond, G.C. and Gilliam, A. 1994. Introduction. In Bond, G.C. and Gilliam, A. (eds), *Social Construction of the Past: Representation as Power*. London: Routledge, pp. 1–22.

Bourdieu, P. 1977. *Outline of a Theory of Practice*. Cambridge: Cambridge University Press.

Boyarin, J. 1992. *Storm from Paradise: The Politics of Jewish Memory*. Minneapolis: University of Minnesota Press.

Chapman, M., McDonald, M., and Tonkin, E. 1989. Introduction. In Tonkin, E., McDonald, M., and Chapman, M. (eds), *History and Ethnicity*. London: Routledge, pp. 1–33.

Childe, G.V. 1929. *The Danube in Prehistory*. Oxford: Clarendon Press.

Childe, G.V. 1940. *Prehistoric Communities of the British Isles*. London: W. and R. Chambers.

Childe, G.V. 1956. *Piecing Together the Past: The Interpretation of Archaeological Data*. London: Routledge and Kegan Paul.

Clifford, J. 1988. *The Predicament of Culture*. Cambridge, MA: Harvard University Press.

Cohen, A. 1974. Introduction: The Lesson of Ethnicity. In Cohen, A. (ed.), *Urban Ethnicity*. London: Tavistock Publications, pp. ix–xxiv.

Cohen, R. 1978. Ethnicity: Problem and Focus in Anthropology. *Annual Review of Anthropology* 7: 379–403.

Colson, E. 1968. Contemporary Tribes and the Development of Nationalism. In Helm, J. (ed.), *Essays on the Problem of Tribe*. Seattle: University of Washington Press, pp. 201–6.

Comaroff, J and Comaroff, J. 1992. *Ethnography and the Historical Imagination*. Boulder: Westview Press.

Conkey, M.W. 1990. Experimenting with Style in Archaeology: Some Historical and Theoretical Issues. In Conkey, M.W. and Hastorf, C.A. (eds), *The Uses of Style in Archaeology*. Cambridge: Cambridge University Press, pp. 5–17.

Danforth, L. 1993. Competing Claims to Macedonian Identity: The Macedonian Question and the Breakup of Yugoslavia. *Anthropology Today* 9(4): 3–10.

Daniel, G. 1978 [1950]. *One Hundred and Fifty Years of Archaeology*. London: Duckworth.

Devalle, S.B.C. 1992. *Discourses of Ethnicity, Culture and Protest in Jharkhand*. London: Sage.

Eriksen, T.H. 1991. The Cultural Contexts of Ethnic Differences. *Man* 26: 127–44.

Eriksen, T.H. 1992. *Us and Them in Modern Societies: Ethnicity and Nationalism in Mauritius, Trinidad and Beyond*. London: Scandinavian University Press.

Eriksen, T.H. 1993. *Ethnicity and Nationalism: Anthropological Perspectives*. London: Pluto Press.

Fabian, J. 1983. *Time and the Other: How Anthropology Makes its Object*. New York: Columbia University Press.

Fardon, R. 1987. 'African Ethnogenesis': Limits to the Comparability of Ethnic Phenomena. In Holy, L. (ed.), *Comparative Anthropology*. London: Blackwell, pp. 168–87.

Fortes, M. 1969 [1945]. *The Dynamics of Clanship Among the Tallensi: Being the First Part of an Analysis of the Social Structure of a Trans-Volta Tribe*. London: Oxford University Press.

Foster, R.J. 1991. Making National Cultures in the Global Ecumene. *Annual Review of Anthropology* 20: 235–60.

Francis, E.K. 1947. The Nature of the Ethnic Group. *American Journal of Sociology* 52: 393–400.

Fried, M.H. 1968. On the Concepts of 'Tribe' and 'Tribal Society'. In Helm, J. (ed.), *Essays on the Problem of Tribe*. Seattle: University of Washington Press, pp. 3–20.

Gifford, J.C. 1960. The Type Variety Method of Ceramic Classification as an Indicator of Cultural Phenomena. *American Antiquity* 25(3): 341–7.

Greengrass, M. 1991. Introduction: Conquest and Coalescence. In Greengrass, M. (ed.), *Conquest and Coalescence: The Shaping of the State in Early Modern Europe*. London: Edward Arnold, pp. 1–24.

Haaland, G. 1969. Economic Determinants in Ethnic Processes. In Barth, F. (ed.), *Ethnic Groups and Boundaries*. London: George Allen and Unwin, pp. 58–73.

Handler, R. 1988. *Nationalism and the Politics of Culture in Quebec*. Wisconsin: University of Wisconsin Press.

Hastrup, K. 1992. Introduction. In Hastrup, K. (ed.), *Other Histories*. London: Routledge, pp. 1–13.

Hawkes, C.F.C. 1940. *The Prehistoric Foundations of Europe to the Mycenean Age*. London: Methuen.

Hodder, I. 1982. *Symbols in Action*. Cambridge: Cambridge University Press.

Jones, S. 1994. Ethnicity and Archaeology: Constructing Identities in the Past and the Present. Ph.D. thesis. University of Southampton.

Just, R. 1989. Triumph of the Ethnos. In Tonkin, E., McDonald, M., and Chapman, M. (eds), *History and Ethnicity*. London: Routledge, pp. 71–88.

Kimes, T., Haselgrove, C., and Hodder, I. 1982. A Method for the Identification of the Location of Regional Cultural Boundaries. *Journal of Anthropological Archaeology* 1: 113–31.

Kohl, P. 1993. Nationalism, Politics, and the Practice of Archaeology in Soviet Transcaucasia. *Journal of European Archaeology* 1(2): 181–8.

Kristiansen, K. 1993. The Strength of the Past and its Great Might: An Essay on the Use of the Past. *Journal of European Archaeology* 1: 3–33.

Leach, E. 1964 [1954]. *Political Systems of Highland Burma: A Study in Kachin Social Structure*. London: G. Bell and Sons.

Llobera, J. 1989. Catalan National Identity: The Dialectics of Past and Present. In Tonkin, E., McDonald, M., and Chapman, M. (eds), *History and Ethnicity*. London: Routledge, pp. 247–61.

Malina, J. and Vasicek, Z. 1990. *Archaeology Yesterday and Today: The Development of Archeology in the Sciences and Humanities*. Cambridge: Cambridge University Press.

Miller, D. 1985. *Artefacts as Categories: A Study in Ceramic Variability in Central India*. Cambridge: Cambridge University Press.

Moerman, M. 1965. Who are the Lue? *American Anthropologist* 67: 1,215–30.

Olsen, B. 1986. Norwegian Archaeology and the People Without (Pre-)History: Or How to Create a Myth of a Uniform Past. *Archaeological Review from Cambridge* 5: 25–42.

Patterson, O. 1975. Context and Choice in Ethnic Allegiance: A Theoretical Framework and Caribbean Case Study. In Glazer, N. and Moyniban, D.P. (eds), *Ethnicity: Theory and Experience*. Cambridge, MA: Harvard University Press, pp. 305–49.

Piggott, S. 1958. *Approaches to Archaeology*. London: Adam and Charles Black.

Piggott, S. 1965. *Ancient Europe: From the Beginnings of Agriculture to Classical Antiquity*. Edinburgh: Edinburgh University Press.

Postone, M., LiPuma, E., and Calhoun, C. 1993. Introduction: Bourdieu and Social Theory. In Calhoun, C., LiPuma, E., and Postone, M. (eds), *Bourdieu: Critical Perspectives*. Cambridge: Polity, pp. 1–13.

Ringer, B.B. and Lawless, E.R. 1989. *Race, Ethnicity and Society*. London: Routledge.

Rowlands, M.J. 1982. Processual Archaeology as Historical Social Science. In Renfrew, C., Rowlands, M.J., and Seagraves, B.A. (eds), *Theory and Explanation in Archaeology*. London: Academic Press, pp. 155–74.

Sahlins, M. 1985. *Islands of History*. Chicago: University of Chicago Press.

Shennan, S.J. 1989. Introduction. In Shennan, S.J. (ed.), *Archaeological Approaches to Cultural Identity*. London: Unwin and Hyman, pp. 1–32.

Shibutani, T. and Kwan, K.M. 1965. *Ethnic Stratification: A Comparative Approach*. New York: Macmillan.

Shore, C. 1993. Inventing the 'People's Europe': Critical Approaches to European Community Cultural Policy. *Man* 18(4): 779–800.

Spencer, J. 1990. Writing within. Anthropology, Nationalism, and Culture in Sri Lanka. *Current Anthropology* 31(3): 283–300.

Tonkin, E., McDonald, M., and Chapman, M. (eds). 1989. *History and Ethnicity*. London: Routledge.

Trigger, B.G. 1978. *Time and Traditions: Essays in Archaeological Interpretation*. Edinburgh: Edinburgh University Press.

Trigger, B.G. 1989. *A History of Archaeological Thought*. Cambridge: Cambridge University Press.

Ucko, P.J. (ed.). 1995. *Theory in Archaeology: A World Perspective*. London: Routledge.

Wallerstein, I. 1960. Ethnicity and National Integration in West Africa. *Cahiers d'Etudes Africaines* 1(3): 129–39.

Wallman, S. 1977. Ethnicity Research in Britain. *Current Anthropology* 18(3): 531–2.

Wiessner, P. 1983. Style and Ethnicity in the Kalahari San Projectile Point. *American Antiquity* 48: 253–76.

Wiessner, P. 1989. Style and Changing Relations Between the Individual and Society. In Hodder, I. (ed.), *The Meanings of Things*. London: Unwin and Hyman, pp. 56–63.

Wolf, E.R. 1982. *Europe and the People Without History*. Berkeley: University of California Press.

Chapter 4

The politics of identity in archaeology

Michael Rowlands

In 1973 David Clarke published a paper in *Antiquity* entitled 'The Loss of Innocence in Archaeology'. He was alluding to a naïvety in archaeological practice as part of a more wide-ranging attack on the subjectivism and parochial forms of empiricism that, he felt, pervaded the subject. His purpose was to advocate greater rigour in the development of explicit theory and method that would build a sustainable body of archaeologically derived generalizations.

Naïvety of course does not represent ignorance. It refers to an unreflective mode of practice that takes for granted the axioms on which established work predetermines the value of future knowledge. By encouraging a commonsense, taken-for-granted conviction in the obvious rightness of simply getting on and 'doing archaeology' rather than discussing the ideological bases of interpretation, a natural defence is formed against accusations of bias. By contrast with some current postmodernist claims, the issue of truth is not an issue for naïve claims to knowledge. Sources and criticism of evidence are as much the methodological underpinnings of commonsense knowledge as explicitness is a priority for positivistic claims.

Yet the dilemma of disciplinary confusion is a more widespread phenomenon. Everywhere the foundations of expert knowledge are being undermined and this reflects a more general crisis in the relationship between intellectuals and society in the late twentieth century. The rapid movement of people, goods, information, and money in the modern world system makes it increasingly difficult for any one group of intellectuals to maintain monopolies on ideas. Scepticism is rife of authority claims from professionals whose impersonal knowledge appears either irrelevant or dangerous – scientists endanger the environment, doctors are bad for you, lawyers are incompetent, professors have nothing to say. At the most fundamental level, it is the claim to science (loosely defined here as an externally validated system of knowledge) that is doubted, coinciding with movements in different disciplines to subvert the traditional division between the thinking subject and passive social object and replace it with a more engaged and equal relationship.

Archaeology suffers from a particular version of this dilemma. One of its claims is that social and personal identity depends on a secure sense of past which archaeologists produce through objective knowledge and the acceptance of its findings in the established structures of academic bureaucracy. Another has been a populist argument that it produces a knowledge open and available to all; that it forms an ethical discipline through its engagement directly with people in society. The politics of archaeological claims to both objective and subjective knowledge have recently become more central to understanding the formation of the discipline. Nationalism and ethnicity (Kohl 1993; Kristiansen 1993), gender and class (Gero and Conkey 1991), and power/knowledge claims (Miller and Tilley 1984; Shanks and Tilley 1987) are some examples of how bias in archaeological knowledge has been exposed. The ideological role of archaeological interpretation was exposed with a second, political, loss of innocence in the furore over the first World Archaeological Congress in Southampton in 1986. That particular event, in fact, demonstrated both the politics of doing academic work as well as the political implications of archaeological representations of alternative pasts. What was striking about this challenge to archaeological naïvety was the role of non-European archaeologies in challenging the metanarratives of principally European- and North American-dominated global archaeology. The convenient forgetting of the political construction of European prehistory was challenged more by the experience of 'writing prehistory' in the periphery as resistance to colonial constructions of indigenous pasts than by political events in the archaeological heartlands of Europe and North America.

This was in spite of the fact that Europe has been the site of some of the greatest controversies in the representation of collective identity in the twentieth century. The search for cultural origins has successfully organized much archaeological writing in the West until recently precisely because of the appeal of collective identity.

> The impulse to preserve the past is part of the impulse to preserve the self. Without knowing where we have been it is difficult to know where we are going. The past is the foundation of individual and collective identity, objects from the past are the source of significance as cultural symbols.
>
> (Hewison 1987: 45)

For cultural heritage to be significant it must therefore be unifying and transcendent and be constitutive of a sense of personal and group identity. Moreover the possession of a collective heritage puts the fragmentation of modern society firmly in its contingent and ephemeral place by locating identity within a sense of enduring time and place. The discovery of cultural origins has become one of the principal means of doing this, and as a trope that authenticates a diverse range of archaeological writings from the academic to the popular, it has arguably been more powerful than naturalization as a metaphor in modernist ideological formation (cf. Rowlands 1987). However, an essentialist line of argument only gains any credence because of a naïve, unreflexive adherence to the belief that neither person nor group exists without a sense of identity. But what is identity and why do we need one?

Identity and categories of the person

We can scarcely do without the word identity these days to describe an almost inviolable right to existence. Usually this requires an adjective that specifies the identity; this provides a singularity which of course is precisely what the term is meant to convey. Yet academic concern with identity, at least, has displayed a considerable growth in attention over the last few decades. The *International Encyclopaedia of Social Sciences* published in 1968 carries two substantial articles on the subject, one on the psychology of identity and the other on the political dimensions of identification as a process. By comparison, the first edition of the same encyclopaedia in the early 1930s does not mention the word. Such a significant shift in the usage of the term, I suggest, can also be correlated to the development of concepts such as cultural heritage and ideas about national character in general intellectual discourse from the 1940s onwards. In anthropology the work of Margaret Mead and the Culture and Personality School was a particularly important element in developing a concern for building national character through an understanding of the transition from 'traditional' to 'modern' societies (see Gleason 1983). The development of a concern with identity has therefore been consistent with the recognition of the problem of the individual in mass society (from de Tocqueville to the present). Modernization produces identity as a problem precisely because it evokes a sense of loss and nostalgic desire (Robertson 1990). Whether it is the effect of an experience of emigration and immigration in the twentieth century or fears of the threat of cultural homogenization or the doubts cast on the unity of the self due to fears of anomie, alienation, and loneliness, identity has become the keyword to describe a sense of loss.

The word identity comes from the Latin root *idem*, the same, and evokes a principle of endurance and continuity, usually in essentialist terms. The *Oxford English Dictionary* (OED) definition conveys much the same meaning: 'the sameness of a person or thing is itself and not something else; individuality, personality. Personal identity (in Psychology) the condition or fact of remaining the same person throughout the various phases of existence; continuity of the personality'.

Both the above usages are consistent with the empiricist philosophy of the individual derived from John Locke's *Essay Concerning Human Understanding* (1690) and David Hume's *Treatise on Human Nature* (1739). For them the unity of the self was not a problem until the traditional Christian notion of the soul gave way to doubt as to the original unity of the person (Langbaum 1977: 25). Both Locke and Hume used the word identity to express doubt as to the naturalness of the self and therefore the necessary unification of mind and body. The possibility of losing identity or the fact that uprootedness, alienation, and loneliness could seriously affect secure possession of a sense of identity was the logical outcome of this position.

Once posed as a question of doubt, broadly speaking, there have been two kinds of response to what forms an identity. The term identification was introduced by Freud to describe the process by which the infant internalizes external persons in the process of socialization. Developed by Melanie Klein and popularized by Erikson (1959), the term identity or identity crisis described a process by which the core of the individual and the core of his/her communal culture become one and the same. This situating of ego formation in the historical context of a particular cultural history meant that the elements of inferiority and continuity were indispensable to the development of a secure sense of self. Regardless of change and crisis in social and historical context, identity as a sense of inner sameness and continuity would be reproduced and survive, as a template, to structure new cultural forms. An alternative sociologizing tradition has consistently maintained that identities are labile and contingent, reflecting particular social circumstances. Symbolic interactionists such as Goffman (1967) and Berger and Luckman (1967) popularized the sociological understanding that social interaction, mediated through symbolic structures, shaped the self-consciousness of the individual. There was no inner core but instead a sense of self, derived circumstantially from processes of socialization. The view that identity is a product of the interaction between the individual and society means that the self is not some inner, historically constituted and unchanging core, but is constantly altered by changes in social situation. Primordialists therefore see identity as deep, internal, and permanent while interactionists see it as shallow, external, and contingent on social circumstance.

The models and theories of identity that developed in archaeology share elements of both these paradigms. Whether this represents the projection of a modernist concern with unified identities on to the past where such entities never existed remains a significant question. But archaeology, as with other disciplines, has been part of the explosive growth of concern with identities in the last few decades. Partly it constitutes a response to the growing recognition of the capacity of ethnic, national, and minority groups to generate disorder when their sense of integrity is threatened, and partly it is due to the growth of mass consumerism and fears about the coca colonization of global culture (Robertson 1990). In response to these anxieties, identity as something perduring and consistent has become a key value that archaeology, due to its access to the long term, is credited with being particularly well situated to exploit. The manipulation of archaeology in the shoring up of identities is now far more widespread than in the 1930s when Kossinna-like racial arguments stalked the archaeological landscape. Whether in the form of cultural heritage where the production of archaeological identities might be seen as admirable in empowering local groups and indigenous rights, or in cases of ethnic nationalism where archaeological accounts of the past may be distorted to serve political goals that most would find distasteful and objectionable, identities are produced as categorial imperatives to serve political ends. This is far removed from the naïve, unreflexive 'good old days' of empiricist archaeology but is consistent with the general relation of intellectual work to society.

Archaeology and nationalism

Nations without pasts are a contradiction in terms and archaeology has been one of the principal suppliers of the raw material for constructing pasts in modern struggles for nationhood. Hobsbawm (1992) has written ironically that the historian is to the nationalist what the poppy grower is to the heroin addict. Archaeology, especially in its modernist form, has been formed on the premise of a sense of loss, its subject matter conceived to be the recovery of tradition and a sense of community in contrast to the feeling of disenchantment for the world in which they live (Robertson 1990). For nationalists the 'imagined community' is often portrayed as an idealized entity that once existed or was under threat and whose demise must be fought against and recovery sustained. Alternatively much of the recent writings on nationalism have been elaborately concerned with demonstrating the fictitious element of such reconstructions of the past – the invention of tradition in the building of new worlds (Hobsbawm and Ranger 1983). Handler writes of the attempts by the Québécois to construct bounded cultural objects as 'a process that paradoxically demonstrates the absence of any such objects' (1988: 191). One of the purposes in seeing the past as a strategic resource to serve current political purposes is to avoid the central issue of historical primordialism. By excluding the passions from this sense of identity, they erupt instead elsewhere as various kinds of personal, often non-academic practices.

Whatever the relative success of the traditionalism that so marks a nation – the battles, flags, great dynastic events – it depends less on claims to possess historical symbolic value and more on how they constitute a community of shared memory.

Anderson (1981) has stressed that where the imagination of collective identity is constituted in memory, nationalisms are shaped as communities of shared feeling or passion. Understanding the construction of British identity after 1870, for example, would be inseparable from understanding how the class politics of the early industrializing period were displaced into the construction of a unified national identity based on custom, tradition, and the creation of royal rituals (Canadine 1983). Custom versus history, as Hobsbawm and Ranger (1983) remind us, is really the politics of timeless inevitability versus social rupture and the politics of change. It is also the difference between a self-knowledge created through writing and an unreflexive sense of self based in the imagination. This is why the battle for custom to become identified with history (or vice versa) is basic to educational practice in the building and preservation of a nation. After Italy had been politically unified Massimo d'Azeglio said 'We have made Italy, now we have to make Italians' (quoted in Hobsbawm 1992: 4).

The real issue is whether the archaeological pasts that archaeologists do or should produce are or should be those wanted by nationalists. Clearly there is one view that all contestatory pasts are equally mythological and are simply desirable or undesirable at any particular moment in time. Another, with which I am more in sympathy, claims to detect error, to show not only how things have become but also how they might have been otherwise. Hobsbawm makes this point by repeating the words of Ernest Renan in his famous lecture 'What is a Nation?' in 1882: 'Forgetting history or even getting history wrong (*l'erreur historique*) are an essential factor in the formation of a nation, which is why the progress of historical studies is often dangerous to a nationality' (Renan quoted in Hobsbawm 1992: 3).

So an archaeologist who writes within a national or ethnic framework cannot help but take a critical stand as to how his/her work is used. There seems little doubt that this is a growing dilemma for archaeologists. However, it is significant that the rise of contestatory archaeological narratives of the past has found its most virulent form in places where the discordance between colonial master narrative and local indigenous identities has been greatest. Perhaps it is particularly significant that such clashes have been most prominent in regions with immigrant population settlement and where appeals to prior origin by minorities will depend on archaeologically derived pasts. Of course the call for contestatory histories in the West – working-class histories, gender, race, etc. – has emphasized struggle in the narrative at home as well, but in a curious way it has also served to neutralize its impact. As Joan Scott has written 'proliferation of others' histories has not so much politicized the discipline (a charge usually leveled by the defenders of orthodoxy) as it has exposed the politics by which one particular viewpoint established its predominance' (Scott 1989: 690, quoted in Dirks 1990). By absorbing these biases it becomes possible still to claim that there are timeless truths 'transcending accidents of class, race and gender, that speak to us all' (Scott 1989: 683, quoted in Dirks 1990).

The debate between Ucko and Cunliffe on the lessons to be drawn from the exclusion of South African academics from the World Archaeological Congress rehearsed similar lines. Ucko claimed that the inexorable conclusion of the 1986 World Archaeological

Congress was that academic work cannot be separated from politics, while Cunliffe argued that the controversy was a clear justification that objective archaeological truth was all-important and should transcend local politics (Ucko 1987: 139–41).

Ironically what makes a sense of past constitutive of a nation is its link with modernity. In the eighteenth and nineteenth centuries, history became part of the enactment of modern nationalisms. From the writing of chronicles and annals of kings and dynasties, history progressed to the narrative of the formation of the nation-state as a community of shared memory. To paraphrase a point made about history by Dirks (1990), archaeology is one of the most important signs of the modern. We are modern because we are historically conscious, and historically conscious because we are modern. But equally, to cite Habermas (1987), we are modern in the belief that we already live in the future. Our present therefore is constituted in the irony of having transcended a sense of the traditional while achieving a future as the triumph of reason. History and Reason have therefore always been in tension with each other and yet dependent upon each other as mutually constituted creations of modernity.

In the Third World, each new nation created by independence from colonial rule had in turn to create its own narrative of possessing an authentic pre-colonial past, suffering the rupture of colonial possession and re-achieving authenticity through its struggle for freedom. The master narrative of nineteenth-century European nation-states was appropriated by the subjects of colonial rule and turned against the master narratives of imperial history. But in the process what has come to be realized is that although defined in opposition, the shape of that historical narrative is still that of the colonizer. If the subject voices were constituted in resistance to colonial rule, then it is not surprising that a sense of past has been colonized as well and frequently gives form to idealized futures. 'Nationalism produced a discourse in which, even as it challenged the colonial claim to political domination, it also accepted the intellectual premises of modernity on which colonial domination was based' (Dirks 1990: 26).

Behind this claim are of course familiar constructs for modelling change. A familiar pattern would be the way in which homogeneous, undifferentiated social solidarities of the past have given way to the fragmentation of modern society – a belief in alternative paths to modernity, in which fragmentation of the Western societies will be avoided by sustaining continuity with an authentic past. The double helix of homogenization and heterogenization is twisted on the axis of historical change such that social fragmentation and cultural homogenization become opposed to each other in temporal succession. As Hobsbawm (1992: 6) argues, classical nineteenth-century liberal nationalism was organized on opposite principles to those of contemporary ethnic politics in former Yugoslavia, Georgia, and elsewhere. It aimed to unify and extend the scale of human social and cultural units by inclusion (via language and education primarily) rather than by separation and exclusion. This is one reason why Third World regimes have found nineteenth-century European traditions so congenial to their problems of integration and unification, while in the same period the exporters of these models have been involved in reinventing local ethnic or regional loyalties as categorical imperatives of the modern bureaucratic state.

Heritage in this setting has diversionary potential in the sense that the aim is to substitute the promotion of local identity for active engagement in national politics. The reason why modern nationalism often means monuments is surely this. The past as property means ownership of what constitutes unity in a chosen sense of place. Whether at national or local levels, the objectification of national spirit and the recognition of the people or races as embodiments of that spirit takes an enduring form that emphasizes long-term continuity. Symbols of transcendence are chosen from the rubble of cultural history in line with their capacity to displace attention from political conflicts. It is not surprising, therefore, that archaeologies have contributed more to the primordialist view of identity, since by escaping the deceit of historical writing, the production of past material cultures has the spontaneity of a kind of unconscious speech, a taken-for-granted, commonsense existence that simply demonstrates that a people have always existed in that place. The origins of naïvety in archaeological interpretation can now be properly contextualized within a nineteenth-century nationalist mode of thought.

Archaeologists and development

Archaeologists, of whatever political persuasion, are involved inevitably as producers of expert knowledges. How are claims to control the materiality of the past defined by expertise, legalization, and the rights of higher authorities to know better? Such disputes hinge on the question of whose expert knowledge carries authority. In a controversy over a sacred site in Hawaii (Spriggs 1989), Kenneth Emory of the Bishopsland Museum claimed that his concern was to protect the integrity of the knowledge that has been passed down by scholars, Hawaiians and otherwise (that is, real knowledge). In this manner he justified his scepticism over the 'springing up of sacred sites' everywhere and the claims by followers of a Hawaiian revivalist cult that the information in museum books is often in error because it is gathered by whites to whom Hawaiian informants did not tell the truth. Could expert archaeological knowledge in Hawaii ever really cope with the Christian revivalist idea that the Hawaiians were one of the lost seven tribes of Israel that migrated to the Pacific via the Red Sea and Indonesia?

Clashes between archaeologists as local experts and carriers of 'local knowledges' have been fought out on the terrain of 'who can speak with authority versus who can speak with authenticity'. Trying to be both is not necessarily any more successful. The Nigerian archaeologist Nwanna Nzewunwa has documented how becoming an archaeologist estranged him from his own ethnic group, in the way that expert knowledge, education, and the city opposes the rural, the traditional, and the village (Nzewunwa 1990: 193–7). Here the historical axis is twisted on a geographical scale to create the urban/rural divide with the village as repository of ancestral knowledge, of craft, folk knowledge, and tradition in tension with modernity identified with urban living and formal education as the fountain of rational expertise – primary health care, literacy, development, and aid technologies. In other words academic archaeology acquires authority due to its association with the signs of urban modernity, while an indigenous sense of past retains veracity due to its association with orality and tradition. The capacity to have a past, either historically or archaeologically constituted, comes with development and is symptomatic of progress.

Of course the fact that the state is concerned only with certain kinds of representations of the past and not others has implications for defining what is conceived to be legitimate archaeology rather than treasure seeking and the evaluation of memory as a cultural resource versus museums and archives. Inventing tradition is therefore a product of the codes creating cultural knowledges, i.e. inclusion/exclusion, same-ness/difference, writing/memory. In other words a tradition that aspires to emphasize what makes a group, community, nation different is somehow immediately suspected of being contrived, self-conscious, and false in the eyes of others. In order to protect them from others, the rituals of distinct traditions have to be bracketed and displaced into some safe place where their performance can be held unhindered and consumed without discomfort. Invented folklores, craftlore, Scottish ballads, festivals, etc. are all well-known features of this kind of privatized traditionalism whatever the scale. The only problem with this anodyne view of tradition – either of the invented or dis-covered kind – is that in much of the world tradition as we know it today was created through contact with modernity in the context of colonialism. In Africa, for example, such timeless features of African society as divine kingship, tribalism, segmentary lin-eages, and fetishism can all be shown to have been produced or transformed in meaning through encounter with colonial rule. The British and other colonial powers were therefore drawn into the production of those components of African tradition that in the post-colonial era have been widely cited as the principal impediments to full-scale modernity. Headlines which despair of the current plight of Africans illus-trate a current view that modernization has failed in Africa because of insuperable, indigenous, cultural blockages rather than because of contemporary, external, politi-cal realities.

The belief that the colonizers had history and the colonized had custom and tradi-tion sustained and in part still does sustain an anthropology/archaeology dualism (Asad 1979). Mignolo (1992) has described the complicity between alphabetic writing and history in the Renaissance view of knowledge and how this denied Amerindian understanding of their own history since how could the memory of past events be pre-served without writing. It is striking that archaeology was least developed in those parts of the colonized periphery where British anthropology in particular was most powerful. We still know virtually nothing in fine-grain detail of the archaeology of vast tracts of west central Africa, for example, whereas ethnographically it formed the backbone for British structural functionalist anthropology. What Dirks (1990) calls the policing of tradition, by which he means the ways in which tradition is codified, controlled, reformed, and suppressed, became not only the discourse of anthropology but also the justification for fieldwork by providing a more controllable access to custom than did objects and museums. It would appear that anthropology and archae-ology were in competition to provide a disciplined account of traditional society, the one based on oral tradition, the other on material culture, and both opposed by the official written histories made by European observers. Ironically the growth of anthro-pological archaeology has tended to encourage this colonization of the prehistories of others by judging their significance in terms of how well they illustrate some general benchmark in human progress, such as the origins of farming, or of metallurgy, or the state. For an African archaeologist, the need to have a suitable piece of generalizable academic capital in order to be invited to conferences in the archaeological heartlands of Europe and North America was and is of great importance since jobs and promo-tion depend on external validation of this kind.

But the very success archaeology has had in evaluating and subsuming local pre-histories by the contributions they make to universal comparative projects of Western origin has also revealed the limitations of the archaeological project on a global scale. Such universalizing goals were suitable in the context of colonial ideologies where a clear separation existed between Us and Them – where the colonized Other could be domesticated and made an example, however crudely, of some more grandiose paradigm. In this sense classical evolutionism may have changed in substance since the nineteenth century but its basic role as a framework for hierarchically ordering societies on a single scale of values has not changed much. But the fear that the growing transnationalization of capital and developments in communication and transport have created a global culture that will extinguish local identities in a gigantic wave of mass consumerism has undermined the desirability of archaeology's older generalizing goals. One response as a counter to global homogenization would obviously be to claim expertise in local knowledge which archaeology could claim as its own constituency. Local prehistories are particular and irreducible by the very method of their excavation and recording, and simply denying the need to abstract and generalize has produced the 'thick description' that provides a localized sense of past. The idea of thousands of local archaeology societies producing their own accounts of local pasts simultaneously on a global scale is not at all far-fetched. If the European experience is anything to go by, this is what follows from a successful creation of a sense of nationhood usually in the guise of the creation of a national museum followed by local museums to re-present subordinated identities.

An alternative to this would be for archaeology to break out of the simplicity of such a scenario by investigating the global processes and forms themselves. An archaeology of colonialism, for example, is barely acknowledged as existing and yet an archaeological version of Eric Wolf's (1982) *Europe and the People Without History* is certainly both feasible and probably more relevant than that based on the ethno-history and ethnography available to him. Immanuel Wallerstein's three volumes on *The Modern World System* (1974–89) provide the most overall account of contemporary and historical processes of globalization since the sixteenth century. The accounts offered so far, however, are still produced within an ambience that evaluates the pasts of others by their closeness or otherwise to that of the 'Europeans' providing the account. While in an evolutionist past, an Old World archaeology would describe Africa or the Americas in terms of what they lacked (writing, true religion, cities, markets, money, or history), now it would be a question of how much they have lost, measured as an absence of otherness itself. Taussig has described this sense of loss as 'This infernal American identity machine...composing a mosaic of alterities around a mysterious core of hubridity seething with instability, threatening the First World quest for a decent fix of straightforward Othering' (1993: 143).

Archaeology and the postmodern

Just as there seemed to be a growing acceptance of a value-committed archaeology and a willingness to debate the kind of archaeological objectivity required to discern between alternative pasts, the whole archaeological enterprise seems beset by the current slippage of historicity announced as a predominant feature of the postmodern. Jameson (1984), in one of the most well-known formulations of the culture of postmodernism, described it 'as an era experiencing a new depthlessness and a consequent weakening of historicity representing an inability to unify past, present and future...leaving a rubble of distinct and unrelated signifiers' (Jameson 1984: 79), and the reduction of experience to a series of pure and unrelated presents in time and a 'general warning of effect with a general accompanying sense of consumer euphoria' (ibid.). In the shift from the modern to the postmodern we witness the replacement of angst about the alienation of the subject by the fragmentation of the self. Such a breakdown in the temporal ordering of things also gives rise to a peculiar treatment of the past – postmodernism abandons memory and sense of historical continuity while simultaneously developing an incredible ability to plunder history and absorb whatever it finds there as some of the present. Moreover archaeology seems willing to provide a postmodern access to the Other that anthropology once promised through primitivism but which is now no longer possible. The likelihood that a primitive Other is now only possible either as science fiction, or by archaeology providing mythical alien pasts to experience personally in museums and theme parks, reveals the true hunger for wholeness and unity which anthropology was always a little inadequate in providing. But these are not temporarily experienced pasts – as would be sequence-explored in some kind of time machine or as an exploration of the collective identity of shared memory. Instead they are rhizome pasts (Deleuze and Guattari 1977) – pasts constructed out of a multiplicity of events that cannot be understood by reference to origin or genesis or deep structures but as social networks of power and desire that nonetheless have trajectories and futures to be understood.

But who is served by this view of the past? The majority of people who visit museums and art galleries are educated, middle-class, and obey Bourdieu's (1984) principle that length of time in higher education determines who visits museums. By comparison the main consumers of postmodern imagery are anything but the educated middle class. As Eagleton (1985) has argued, postmodernism in historical effect is conservative – not only in terms of the complacency it generates in creating perfect consumers but also because the images it produces are consumed by those whose historical voice would not be heard anyway. Postmodern art forms and cultural artefacts have also been described as self-embracing and incapable of referring to conditions outside of the problem of image creation (Harvey 1989: 323). We have no means of distinguishing class or gender relations in the differential consumption of such images. Instead the postmodernist collapse of metanarrative – in its deconstructionist sense – was celebrated precisely as play on tropes, privileging writing over language, and as a radical approval of the loose play of difference in the creation of individual realities. Totalizing concepts such as class, race, society, etc. had no prior existence, nor could they be deemed to be the hidden determinants of postmodern identities. In fact, identity itself becomes a fictitious and doubtful concept based on the heady modernist desire to deny Lockean doubt and assert a commonsense acceptance of a unified self.

If identities are not given, then the politics of postmodernism must deny that relevance of a sense of past and replace it with a temporarily indeterminate consumption of the past as image. In this respect the point made by Harvey (1989) that postmodernism is a movement within modernity is well made. Little has changed in the sense that the seeking of coherent narratives of the past is still the major legitimation of elite status in advanced capitalism. Sub-categories, such as gender, class, and race, have a potential historical consciousness to be realized rather than repressed through the unsettling disorder of the loose play of difference. However, even if we allow alternative narratives of how things came to be, the postmodern as a dominant ideology which proposes the existence of a plurality of archaeological voices is accompanied by the suspicion that some of these are more authentic than others. The aestheticization of politics to stifle social aspirations and revolutionary movements has happened before. However, it is a new twist to promote alternative historical voices while at the same time making clear that some are not to be taken as seriously as others. This is not because the deconstructionist approach threatens an open play of meaning unchecked by the realities of the archaeological record (Hodder 1992: 166), but precisely because eventually the latter has to be introduced to rank the relative claims made by minority voices. Shanks and Tilley (1987: 192) have made much the same point in criticizing Habermas's naïve faith that debate and discussion in a liberal society will make any difference in a subject like archaeology where the system only allows certain people to do or write archaeology. Probably few will have the courage to pursue the post-structuralist argument in archaeology this far and instead a revisionist faith will be expressed, confirming the objectivity of the archaeological record and its independence and capacity to resist any account imposed upon it (cf. Hodder 1992: 166). This clearly does not go far enough since achieving objectivity still relies on meaning, text, and 'ideas in people's heads' which are precisely the subject of the deconstructionist critique. Such an intention requires what Bourdieu has called 'methodological objectivism', a necessary moment in all research, by which he meant 'the break with primary experience and the construction of objective relations which once accomplished, demands its own supersession' (1977: 72). It must also assume the existence of a more dialectical relationship between past and present in which answering 'how things might have been otherwise' requires equal understanding of the play of structure that escapes human consciousness and effectively prohibits certain kinds of action either to enter historical consciousness or to be stifled in the event.

Conclusion

The social construction of archaeological pasts is more than personal values getting involved in the academic enterprise. In the differing contexts of nationalism, development, and the postmodern, we encounter the silences and gaps in archaeological explanations that determine which sites are excavated, what kinds of artefacts are privileged in the legitimizing of expert archaeological knowledges. The fact that the materiality of the archaeological record can resist these selective pressures or that silences can be exposed does not deny the obvious effects of such value commitment in archaeological practice. What I would suggest has been the key value motivating archaeological work is the notion of identity employed. If archaeology has tended traditionally to be on the primordialist side, current interest in notions of agency and the individual suggest a late but necessary move towards the interactionist perspective. Pushed to its limit, a postmodern denial of identity, except as temporary and fleeting refusal of anxiety, would have more serious implications for a future demand of archaeological narratives.

Of the motivations considered in this chapter, the expansion of archaeology's relation to nationalism and ethnicity in the construction of collective identity seems certain to continue. Partly the materiality of the archaeological record will assure this.

Partly also the creation of alternative pasts is increasingly being used to legitimize land claims, ethnic territories, and access to economic resources. Representations of communities of shared memory are diversifying, often outside the museum into settings that are more immediately graspable and open to appropriation. What seems clear is that while the relation of archaeology to nationalism has been the dominant force historically in Europe and for new nations creating themselves out of the exigencies of colonial rule, the wider issue is that of the construction of communities of shared memory. From the standpoint of modernity, every age is thus judged to attain the fullness of its time not by being but by becoming.

Acknowledgements

I am particularly grateful for Chris Tilley's comments on this chapter and to Bruce Kapferer for his insights on the subject of identity.

Bibliography

Anderson, B. 1981. *Imagined Communities*. London: Verso.

Asad, T. 1979. Anthropology and the End of Ideology. *Man* 14: 607–28.

Berger, P. and Luckman, T. 1967. *The Social Construction of Reality*. New York: Doubleday.

Bintliff, J. 1992. Postmodernism, Rhetoric and Scholasticism at TAG: The Current State of British Archaeological Theory. *Antiquity* 65: 274–8.

Bourdieu, P. 1977. *Outline of a Theory of Practice*. Cambridge: Cambridge University Press.

Bourdieu, P. 1984. *Distinction*. London: Routledge.

Canadine, D. 1983. The Context, Performance and Meaning of Ritual: The British Monarchy and the Invention of Tradition. In Hobsbawm, E. and Ranger, T. (eds), *The Invention of Tradition*. Cambridge: Cambridge University Press, pp. 101–65.

Deleuze, G. and Guattari, F. 1977. *Anti-Oedipus*. New York: Viking.

Dirks, N. 1990. History as a Sign of the Modern. *Public Culture* 2: 25–33.

Eagleton, T. 1985. Capitalism, Modernism and Postmodernism. *New Left Review* 152: 60–73.

Erikson, E.H. 1959. *Identity and the Life Cycle: Selected Papers*. New York: International Universities Press.

Frank, G. 1993. Was There a Bronze Age World System? *Current Anthropology* 34: 383–430.

Gero, J. and Conkey, M. 1991. *Engendering Archaeology: Women and Prehistory*. Oxford: Blackwell.

Gleason, P. 1983. Identifying Identity: A Semantic History. *Journal of American History* 69: 910–31.

Goffman, E. 1967. *The Presentation of Self in Everyday Life*. London: Allen Lane.

Habermas, J. 1987. *The Philosophical Discourse of Modernity*. Cambridge, MA: MIT Press.

Handler, R. 1988. *Nationalism and the Politics of Culture in Quebec*. Madison, WI: University of Wisconsin Press.

Harvey, D. 1989. *The Condition of Postmodernity*. Oxford: Blackwell.

Hewison, R. 1987. *The Heritage Industry*. London: Methuen.

Hobsbawm, E. 1992. Ethnicity and Nationalism in Europe Today. *Anthropology Today* 8: 3–13.

Hobsbawm, E. and Ranger, T. (eds). 1983. *The Invention of Tradition*. Cambridge: Cambridge University Press.

Hodder, I. 1992. *Theory and Practice in Archaeology*. London: Routledge.

Jameson, F. 1984. Postmodernism or the Cultural Logic of Late Capitalism. *New Left Review* 146: 53–92.

Kohl, P. 1993. Nationalism, Politics and the Practice of Archaeology in Soviet Transcaucasia. *Journal of European Archaeology* 2: 179–86.

Kristiansen, K. 1993. The Strength of the Past and its Great Might: An Essay on the Use of the Past. *Journal of European Archaeology* 1: 3–33.

Langbaum, R. 1977. *The Mysteries of Identity: A Theme in Modern Literature*. New York: Oxford University Press.

Merriman, N. 1989. Heritage from the Other Side of the Glass Case. *Anthropology Today* 5: 14–15.

Mignolo, W. 1992. On the Colonization of Amerindian Languages and Memories. *Comparative Studies of Sociology and History* 34: 301–34.

Miller, D. and Tilley, C. 1984. *Ideology: Power and Prehistory*. Cambridge: Cambridge University Press.

Nzewunwa, N. 1990. Cultural Education in West Africa: Archaeological Perspectives. In Gathercole, P. and Lowenthal, D. (eds), *The Politics of the Past*. London: Unwin Hyman, pp. 189–202.

Robertson, R. 1990. After Nostalgia: Wilful Nostalgia and Modernity. In Turner, B. (ed.), *Theories of Modernity and Postmodernity*. London: Sage, pp. 31–45.

Rowlands, M. 1987. Repetition and Exteriorization in Narratives of Historical Origins. *Critique of Anthropology* 8: 43–62.

Scott, J. 1985. *Weapons of the Weak*. New Haven: Yale University Press.

Scott, J. 1989. History in Crisis? The Others' Side of the Story. *American Historical Review* 94: 688–700.

Shanks, M. and Tilley, C. 1987. *Reconstructing Archaeology: Theory and Practice*. London: Routledge.

Spriggs, M. 1989. God's Police and Damned Whores: Images of Archaeology in Hawaii. In Gathercole, P. and Lowenthal, D. (eds), *The Politics of the Past*. London: Unwin Hyman, pp. 118–29.

Taussig, M. 1993. *Mimesis and Alterity: A Particular History of the Senses*. New York: Routledge.

Ucko, P.J. 1987. *Academic Freedom and Apartheid*. London: Duckworth.

Wallerstein, I. 1974–89. *The Modern World System*. New York: Academic Press.

Wolf, E. 1982. *Europe and the People Without History*. Berkeley: University of California Press.

Part II

Gender and age

An introduction

Timothy Insoll

The second part of this book is concerned with exploring the archaeology of gender and age. The former, gender, as the contributors here indicate, was possibly one of the first areas within the archaeology of identities to have been considered, whereas the latter, age, has only been approached by archaeologists much more recently, and Sofaer's chapter was one of the first to do this. Moreover although the archaeological study of gender might now, comparatively, have a reasonable history of research, frequently only one gender is considered, female, and the contributions chosen here crucially redress this in also evaluating the construction of male identity, and where relevant the cultural construction of further genders as well. The life cycle, as previously noted with reference to Meskell's chapter, is again emphasized as important in acting as a framework into which various identities can be slotted as they might wax and wane in importance as this cycle is completed (see also Gilchrist 2000); childhood, for instance, is obviously of great significance to the individual which then of course usually ceases to be, except in memory, as biologically and socially he or she progresses beyond this stage.

Rosemary Joyce in the first of the chapters in this section looks at both gender and age by focusing upon sixteenth-century Aztec children and their life cycles. Joyce is fortunate in being able to enrich her interpretations through the use of texts and pictorial documents, obviously not always available to those considering the archaeology of identities. The notion of 'repeated performance' is considered as an agent of socialization along with the use of material culture items such as costume or ornaments in creating engendered and socialized adults. In emphasizing 'repeated performance' Joyce draws upon the work of Judith Butler (1993). Performance and repetition are thus posited as key, besides biology, in creating gender in a social context.

Also significant, once again, is the unstated emphasis that we cannot take anything for granted in the archaeological study of identities, and Joyce indicates that in Aztec society three genders were created: potentially reproductive female, potentially reproductive male, and celibate. What is also evident is that the archaeology of childhood is not necessarily how we might conceptually configure childhood today. This is apparent in Joyce's forceful description of how punishments, including body piercing, were used on children over the age of seven to induce the notions of discipline, conformity, and regulation. The whole adding to what she terms the 'materialization of embodied subjectivity'.

The theme of engendering children is continued in the chapter by Joanna Sofaer. Furthermore she critically analyses some of the problems inherent in the archaeological study of identity, including the epistemological foundations which have largely precluded, until recently, an 'archaeology of childhood'. These primarily revolve around the neglect of the gender development of children or their socio-economic roles, as Sofaer notes, in favour of looking at adult gender roles, especially those associated with females. Alternatively recourse was made to the argument that the absence of evidence pertaining to childhood in the archaeological record necessitated this neglect.

Sofaer redresses this through discussing both the concepts of 'child' and 'childhood'. In so doing she indicates that the modern Western usage of the term 'child' is problematic in shoehorning a great range of diversity both in stages of development and differing levels of independence and dependence within its definitional boundaries. Again, complexity in how we configure identities is plainly required. Sofaer also provides a review of cognate literature drawn from, for example, linguistics and developmental psychology, of how gender is understood by children. The implications resulting from this for the examination of gender in archaeological contexts are varied with the important point being that its overall study may well benefit from the discussion of the gender development of children. Significantly, she indicates how interaction with gender-specific forms of material culture along with genital identification and linguistic involvement all help in developing gender identity. Too often the last two categories are given prominence or taken for granted, while the former, of obvious importance for archaeologists, might be neglected. However, the simple reduction of gender to artefact equivalence has to be, as Sofaer notes, obviously avoided.

The final chapter in this part of the book, by Alison Wylie, is thought provoking and has a resonance beyond the archaeological study of gender, at first sight, its immediate concern. This is because she provides a synthesis of critiques, defined as 'five levels and types of critique' which are applicable across the range of identities considered here. These include what Wylie describes as 'explanatory critiques' – why, literally, areas of research, including those pertaining to the archaeology of identities, are neglected, and this is of obvious relevance to the archaeology of childhood as just described. Wylie's chapter is also valuable in contextualizing how and why, for example, in relation to the political impetus which existed, gender came to assume the prominence that it has since been accorded by many archaeologists. Once again the theme of complexity recurs: in Wylie's emphasis that feminist research cannot place allegiance on either 'uncompromising constructivism' or 'relativism', both of which serve, she notes, to 'trivialize' experiences. Thus the sound conclusion is proposed that no general 'epistemic stance' is appropriate for all situations, rather this is down to local context. A point which serves well across the archaeology of identities per se.

Bibliography

Butler, J. 1993. *Bodies That Matter: On the Discursive Limits of 'Sex'*. New York: Routledge.
Gilchrist, R. 2000. Archaeological Biographies: Realizing Human Lifecycles, -Courses and -Histories. *World Archaeology* 31: 325–8.

Chapter 5

Girling the girl and boying the boy

The production of adulthood in ancient Mesoamerica

Rosemary A. Joyce

Introduction

Most Mesoamerican archaeology has taken adults as its representative subjects. Childhood is a significant focus in some demographic studies (Storey 1992). Mortuary analyses include discussion of burial treatment of infants and juveniles, rarely considering the experience of childhood or transitions in the life course. Some discussion of life-cycle rituals is embedded in historical accounts of specific Classic Maya rulers (Schele and Miller 1986: 114, 136–7, 148–50; Schele and Freidel 1990: 235–40, 470–1). Studies of figurines have led analysts to suggest connections with stages in the life course and life-cycle rituals (Cyphers Guillén 1993; Lesure 1997; Serra Puche and Durand 1998).

The most extensive discussions of childhood and the life cycle in Mesoamerica, based on sixteenth-century ethno-historic sources, examine the experience of childhood and adult concerns with control of children among the Aztecs (e.g. Calnek 1974, 1988, 1992; Clendinnen 1991; Kellogg 1995: 88–91). I use Aztec narratives about the social construction of adults to inform an understanding of archaeological artefacts and sites as media and settings for such life-cycle transformations. These complex verbal and visual narratives describe events in the lives of infants, children, and young adults of both sexes and a variety of social classes and occupational statuses.

I deliberately juxtapose discussion of early village sites in Mesoamerica, dating to the Formative period (*c.* 1500–500 BC), with the Aztec material because they were linked in a historical *longue durée*. The Mesoamerican *longue durée* was shaped not only by conservative reproduction of basic economic relations but also by conservatism in the reproduction of social personhood (Joyce 1998, 2000; cf. Cobb 1991: 171–4; Smith 1992). While specific conjunctures within the *longue durée* experienced significant change, not all practices were equally transformed. I argue that social construction of the person, beginning within the household, was as conservative as subsistence technology. Mesoamerican archaeology provides abundant evidence of material practices through which basic ways of being in the world were continually re-created throughout this *longue durée* (Joyce 2000).

Aztec texts emphasize physical discipline of the body of the child to produce a properly decorous adult. This, I argue, is due to the social value placed on reproduction of embodied identification with tradition. Judith Butler (1993: 12–16, 101–19) describes the social production of embodied existence as resulting from repeated *performance* of particular ways of being that are represented within a society as *citational precedents*.

The admonitions and physical discipline recorded in Aztec sources were directed towards instilling in youth a desire to match citational precedents presented by the examples and words of their elders. Life-cycle rituals involved careful repetition of actions, a compulsive iteration like that which Butler suggests is an inevitable outcome of consciousness of the unavoidable gap between a citational precedent and an individual performance (Butler 1993: 95, 107–9).

Presented at birth as raw materials like precious stones and feathers that were shaped into body ornaments, Aztec children were gradually socialized through habitual action, costume, and ornaments. They achieved a peak of differentiated gender identity in the early teens, when three approved genders (potentially reproductive male, potentially reproductive female, and celibate) were distinguished. Through life-cycle rituals, punctuating the continuous experience of embodied difference, individual chronological age was subordinated to socially recognized membership in common age grades.

Sources for the Aztecs are unusually rich, allowing construction of a more complete narrative of life-cycle transformations than is possible for other Mesoamerican societies. Bodily markings and disciplines of work, worship, and appearance were also deployed in life-cycle rituals described in much less detail in ethno-historic accounts of Post-classic Yucatec Maya states (Joyce 1994). These late Aztec and Maya case studies suggest avenues for interpretation of material culture and social and political life of earlier societies. The conservative and repetitive nature of Mesoamerican life-cycle rituals results in their archaeological visibility as ordered material remains, for example, burials. The Mesoamerican emphasis on creating bodily signs as part of life-cycle rituals confers on even disordered material remains the potential to inform us about changes in the life course.

Items of costume should be considered as potential media for life-cycle transitions, and contrasts in their patterns of use evaluated in light of the possible importance of costume as a medium for materializing properly socialized embodied persons. Indeed if distinctions in body modification like those described for the Aztec were already being employed earlier, then all distinctions in bodily appearance, as abstracted in representational media, must be considered potential evidence of life-cycle transitions. Finally even understandings of the use of different spatial settings must be re-evaluated with the potential enactment of life-cycle rituals in mind.

Aztec sources and their limits

Out of the sixteenth-century collision between European conquerors and native peoples came a literature reflecting the mutual task of understanding the other that united native peoples and Spanish newcomers. Because they served many purposes in dialogues about power, these texts cannot be uncritically treated as documentation about the pre-Hispanic world, but must be read as products of interested writers (Gillespie 1998). I employ two major sources to examine Aztec life transitions. In the *Florentine Codex* (Sahagún 1951, 1953, 1954, 1961, 1969), Sahagún assembled texts in Nahuatl provided by elite male informants to native students trained to read Spanish and their own Nahuatl, and glossed them in Spanish (see Calnek 1974, and essays in Klor de Alva *et al.* 1988). It is believed that Sahagún made use of a questionnaire to elicit information, channelling responses. Surviving versions of the work assembled these already structured responses in successive European orders. In the version represented in the *Florentine Codex*, we are faced with a document far from a straightforward description of life in the Aztec world. Obvious biases include substitution in the text of a normative male actor for mixed males and females (Brown 1983), and clerical concerns with labelling indigenous religious beliefs and practices as errors (Burkhart 1997: 27). Because life-cycle ceremonies were religious, these concerns affected the way they were recorded. Performance of life-cycle rituals was noted only where Sahagún's interests intersected the individual life course. Most information available about birth and marriage, both times of marked change in the life course, comes from speeches included only as examples of laudable rhetoric. A second issue is fragmentation. Text about transformations in the life-cycle comes from four volumes. There is no reason to think the aggregate description is ethnographically complete, since Sahagún was not trying to provide a single coherent account of everyday life.

Codex Mendoza is a pictorial document painted in 1541 by a master scribe trained in native traditions (see Berdan and Anawalt 1992, 1997: xi–xiii). It includes short glosses resulting from consultation with a group of Aztec elders and longer commentary. The section depicting childhood was a visual innovation without any pre-conquest model, which Calnek (1992) shows parallels texts collected by Sahagún. Like the *Florentine Codex*, the *Codex Mendoza* presented to the colonizing power an idealization of correct behaviour, and its just rewards, and of transgression and punishment. While this reduces their utility as accounts of everyday life, it makes them more useful sources for an investigation of attempts to define and impose norms through the life course.

The existential status of Aztec children

Sixteenth-century Nahuatl texts describe Aztec infants initially as raw materials that needed to be worked into specific forms. Life-cycle rituals were the context where continued refinement of this raw material was effected. The natural background from which humans were to be differentiated was as much vegetal or mineral as animal (cf. Clendinnen 1991: 153–67, 184–93, 223–8, 244–8, 250–3). In speeches to expectant mothers, children were characterized as the thorn that grows from the tip of the maguey leaf, and as maguey about to sprout and blossom (Sahagún 1969: Ch. 25). Identification of the child with unmodified raw materials worked into valued forms within the household-based productive economy was emphasized by equating infants with feathers and precious stones. Before and at birth, the child was described as a product made by the gods:

> the one who has arrived, the precious necklace, the precious feather, the baby, which has been flaked off here. Our lord the creator, the master, Quetzalcoatl, flakes a precious necklace, places a precious feather, here on your neck, at your breast, in your hands he places a precious necklace.
>
> (Sahagún 1969: Ch. 33)

During the ritual burial of the umbilical cord, the newborn child was still described as a sprouting plant, a chip of stone, and even as a wild bird in a nest (Sahagún 1969: Ch. 31). A shift in balance towards symbols drawn from the social universe came with the reading of the calendrical fortune of the child's birthdate (Sahagún 1969: Ch. 36). During the formal bathing ritual which followed, verbal rhetoric was given material form through the use of specific objects, for the boy 'a little shield, a little bow, little arrows...his little loin-cloth, his little cape', for the girl, 'the equipment of women – the spinning whorl, the weaving sword, the reed basket, the spinning bowl, the skeins, the shuttle, her little skirt, her little shift' (Sahagún 1969: Ch. 37). The midwife urged the baby to take and use small versions of adult tools. She named the baby and dressed it in small versions of adult cloth-ing that had been provided, not the everyday garments of infants.

This verbal and material rhetoric of labour and dress began to impose distinct adult male and female statuses on the newborn, 'boying' and 'girling' (Butler 1993: 7–8) these as-yet unfixed human subjects. The initial act of dressing did not make adults of infants, a task that lasted many years. But it did begin to treat children as social beings of the same kind as adults, with whom they shared this manner of dress. It began a sequence of changes in hair, costume, and ornaments that gradually created distinct social identities, above all those of adult genders and labour roles.

Making Aztec adults

The work of transforming the raw material of Aztec children into properly socialized adults was advanced through a series of life-cycle rituals, often including preparation for, or provision of, new forms of body modification. Kellogg (1995: 89–91) suggests that birth rituals involved gradually expanding groups of actors, from the midwife and parents present at birth, to kin who witnessed bathing and naming in the house compound, to non-kin at later, more public, ceremonies. Images in *Codex Mendoza* illustrate the actions of the midwife during the bathing ceremony (Berdan and Anawalt 1997: folio 57; cf. Sahagún 1969: Ch. 18; 1954: Ch. 16; 1953: Appendix 4). A baby in a cradle is linked by a dotted line to an older woman labelled 'midwife' holding an infant near a pottery vessel full of water set on a mat. Footprints around the mat form a counterclockwise path. Two dotted lines link the baby to a shield and spears, and to a broom and spinning basket, alternative insignia of dichotomous adult genders in the *Florentine Codex* (see McCafferty and McCafferty 1988, 1991; Brumfiel 1991; Burkhart 1997: 33–8, 45–52). In the image, the male emblems are augmented by tools for woodworking, feather-work, scribal prac-tice, and metalworking, described as tools of the child's father's profession.

The parallel between the sources continues with dedication of the baby to either the religious schools, the *calmecac*, or the secular *telpochcalli* or 'house of youths' (Calnek 1988). Directly below the drawings of the bathing and naming ceremony, the cradled infant is shown in front of its parents (Berdan and Anawalt 1997: folio 57). Dotted lines link the cradle to two seated figures, labelled as the master of the *telpochcalli* and the priest who headed the *calmecac*. Sahagún noted that a feast accompanied the promise of a child to the *calmecac*, taking place in the temple precincts because the head priest could not enter houses of commoners. A feast for the masters of the house of youths was celebrated at the house of a child promised to the *telpochcalli*. On that occasion the Masters of Youths 'cradled [the child] in their arms to possess it, to make it forever their possession, until it reached a marriageable age' (Sahagún 1969: Ch. 39).

In its first use, the either/or convention of the dotted line in *Codex Mendoza* dif-ferentiates the gender of the child. In its second use, it marks the institutional basis for the child's adult role. Assignment of children to the temple destined them to a life of chastity (Sahagún 1969: Ch. 39*)*. Through ceremonies of dedication to adult institutions, significantly different adult sexualities were predicted for newborn infants, conditioning the entire course of childhood towards these adult statuses.

Infants whose cultural shaping was initiated by these birth rituals underwent their next life-cycle ritual as early as four years old. Sahagún describes this ceremony in relative detail because it was tied to the civil calendar. Every fourth year in the month Izcalli a feast was held 'when children were grabbed by the neck to make them grow tall' (Sahagún 1951: Ch. 37). It marked the transition from the freedom of infants to the structured training of older children. As Inga Clendinnen (1991: 189–92) noted, the timing of the feast at four-year intervals means the children participating were not all the same age. Izcalli rituals established an age grade of four years.

The ceremony began at midnight at the local temple with piercing of the children's ears (Sahagún 1951: Chs 37–8). At dawn the children and their sponsors, adult non-kin, returned to the house compound, initiating a round of feasting, drinking the intoxicating beverage *pulque*, singing and dancing. In the afternoon, the sponsors took the children to the temple again, bringing *pulque* and special child-size drinking vessels (Sahagún 1951: Ch. 37). Everyone continued drinking throughout the day and, after returning to the house, throughout the evening.

Children who experienced the Izcalli ritual together were introduced to the repertoire of actions that would characterize all their later participation in religion: singing, dancing, ceremonial drinking, and shedding sacrificial blood. They also began the process of expanding a perforation in the ear lobe to eventually allow use of adult ear ornaments. Sahagún, while emphasizing production of sacrificial blood from the ear as the goal of piercing, also explicitly notes that a cotton thread was placed in the pierced opening. This would have prevented it from closing again. A process of gradual expansion of these pierced holes would have to have ensued to ensure that young adults could later wear adult ear ornaments, whose shafts average over 2cm wide.

Visual images in *Codex Mendoza* showing training of a boy and girl depict the introduction of serious adult expectations at the age when children would have completed the Izcalli ritual. Four-year-old children are shown beginning instruction in adult work. Between ages seven and eight, children are shown subjected to punishments for the first time, including use of maguey spines to pierce the body. The nine-year-old boy is specifically shown with a spine inserted in his ear lobe, the site first pierced at Izcalli. The children between ages four and seven depicted in *Codex Mendoza* were already beginning adult training. Only after age seven were they subject to full discipline, and to forms of punishment that employed a method introduced as the bodily mark of passage through the Izcalli ritual. Discipline, both in the sense of regulation through punishment and of the creation of subjectivity through conformity to a norm, was a reality for Aztec children once they underwent this life-cycle event.

Bodily discipline and the achievement of adult status

Figures of speech relating Aztec children to precious raw materials used for ornaments evoke the symbolic importance of body ornaments as media that transformed and displayed age status. Approximately every four years from birth to the early teens, transitions in the life-cycle were visibly marked through changes in practices of body ornamentation and dress. Childhood was divided by these transitions into three uniform segments, followed by an adulthood of more individualized transitions.

Through the coordination of social age grades, life-cycle rituals reproduced individual performances of embodied subjectivity as citations of approved precedents (Butler 1993: 12–16). These precedents were so clear that they could be reproduced in visual and verbal records decades after their disruption.

With the dedication of children to the *calmecac* or *telpochcalli* the first body markings were directly applied to the flesh. Speeches made at the feast dedicating a child to the *calmecac* described the distinctive haircut of religious life that would be adopted with adulthood. In the meantime, the child's body was marked by ritual scarification on the hip and chest. For those destined to the non-religious life, 'to make it known that he belonged to the *telpochcalli*, the lip was pierced in order to place the lip plug there', although use of lip plugs was deferred until adulthood. Distinctions in adult destiny were literally marked on the bodies of children, prefigured in speech, and anticipated through the provision of sites of body ornaments that would not be used until much later.

Modification of the body, begun for many in infancy, extended to all children by the time they were eight years old, through the Izcalli ritual. The creation of the site to be occupied by the ear spools of adults was like the piercing of the lip for a labret that was not adopted until adulthood. *Codex Mendoza* depicts ear spools on a boy of age 15 going to the *telpochcalli*, and on a girl of the same age being married (Berdan and Anawalt 1997: folio 61). A later scene, glossed as a feast held by a newly married youth to beg leave from his peers in the *telpochcalli* for spending time away from them, shows six young men and the young bride, each with carefully detailed ear spools (Berdan and Anawalt 1997: folio 68). Use of labrets waited until the boy's achievements in warfare, marked by adoption of variants described in the *Florentine Codex* and shown in *Codex Mendoza*. Initial lip piercing or scarification and later ear piercing punctuated the continuous bodily development of the child, and prefigured adoption of adult practices. Ornamentation for which these sites were prepared were citations of practices visible to the child in the bodies of adults working to transform their infant raw material into disciplined social form. These piercings consequently had precisely the ambiguous status of the 'repetition of what cannot be recollected' that Butler (1993: 244) argues is central to materialization of embodied subjectivity.

A second set of disciplines of bodily materiality began with presentation of adult garments to the newborn infant. These symbolic garments were not the clothing of infancy. At age three, the girl and boy each wore only the appropriate upper garment, the blouse or cape (Berdan and Anawalt 1997: folio 58). A skirt was added to the girl's costume at age four, and a loincloth to the boy's costume by age seven (Berdan and Anawalt 1997: folio 59). By the time they had passed through the Izcalli ritual, children were wearing the garments of adulthood and learning through them the decorous postures and ways of moving of Aztec men and women.

The central action in wedding ceremonies reiterated use of clothing in birth ceremonies as synecdoches (Burkhart 1997: 46–7) for normative male and female subject positions:

> The mother of the man went to give gifts to the bride. She placed a blouse on her, and a skirt before her. And the mother of the woman also went to give gifts. She tied a cape on the groom, but his breech clout she placed before him....And the elderly matchmakers tied them together. They took the corner of the man's cape, they drew up the woman's blouse, then they tied these together.
>
> (Sahagún 1969: Ch. 23; cf Berdan and Anawalt 1997: folio 61)

Clothing served at life transitions as a form of insistently stable gendered materiality that had the power to impose particular ways of being adult on children. Unlike the punctuated changes of piercing for body ornaments, use of static adult garments denied the gradual transformation of raw child to shaped adult, asserting instead an essential stability of form.

Hair treatment was another aspect of bodily materiality incorporated in Aztec life-cycle transitions. The hair of boys and girls is depicted as identical, cropped short over the entire head, to age 11. At age 12, the girl's hair is noticeably long at the back, typical also of depictions of sexually active young women being punished for their transgressions (Berdan and Anawalt 1997: folios 60, 61, 63). Images of young men early in their training show a long tail of hair indistinguishable from that of young women (Berdan and Anawalt 1997: folios 60, 61, 62). This was named the 'young girl's lock of hair' in a summary of Aztec noble women's appearance and in admonitions to young men seeking their first captive (Sahagún 1954: Chs 15, 21).

Transformations of Aztec boys' hair are related to their distinction as warriors:

At first, while still a small boy, his hair was shorn. And when he was already ten years old, they then let a tuft of hair grow on the back of his head. And when he was fifteen years old, then the tuft of hair became long...when he had nowhere taken captives. And if he took a captive...then the lock of hair was removed....And when the tuft on the back of his head was removed, he was shorn so that he was left [another] lock: his hair dress kept, on the right side, the hair hanging low, reaching the bottom of his ear; to one side [only] was his lock of hair set....And he who then did not take a captive...might not remove his lock of hair....Thus was his hair shorn: it was cut like a ring-shaped carrying pad; they shaved only the crown of his head.

(Sahagún 1954: Ch. 21)

Men who continued as warriors were allowed a new hairstyle when they captured their fourth captive on their own.

Transformation of Aztec girls' hair is described only briefly. Distinctions were noted between noble girls with 'hair all cut the same length', with the 'young girl's lock of hair', and with the hairstyle of women 'wound about the head', but neither the ages nor circumstances of these changes are detailed (Sahagún 1954: Ch. 15). Commentary on another ethnic group, the Otomí, characterized as having 'a civilized way of life', describes their costume as comparable to the Aztecs', and presents identical information about male hairstyles as for the Aztecs. The section on women's appearance provides details:

When the women were still young girls, they cut their hair short; but when [they were] grown, when [they were] young women, the hair covered their shoulders....And when one was a mature woman, when perhaps she also [had delivered] her child, the hair was bound around her head.

(Sahagún 1961: Ch. 29)

This suggests that the standard adult woman's hairstyle (Berdan and Anawalt 1997: folio 68) was adopted following childbirth, structurally equated with the capture of prisoners in battle that initiated new hair treatment for boys (Sahagún 1969: Chs 28, 30, 33).

For boys and girls alike, passage into adult status was accompanied by adoption of a complex hairstyle that required continual maintenance, ensuring that, although the shared life-cycle rituals of childhood were completed, each adult would individually continue to perform disciplines of appearance that were major means through which adult status was formalized, internalized, and externally signalled. Children's bodies were worked as raw material by adult authorities. Adults carried out their own regimes of bodily control.

Discussion

Aztec childhood was divided through life-cycle rites into phases. The bodies of children were systematically laden with signs of difference in gender, achievement, and status. Physical differences observable at birth had to be transformed through ritual and everyday action into socially interpretable forms. Youths were literally products of adult action, just as were materials used to mark their bodies – items of clothing and ornaments. While appearance, achievement, and destiny did not stop unfolding after childhood, marking of changes became less social and public, and more private, personal, and individual, as daily practices to maintain adult discipline replaced the punctuated experiences of childhood.

Material previously viewed simply as 'costume' must now be considered as active mechanisms for socialization and materialization of preferred forms of embodied subjectivity. The practices important for the Aztecs as means through which children were transformed into adults also vary by age in earlier Mesoamerican societies. The only consistent difference in use of costume ornaments in burials from several early village sites (dated 1500–400 BC) was the restriction of ear ornaments to adults, even when burials of children otherwise included the greatest number and diversity of goods, including other ornaments (Joyce 1999). I suggest that these children belonged to societies in which ear ornaments were media for life-cycle transitions, incomplete at the time of their death. This observation marks fragments of ear ornaments, routinely recovered in such sites, as possible evidence of life-cycle ceremonies. It draws attention to the relative stability of ear ornament form over three millennia (Joyce 1998). Careful attention to distributions of ear spools of different diameters should allow documentation of the physical process through which children's ears were gradually made suitable sites for use of adult ornaments.

Contemporary with these burials, hand-modelled figurines representing human subjects were created. Playa de los Muertos-style figurines from northwest Honduras were particularly carefully detailed, depicting a great diversity of hairstyles and body ornaments. Attempts to subdivide these figurines using traditional evolutionary criteria were unsuccessful (Agurcia 1978). By examining differences in hair treatment, a feature significant in Aztec accounts of the life course, I was able to subdivide the group into four classes in which posture, dress, and ornamentation varied predictably along with hairstyle (Joyce 1997; cf. Serra Puche and Durand 1998). Two of the classes feature physical marks of relative age, demarcating infant and elderly categories. The remaining figurines, neither infant nor elderly, vary in elaboration of hair treatment. I consider them stylized representations of transitions in bodily appearance at a point during the life-cycle when the long unornamented hair of infancy was transformed through shaving, beading, braiding, and binding into elaborate fashions of young adulthood. Like contemporary burials, figurines document that the materialization of adult bodies was already the subject of standardized practices in Mesoamerica's earliest villages, practices deploying techniques of body modification that left behind substantial material traces.

Just as the Mesoamerican world of things is transformed by considering the use of objects as media for life-cycle rituals, so also the space of Mesoamerican sites must be reconsidered in light of these practices. Life-cycle rituals described in post-Hispanic sources took place in and around the house compound. Entry into the house compound of neighbours, kin, and fictive kin called to witness the events were occasions for hosting feasts and for formalized drinking. Recent discussions of the significance of feasting as a political tactic in Mesoamerica seldom consider what events provided occasions for employment of such strategies. Transitions in the life-cycle presented significant opportunities for hosting others without seeming overtly self-aggrandizing. On these occasions, the residential character of the house compound was thoroughly imbued with social strategizing. Facilities incorporated in house compounds – seating platforms, formal food-preparation facilities, domestic altars, and sweatbaths – must be re-examined as conditioned not simply by economic requirements, but also by the needs of effective and persuasive hosting of regularly timed, intimate rituals where the life of society intersected the biographies of individuals.

Bibliography

Agurcia, R. 1978. Las Figurillas de Playa de los Muertos, Honduras. *Yaxkin* 2: 221–40.

Berdan, F.F. and Anawalt, P. (eds). 1992. *The Codex Mendoza*. Berkeley: University of California Press.

Berdan, F.F. and Anawalt, P. 1997. *The Essential Codex Mendoza*. Berkeley: University of California Press.

Brown, B.A. 1983. Seen But Not Heard: Women in Aztec Ritual – the Sahagún Texts. In Berlo, J.C. (ed.), *Text and Image in Pre-Columbian Art*. BAR International Series. Oxford: BAR, pp. 119–54.

Brumfiel, E.M. 1991. Weaving and Cooking: Women's Production in Aztec Mexico. In Gero, J. and Conkey, M. (eds), *Engendering Archaeology*. Oxford: Blackwell, pp. 224–51.

Burkhart, L.M. 1997. Mexican Women on the Home Front. In Schroeder, S., Wood, S., and Haskett, R. (eds), *Indian Women of Early Mexico*. Norman: University of Oklahoma Press, pp. 25–54.

Butler, J. 1993. *Bodies That Matter: On the Discursive Limits of 'Sex'*. New York: Routledge.

Calnek, E.E. 1974. The Sahagún Texts as a Source of Sociological Information. In Edmonson, M. (ed.), *Sixteenth-Century Mexico: The Work of Sahagún*. Albuquerque: University of New Mexico Press, pp.189–204.

Calnek, E.E. 1988. The Calmecac and the Telpochcalli in Pre-Conquest Tenochtitlan. In Klor de Alva, J.J., Nicholson, H.B., and Quiñones Keber, E. (eds), *The Work of Bernardino de Sahagún*. Albany: Institute for Mesoamerican Studies, State University of New York, pp. 169–78.

Calnek, E.E. 1992. The Ethnographic Context of the Third Part of the *Codex Mendoza*. In Berdan, F. and Anawalt, P. (eds), *The Codex Mendoza, Volume 1: Interpretation*. Berkeley: University of California Press, pp. 81–91.

Clendinnen, I. 1991. *Aztecs: An Interpretation*. Cambridge: Cambridge University Press.

Cobb, C.R. 1991. Social Reproduction and the *Longue Durée* in the Prehistory of the Midcontinental United States. In Preucel, R.W. (ed.), *Processual and Postprocessual Archaeologies*. Carbondale: Center for Archaeological Investigations, Southern Illinois University, pp. 168–82.

Cyphers Guillén, A. 1993. Women, Rituals, and Social Dynamics at Ancient Chalcatzingo. *Latin American Antiquity* 4(3): 209–24.

Gillespie, S.D. 1998. The Aztec Triple Alliance: A Postconquest Tradition. In Boone, E.H. and Cummins, T. (eds), *Native Traditions in the Postconquest World*. Washington, DC: Dumbarton Oaks, pp. 233–63.

Joyce, R.A. 1994. Looking for Children in Prehispanic Mesoamerica. Paper presented at the annual meeting of the Society for American Archaeology, Anaheim, CA.

Joyce, R.A. 1997. Playa de los Muertos Figurines and their Predecessors. Ms.

Joyce, R.A. 1998. A Mesoamerican History of Body Ornamentation. Paper presented at the conference 'Thinking Through the Body', University of Wales, Lampeter.

Joyce, R.A. 1999. Social Dimensions of Pre-classic Burials. In Grove, D.C. and Joyce, R.A. (eds), *Social Patterns in Pre-Classic Mesoamerica*. Washington, DC: Dumbarton Oaks, pp. 15–47.

Joyce, R.A. 2000. High Culture, Mesoamerican Civilization, and the Classic Maya Tradition. In Richards, J. and Van Buren, M. (eds), *Order, Legitimacy, and Wealth in Early States*. Cambridge: Cambridge University Press, pp. 64–76.

Kellogg, S. 1995. *Law and the Transformation of Aztec Culture, 1500–1700*. Norman: University of Oklahoma Press.

Klor de Alva, J.J., Nicholson, H.B., and Quiñones Keber, E. (eds). 1988. *The Work of Bernardino de Sahagún*. Albany: Institute for Mesoamerican Studies, State University of New York.

Lesure, R. 1997. Figurines and Social Identities in Early Sedentary Societies of Coastal Chiapas, Mexico. In Claassen, C. and Joyce, R. (eds), *Women in Prehistory: North America and Mesoamerica*. Philadelphia: University of Pennsylvania Press, pp. 227–48.

McCafferty, S.D. and McCafferty, G.G. 1988. Powerful Women and the Myth of Male Dominance in Aztec Society. *Archaeological Review from Cambridge* 7: 45–59.

McCafferty, S.D. and McCafferty, G.G. 1991. Spinning and Weaving as Female Gender Identity in Post-Classic Mexico. In Berlo, J.C., Schevill, M., and Dwyer, E.B. (eds), *Textile Traditions of Mesoamerica and the Andes*. New York: Garland, pp. 19–44.

Sahagún, B. de (trans. Anderson, A.J.O. and Dibble, C.E.). 1951. *Florentine Codex, Book 2 – The Ceremonies*. School of American Research Monographs, Number 14, Part III. Salt Lake City: University of Utah Press.

Sahagún, B. de (trans. Anderson, A.J.O. and Dibble, C.E.). 1953. *Florentine Codex, Book 3 – The Origins of the God*. School of American Research Monographs, Number 14, Part IV. Salt Lake City: University of Utah Press.

Sahagún, B. de (trans. Anderson, A.J.O. and Dibble, C.E.). 1954. *Florentine Codex, Book 8 – Kings and Lords*. School of American Research Monographs, Number 14, Part IX. Salt Lake City: University of Utah Press.

Sahagún, B. de (trans. Anderson, A.J.O. and Dibble, C.E.). 1961. *Florentine Codex, Book 10 – The People*. School of American Research Monographs, Number 14, Part XI. Salt Lake City: University of Utah Press.

Sahagún, B. de (trans. Anderson, A.J.O. and Dibble, C.E.). 1969. *Florentine Codex, Book 6 – Rhetoric and Moral Philosophy*. School of American Research Monographs, Number 14, Part VII. Salt Lake City: University of Utah Press.

Serra Puche, M.C. and Durand, K.R. 1998. Las Mujeres de Xochitecatl. *Arqueologia Mexicana* 5(29): 20–7.

Schele, L. and Freidel, D. 1990. *A Forest of Kings*. New York: William Morrow.

Schele, L. and Miller, M.E. 1986. *The Blood of Kings*. Fort Worth: Kimball Art Museum.

Smith, M.E. 1992. Rhythms of Change in Postclassic Central Mexico: Archaeology, Ethnohistory and the Braudelian Model. In Knapp, A.B. (ed.), *Archaeology, Annales and Ethnohistory*. Cambridge: Cambridge University Press, pp. 51–74.

Storey, R. 1992. Children of Copan: Issues in Paleopathology and Paleodemography. *Ancient Mesoamerica* 3: 161–7.

Chapter 6

Engendering children, engendering archaeology

Joanna Sofaer

Chief of our aunts - not only, I,
But all your dozen of nurslings cry –
What did the other children do?
And what were childhood, wanting you?
R.L. Stevenson, *To Auntie*, 1885

Since the inception of gender archaeology in the 1970s, archaeologists have succeeded in highlighting a variety of methodological problems and prejudices within the discipline. Importantly they revealed the extent of androcentric bias in archaeological interpretation and in doing so pushed for recognition of the value of women's contributions to ancient and modern societies (Gero 1988). An initial emphasis on the 'finding of women' gradually translated into greater awareness of their socio-economic contributions, manifest in the growing number of studies of the gendered division of labour (Spector 1982, 1991; Conkey and Spector 1984; Gero 1991; Hollimon 1992; Joyce 1992). However, the range of activities attributed to women has often been influenced by assumptions of logistical or biological constraints derived from controversial cross-cultural anthropological models (Peacock 1991). Women's activities were defined as those compatible with childcare, confined to limited areas in and around settlement sites. These interpretations proved unacceptable to feminist scholars who opposed sociobiological perceptions of sex and gender as interchangeable concepts, arguing that gender differences and male/female power relations were not the natural and inevitable product of biological difference (Fausto-Sterling 1985; Lorber 1994).

Under feminist influence the terms 'male' and 'female' were increasingly questioned. Concepts of biological sex (concrete and categorical) were separated from gender (the social construction) as researchers demonstrated enormous cultural diversity in fe/male tasks and roles (Ortner and Whitehead 1981; Conkey and Spector 1984; Moore 1986, 1988; Collier and Yanagisako 1987; Hess and Ferree 1987; Wylie 1991). Others saw sex itself as a socio-political construction (McDonald 1989) or as a function of discourse (Foucault 1984).

Yet, paradoxically, the feminist-inspired reaction against the emphasis on 'woman as mother', and associated assumptions regarding the need to feed and nurture infants, did not precipitate an interest in the socio-economic roles or gender development of children – the very individuals who were deemed axiomatic to the development of gender systems. This is perhaps even more surprising given the recent anthropological emphasis on kinship relations as gendered structures (Collier and Yanagisako 1987; Howell and Melhuus 1993). A number of basic questions necessary to the project of an engendered archaeology which might have been addressed through an examination of children were, therefore, left unexplored. For example: what is the relationship between sex and gender? If gender is not biologically defined, then how are gender structures actively constructed, mediated, and passed on from generation to generation? How might this be recognized in the archaeological record? What are the socio-economic roles of children in relation to the gendered division of labour?

The reasons for this apparent reluctance to explore an archaeology of children are twofold. First, it is often argued that the under-representation of children in the archaeological record, particularly in cemeteries, precludes their examination (Moore et al. 1975; Boddington 1987). Nonetheless we know that just as women and men existed in the past, children must also have existed. Lacking the evidence of the body from which to construct evidence of the person, the development of a theoretical frame of reference within which the roles of perceptions of children as human beings could be accommodated was rather perversely deemed unnecessary. This 'under-representation' argument follows strikingly similar lines to that advocating a need to 'find' hidden women and render them visible. Yet it is now increasingly recognized that the activities of women have always been part of the archaeological record, a realization which should also be extended to children. Bonnichsen (1973) and Hammond and Hammond (1981) have emphasized the role of children in site-formation processes. Thus the perceived difficulty lies not in the invisibility of children but in the identification of their activities as opposed to other agents in the archaeological record.

The second reason lies in the concepts 'childhood' and 'child' themselves. These only exist in relation to the concepts 'adult' and 'maturity' and Western notions of the compartmentalization of the human life-cycle (MacCormack 1980a; Burman 1994). Backwards inference from our own culturally specific concepts of childhood, as a prolonged period of dependence on the parent and an age of innocence, leads to an assumption that it is adults (i.e. fertile and sexually mature individuals) who have political and social control over the production of material culture and social ideologies. Nonetheless, the activities of children are often vital to communal economic survival in traditional societies (Draper 1975; Friedl 1975; Claassen 1992). It is therefore plausible that the experiences of children also moulded the past.

The term 'children' is culturally loaded and the product of Western culture, which marginalizes their activities. By universal extension 'children' are therefore rendered invisible in the archaeological record. The modern Western usage of the term 'child' is problematic in that it is a blanket term for individuals at a variety of stages of development with widely differing levels of dependence and independence. This need not be congruent with age categories and conception of maturity or immaturity in other societies. There is a need to problematize the investigation of children along with a reconceptualization of the concept of 'child'. Age and sex classifications alone cannot account for cultural variation in attitudes and classifications of children (Friedl 1975; MacCormack and Strathern 1980). One possibility lies in regarding not only age and dependence but also the development of gender sensibilities as defining parameters of childhood. A child may be regarded as a cultural tabula rasa gradually engendered as s/he develops an awareness of gender identity, gender roles, and gender ideology. These evolve and change as the individual absorbs, learns, and complies with culturally defined gender rules. At the same time, society's gendered perceptions of that individual may change in line with his or her development. Even if an individual is assigned to a sex-based gender category at birth (Scheffler 1991) s/he must still learn and accept gender appropriate behaviours.

I therefore suggest that the study of gender in the archaeological record may benefit from a discussion of the gender development of children. I do not wish to discuss notions of *socialization* per se. This concept is often associated with Freudian theories of suppression, assuming that children need to be moulded to a certain pattern, along the same lines as the primitive eventually becomes civilized (Burman 1994). Indeed, the notion of socialization may itself be culturally specific, existing in some cultures, but not in others (MacCormack and Strathern 1980). Instead I wish to link models drawn from developmental psychology and gender theory to argue that it is possible to theorize about the activities of children by examining the mediation of gender within the archaeological record. Children can be regarded as learners and practisers of gender.[1]

The assumption that aspects of material culture act as repositories of gender symbolism, and thus that artefacts behave as contextually determined gender markers, underlies much of the project of an engendered archaeology. This assumption is necessary if archaeologists are to be successful in interpreting gendered social structures in the past. Used in conjunction with post-processualist concepts of the active object (Hodder 1982, 1987), everyday items such as clothing have been regarded as media for gendered communication and mediators of ideology, producing some of the most successful attempts at engendering archaeology (Gibbs 1987; Sørensen 1991).

Yet material culture may function not only as a communicative vehicle for the maintenance of symbolic structures or social values, but may also be instrumental in actively constructing the world of the individual on the most fundamental level. Cole *et al.* (1971) found that different interactions and observations of interactions may lead to culturally specific learning outcomes and world perceptions. When asked to organize piles of food and household items, the Kpelle of Liberia consistently distributed the objects in terms of functional relations reflecting the way the items were used (potato-pot: food-tool). When asked how 'a fool' would carry out the task, participants demonstrated a typical Western classification system based on type (potato-orange: food-food). Thus, it is through observing the behaviour of his/her elders interacting with material culture and through his/her own interaction with it that the child learns abstract principles, is stimulated, and learns about the nature of the world. The nature of individual interaction need not follow the Western pattern of children playing with toys and the result of this interaction is not 'given' or germane, otherwise universal 'laws' would be applicable to all cultures.

This perspective assumes that children make sense of their world in qualitatively different ways at different points in their development. Thus children's understanding of gender may be quite different at different ages, with the development of gender understanding paralleling the development of children's growing abilities to reason about other aspects of the world (Golombok and Fivush 1994). In their book *Gender Development*, Golombok and Fivush (1994) describe Kohlberg's (1966) findings regarding children's developing concept of gender in Western society. He argued that the major developmental task facing children is coming to understand that gender is constant and cannot be changed regardless of superficial characteristics.[2] Children develop through three stages in coming to understand gender. In the beginning children do not use gender to categorize themselves or others at all. If asked if they are female or male, they may respond 'female' when asked the first time and 'male' when asked again. He interpreted this as a lack of understanding of gender as an unchanging characteristic of an individual. At about two years of age children enter stage one called gender identity. They are now able to consistently label themselves and others as male or female, but base this categorization on physical characteristics. Thus a person is female because she has long hair and wears skirts, and a person male because he has short hair and wears a tie. If external appearance changes, then gender changes as well. Similar gender identifications with different objects or aspects of dress are possible in other non-Western cultures and need not be limited to bipolar associations with biological sex. Thus in cultures with more than two genders, where these are 'marked' in some way, for instance by clothing or jewellery (Sørensen 1991), children might learn to identify them in a similar way.

At about three to four years children move on to stage two called *gender stability*. They now understand that if an individual is fe/male at the present time then s/he was fe/male earlier in life and will later remain so. Stage-two children understand that gender is stable across time but do not yet understand that gender is constant across situations. If a male engages in female-typed activities, stage-two children believe that the male might change into a female. In Kohlberg's model, children progress to stage three, called *gender constancy*, at about age five. Bem (1989) related this to an understanding of the biological basis of gender identity. Children now understand that gender is constant across time and situations. They assert that gender will not change regardless of the clothes worn or the activities engaged in. They have come to realize that gender is an underlying, unchanging aspect of identity.[3]

Even very young children know a great deal about culturally defined stereotypes and 'may only need to know some very basic information about gender to begin to use gender as a way of thinking about the world' (Golombok and Fivush 1994: 95). This knowledge is intimately linked to gendered associations with material culture. Two types of tasks have been used to assess Western children's understanding of gender: gender-knowledge tasks and gender-preference tasks. Gender-knowledge tasks measure how much information children know about gender and gender stereotypes. Typical versions of these tasks include examining children's knowledge of gender-typed clothing and toys. Children are shown pictures of a boy and a girl and asked to match the items with the 'appropriate' person. In gender-preference tasks children are asked to rate how much they would like to play with toys that are either gender consistent (e.g. a truck for a boy) or gender inconsistent (e.g. a doll's house for a boy). These tasks indicate that gender knowledge and gender preferences do not appear to be interdependent. A child may know a lot about gender but show little preference for gender-typed activities and vice versa.

While neither of the tasks described above is free from problems and limitations (Golombok and Fivush 1994), they reveal the role and power of aspects of material culture as signifiers and mediators of gender. Material culture influences gender development since it acts as a reflector of gender and is associated with culturally defined gender stereotypes from a very early age. It is, therefore, of great importance as a repository of cultural values with which the child and those around him/her interact. Shanks and Tilley (1987a, 1987b, 1989) describe the individual as an active social agent. Thus children actively engage in the creation and maintenance of gender structures through material culture, while an individual's experience of the world is in turn described by gendered interactions with a material culture which itself actively constructs social relations. Material culture is vital in perpetuating gender differences and similarities as the child continues to develop his/her knowledge of gender throughout childhood and it provides a framework for the organization of that knowledge as objects become associated with gendered behaviours.

Gender identity is not developed solely as the result of genital identification (Nordbladh and Yates 1990) or linguistic involvement (Vygotsky 1962, 1978) but is also a consequence of interaction with gender-specific forms of material culture. If it is possible to examine gender in the archaeological record through the identification of gender markers, then, by extension, those markers are also perpetuators of gender. They are symbolic messengers passing on gendered meanings and constructs to the next generation. Interaction and observation of interaction with those objects conveys that gendered meaning to other individuals, including children, who learn socially defined gender structures and socially acceptable gendered behaviours from those interactions. Acceptance of those meanings leads to their perpetuation. Material culture constructs and maintains gender interactions on a macro-societal level, but may also construct gender awareness on an individual level from a very early age. The logical extension to this is that gender structures cannot be present or relayed without the existence of a gendered material culture. Hence, material culture in gendered societies must carry gendered nuances.

The engendering of children is, therefore, the development of an understanding of the use of material culture as a repository of gendered symbolic meanings, followed by the decoding and learning of those embedded meanings and finally the organization of that symbolic knowledge.[4] The developing child imports, transfers, and ascribes gendered meanings to objects and actively transforms them into the gendered world in which s/he lives. Those objects are recoverable as archaeological artefacts. I am not advocating artefact association as an archaeological methodology. The fallacy of this has already been well demonstrated (Conkey and Gero 1991). However, by following current archaeological assumptions regarding the gender symbolism of artefacts, it is possible to pursue a chain of logic which uses the engendering of children to examine gender in the archaeological record and, therefore, to include children and view the archaeological record in a new light.

How then is it possible to account for a variety of gendered behaviours within a single society and for the complexity of gender systems, given that individuals may be born into the same cultural milieu? Social learning theory suggests that children engage in behaviour for which they are rewarded, with differential reinforcement acting on individuals to produce different genders. Gender-typed behaviour is initially guided by children's anticipations of the responses of others. Children are more likely to imitate behaviour which will be favourably received (Bussey and Bandura 1992).

> Girls and boys learn(ed) the symbolic behaviour appropriate to their future adult gender status. Where there is significant separation of women and men, much of this symbolic behaviour relates the person to the members of the other status and

is age graded. That is, girls and boys had to be taught not only how to work as women and men but how to behave toward girls and boys their own age and toward women and men their parents' and grandparents' age. They also learned how women and men were supposed to act toward each other as well as how every-one actually did act toward each other. In the process, the children identified with the members of their gender category, and because they were rewarded for it, they came to want to act in the prescribed ways. In this way gender statuses were repro-duced in daily activity.

(Lorber 1994: 130)

The influence of gendered parenting in providing such models is unconfirmed, although in Western society parental choice, provision, and promotion of gender-typed activities appear to be important aspects of gender development (Golombok and Fivush 1994). Nonetheless, gender influences may come from other than parental sources since the care and teaching of children may be assigned to individuals who are not their biological parents (Yanagisako and Collier 1987).

Children often display a preference for their own sex-typed activities and display more knowledge about their own gender (Golombok and Fivush 1994). Cognitive developmental theories attribute this to 'schema driven memory bias', whereby chil-dren pay more attention to information that conforms to their stereotyped beliefs and predictions about gender. Younger children show greater attachment to gender stereotypes than older children (Golombok and Fivush 1994). As children grow older and acquire more complex, problematic, and ambiguous knowledge they incorporate this and show increasing flexibility, and schemas will be culturally specific. As chil-dren get older they build personal standards based on their cognitive understanding of gender and on their history of reinforcements. They start to evaluate their own behaviour, and gender appropriateness becomes an important dimension of children's own self-evaluations. We therefore see children participating in, practising, or being allowed and encouraged to carry out gender-appropriate predominantly 'adult' tasks (Friedl 1975). This has implications for archaeological analyses of the gendered divi-sion of labour, which may be more complex than is currently perceived.

In Western culture childhood is generally regarded as one continuous block of undi-vided time with adulthood attributed to an individual upon the attainment of a birthday between the ages of 16 and 25, depending on the law of an individual country. Yet in other societies individuals may pass through stages in the achievement of maturity through rites of passage or initiation rituals. The importance of different age stages in the social accom-plishment of gender has been ignored in archaeology because Western culture views all sub-adults as children, although Friedl (1975: 82) explicitly refers to 'age as a modifier of sex roles'. Gender learning may be informal or formal. Many initiation rituals exist specif-ically to teach or test gendered skills or gendered behaviour. Moogk (1991) has described the construction of 'woman' in the Nuu-chah-nulth girls' puberty ceremony. The Laymi Indians view growth to maturity through language and gender-attributed language skills (Harris 1980). In Sherbro society children are considered to be proto-social. 'They talk a great deal about children who do not have "sense" and who need "training"' (MacCormack 1980b: 95). MacCormack describes sexual division of labour in produc-tive tasks in which children are intensively and carefully trained, especially during their liminal status in the initiation ritual. During this period adolescent males learn masculine farming skills and other male skills such as weaving cloth. Adolescent females demonstrate mastery of feminine farming skills and spin cotton. The complementary nature of these tasks demonstrates the interdependence of the genders. 'Both men and women, after initiation, are designated "those who may procreate" and are publicly recognized as having a minimal level of "adeptness" in adult roles' (ibid.).

> Gendering extends to children because men and women separately train them in order to reproduce themselves socially. This training is an investment in the children's future labor, a 'lien over time, the claim of both men and women over the future production of children' (Siskind 1978: 864). Unless they are strictly segregated, however, girls and boys can learn each other's work. If they persist in doing the work of the other gender, and the work is strictly divided between women and men with little overlap, they will be ostracized unless their society permits gender shifts, as happens when boys become berdaches; they will be women and do women's work when they grow up.
>
> (Lorber 1994: 131–2)

Yet gender-related knowledge goes further than merely to describe 'who does what'. Gender schema theory describes developmental differences in gender-related knowledge. It divides gender knowledge into a number of components including behaviours, roles, occupations, and traits (Martin 1993). In Western culture, therefore, 'male' is stereotypically associated with playing football, father, engineer, and aggressive. Knowledge is organized and distinct so that knowing the gender label 'male' or 'female' leads to clear links about its gender-related components and associations. Each component of knowledge is independent so one might know a great deal about female-related behaviours but little about female-related occupations. Knowledge becomes organized so that associations are made both within and across components, allowing increasingly complex predictions about gender attributes to be made as the complexity of knowledge increases (Martin and Halverson 1981; Martin 1993). This theory has parallels in archaeology where Renfrew (1994: 10) proposed the concept of the 'mappa', in which each individual possesses 'a cognitive map of the world, built up in the light of one's own experience and activities, so that this map or world-view serves as the referant used by the individual in determining his or her future activities'.

This chapter has been intended as an exploration of some of the issues, problems, and potential that an investigation of children raises for the examination of gender in archaeological contexts. Childhood can be regarded as a time of apprenticeship to a culturally defined gendered norm. The cognitive world of the child is influenced by the gendered world in which s/he lives, that world being encapsulated in symbolic gendered meanings encoded within material culture. I do not wish to suggest that all individuals conceive of the world in the same way or that the models described above are universally applicable today or in the past. However, they do indicate that objects can play significant roles in the gender development of children. An examination of this development may go some way to accounting for the plurality of gender concepts and how they are passed on from generation to generation. It also emphasizes flexibility and age-related dimensions of gender, providing interesting avenues for the further examination of the negotiation of gender structures in archaeological contexts.

Notes

1. Developmental psychology is perhaps the one field with children (or more often 'the child') as its central focus. While it is recognized that research in this field is heavily biased towards North American and European values, it is felt that certain aspects may still be useful to the examination of children in antiquity.
2. The constancy of gender has recently been debated (Moore 1993). Kohlberg views gender in bipolar terms seeing it as intimately related to the biological sex of the individual.
3. Kohlberg's model has been corroborated by a number of researchers (e.g. Stagnor and Ruble 1987), although controversy exists regarding the age at which the stages occur and the meaning and importance of 'gender constancy' (Golombok and Fivush 1994).
4. As children learn more about gender, their knowledge about it becomes more organized (Golombok and Fivush 1994).

Bibliography

Bem, S. 1989. Genital Knowledge and Gender Constancy in Preschool Children. *Child Development* 60: 649–62.

Boddington, A. 1987. From Bones to Population: The Problem of Numbers. In Boddington, A., Garland, A.N., and Janaway, R.C. (eds), *Death, Decay and Reconstruction*. Manchester: Manchester University Press, pp. 180–97.

Bonnichsen, R. 1973. Millie's Camp: an Experiment in Archaeology. *World Archaeology* 4: 277–91.

Burman, E. 1994. *Deconstructing Developmental Psychology*. London: Routledge.

Bussey, K. and Bandura, A. 1992. Self-regulatory Mechanisms Governing Gender Development. *Child Development* 63: 1,236–50.

Claassen, C. 1992. Questioning Gender: An Introduction. In Claassen, C. (ed.), *Exploring Gender Through Archaeology: Selected Papers from the 1991 Boone Conference*. Madison, WI: Prehistory Press, pp. 1–9.

Cole, M., Gay, J., Glick, J.A., and Sharp, D.W. 1971. *The Cultural Context of Learning and Thinking: An Exploration in Experimental Anthropology*. New York: Basic Books.

Collier, J.F. and Yanagisako, S.J. (eds). 1987. *Gender and Kinship: Essays Toward A Unified Analysis*. Stanford, CA: Stanford University Press.

Conkey, M.W. and Gero, J.M. 1991. Tensions, Pluralities and Engendering Archaeology: An Introduction to Women and Prehistory. In Gero, J.M. and Conkey, M.W. (eds), *Engendering Archaeology: Women and Prehistory*. Oxford: Blackwell, pp. 3–30.

Conkey, M.W. and Spector, J.D. 1984. Archaeology and the Study of Gender. In Schiffer, M.B. (ed.), *Advances in Archaeological Method and Theory* 7. New York: Academic Press, pp. 1–38.

Draper, P. 1975. Kung Women. In Reiter, R.R. (ed.), *Toward an Anthropology of Women*. London: Monthly Review Press, pp. 77–109.

Fausto-Sterling, A. 1985. *Myths of Gender: Biological Theories About Women and Men*. New York: Basic Books.

Foucault, M. 1984. *History of Sexuality, An Introduction, Vol. 1*. London: Penguin.

Friedl, E. 1975. *Women and Men: An Anthropologist's View*. New York: Holt, Rinehart, and Winston.

Gero, J.M. 1988. Gender Bias in Archaeology: Then and Now. In Rosser, S.V. (ed.), *Feminism Within the Science and Health Care Professions: Overcoming Resistance*. Oxford: Pergamon Press, pp. 33–43.

Gero, J.M. 1991. Gender Lithics: Women's Roles in Stone Tool Production. In Gero, J.M. and Conkey, M.W. (eds), *Engendering Archaeology: Women and Prehistory*. Oxford: Blackwell, pp. 163–93.

Gibbs, L. 1987. Identifying Gender Representation in the Archaeological Record: Contextual Study. In Hodder, I. (ed.), *The Archaeology of Contextual Meanings*. Cambridge: Cambridge University Press, pp. 79–89.

Golombok, S. and Fivush, R. 1994. *Gender Development*. Cambridge: Cambridge University Press.

Hammond, G. and Hammond, N. 1981. Child's Play: a Distorting Factor in Archaeological Distribution. *American Antiquity* 46: 634–6.

Harris, O. 1980. The Power of Signs: Gender, Culture and the Wild in the Bolivian Andes. In MacCormack, C.P. and Strathern, M. (eds), *Nature, Culture and Gender*. Cambridge: Cambridge University Press, pp. 70–94.

Hess, B.B and Ferree, M.M. (eds). 1987. *Analyzing Gender*. Newbury Park: Sage.

Hodder, I. 1982. *Symbols in Action*. Cambridge: Cambridge University Press.

Hodder, I. 1987. The Contextual Analysis of Symbolic Meanings. In Hodder, I. (ed.), *The Archaeology of Contextual Meanings*. Cambridge: Cambridge University Press, pp. 1–10.

Hollimon, S. 1992. Health Consequences of Sexual Division of Labor Among Prehistoric Native Americans: The Chumash of California and the Arikara of the North Plains. In Claassen, C. (ed.), *Exploring Gender Through Archaeology: Selected Papers from the 1991 Boone Conference*. Madison, WI: Prehistory Press, pp. 81–8.

Howell, S. and Melhuus, M. 1993. The Study of Kinship; the Study of Person; A Study of Gender? In del Valle, T. (ed.), *Gendered Anthropology*. European Association of Social Anthropologists. London: Routledge, pp. 38–53.

Joyce, R. 1992. Images of Gender and Labor Organization in Classic Maya Society. In Claassen, C. (ed.), *Exploring Gender Through Archaeology: Selected Papers from the 1991 Boone Conference*. Monographs in World Archaeology 11. Madison, WI: Prehistory Press, pp. 63–71.

Kohlberg, L. 1966. A Cognitive-Development Analysis of Children's Sex-Role Concepts and Attitudes. In Maccoby, E.E. (ed.), *The Development of Sex Differences*. Stanford, CA: Stanford University Press, pp. 82–173.

Lorber, J. 1994. *Paradoxes of Gender*. New Haven: Yale University Press.

MacCormack, C.P. 1980a. Nature, Culture and Gender: A Critique. In MacCormack, C.P. and Strathern, M. (eds), *Nature, Culture and Gender*. Cambridge: Cambridge University Press, pp. 1–24.

MacCormack, C.P. 1980b. Proto-Social to Adult: a Sherbro Transformation. In MacCormack, C.P. and Strathern, M. (eds), *Nature, Culture and Gender*. Cambridge: Cambridge University Press, pp. 95–118.

MacCormack, C.P. and Strathern, M. (eds). 1980. *Nature, Culture and Gender*. Cambridge: Cambridge University Press.

McDonald, M. 1989. *We Are Not French! Language, Culture and Identity in Brittany*. London: Routledge.

Martin, C.L. 1993. New Directions for Assessing Children's Gender Knowledge. *Developmental Review* 13: 184–204.

Martin, C.L. and Halverson, C. 1981. A Schematic Processing Model of Sex Typing and Stereotyping in Children. *Child Development* 52: 1,119–34.

Moogk, S. 1991. The Construction of 'Woman' in the Nuu-chah-nulth Girls' Puberty Ceremony in 1910. In Walde, D. and Willows, N.D. (eds), *The Archaeology of Gender: Proceedings of the 22nd Annual Chacmool Conference*. Calgary: University of Calgary, pp. 86–103.

Moore, H. 1986. *Space, Text and Gender*. Cambridge: Cambridge University Press.

Moore, H. 1988. *Feminism and Anthropology*. Cambridge: Polity.

Moore, H. 1993. The Differences Within and the Differences Between. In del Valle, T. (ed.), *Gendered Anthropology*. London: Routledge, pp. 193–204.

Moore, J.A., Swedlund, A.C., and Armelagos, G.J. 1975. The Use of Life Tables in Palaeodemography. *American Antiquity* 40: 57–70.

Nordbladh, J. and Yates, T. 1990. This Perfect Body, This Virgin Text: Between Sex and Gender in Archaeology. In Bapty, I. and Yates, T. (eds), *Archaeology After Structuralism*. London: Routledge, pp. 222–37.

Ortner, S.B. and Whitehead, H. (eds). 1981. *Sexual Meanings: The Cultural Construction of Gender and Sexuality*. Cambridge: Cambridge University Press.

Peacock, N.R. 1991. Rethinking the Sexual Division of Labor: Reproduction and Women's Work Among the Efe. In di Leonardo, M. (ed.), *Gender at the Crossroads of Knowledge: Feminist Anthropology in the Post-Modern Era*. Berkeley, CA: University of California Press, pp. 339–60.

Renfrew, C. 1994. Towards a Cognitive Archaeology. In Renfrew, C. and Zubrow, E.B.W. (eds), *The Ancient Mind: Elements of Cognitive Archaeology*. Cambridge: Cambridge University Press, pp. 3–12.

Scheffler, H.W. 1991. Sexism and Naturalism in the Study of Kinship. In di Leonardo, M. (ed.), *Gender at the Crossroads of Knowledge: Feminist Anthropology in the Postmodern Era*. Berkeley, CA: University of California Press, pp. 361–82.

Shanks, M. and Tilley, C. 1987a. *Re-constructing Archaeology*. Cambridge: Cambridge University Press.

Shanks, M. and Tilley, C. 1987b. *Social Theory and Archaeology*. Cambridge: Polity.

Shanks, M. and Tilley, C. 1989. Archaeology into the 1990s. *Norwegian Archaeological Review* 22: 1–54.

Siskind, J. 1978. Kinship and Mode of Production. *American Anthropologist* 80: 860–71.

Sørensen, M.-L.S. 1991. The Construction of Gender through Appearance. In Walde, D. and Willows, N.D. (eds), *The Archaeology of Gender: Proceedings of the 22nd Annual Chacmool Conference*. Calgary: University of Calgary, pp. 121–9.

Spector, J.D. 1982. Male/Female Task Differentiation among the Hidatza: Toward the Development of an Archaeological Approach to the Study of Gender. In Albers, P. and Medicine, B. (eds), *The Hidden Half: Studies of Native Plains Women*. Washington, DC: University Press of America, pp. 77–99.

Spector, J.D. 1991. What this Awl Means: Toward a Feminist Archaeology. In Gero, J.M. and Conkey, M.W. (eds), *Engendering Archaeology: Women and Prehistory*. Oxford: Blackwell, pp. 388–406.

Stagnor, C. and Ruble, D.N. 1987. Development of Gender Role Knowledge and Gender Constancy. In Liben, L.S. and Signorella, M.L. (eds), *Children's Gender Schemata: New Directions for Child Development*. San Francisco: Jossey-Bass, pp. 5–22.

Vygotsky, L.S. 1962. *Language and Thought*. Cambridge, MA: MIT Press.

Vygotsky, L.S. 1978. *Mind in Society: The Development of Higher Psychological Processes*. Cambridge, MA: Harvard University Press.

Wylie, A. 1991. Feminist Critiques and Archaeological Challenges. In Walde, D. and Willows, D.E. (eds), *The Archaeology of Gender, Proceedings of the 22nd Annual Chacmool Conference*. Calgary: University of Calgary, pp. 17–23.

Yanagisako, S.J. and Collier, J.F. 1987. Toward a Unified Analysis of Gender and Kinship. In Collier, J.F. and Yanagisako, S.J. (eds), *Gender and Kinship: Essays Toward a Unified Analysis*. Stanford, CA: Stanford University Press, pp. 14–50.

Chapter 7

The constitution of archaeological evidence

Gender politics and science

Alison Wylie

Introduction

I begin with a digression that will situate my discussion of archaeological uses of evidence in the wider context of debate about the objectivity and value neutrality of archaeological understanding. My aim is to show that although archaeology is a thoroughly social and political enterprise, evidential constraints are not reducible to the interests of individual archaeologists or to the macro- and micro-political dynamics of the contexts in which they operate. In fact they are in some respects constitutive of political interests. My thesis is that although archaeological evidence is thoroughly laden with theory – although it is unavoidably a construct, open to question and revision – it can nonetheless impose decisive limitations on what can be claimed about past cultural systems, their internal dynamics, and their trajectories of development and transformation. I elaborate this model and illustrate it with examples drawn from the rapidly growing corpus of archaeological research on questions about women and gender, some of which is explicitly feminist in perspective.

From the outset, critics of scientific, processual archaeology have advocated feminist approaches, usually in the abstract and in prospect, as exactly the sort of politically engaged research they hope will displace the scientism and pretensions to value neutrality that they associate with the New Archaeology (Hodder 1986: 159–61; 1991: 7; Shanks and Tilley 1987: 246). It is striking, however, that they rarely made feminist problems a primary focus of their own research (see critiques by Engelstad 1991; Gilchrist 1992), and that few of those who have pursued feminist lines of enquiry embrace the strongly constructivist, often ironic view of the research enterprise associated with post- and anti-processual critique. Indeed, the feminist analysts typically make effective use of quite conventional appeals to evidential constraints to demonstrate the need for substantially rethinking explanatory and reconstructive models that leave women and gender out altogether or that depend on ethnocentric and androcentric presuppositions about gender relations. And in the process, they routinely produce results that diverge sharply from expectations, sometimes calling into question the presuppositions that informed their own reframing of questions and reinterpretation of the archaeological data. Central to this programme of research is an interplay between evidential constraints and social, political factors that is poorly comprehended by positions articulated at either the objectivist or the anti-objectivist extremes that dominate current archaeological discussion, an interplay that figures in parallel debates in other social sciences and in the sociology and philosophy of science.

Archaeology as politics by other means

It is by no means a new insight that archaeology is a deeply political enterprise. However pervasive and influential the rhetoric of (unmitigated) objectivity may be among professional archaeologists, the practice and products of archaeology do reflect the standpoint and interests of its makers. But even though this observation is by now a commonplace in the archaeological literature, it is still regarded with suspicion, if not outright hostility, by a great many archaeologists. It constitutes a profound challenge to the conviction – a central and defining tenet of North American archaeology – that the social and political contexts of enquiry are properly external to the process of enquiry and to its products. In general terms, as Rouse describes these ideals, it is assumed that, 'knowledge acquires its epistemological status independent of the operations of power....Power can influence our motivation to achieve knowledge [in specific areas] and can deflect us from such achievement, but it can play no constructive role in determining what knowledge is' (1987: 13, 14).

Archaeologists have long nourished the hope that if properly scientific modes of enquiry were adopted, they might secure a body of evidence that is autonomous of, and provides a decisive check on, the range of idiosyncratic and contextual interests that influence archaeological interpretation, either as a consequence of internal dynamics (the micro-politics of the discipline or the interests of individual practitioners) or as forces that impinge on the discipline from outside (external, socio-political factors). Despite the continuing influence of these ideals, however, there has been no shortage of critical analyses that demonstrate (with hindsight) how profoundly some of the best, most empirically sophisticated archaeological practice has reproduced manifestly nationalist, racist, and, on the most recent analyses, sexist understandings of the cultural past; confronting test hypotheses with evidence seems not to be proof against intrusive bias. These critiques take a number of forms. By way of a short and selective summary, I here distinguish five levels and types of critiques that have appeared in recent years. Later in the chapter I return to a detailed analysis of several examples of critical analysis that exposes sexist bias.

Critiques of erasure

First are the critiques that expose straightforward erasure, where the choice of research problem or the determination of significant sites or periods or cultural complexes systematically directs attention away from certain kinds of subjects – namely those that might challenge the tenets of a dominant ideology or might be particularly relevant to the self-understanding of subordinate and oppressed groups. These include the critiques of colonial period archaeology in North America that have given rise to vigorous new areas of research: for example the archaeology of slavery, share-cropping, and free black settlements in contexts where it had been assumed none existed, or where the great houses of prominent planters had been the exclusive focus of attention (Singleton 1985; Epperson 1990; Orser 1990, 1999; Yentsch 1994), and a range of studies that are now documenting the enormous diversity of those who populated the West (Wylie 1993). What gave rise to these new fields of interest was, in part, a concern that where archaeologists had failed to consider the material record of slavery and of poverty, of African American settlements and a highly diverse frontier, they had helped ensure that silence on these aspects of US history would be enforced by a lack of relevant data. Critiques from South and Central America and from various parts of Africa make it clear that the typical preoccupations of First World and neo-colonial research programmes – such as discovery of the most primitive human and hominid remains (e.g. palaeoanthropology in the Rift Valley) and documentation of the now eclipsed glories of ancient civilizations (in Mesoamerica and South America) – systematically obscure the history of oppression and colonization that is crucially relevant to contemporary indigenous and mestizo populations in these areas (Vargas Arenas and Sanoja 1990; Irele 1991, as cited by Vargas Arenas 1995; Patterson 1995; Schmidt 1995; Vargas Arenas 1995). And since the late 1980s a rapidly expanding body of feminist critique documents how women and gender have been left out of account even when they are a crucial part of the story to be told (see below; Conkey and Spector 1984; Spector and Whelan 1989).

Critiques of distortion

Even when marginal subjects are acknowledged and investigated as part of the subject domain of archaeology, they are often characterized in terms that legitimate a different kind of colonizing representation. A common second type of critique focuses attention not on erasure but on systematic, and manifestly interested (standpoint-specific), distortion in how various archaeological subjects are understood. Some critics have argued that this distortion is evident even in the new work on African American sites and heritage (e.g. Potter 1991). Most often, such critiques challenge the presuppositions of long-established research programmes. Renewed studies of early Spanish exploration and settlement in the Americas undermine conventional contrasts and stereotypes (Deagan 1990; Thomas 1991a; contributors to Thomas 1991b), and, in an early discussion of 'the image of the American Indian', Trigger (1980) traces the legacy of nineteenth-century evolutionary beliefs that compromises archaeological thinking about the complexity and diversity of Native American cultures. He subsequently extends this analysis to the presuppositions that lie behind a pervasively romantic view of early Native American responses to contact with Europeans, a view that was intended to correct earlier accounts but represents Native Americans as essentially tradition – and culture – bound. Such representations selectively deny these subjects a capacity for rational self-determination, obscuring the considerable diversity in the response of the First Nations to Europeans that, Trigger (1991) argues, the archaeological record of the period reveals in a number of ways.

Trigger's critique has been extended by Handsman (1989, 1990) and by Handsman and Richmond (1995), among others. They decry the dependence of North American archaeologists on Eurocentric models of community and settlement, documenting how this failure to recognize native presence in anything but European-style settlements was crucial in legitimating rhetoric of absence that has been used, throughout the long history of native dispossession, to justify the appropriation of native lands. In a similar vein, Hall documents the inherent racism of 'archaeolog[ies] of the colonized...mostly practiced by the descendants of the colonizers' (1984: 455) in southern Africa, where the presumption of indigenous absence and an erasure of class conflict have been reinforced by the dependence of archaeological analysis on reified, externally imposed concepts of tribal identity (see also Miller 1980). Feminist critiques of androcentrism in archaeological research often operate at this second level of analysis; they draw attention not just to the absence of any consideration of women and gender but also to the projection on to pre-history of presentist and ethnocentric assumptions about sexual divisions of labour and the status and roles of women in prehistory (see, e.g., Spector and Whelan 1989, and Conkey and Spector 1984 on 'man the hunter' models of human evolution).

In all these cases the imposition of prejudgements about what must have been the case in the cultural past determines not just what range of reconstructive models will be considered but also what sorts of data will be recovered and how they will be interpreted as evidence. At their most radical and pessimistic, the critics responsible for this second type of critique insist that the stereotypes, evaluative commitments, and 'mythologies' (Thomas 1991a) that inform archaeological research are unavoid-ably self-perpetuating: they foreclose the collection or serious consideration of counter-evidence that might call these presuppositions into question.

Political resonance

At a more general level, a number of synthetic critiques have been advanced that delineate broad patterns of congruence or 'resonance' (Patterson 1986a, 1986b) between the interests of large-scale geopolitical elites and entrenched archaeological research programmes. For example in his compendious history of archaeological thought, Trigger (1989) documents the entanglement of archaeology, in every context in which it has flourished, with nationalist programmes of territorial expan-sion and cultural legitimation. At a less global scale, Patterson has argued that one can discern in the training and interpretive practices of North American archaeolo-gists – in the discourse, the 'content and form, level of exposition, and the chosen vehicles for publication' typical of the field (1986a: 21; see also 1986b) – two dis-tinct communities whose views of the past resonate with the interests of the eastern establishment (that is, international capital and its allies) on the one hand, and with the core culture (midwestern, national capital, and its power base) on the other.

The politics of objectivism

At an even more general level are critiques of the enterprise of archaeology as a whole that indict its methodological and epistemic stance – its commitment to scientific ideals of objectivity – on the grounds that these effectively reinforce, rather than counter, the partiality of its makers. The British post-processual critics of the posi-tivism associated with the New Archaeology are among the most outspoken in this vein. For example Tilley has argued that 'living in Western society of the 1980s is to be involved with and, in part, responsible for prevailing [grossly inequitable] social conditions' (1989: 105); under these conditions the attempts made by archaeologists to maintain a stance of political neutrality and professional disengagement serve not to defuse the problem but to sustain and legitimate the existing order.

Explanatory critiques

While the foregoing types of critiques reveal, at various levels of analysis, systematic gaps, biases, and distortions in the results of archaeological enquiry that we should be prepared to question, for the most part they provide no detailed explanation of how these compromising effects are produced or why they persist. That is, they offer little account of the conditions under which, or the mechanisms by which, local and global political interests come to shape the content of archaeological understanding, generating the sorts of resonances and congruencies – the systematic silences and replication of stereotypes – that arise at the four different levels of analysis I have identified. A fifth form of critique, perhaps the least developed but one that is crucially important in its potential to provide these missing explanatory links, consists of analyses of how the internal conditions of archaeological practice – the micro-politics of archaeology conceived as a community and as a discipline articulated with a range of institutions – shape the direction and results of enquiry.

Several studies along these lines were reported in a landmark collection of essays, *The Socio-politics of Archaeology* (Gero *et al.* 1983); they illustrate how, for example, the structure of rewards institutionally entrenched in archaeology may reinforce a disproportionate interest in origins research and regional syntheses, much beyond the intellectual warrant for such research (Wobst and Keene 1983). Feminist scrutiny of the discipline has resulted in a number of critical sociological analyses of familiar patterns of differential support, training, and advancement of women in the field, as well as of strong patterns of gender segregation in the areas in which women typically work (e.g. as reported in Nelson *et al.* 1994), but much of this equity research remains disconnected from questions about androcentric or sexist bias in the content of archaeological accounts. One study that does make this connection is Gero's analysis (1993) of the assumptions and conditions that have shaped Palaeoindian research on the earliest human populations in the Americas. Gero notes a strong pattern of gender segregation in the field. The predominantly male community of Palaeoindian researchers had focused almost exclusively on stereotypically male activities: specifically, large-scale mammoth and bison kill sites, technologically sophisticated hunting tool assemblages, and the replication of these tools and of the hunting and butchering practices they are thought to have facilitated. The women in the field have largely been displaced from these core research areas; they work on expedient blades, flake tools, and so-called domestic sites, and they have focused on edge-wear analysis. This pattern of segregation in the workplace is reinforced by gender bias in citation patterns. In the field of lithics analysis generally, Gero argues, women are much less frequently cited than their male colleagues, even when they do research that is more typical of men in the field, except when they publish with a male co-author. Not surprisingly, their work on expedient blades and edge-wear patterns is almost completely ignored, even though these analyses provide evidence that Palaeoindians exploited a wide range of plant materials, presumably foraged as a complement to their diet of Pleistocene mammals.

At the very least, these disciplinary dynamics, these 'social *relations* of palaeo research practice' (Gero 1993: 36, emphasis in the original), have reinforced an unfortunate incompleteness in entrenched accounts of Palaeoindian culture. More seriously, Gero charges, they substantially derail or, as she puts it, impose a limiting 'en-railment' on the research programme as a whole: 'women's exclusion from Pleistocene lithic and faunal analysis...is intrinsic to, and necessary for, the bison-mammoth knowledge construct' (ibid.: 37). The central problematic of Palaeoindian research is created by the technology, subsistence activities, social organization, and mobility, and patterns of occupation of the landscape are characterized primarily in terms of male-associated hunting activities. It is this focus that generates the puzzles that dominate Palaeoindian research: how to explain or reconstruct what happened to the mammoth hunters when the mammoths went extinct. Did Palaeoindians disappear or die out, to be replaced by the small-game – and plant-foraging – groups that succeeded them? Did they effect a miraculous transformation of their entire form of life as the subsistence base changed? These questions only arise, Gero argues, if researchers ignore the evidence that Palaeoindians depended on a much more diversified set of subsistence strategies than acknowledged by standard 'man the (mammoth/bison) hunter' models – precisely the evidence produced (largely) by women working on microblades and use-wear patterns. To overcome this incompleteness requires not just that practitioners take into account female-associated tools but, in addition, that they revalue women's work – the work of both contemporary women archaeologists and of Palaeoindian women in prehistoric contexts – and systematically rethink the ways Palaeoindian culture has been conceived as a subject of archaeological enquiry.[1]

Taken together, critiques at these five levels are understood by many to demonstrate more than just that archaeology is partial, in the sense that external interests and power relations may determine what questions will be taken up and what uses will be made of the results of enquiry. This admission would leave disciplinary practice and its products uncompromised by values, interests, and the social relations and material conditions of its operation. Rather, critiques of the kinds I have described are often seen to reveal socio-political dynamics that are intrinsic to disciplinary practice and are constitutive of its results at all levels. They show how external (non-cognitive) factors determine what data will be collected and how they will be construed as evidence, what interpretive and explanatory hypotheses will be taken seriously and accepted (sometimes evidence notwithstanding), and what range of revision or corrections will be considered when evidence resists being appropriated in terms of entrenched presuppositions. As Rouse has put this point with reference to general challenges to objectivism, such critiques make it clear that 'power does not merely impinge on science and scientific knowledge from without. Power relations permeate the most ordinary activities in scientific research. Scientific knowledge arises out of these power relations rather than in opposition to them' (1987: 24). It is this extension of socio-political critique, especially as attributed to feminists, that many archaeologists reject out of hand as a reduction ad absurdum of the central arguments of post-processualism.

Gender research and theoretical ambivalence

Conkey and Spector made the first widely influential argument for feminist approaches to archaeological research in 1984, and a watershed collection of essays devoted to work in this area appeared seven years later (Gero and Conkey 1991), the outgrowth of a small working conference organized by Conkey and Gero in 1988. In organizing this conference, Conkey and Gero approached a number of colleagues working in widely different areas of prehistoric archaeology and asked if they would be willing to explore the implications of taking gender as a focus for analysis in their various fields; even several years after the appearance of Conkey and Spector (1984) there was little feminist work in print or in process. Most of those approached had never considered such an approach and had no special interest in feminist initiatives, but they agreed to see what they could do. In effect Gero and Conkey commissioned a series of pilot projects on gender that they hoped might demonstrate the potential of research along the lines proposed by Conkey and Spector in 1984. Their motivation was explicitly feminist: they sought to engage potentially sympathetic and influential colleagues in the investigation of new questions they thought should be asked concerning women and gender, questions they had come to see as important because of their own political commitments. Although a number of other contextual factors of a socio-political nature fed the subsequent groundswell of interest in work in this area, these feminist efforts to mobilize support for research on questions about gender and women in prehistory were a crucial catalyst for the considerable body of work that has since appeared.[2] In short, political interests have played a key role in shaping the direction of this programme of research.[3]

Yet despite the political impetus that gave rise (directly and indirectly) to the diverse programmes of research that now address feminist questions about women and gender, the practice and the products of research in this area do not support or instantiate the strongest relativist claims sometimes attributed to post-processualism. Far from displacing evidential considerations, a feminist standpoint, if anything, enhances a commitment to empirical rigour, especially in the critical inspection of sexist, androcentric presuppositions that have framed much otherwise exemplary research in the field. Indeed, the new research on gender frequently reflects a wariness of strong constructivist conclusions, and in this attitude feminist archaeologists are not alone. Feminist practitioners in a number of contexts have been alert to the relativist implications that are often presumed to follow from their own wide-ranging critiques of extant traditions of scientific practice and its claims to objectivity. Even those who recommend a postmodern stance as a resource for feminist research acknowledge the dilemma that it creates for feminists or for any who would use postmodern insights 'in the interests of emancipation' (Lather 1991: 154). In this connection, and with special reference to feminist critiques of science, Harding argues the need to cultivate strategic 'ambivalence' – to embrace both 'successor science' projects which use the tools of existing research traditions to expose their inherent androcentric bias, and the vision of alternatives embodied in postmodern disruption of these projects (1986: 195). Many who are less optimistic express concern that, at the very least, a postmodern stance has 'both emancipatory and reactionary effects'; indeed it may be 'especially dangerous for the marginalized' (Lather 1991: 154). The worry is that deconstructive arguments intended to destabilize Enlightenment myths of objectivity and truth are themselves 'merely an inversion of Western arrogance' (Mascia-Lees et al. 1989: 15); they are an inversion that serves the interests of those who have always benefited from gender, race, and class privilege: 'The postmodern view that truth and knowledge are contingent and multiple may be seen to act as truth claim itself, a claim that undermines the ontological status of the subject at the very time when women and non Western peoples have begun to claim themselves as subject' (ibid.).

The tension between postmodern and emancipatory projects is evident in much feminist practice in the social and life sciences. On the one hand feminist critics of science have exposed such pervasive androcentric bias that whatever their intentions, they seem to call into question not just 'bad science' but much that passes for 'good science', even exemplary science (see Longino and Doell 1983: 207–8; Harding 1986; Longino 1990: 3–15; Wylie 1991: 38–44). Where this erodes confidence that scientific method is self-cleansing, a guarantor of objectivity, it is often presumed that feminist critics undermine any possibility of claiming greater credibility for their own insights in any but a purely political sense. And yet, the feminists responsible for these critiques are by no means prepared to concede that their accounts are just equal but different alternatives to those they challenge. Where women and gender have been characterized in stereotypically androcentric terms, or ignored in what purport to be humanly inclusive accounts of societies or cultural groups (e.g. in hunting-focused accounts of foraging societies; Slocum 1975 [1974]), historical epochs (e.g. the Renaissance that women did not have; Kelly-Gadol 1977), psychological processes (e.g. the 'different voice' in moral reasoning documented by Gilligan 1982), or physiological and cognitive capacities (Fausto-Sterling 1985), the result has frequently been pervasive error and misrepresentation as measured by such standard criteria as empirical adequacy and internal coherence. Indeed the claim made on behalf of research informed by a feminist angle of vision is often that it is simply *better* science in quite conventional terms (Fausto-Sterling 1985: 9). In a close analysis of exactly how and where androcentrism arises in biology (evolutionary theory and endocrinology), Longino and Doell argue such critiques of science should not put feminists in the position of having to choose for or against science; we should not have to 'turn our backs on science as a whole...or condemn it as an enterprise' (1983: 227). Their reason for cautioning against such simple, polarized responses is immediately relevant for understanding feminist practice in archaeology: 'the structure of scientific knowledge and the operation of bias are much more complex than either of these responses suggests' (ibid.: 208). Longino has since argued for the viability of a sophisticated 'contextual empiricism' as a philosophical position (Longino 1990: 215–32), as well as an option for feminist research practice for 'doing science as a feminist' (ibid.: 188) – which preserves a (mitigated) claim to objectivity.

It should not be surprising that the epistemological analysis offered by Longino and Doell and the research practice of many feminist scientists reflect a reticence to embrace a thoroughgoing constructivism about empirical enquiry. At its best, feminist research grows out of a commitment to understand, accurately and in detail, the institutions, attitudes, and practices that oppress women in a diversity of contexts and ways, *so that we can be effective in changing them*. And in this case its roots and inspiration lie in the varied experiences of constraint and dispossession that mark women's lives. Uncompromising constructivism and relativism trivialize these experiences; they deflect attention from questions about how and why they arise and from questions about the structures and conditions that constitute, for any who lack power, intransigent realities that impinge on their lives at every turn. In this respect, such positions embody what seems patently an ideology of the powerful. Certainly a central part of the activist experience of feminists who attempt to change oppressive conditions of life is the realization that effective intervention requires, first and foremost, a sound understanding of the forces we oppose. In short a commitment to the emancipatory potential of feminism and a respect for the very real constraints we encounter in practice persistently force feminist researchers, theorists, and activists alike back from the extremes of both objectivism and relativism that emerge in abstract debate about the status of empirically grounded knowledge claims (see, e.g., Fraser and Nicholson 1988: 83; Wylie 1992: 63–4).

These sorts of concerns, which are ubiquitous in discussions of the apolitical and even reactionary implications of (some) deconstructive and postmodern positions (Norris 1990), are not lost on the proponents of an explicitly political (post-processual) archaeology. The most outspoken critics of objectivist, processual archaeology can be seen to retreat from an uncompromising constructivism as soon as it becomes clear that such a position threatens to undermine their own social and intellectual agenda as surely as it does those of the positivists they repudiate. Hodder qualifies his arguments from underdetermination with the striking observation that even though all facts are constructs, there does exist a real world – and, what is more, 'the real world does constrain what we can say about it' (1986: 16); Shanks and Tilley declare themselves realists and invoke a dialectical relationship between object and subject that ensures that archaeological construction is not 'free or creative in a fictional sense' (1987: 104). They make it clear that they are not prepared to embrace the view that all claims about the past must be considered equal (ibid.: 245), insisting that 'the archaeological record itself' is a source of constraints that may 'challenge what we say as being inadequate in one manner or another' (ibid.: 104).

This recurrent ambivalence about 'anything goes' relativism among critics of naïve objectivism – among post-processual archaeologists as much as feminist critics of science – raises the question of how empirical (scientific) enquiry can be conceptualized so as to recognize, without contradiction, *both* that knowledge is constructed – it bears the marks of its makers – *and* that it is constrained, to a greater or lesser degree, by conditions that we confront as external realities not entirely of our own making. A fruitful point of departure is the acknowledgement of all parties to the current debate that although archaeological data must be richly interpreted to stand as evidence, they do (sometimes) have a capacity to challenge and constrain what we claim about the past: they routinely turn out differently than expected; they generate puzzles, pose challenges, force revisions, and canalize reconstructive and explanatory thinking, sometimes raising doubts about even the most well-entrenched presuppositions.

Theory-ladenness reconsidered

A concern with just this nexus of problems can be discerned in the work of those (post-positivist) philosophers of science, including feminist philosophers of science, who have undertaken analyses of how observational and experimental results are stabilized such that, in practice, they often show less arbitrariness of construction than has been insisted on by some of the stronger sociological critics. I have in mind, for example, Longino and Doell's analysis of the role played by background assumptions in traversing the distance between data, evidence, and hypotheses (1983: 208–10); Longino's subsequent analysis of ideals of objectivity (1990: 62–82); Shapere's account of the role played by prior information in determining what will count as an observation in physics (1982: 505); and the substantial philosophical and historical literature that has grown up since the mid-1980s on experimental practice (see, e.g., Galison 1987: 7–9; 1988, 1989; Hacking 1988a, 1988b, 1989). The key to understanding how archaeological evidence can (sometimes) function as a semi-autonomous constraint on claims about the cultural past is to recognize that archaeologists exploit an enormous diversity of evidence – not just different kinds of *archaeological* evidence, but also evidence that depends on background knowledge derived from a number of different sources, that enters interpretation at different points, and that can be mutually constraining when it converges, or fails to converge, on a coherent account of a particular past context.

To summarize the earlier discussion, my thesis is that archaeological evidence derives its stability and autonomy from two sources: the *security* of the background knowledge invoked to establish a link between the surviving record and the past events or conditions that produced it and the epistemic *independence* of the evidence thus constituted. The kinds of security at issue here include the credibility of the background knowledge in the context from which it derives and the security of the inferences in which this knowledge is deployed: this last is a function of the nature of the linkages between surviving traces and antecedent causes (the degree to which they are unique or deterministic) and the directness and complexity of the inferential chain required to reconstruct the antecedents. And there are two dimensions on which independence is crucial: the vertical independence of background assumptions from test hypotheses (this is the independence captured in especially stringent terms by bootstrapping models of confirmation) and the horizontal independence from *one another* of linking hypotheses that arises when a number of different sources are used to establish the evidential import of archaeological data (independence in this sense obtains if no one set of uniting principles entails the others as a proper subset of itself, or is confirmed by the same evidence). Horizontal independence allows archaeologists to exploit a strategy of triangulation, setting up a system of mutual constraint among lines of evidence bearing on a common archaeological subject.

It is a significant irony that the role of these evidential constraints is nowhere clearer than in the new feminist work on gender, which is so often identified as precisely the sort of explicitly political research that leads inevitably to corrosive relativism. I will consider here a number of examples from contributions to the ground-breaking 1988 conference on gender research in archaeology that subsequently appeared in *Engendering Archaeology* (Gero and Conkey 1991).

Although, as I have indicated, most contributors to this conference remarked that they began with serious reservations about the approach urged on them by Gero and Conkey – they did not see how questions about gender, which had never arisen before, could bear on research in their fields or sub-fields – even the most sceptical found that attention to such questions brought to light striking instances of gender bias in existing archaeological research and opened up a range of constructive possibilities for enquiry that had been completely overlooked. One especially compelling critical analysis, developed by Patty Jo Watson and Kennedy (1991), exposes pervasive androcentrism in explanations of the emergence of agriculture in the eastern United States. Whatever the specific mechanisms or processes postulated, the main contenders all assume that women could not have been actively responsible for the development of cultigens even though they also assume that women were responsible for gathering plants (as well as small game) under earlier foraging adaptations, and were responsible for the cultivation of domesticates when horticulture was established. One model turns on the blatantly ad hoc proposal that shamans, who are consistently identified as male, were the instigators of this culture-transforming development; it was their knowledge of plants used for ritual purposes that informed the development of the cultigens on which Eastern Woodlands horticultural practices were based. In effect, women passively followed plants around when foraging, and then passively tended them when the plants were (re)introduced as cultigens by men (Watson and Kennedy 1991: 263–4). The dominant alternative postulates a process of co-evolution by which horticulture emerged as an adaptive response to a transformation of the plant resources that occurred without the benefit of any deliberate human intervention; at most, human patterns of refuse disposal in 'domestilocalities' unintentionally introduced artificial selection pressures that generated the varieties of indigenous plants that became cultigens. On this account the plants effectively 'domesticate themselves', and women are, once again, represented as passively adapting to imposed change (ibid.: 262).[4]

Watson and Kennedy make much of the artificiality of both models. Why assume that shamans were men, or that dabbling for ritual purposes would be more likely to produce the knowledge and transformations of the resource base necessary for horticulture than the systematic exploitation of these resources as a primary means of subsistence? Why deny human agency altogether and represent the emergence of horticulture as an 'automatic process' (ibid.: 262) when it seems that the most plausible ascription of agency (if any is to be made) must be to women (ibid.: 262–4)? Indeed, Watson and Kennedy observe that they are 'leery of explanations that remove women from the one realm that is traditionally granted them, as soon as innovation or invention enters the picture' (ibid.: 264). The common and implicit basis for both theories is, they argue, a set of underlying assumptions, uncritically appropriated from popular culture and traditional anthropology, to the effect that women could not have been responsible for any major culture-transforming exercise of human agency.

In a constructive vein Hastorf, a contributor who works on pre-Hispanic sites in the central Andes, drew on several lines of evidence to establish that gendered divisions of labour and participation in the public, political life of the highland communities in question were profoundly altered through the period when the Inka extended their control in the region; the household structure and gender roles encountered in historical periods cannot be treated as a stable, traditional feature of Andean life that pre-dates state formation (1991: 139). In a comparison of the density and distribution of palaeobotanical remains recovered from household compounds dating to the periods before and after the advent of Inka control, Hastorf found evidence within the sites that over time both maize production and processing intensified and the degree to which female-associated processing activities were restricted to specific locations increased. In addition she reports a striking comparison between the sexes of skeletal remains recovered from these sites and the results of a stable-isotope analysis of bone composition for evidence of variability in dietary intake. Although the lifetime dietary profiles of males and females are undifferentiated preceding the advent of Inka control in the region, Hastorf finds that they diverge sharply in the period when evidence of an Inka presence begins to appear. Specifically, males show higher rates of consumption of foods that have the isotope values Hastorf identifies with maize than do females. To interpret this result Hastorf turns to ethno-historic records that document Inka practices of treating men as the heads of households and communities, drawing them into ritualized negotiations that involve the consumption of maize beer (*chicha*) and require them to serve on obligatory workforces away from their villages, for which they were compensated with maize and *chicha*. She concludes that through this transitional period, the newly imposed political structures of the Inka empire had forced a realignment of gender roles on local communities and households. Women 'became the focus of [internal social and economic] tensions as they produced more beer while at the same time they were more restricted in their participation in the society' (ibid.: 152).

Parallel results are reported by Brumfiel (1991) in an analysis of changes in production patterns in the Valley of Mexico in the period when the Aztec state was establishing a tribute system in the region. Through analysis of the density and distribution of spindle whorls, she argues that fabric production, largely the responsibility of women (on ethno-historic and documentary evidence), increased dramatically in outlying areas but decreased in the vicinity of the urban centres as the practice of extracting tribute payments in cloth developed. On further analysis she found evidence of an inverse pattern of distribution and density in artefacts associated with the production of labour-intensive and transportable cooked food based on tortillas; the changing proportion of griddles to pots suggests that the preparation of griddle-cooked foods increased near the urban centres and decreased in outlying areas, where the less demanding (and preferred) pot-cooked foods continued to predominate. She postulates, on this basis, that cloth may have been exacted directly as tribute in the hinterland, while populations living closer to the city centre intensified their production of transportable food so that they could participate in the markets and 'extra-domestic institutions' then emerging in the Valley of Mexico that required a mobile labour force (Brumfiel 1991: 241). In either case, Brumfiel points out, the primary burden of meeting the tribute demands for cloth imposed by Aztec rule was shouldered by women and caused strategic realignments of their household labour. Where the Aztec state depended on tribute to maintain its political and economic hegemony, its emergence, like that of the Inka state studied by Hastorf, must be understood to have been dependent *on* a transformation that it caused in the way predominantly female domestic labour was organized and deployed.

Finally several contributors consider assemblages of artistic material, some of them rich in images of women, and explore the implications of broadening the range of conceptions of gender relations that inform their interpretation. In a discussion of the British exhibition *The Art of Lepenski Vir*, Handsman challenges the notion that gender can be treated in essentialist terms, reassessing the ideology of gender difference and the presumption of a timeless, natural, and hierarchical opposition between men and women (1991: 360). He suggests several interpretive options that might be pursued in constructing 'relational histories of inequality, power, ideology and control, and resistance and counter-discourse' where gender dynamics are concerned (ibid.: 338–9). In the process he points to a wide range of evidence – features of the images themselves and associations with architectural and artefactual material that might provide them context – that constitutes 'clear signs' of complexities, contradictions, 'plurality and conflict' (ibid.: 340, 343), undermining the simple story of natural opposition and complementarity told by the exhibit. In a similar vein Conkey has developed an analysis of interpretations of Palaeolithic art, especially images of females or purported female body parts, in which she shows how 'the presentist gender paradigm has infused most reconstructions of Upper Palaeolithic "artistic" life', yielding accounts in which 'sexist twentieth-century notions of gender and sexuality are read into the cultural traces of "our ancestors"' with remarkable disingenuity (Conkey with Williams 1991: 121). She concludes that whatever the importance of these images and objects, it is most unlikely that they were instances of either commodified pornography or high art, as produced in contemporary contexts.

Evidential constraints in practice

In all the cases discussed above, both critical and constructive results turn on the appraisal of evidential constraints. And in all cases, the evidence appraised plays a role that is to varying degrees autonomous and corrective of the expectations and presuppositions that laden it, that bring it into view, or give it specific evidential import. Considerations operating on a number of dimensions have this capacity to constrain, as Kosso (1988) argues. Nevertheless, these multiple factors generate cases that fall along a rough continuum defined chiefly by degrees of independence in the first sense (the independence of linking hypotheses from claims or presuppositions about the subject past they help establish) and by the nature of the linkage invoked (the degree to which it is uniquely determining, establishing security in the second sense).

At one end of the continuum, the end that draws the attention of anti-objectivist critics, ascriptions of evidential significance are entirely determined by theoretical commitments, a set of precepts about the nature of the cultural subject, that are also embodied in the broader interpretive and explanatory claims that this evidence will be used to test or support. This predetermination is, in part, what Watson and Kennedy object to in explanations for the emergence of horticulture in the Eastern Woodlands. Sexist assumptions about the nature and capabilities of women underlie standard models of the horticultural transition (consistently reading women out of the account) and they infuse interpretations of the archaeological data used to evaluate these models, ensuring that these data will be seen as evidence for models that project on to the past a natural sexual division of labour in which women are consistently passive and associated with plants.

But even in these worst cases it is often possible, as Watson and Kennedy demonstrate, to establish grounds for questioning the assumptions that frame both the favoured hypotheses and the constitution of data as the evidence from which these hypotheses derive support. Two strategies for critique are evident in their analysis. The first is to exploit non-archaeological resources, both conceptual and empirical, in an independent assessment of the framing assumptions. In this connection, Watson and Kennedy draw attention to a straightforward contradiction inherent in current theorizing about the emergence of horticulture in the Eastern Woodlands: women are persistently identified as the tenders of plants, whether wild or under cultivation, and yet are systematically denied any role in the transition from foraging to horticulture, whatever the cost of that denial in terms of theoretical elegance, plausibility, or explanatory power. To indicate just how high the cost may be, they draw on background (botanical) knowledge about the range and environmental requirements of the plant varieties that became domesticates to establish that they routinely appear in prehistoric contexts that were far from optimal (Watson and Kennedy 1991: 266). Watson and Kennedy argue that it is most implausible that these domesticates could have arisen under conditions of neglect, as suggested in the co-evolution model. Regarding the shaman hypothesis, their analysis is informed by an appreciation that since the 1970s, feminist anthropologists have documented enormous variability in the roles played by women and in the degrees to which women are active rather than passive, mobile rather than bound to a home base, and politically powerful rather than stereotypically dispossessed and victimized. This undermines any presupposition that women are inherently less capable of innovation, self-determination, and strategic manipulation of resources than their male counterparts and it renders suspect any interpretation that depends on such an assumption, regardless of its archaeological implications. In this way Watson and Kennedy challenge the credibility of the interpretive principles used to bring archaeological evidence to bear on questions about the transition to horticulture, questioning the more fundamental framework assumptions that underlie the explanatory models of this transition that they find inadequate.

But in addition, even when circularity threatens – when linking principles are drawn from the same theory as underpins the test hypothesis – archaeological data can sometimes function as a locus of evidential constraint, thereby making possible a second strategy for critique. The predisposition to interpret archaeological data in terms of sexist assumptions about the nature and capabilities of women does not necessarily ensure (indeed, as Watson and Kennedy point out, it has not ensured) that the record will obligingly provide evidence that activities that are assumed to be male associated will prove to have mediated the transition from a foraging to a horticultural way of life, however strong the expectation that they must have done so. In fact most of the activities that the co-evolution model deems responsible for the creation of the 'domestilocalities' in which cultigens emerged were women's activities, if the archaeological record of such sites is interpreted in light of the traditional assumptions about gender relations that Watson and Kennedy find presupposed by this account (1991: 262). If the interpretive assumptions in question constituted a more closely specified theory, the outlines of Glymour's bootstrapping inference might emerge in cases like these, complete with internal-to-theory independence between linking and test hypotheses (Glymour 1980).

Straightforward circularity is generally not the central problem in archaeological interpretation, however. Given the state of knowledge in the relevant fields and the complexity of most archaeological subjects, it is almost unimaginable that a single encompassing theory could provide both the linking principles necessary to interpret archaeological data as evidence of the cultural past and a suite of hypotheses capable of explaining the events and conditions that this evidence brings into view. Usually the basis for ascribing evidential significance to archaeological data is some form of analogical inference that draws on diverse sources, most of which are understood in terms of highly localized theory. Here the worry is not overdetermination by an all-encompassing conceptual framework, but underdetermination due to a lack of generalizable knowledge about the conditions under which observed linkages between (archaeological) statics and (cultural, behavioural) dynamics may be projected on to past (or otherwise unobserved) contexts. The inferential distance that must be crossed, in all of Longino and Doell's senses (1983), remains considerable, and there are relatively sparse resources for helping to bridge it. As has been widely argued by both critics and advocates of analogical inference, there is a pressing need to strengthen the grounds for supposing that surviving traces are linked to antecedents in the same manner as observed in better-known contexts, as well as for eliminating alternatives when alternative linkages are known to be possible. That is, there is a need to establish the security of the inferences from present to past in both of the senses identified above.

Analogical inference is typically constructed and evaluated in terms of two sets of evidential constraints that establish security in just these senses when effectively deployed. These are constraints on what can be claimed about the analogue, given background knowledge of the source contexts from which they are drawn, and constraints on the applicability of the analogue to a specific subject context that derive from the archaeological record. For example in associating women with the use of spindle whorls in weaving and with the use of griddles in food preparation, Brumfiel (1991) relies on a direct historic analogy, arguing that these artefacts are so extensively and stably associated with weaving/cooking and women in historically related ethnographic and ethno-historic contexts that it is reasonable to assume that these associations held for prehistoric contexts as well. Similarly, archaeologists dealing with evidence of horticultural practice routinely postulate a division of labour in which women are assumed to have had primary responsibility for agricultural activities (Ehrenberg 1989: 77–141), but they base this assumption not on an appeal to the completeness of mapping between source and subject (which Brumfiel's case illustrates) but on the persistence of the association of women with horticulture across historically and ethnographically documented contexts, however different they may be in other respects.

In these cases completeness of mapping and reliable correlation figure as evidence that a common 'determining structure' (Weitzenfeld 1984) links a distinct type of artefactual material to specific functions, gender associations, or activity structures securely enough in present contexts to support an ascription of the same functions and associations to the archaeological subject. These interpretive claims can be as decisively undermined by a change in background knowledge about the sources of these analogues (e.g. evidence that the material/behavioural linkage projected on to the past is not stable in source contexts) as by what archaeologists find in the record of the contexts on to which they are projected (e.g. evidence that a particular association or function could not have obtained in the context in question). Conversely where the linking principles based on background knowledge of source (or actualistic) contexts are uncontested and their credibility is independent of any of the hypotheses archaeologists want to evaluate against the evidence these principles help to establish, they can very effectively stabilize debate.

The power of the challenge posed by Brumfiel to extant models of the economic base of the Aztec empire depends on precisely this sort of stabilizing analogy. The association she posits between women and spindle whorls, pots, and griddles is not questioned by those she engages in debate and is independent of both the hypotheses she challenges and those she promotes. Given this provisional foundation, she brings into view new features of the structure of otherwise well-understood assemblages – formerly undocumented patterns of distribution and association among components of these assemblages – that standard models cannot account for, even when constituted and interpreted in terms that are shared by proponents of these models. She thus challenges not (just) the conceptual integrity or prior plausibility of conventional models (as Watson and Kennedy had done) but their empirical and explanatory adequacy as an account of the political economy of states that rose in pre-Columbian

Mesoamerica and South America. Perhaps most importantly, Brumfiel identifies implausible assumptions about the stability of gender structures as the source of the inadequacies of these models; she argues for an alternative predicated on the thesis that gender relations and household divisions of labour are not only dynamic – genuinely historical and cultural, not natural – but are also crucial co-determinants of political and economic processes of state formation that had been treated as a public, male preserve. Her account is compelling in as much as she effectively fills some of the gaps and solves some of the puzzles that arise for extant theories because of their dependence on these assumptions.

The limiting case on this continuum of theory-ladening inferences, the ideal of security in the ascription of evidential significance to data described earlier, arises when archaeologists can draw on completely independent, non-ethnographic sources that specify unique causal antecedents for components of the surviving record. Among the cases considered here, Hastorf's analysis of bone composition comes the closest to this ideal. If the background knowledge deployed in stable-isotope analysis is reliable (a question always open to critical reassessment), then it can establish, in chemical terms, what dietary intake would have been necessary to produce the reported composition of the bone marrow recovered from archaeological contexts. Where its results can be linked, through palaeobotanical analysis, to the consumption of specific plant and animal resources and through skeletal analysis to a pattern of sex-linked differences in consumption, isotope analysis can underwrite the inference of dietary profiles that is substantially independent and can provide a genuine test of interpretive or explanatory presuppositions about subsistence patterns or gender-structured social practices affecting the distribution of food. The independence and security of linking arguments based on background knowledge of this physical, chemical, bioecological sort are exploited in many other areas of gender research: in morphological analyses of skeletal remains that provide evidence of pathologies, physical stress, and fertility (Bentley 1996) and in materials analysis and reconstructions of prehistoric technology (e.g. in connection with ceramic production, Wright 1991; and architecture, Tringham 1991), to name a few such examples. As this limiting ideal of (vertical) independence between linking principles and test hypotheses or framework assumptions is approximated, archaeologists secure a body of evidence that establishes provisionally stable parameters for all other interpretation and a stable (if never uncontestable) basis for piecemeal comparison between contending claims about the cultural past.

It is important to note, however, that the evidence provided by these sorts of linking principles has limited significance, taken on its own. Hastorf must rely on a number of collateral lines of evidence to establish that the anomalous shift in diet evident in male skeletons was due to increased consumption of maize beer, and to link the change in consumption to the advent of Inka-imposed systems of political control in the region and to a restructuring of gender relations at the level of the household. This reliance on multiple lines of evidence is an important feature of archaeological reasoning that cuts across the considerations of (vertical) independence and of security I have described. In fact evidential significance is rarely ascribed to items taken in isolation. Context is crucial and is defined in a number of ways; if it is relevantly cultural, rather than geological or ecological, it may be characterized by associations among artefacts or features that are recovered together in undisturbed deposits, which have close spatial or temporal proximity, or which show technological, formal, or stylistic affinity even if widely dispersed.

When elements of the archaeological record can be assumed to bear on a particular past context in one of these senses and, most important, when these elements are ascribed significance on the basis of diverse linking principles (i.e. principles derived from independent bodies of background knowledge), then a network of horizontal constraints may come into play *between* distinct (vertical) lines of interpretive inference that can vastly increase their individual and collective credibility. Each vertical linkage between data, evidence, and hypothesis may be compelling individually – each may be secure in the relevant senses, and independence between linking principles and test hypotheses may ensure against vicious circularity – but if the linking principles determining evidential significance are independent of one another in the second sense, it becomes possible to triangulate on a postulated set of conditions or events. And if diverse evidential strands all converge on a given hypothesis about the past, they can provide that hypothesis compelling support, to the degree that it is implausible that such convergence could be the result of compensatory error in all the lines of inference establishing its evidential support (Hacking 1983: 183–5; Kosso 1988: 456). Most often the problem in archaeology is not to adjudicate between a number of equally plausible, well-supported, explanatory alternatives but to find one account, one reconstructive or explanatory hypothesis, that is consistent with all the lines of evidence that are constructed using diverse resources.

While Hastorf most explicitly exploits the constraints imposed by a requirement of convergence across horizontally independent lines of evidence, it is clear that Brumfiel relies on horizontal independence as well. When she identifies an anomalous distribution of artefacts related to cloth production over time and space, and then reassesses the evidence related to different sorts of food processing, the new (unexpected) convergence she documents provides her own account with especially strong support precisely because nothing in the linking principles ensures such convergence; the evidence could have turned out otherwise. More significant still are cases in which independently constituted lines of interpretation fail to converge. Even when each line of evidence relevant to a particular account of the past enjoys strong collateral support taken on its own (i.e. each is secure), undetected error may become evident when one line of evidence persistently runs counter to the others, when dissonance emerges among lines of interpretation. The failure to converge on a coherent account clearly indicates an error somewhere in the system of background knowledge – the auxiliary assumptions and linking principles – however well-entrenched they may be.

In cases of extreme dissonance, which are approximated by the interpretations of artistic images and traditions considered by Handsman (1991) and by Conkey (with Williams 1991), a persistent failure to converge may call into question the efficacy of *any* interpretive constitution of the data as evidence in a particular area. These authors conclude that many familiar and influential interpretive options must be abandoned, given the lack of convergence between the interpretive claims based on material identified as art and reconstructions based on other forms of evidence that bring into view the larger cultural contexts in which the artistic tradition occurs. Indeed, all indications are that the prehistoric cultures they consider must have been so profoundly different from any with which we are familiar that the images constituting their artistic record cannot be assumed to have any transculturally stable meaning; they cannot be taken as evidence of many, or indeed any, of the range of activities, beliefs, or sensibilities that we associate with art. Such discontinuity may suggest that there is no determinate fact of the matter where the symbolic import of gender imagery is concerned; or, as Conkey suggests, it may require us to acknowledge that in such cases we simply are not and may never be in a position to determine what the fact of the matter is. But even in these most enigmatic cases the data often do effectively resist the imposition of favoured interpretations, thereby undermining a number of formerly plausible claims about the past. Thus dissonance among lines of interpretation may make clear what we *cannot* claim in connection with a particular past; it may force a reconsideration of fundamental assumptions about the nature of the subject domain – about art and artistic production – and about the limits or prospects for success in investigating it. Paradoxically, the fragmentary nature of the archaeological record is at the same time its strength in setting up such evidential constraints, even in establishing the limits of enquiry.

The explicitly feminist initiatives that have emerged in archaeology make clear the centrality of values, interests, and socio-political standpoint to archaeological practice, and for this they are sometimes decried as 'just political' (Wylie 1990). At the same time, however, they illustrate how a range of empirical and conceptual resources can be used to critically evaluate not only conventional interpretations of the cultural past but also the assumptions that inform them, assumptions that are sometimes so deeply entrenched in our thinking as to be invisible. The strategies that feminists use to mobilize these resources are common in archaeological practice. When successful, they sometimes put us in a position to say we have discovered a fact about the world, or have shown a formerly plausible claim to be simply false; the critical analysis by Watson and Kennedy and the constructive proposals of Hastorf and of Brumfiel are examples in point; in other cases the outcomes of enquiry are more equivocal. As Handsman and as Conkey (with Williams) illustrate, sustained investigation may call into question basic assumptions about the accessibility, or even the existence, of certain facts about a given subject domain. In short some objects of knowledge and epistemic situations do sustain a moderate objectivist and realist stance, while others do not; they are text-like in their interpretive openness, and it may never be appropriate to claim evidential security for descriptive or explanatory claims about them.

The conclusion I draw is that we should resist the pressure to adopt a general epistemic stance as appropriate to all evidential claims and all reconstructive or explanatory claims warranted by a particular discipline. Any question about the status of evidence and the relationship between evidential and socio-political interests in the construction of knowledge – whether we should be relativist or objectivist – must be settled locally, in light of what we come to know about the nature of specific subject matters and about the resources we have for their investigation.

Notes

1. Gero's analysis parallels non-gendered critiques of the 'Clovis adaptation' that had begun to appear in the late 1980s (e.g. Meltzer and Smith 1986; Meltzer 1993). Adavasio subsequently argued that 'the official mammoth-centric picture of early Americans completely neglects the role of women, children and grandparents' (as quoted in Nemecek 2000: 84).

2. Interest in feminist and gender research in archaeology has grown dramatically since the late 1980s; a number of monographs, anthologies, and several bibliographies are now available that provide access to this literature (e.g. Gilchrist 1993; Spector 1993; Wall 1994; Claassen and Joyce 1997; Nelson 1997; Hays-Gilpin and Whitley 1998). I give a more detailed account of why this interest in questions about women and gender arose so quickly and so late in archaeology in Wylie 1990, 1991, and 1997.

3. Although they had not yet coalesced into a research programme at this point, feminist themes were explored by North American archaeologists before 1984 and they were actively engaged in other contexts (e.g. Scandinavia and the UK) as early as 1979. For a detailed discussion, please see the original (Wylie 2002: 279, note 8).

4. See Fritz (1999) for a reassessment of this analysis in light of evidence that gourds may have been used as net floats and domesticated prior to the transition to horticulture.

Bibliography

Bentley, G.R. 1996. How Did Prehistoric Women Beat 'Man the Hunter'? Reconstructing Fertility from the Archaeological Record. In Wright, R.P. (ed.), *Gender and Archaeology*. Philadelphia: University of Pennsylvania Press, pp. 23–51.

Brumfiel, E.M. 1991. Weaving and Cooking: Women's Production in Aztec Mexico. In Gero, J.M. and Conkey, M.W. (eds), *Engendering Archaeology: Women and Prehistory*. Oxford: Blackwell, pp. 224–53.

Claassen, C. and Joyce, R.A. (eds). 1997. *Women in Prehistory: North America and Mesoamerica*. Philadelphia: University of Pennsylvania Press.

Conkey, M.W. and Spector, J.D. 1984. Archaeology and the Study of Gender. *Advances in Archaeological Method and Theory* 7: 1–38.

Conkey, M.W., with Williams, S.H. 1991. Original Narratives: The Political Economy of Gender in Archaeology. In di Leonardo, M. (ed.), *Gender, Culture, and Political Economy: Feminist Anthropology in the Post-Modern Era*. Berkeley: University of California Press, pp. 102–39.

Deagan, K. 1990. Accommodation and Resistance: The Process and Impact of Spanish Colonization in the Southeast. In Thomas, D.H. (ed.), *Archaeological and Historical Perspectives on the Spanish Borderlands East*. Washington, DC: Smithsonian Institution Press, pp. 297–314.

Ehrenberg, M. 1989. *Women in Prehistory*. Norman: University of Oklahoma Press.

Engelstad, E. 1991. Images of Power and Contradiction: Feminist Theory and Postprocessual Archaeology. *Antiquity* 65: 502–14.

Epperson, T.W. 1990. Race and the Disciplines of the Plantation. *Historical Archaeology* 24(4): 29–36.

Fausto-Sterling, A. 1985. *Myths of Gender: Biological Theories about Women and Men*. New York: Basic Books.

Fraser, N. and Nicholson, L. 1988. Social Criticism without Philosophy: An Encounter between Feminism and Postmodernism. In Ross, A. (ed.), *Universal Abandon? The Politics of Postmodernism*. Minneapolis: University of Minnesota Press, pp. 83–104.

Fritz, G.J. 1999. Gender and the Early Cultivation of Gourds in Eastern North America. *American Antiquity* 35: 405–12.

Galison, P. 1987. *How Experiments End*. Chicago: University of Chicago Press.

Galison, P. 1988. Philosophy in the Laboratory. *Journal of Philosophy* 85: 525–7.

Galison, P. 1989. Multiple Constraints, Simultaneous Solutions. In Fine, A. and Leplin, J. (eds), *PSA 1988*. East Lansing, MI: Philosophy of Science Association, pp. 157–63.

Gero, J.M. 1993. The Social World of Prehistoric Facts: Gender and Power in Paleoindian Research. In du Cros, H. and Smith, L. (eds), *Women in Archaeology: A Feminist Critique*. Canberra: Australian National University, pp. 31–40.

Gero, J.M. and Conkey, M.W. (eds). 1991. *Engendering Archaeology: Women and Prehistory*. Oxford: Blackwell.

Gero, J.M., Lacy, D.M., and Blakey, M.L. (eds). 1983. *The Socio-Politics of Archaeology*. Amherst: University of Massachusetts.

Gilchrist, R. 1992. Review of *Experiencing Archaeology* by Michael Shanks. *Archaeological Review from Cambridge* 11: 188–91.

Gilchrist, R. 1993. *Gender and Material Culture: The Archaeology of Religious Women*. London: Routledge.

Gilligan, C. 1982. *In a Different Voice: Psychological Theory and Women's Development*. Cambridge, MA: Harvard University Press.

Glymour, C. 1980. *Theory and Evidence*. Princeton: Princeton University Press.

Hacking, I. 1983. *Representing and Intervening: Introductory Topics in the Philosophy of Natural Science*. Cambridge: Cambridge University Press.

Hacking, I. 1988a. On the Stability of the Laboratory Sciences. *Journal of Philosophy* 85: 507–14.

Hacking, I. 1988b. The Participant Irrealist at Large in the Laboratory. *British Journal for the Philosophy of Science* 39: 277–94.

Hacking, I. 1989. Philosophers of Experiment. In Fine, A. and Leplin, J. (eds), *PSA 1988*. East Lansing, MI: Philosophy of Science Association, pp. 147–56.

Hall, M. 1984. The Burden of Tribalism: The Social Context of Southern Africa Iron Age Studies. *American Antiquity* 49: 455–67.

Handsman, R.G. 1989. Native Americans and an Archaeology of Living Traditions. *Artifacts* 17(2): 3–5.

Handsman, R.G. 1990. The Weantinock Indian Homeland Was Not a 'Desert'. *Artifacts* 18(2): 3–7.

Handsman, R.G. 1991. Whose Art Was Found at Lepenski Vir? Gender Relations and Power in Prehistory. In Gero, J.M. and Conkey, M.W. (eds), *Engendering Archaeology: Women and Prehistory*. Oxford: Blackwell, pp. 329–64.

Handsman, R. and Richmond, T.L. 1995. Confronting Colonialism: The Mahican and Schaghticoke Peoples and Us. In Schmidt, P.R. and Patterson, T.C. (eds), *Making Alternative Histories: The Practice of Archaeology and History in Non-Western Settings*. Santa Fe: School of American Research, pp. 87–119.

Harding, S. 1986. *The Science Question in Feminism*. Ithaca, NY: Cornell University Press.

Hastorf, C.A. 1991. Gender, Space, and Food in Prehistory. In Gero, J.M. and Conkey, M.W. (eds), *Engendering Archaeology: Women and Prehistory*. Oxford: Blackwell, pp. 132–59.

Hays-Gilpin, K. and Whitley, D.S. (eds). 1998. *Reader in Gender Archaeology*. New York: Routledge.

Hodder, I. 1986. *Reading the Past: Current Approaches to Interpretation in Archaeology*. Cambridge: Cambridge University Press.

Hodder, I. 1991. Interpretive Archaeology and its Role. *American Antiquity* 56:7–18.

Irele, A. 1991. The African Scholar: Is Black Africa Entering the Dark Ages of Scholarship. *Transition* 51: 51–69.

Kelly-Gadol, J. 1977. Did Women Have a Renaissance? In Bridenthal, R. and Koontz, C. (eds), *Becoming Visible: Women in European History*. Boston: Houghton Mifflin, pp. 137–64.

Kosso, P. 1988. Dimensions of Observability. *British Journal for the Philosophy of Science* 39: 449–67.

Lather, P. 1991. Deconstructing/Deconstructive Inquiry: The Politics of Knowing and Being Known. *Educational Theory* 41: 153–73.

Longino, H.E. 1990. *Science as Social Knowledge: Values and Objectivity in Scientific Inquiry.* Princeton: Princeton University Press.

Longino, H. and Doell, R. 1983. Body, Bias, and Behaviour: A Comparative Analysis of Reasoning in Two Areas of Biological Science. *Signs* 9: 206–27.

Mascia-Lees, F.E., Sharpe, P., and Cohen, C.B. 1989. The Postmodernist Turn in Anthropology: Cautions from a Feminist Perspective. *Signs* 15: 7–33.

Meltzer, D.J. 1993. Is There a Clovis Adaptation? In Soffer, O. and Praslov, N.D. (eds), *From Kostenki to Clovis: Upper Palaeolithic – Palaeo-Indian Adaptations.* New York: Plenum, pp. 293–310.

Meltzer, D.J. and Smith, B.D. 1986. Palaeoindian and Early Archaic Subsistence Strategies in Eastern North America. In Neusius, S.W. (ed.), *Foraging, Collecting, and Harvesting: Archaic Period Subsistence and Settlement in the Eastern Woodlands.* Carbondale: Southern Illinois University at Carbondale.

Miller, D. 1980. Archaeology and Development. *Current Anthropology* 21: 709–26.

Nelson, S.M. 1997. *Gender in Archaeology: Analyzing Power and Prestige.* Walnut Creek, CA: AltaMira Press.

Nelson, M.C., Nelson, S.M., and Wylie, A. (eds). 1994. *Equity Issues for Women in Archaeology.* Arlington, VA: American Anthropological Association.

Nemecek, S. 2000. Who Were the First Americans? *Scientific American* September: 80–7.

Norris, C. 1990. *What's Wrong With Postmodernism: Critical Theory and the Ends of Philosophy.* Baltimore: Johns Hopkins University Press.

Orser, C.E. Jr. (ed.). 1990. The Historical Archaeology of Southern Plantations and Farms. *Historical Archaeology* 24(4).

Orser, C.E. Jr. 1999. Profits in the Fields: Farm Tenancy, Capitalism, and Historical Archaeology. In Leone, M.P. and Potter, P.B. (eds), *Historical Archaeologies of Capitalism.* New York: Kluwer Academie, pp. 143–67.

Patterson, T.C. 1986a. The Last Sixty Years: Toward a Social History of Americanist Archaeology in the United States. *American Anthropologist* 88: 7–22.

Patterson, T.C. 1986b. Some Postwar Theoretical Trends in U.S. Archaeology. *Culture* 11: 43–54.

Patterson, T.C. 1995. *Toward a Social History of Archaeology in the United States.* Orlando: Harcourt Brace.

Potter, P.B. Jr. 1991. What Is the Use of Plantation Archaeology? *Historical Archaeology* 25: 94–107.

Rouse, J. 1987. *Knowledge and Power: Toward a Political Philosophy of Science.* Ithaca, NY: Cornell University Press.

Schmidt, P.R. 1995. Using Archaeology to Remake History in Africa. In Schmidt, P.R. and Patterson, T.C. (eds), *Making Alternative Histories: The Practice of Archaeology and History in Non-Western Settings.* Santa Fe: School of American Research, pp. 119–48.

Shanks, M. and Tilley, C. 1987. *Re-constructing Archaeology: Theory and Practice.* Cambridge: Cambridge University Press.

Shapere, D. 1982. The Concept of Observation in Science and Philosophy. *Philosophy of Science* 49: 485–525.

Singleton, T.A. (ed.). 1985. *The Archaeology of Slavery and Plantation Life.* New York: Academic Press.

Slocum, S. 1975 [1974]. Women the Gatherer: Male Bias in Anthropology. In Reiter, R. (ed.), *Toward an Anthropology of Women.* New York: Monthly Review Press, pp. 36–50.

Spector, J.D. 1993. *What This Awl Means: Feminist Archaeology at a Wahpeton Dakota Village.* St Paul: Minnesota Historical Society Press.

Spector, J.D. and Whelan, M.K. 1989. Incorporating Gender into Archaeology Courses. In Morgen, S. (ed.), *Gender and Anthropology: Critical Reviews for Research and Teaching.* Washington, DC: American Anthropological Association, pp. 65–94.

Thomas, D.H. 1991a. Cubist Perspectives on the Spanish Borderlands. In Thomas, D.H. (ed.), *The Spanish Borderlands in Pan-American Perspective*. Washington, DC: Smithsonian Institution Press, pp. xiii–xxix.

Thomas, D.H. (ed.). 1991b. *The Spanish Borderlands in Pan-American Perspective*. Washington, DC: Smithsonian Institution Press.

Tilley, C. 1989. Archaeology as Socio-Political Action in the Present. In Pinsky, V. and Wylie, A. (eds), *Critical Traditions in Contemporary Archaeology: Essays in the Philosophy, History, and Socio-Politics of Archaeology*. Cambridge: Cambridge University Press.

Trigger, B.G. 1980. Archaeology and the Image of the American Indian. *American Antiquity* 45: 662–76.

Trigger, B.G. 1989. *A History of Archaeological Thought*. Cambridge: Cambridge University Press.

Trigger, B.G. 1991. Early Native North American Responses to European Contact: Romantic versus Rationalistic Interpretations. *Journal of American History* 4: 1,195–215.

Tringham, R. 1991. Households with Faces: The Challenge of Gender in Prehistoric Architectural Remains. In Gero, J.M. and Conkey, M.W. (eds), *Engendering Archaeology: Women and Prehistory*. Oxford: Blackwell, pp. 93–131.

Vargas Arenas, I. 1995. The Perception of History and Archaeology in Latin America: A Theoretical Approach. In Schmidt, P.R. and Patterson, T.C. (eds), *Making Alternative Histories: The Practice of Archaeology and History in Non-Western Settings*. Santa Fe: School of American Research, pp. 47–68.

Vargas Arenas, I. and Sanoja, M. 1990. Education and the Political Manipulation of History in Venezuela. In Stone, P. and McKenzie, R. (eds), *The Excluded Past: Archaeology in Education*. London: Unwin Hyman, pp. 50–60.

Wall, D. di Zerega. 1994. *The Archaeology of Gender: Separating the Spheres in Urban America*. New York: Plenum.

Watson, P.J. and Kennedy, M.C. 1991. The Development of Horticulture in the Eastern Woodlands of North America: Women's Role. In Gero, J.M. and Conkey, M.W. (eds), *Engendering Archaeology: Women and Prehistory*. Oxford: Blackwell, pp. 255–75.

Weitzenfeld, J.S. 1984. Valid Reasoning by Analogy. *Philosophy of Science* 51: 137–49.

Wobst, M.H. and Keene, A.S. 1983. Archaeological Explanation as Political Economy. In Gero, J.M., Lacy, D.M., and Blake, M.L. (eds), *The Socio-Politics of Archaeology*. Amherst: University of Massachusetts.

Wright, R.P. 1991. Women's Labor and Pottery Production in Prehistory. In Gero, J.M. and Conkey, M.W. (eds), *Engendering Archaeology: Women and Prehistory*. Oxford: Blackwell, pp. 194–223.

Wylie, A. 1990. Feminist Critiques and Archaeological Challenges. In Walde, D. and Willows, N. (eds), *The Archaeology of Gender*. Calgary: University of Calgary Archaeological Association.

Wylie, A. 1991. Gender Theory and the Archaeological Record: Why Is There No Archaeology of Gender? In Gero, J.M. and Conkey, M.W. (eds), *Engendering Archaeology: Women and Prehistory*. Oxford: Blackwell, pp. 31–54.

Wylie, A. 1992. Feminist Theories of Social Power: Some Implications for a Processual Archaeology. *Norwegian Archaeology* 25: 51–68.

Wylie, A. 1993. Invented Lands/Discovered Pasts: The Westward Expansion of Myth and History. *Historical Archaeology* 27(4): 1–19.

Wylie, A. 1997. The Engendering of Archaeology: Refiguring Feminist Science Studies. *Osiris* 12: 80–99.

Wylie, A. 2002. The Constitution of Archaeological Evidence: Gender Politics and Science. In Wylie, A., *Thinking from Things: Essays in the Philosophy of Archaeology*. Berkeley: University of California Press, pp. 185–99.

Yentsch, A. 1994. *A Chesapeake Family and Their Slaves*. Cambridge: Cambridge University Press.

Part III

Sexuality

An introduction

Timothy Insoll

Sexual identity has only very recently become a focus of, as-yet, limited archaeological attention (Schmidt and Voss 2000). Hence as children have themselves been neglected by archaeologists it is fair to surmise that the activities by which they are produced, in addition to many other aspects of sexual identity and activity, have been almost wholly ignored by archaeologists as well. Barbara Voss explores the absence of sexuality within archaeological literature with particular reference to considering how feminist archaeology and queer theory articulate with archaeological investigations of sexuality. This is achieved primarily through a cogent analysis of citation practices within relevant archaeological literature. Hence the chapter by Voss provides a theoretical overview and thus complements those of Alberti and Hays-Gilpin in this part of the Reader, which are more concerned with specific bodies of archaeological material. The three chapters together therefore provide a useful sample of this, fortunately, now growing area of archaeological interest, and one of fundamental importance in reconstructing past identities because these are wholly incomplete when we create asexual or non-sexual pasts, even if the evidence allows us to do otherwise.

Voss's chapter especially shows how the intersection between different identities has to be acknowledged. Here the concern is with gender and sex, but in many other ways identities obviously interrelate and to look at one in isolation is perhaps to only gain a partial view. The different strands of the archaeology of identities function together to create the person (see Conlin Casella and Fowler 2005). Definitional and interpretive complexity is again demanded by Voss because an equivalence between sexuality as an extension of gender is rightly questioned and sexuality in all its manifestations, rather than a simplistic heterosexual model, is explored. Thus the development and application of the term 'queer' is considered and interesting points are made, again through drawing upon the work of Judith Butler (1993a, 1993b), that the 'normative' – essentially what is challenged in Voss's contribution – is created through reference to deviance and in so doing the latter becomes foundational and the normative the 'unstable' edifice. Although the universal aspect of this can be questioned (see my introductory chapter), it further underscores the necessity of at least questioning all our assumptions when it comes to configuring identities within the archaeological record.

The second chapter, by Benjamin Alberti, is concerned with an area of archaeology otherwise under-represented in this Reader, that which can be loosely defined as 'classical', here, late Bronze Age Knossos, Crete. This is an absence in part attributable to the simple fact that the archaeological study of identities still remains an under-researched area in classical archaeology. Moreover Alberti deals with an area of material culture, visual imagery or art, which is perhaps at first glance one of the easiest in which to explore past sexuality. However, this is delusional for pitfalls exist for the unwary for not all is as it may seem if we directly transfer present understandings on to past materials. As Alberti notes, art is not passively reflective of societies' norms, and the deceptive familiarity of art from sites such as Knossos may be, as he further notes, analytically hazardous. This again is a point which can be extended beyond the consideration of sexuality to all the identities under consideration here where art may form the basis, or part thereof, of analysis.

Alberti's chapter in focusing upon 'art' also touches upon themes little explored by other contributors who are more strictly concerned to a greater or lesser extent with archaeological material as more usually defined. Hence the concept of aesthetics is explored, especially in relation to the recently emergent anthropology of aesthetics, and the influence of Judith Butler (1990, 1993, 1993b) with the notion of performance or the 'performative' again acknowledged. Ultimately the construct of an identity 'blueprint' is further shown to be flawed for it is evident from Alberti's work that the 'Knossian sexed body' only emerges in the figurative repertoire in association with specific types of adornment and clothing and in certain performative instances.

The third and final chapter in this section is also concerned with examining gender and sex via the analysis of visual material. However, Kelley Hays-Gilpin's chapter is quite different from Alberti's, obviously in terms of time and space, but also through the primary media being considered – rock art and pottery decoration – and in the use made of ethnography to support and enrich interpretation of the prehistoric imagery considered from the southwest of the United States. Complexity is again signalled in, for instance, her point that if one were to focus upon the female dimension alone and thus neglect the male role in religions in the area, the central point of Navajo and Pueblo religions would be missed – i.e. gender complementarity.

Similarly it is also evident from her analysis that the importance of sex and/or gender identity develops over time and is far from fixed. Additionally these were not always, as Hays-Gilpin notes, necessarily, important attributes of the figures depicted. The two-gender assumption is also challenged, for the existence of gender beyond male and female is also indicated via depictions of cross-gender individuals who appear, specifically, in the Basketmaker III period. What Hays-Gilpin's chapter indicates is the impossibility of achieving the degree of interpretation she can proffer without the accompanying narrative traditions and ethnographic evidence. The juxtaposition with Alberti's contribution is thus salient in this respect: the evidential constraints of the latter, which obviously lacks the ethnography, are noticeable, and hence the recourse made to alternative approaches and data sources, primarily, as described, focusing around aesthetics. Thus the multi- or interdisciplinary approach which the archaeology of identities frequently requires is well indicated by the chapters in this part of the Reader.

Bibliography

Butler, J. 1990. *Gender Trouble: Feminism and the Subversion of Identity*. London: Routledge.
Butler, J. 1993a. *Bodies That Matter: On the Discursive Limits of 'Sex'*. London: Routledge.

Butler, J. 1993b. Imitation and Gender Insubordination. In Abelove, H., Barale, M.A., and Halperin, D. (eds), *The Lesbian and Gay Studies Reader*. New York: Routledge, pp. 307–20.

Conlin Casella, E. and Fowler, C. (eds). 2005. *The Archaeology of Plural and Changing Identities*. New York: Kluwer.

Schmidt, R. and Voss, B. (eds). 2000. *Archaeologies of Sexuality*. London: Routledge.

Chapter 8

Feminisms, queer theories, and the archaeological study of past sexualities

Barbara L. Voss

> There is another social function of gender to be considered and that is the social marking of sexually appropriate partners....If the reader accepts this social function of gender, then an archaeology of gender is an archaeology of sexuality.
>
> Claassen, *Exploring Gender Through Archaeology*

> Gender is out – sex is in.
>
> Dig house graffiti, Çatalhöyük, Turkey, 1998

It has been eight years since Claassen observed that sexuality is intrinsically linked to the archaeological study of gender in the past, but until recently only a few archaeologists have seriously considered how the archaeological record can be used to produce knowledge about past sexualities. Fortunately, in the last three years this situation has significantly changed. There is now emerging a significant corpus of discourse about sexuality and the archaeological record, a constellation of recent publications and theses that demonstrate that an ever-increasing range of sexual topics can be investigated and interrogated through archaeological research.

A review of archaeological studies of sexuality is in some ways premature, for (despite an anonymous archaeologist's glib assertion that 'sex is in') the undertaking is still controversial and contested. Yet even at this early date it is clear that archaeological investigations of sexuality are being informed and influenced by several distinct – and at times competing – intellectual traditions. In this chapter, I particularly consider how feminist archaeology and queer theory articulate with archaeological investigations of sexuality. To do so I step back in time, as archaeologists are wont to do, and discuss the genesis of both feminist archaeology and queer theory in the 1980s and 1990s, examining their relationship to each other through an analysis of citational practices in archaeology. This discussion not only contributes to a review of archaeological research on sexuality but also towards discussions on the sociology of knowledge in archaeology.

Feminist archaeologies: gender, status, and the division of labour

The emergence of feminist archaeology is generally attributed to the 1984 publication 'Archaeology and the Study of Gender' (Conkey and Spector 1984). By the late 1980s, symposia, workshops, and dedicated conferences brought together researchers interested in integrating archaeology, feminist theory, women's studies, and the interpretation of a gendered past. A bloom of publications followed, including the edited volume *Engendering Archaeology* (Gero and Conkey 1991), five conference proceedings (Miller 1988; Willows 1991; Claassen 1992a; du Cros and Smith 1993; Balme and Beck 1995), a special issue of *Historical Archaeology* (Seifert 1991), and several topical monographs (e.g. Ehrenberg 1989; Spector 1993; Gilchrist 1994; Wall 1994). Not all the researchers involved in these projects necessarily identified themselves or their work as 'feminist' (Wylie 1997b). Recent commentaries have thus referred to this body of literature as 'womanist' or 'gender' archaeology (e.g. Joyce and Claassen 1997; Nelson 1997; Gilchrist 1999; Wright 2000). These commentators and others are correct in emphasizing that research on women or gender is not automatically 'feminist'. Nonetheless, I believe that most of the works listed above can be accurately described as 'feminist-inspired', informed by popular, political, and/or academic feminist thought. Additionally, feminist practice in archaeology certainly has not been limited to research on women or gender (Conkey and Wylie 1999; Wylie 2001). Because of this, for the purposes of this chapter I have chosen to refer to this body of work as 'feminist archaeology'.

The development of this diverse body of 'feminist' and 'feminist-inspired' archaeologies occurred at a time when feminist theory and politics in the United States and elsewhere were at a crossroads. In the late 1970s and early 1980s, when Conkey and Spector were authoring their 1984 manifesto, North American feminist politics were focused on what then appeared to be the universal oppression of women by patriarchy. Although the exact nature and mechanisms of patriarchal oppression were debated, this focus was generally (but of course not completely) shared by Marxist, socialist, radical, liberal, and cultural feminisms of the time (Jagger 1983: 5–8). In both the humanities and sciences, the omission of women's experiences and accomplishments in academic and popular discourse was identified as one mechanism by which patriarchal ideology replicated itself by privileging male experience. Feminist scholars in anthropology and other disciplines thus prioritized research that documented women's experiences cross-culturally, especially regarding gender roles and the ways that patriarchy acted on women's lives (Rosaldo and Lamphere 1974; Reiter 1975; Rubin 1975).

Informed by this political and academic climate, Conkey and Spector's 1984 article presented a substantial critique of androcentrism in archaeology. They called for new approaches to archaeological interpretation that would promote gender-inclusive models of the past, question the universality of a rigid sexual division of labour, and challenge the ways that men's purported activities are valued more than those believed to be performed by women. In this way feminist theory would be used in archaeology to combat the effects of present-day sexism on archaeological interpretations. Simultaneously, the critical study of gender in the past would provide new information about the long-term history of gender relations. This core agenda was later reiterated by Conkey and Gero in their 1991 edited volume *Engendering Archaeology* with the added aim of problematizing 'underlying assumptions about gender and difference' (Conkey and Gero 1991: 5). Throughout the late 1980s and early 1990s, these goals were largely adopted by most researchers who identified their research as feminist archaeology, gender archaeology, or the archaeology of women. It is perhaps worth noting that these general aims of feminist archaeology are broadly congruent with feminist interventions into the social sciences in general (Harding 1986, 1987; Wylie 1992, 1997a).

Because Conkey and Spector's 1984 article was widely adopted as a central agenda for feminist archaeological studies for the decade to come, the political and intellectual climate within which they wrote significantly affected the way that sexuality has been addressed within archaeological interpretations. Most of the early studies in archaeology that consciously adopted a feminist approach emphasized the sexual (or gendered) division of labour and indices of gender status, an emphasis typified by Spector's task differentiation framework (Conkey and Spector 1984; Spector 1991). There was a particular emphasis on 'finding' women in the archaeological record by debunking androcentric methods and interpretations, and on highlighting the contributions of women to the past (e.g. Brumfiel 1991; Gero 1991; Wright 1991). At the same time many studies used a materialist approach that viewed women as a gender class, trying to understand how archaeologically identified conditions such as environmental change, state formation, or the introduction of agriculture intensified or changed women's status (e.g. Claassen 1991; Hastorf 1991; Watson and Kennedy 1991). The prominence of materialist and empiricist research in North American feminist archaeology has been discussed elsewhere (e.g. Wylie 1996: 320–5; Nelson 1997: Ch. 5; Gilchrist 1999: Ch. 3) and is attributable to both the then-dominant 'New Archaeology' paradigm and also the emphasis on socialist political theory in North American feminism in the 1970s and early 1980s.

These shared emphases in early feminist archaeological studies had significant implications for the ways that issues of sexuality began to be discussed in archaeological interpretation. Feminist archaeologists usually adopted the sex/gender system model, in which gender is taken to be the cultural expression of biological sex (Rubin 1975). Within this framework, sexuality is generally seen as derivative of gender, one of many aspects of social life that is structured by sex/gender systems. As a result, to paraphrase Brumfiel (1992), during the first decade of feminist archaeological practice, 'Gender...[stole] the show'. Feminist archaeological research rarely addressed the topic of sexuality, instead treating sexuality predominantly as a function of gender rather than as a distinct aspect of social relations (see Rubin 1984: 309 for a general discussion of this point). For example heterosexual marriage has been examined by many feminist archaeologists as a locus for the gendered organization of labour (which, of course, it often is) but only rarely with a consideration of how marriage relates to the regulation and expression of sexuality (e.g. Deagan 1983; Gibb and King 1991; Jackson 1991; Wright 1991; Wall 1994).

In noting these trends, I am not suggesting that the initial goals of feminist-inspired archaeological projects negatively affected archaeological interpretations of sexuality. On the contrary, by highlighting gender as a subject of archaeological research, and by foregrounding interpersonal relationships as an arena of social action, feminist interventions in archaeology created an intellectual climate within which research on sexuality became increasingly viable. Exactly how the priorities and conventions of feminist archaeological practices came to influence archaeological investigations of sexuality is, however, of great interest, and is a topic that I return to later in this essay.

The Sex Wars, AIDS, and queer theory: sexuality moves front and centre

During the emergence of feminist archaeologies in the 1980s and early 1990s, North American feminist politics negotiated a series of epistemological crises that shifted feminist attention towards an examination of differences between women. Among other issues such as race and class, feminist scholars and activists undertook projects that theorized sexuality in ways markedly different from previous treatments of sexuality as some sort of an extension of gender. In the late 1970s works by lesbian and gay scholars (e.g. Katz 1976; Rowbotham and Weeks 1977; Weeks 1977; Smith-Rosenberg 1979), the English translation of Foucault's *The History of Sexuality* (1978), and, in anthropology, Ortner and Whitehead's *Sexual Meanings* (1981) challenged conventional feminist wisdom about the primacy of gender as a vector of oppression. By the early 1980s sexuality had become a flashpoint of feminist debate (the so-called 'Sex Wars'), and the relationship of sexuality to patriarchy and liberation was hotly contested (Rubin 1984; Vance 1984; Duggan and Hunter 1995). Homosexuality, pornography, sadomasochism, prostitution, monogamy, rape, promiscuity, butch–femme relationships, interracial and inter-generational sex – these and other sexual practices became prominent topics of often acrimonious public forums and written discourse. Concurrently, the emerging AIDS pandemic propelled male same-sex sexual practices and commercial sex into explicit public discussion through medical, public health, and activist movements, bringing coverage of condom distribution, prostitution, anal and oral sex, and public sex into mainstream print and television media.[1]

Discussions about the politics of sexuality during the early and mid-1980s were at times bitter (see, for example, Vance's discussion of the 1982 Barnard College conference [Vance 1984] or Crimp and Roston's pictorial history of ACT UP [Crimp and Rolston 1990]), but it would be a mistake to characterize this period solely as an era of contentious debate. As Rubin urged, 'The time has come to think about sex' (1984: 267), and thinking about sex was precisely what many feminist, lesbian, and gay researchers, writers, and activists did. What emerged was a sense that theories of gender were not fully adequate to address sexuality, either as a social practice or as a vector of oppression (Vance 1984: 10): that 'it is essential to separate gender and sexuality analytically to more accurately reflect their separate social existence' (Rubin 1984: 308). By the late 1980s and early 1990s, the call to develop theories of sexuality was being answered by an expanding body of literature that addressed the political and cultural positions of gays, lesbians, bisexuals, transsexuals, sex workers, sadomasochists, and others – a diverse conglomeration of sexual 'minorities' who were increasingly identified as 'queer' (de Lauretis 1991: v). Sedgwick's *Epistemology of the Closet* (1990), Butler's *Gender Trouble* (1990) and *Bodies That Matter* (1993a), Warner's *Fear of a Queer Planet* (1993), and two special issues of *differences* (vol. 5 no. 2 and vol. 6 nos. 2 and 3) all signalled the consolidation of an approach to theorizing sexuality that crossed gender lines, integrating (but not collapsing) sexual theories related to masculinity and femininity and to heterosexuality and homosexuality.

Most importantly the emergence of queer theory within academia marked a radical shift towards positioning abject and stigmatized sexual identities as important entry points to the production of knowledge (Butler 1993b). A move to destabilize sexual and gender categories was and still is an integral part of this process. The adoption of the inclusive moniker 'queer' reflected the rejection of taxonomic sexual categories (e.g. homosexual, heterosexual, fetishist, pederast) that initially had been established through sexological discourse in the late 1800s and early 1900s (see Bland and Doan 1998 for a discussion of sexology and sexual taxonomies). Instead the term 'queer' reflects an inclusive standpoint based on difference from or opposition to the ideology of hetero-normativity (Warner 1993: xxiii). Thus queer theory and queer politics represent a critical moment in the history of Western sexuality in which sexual minorities and deviants who were previously deemed by legal statutes and medical/psychological diagnoses are instead creating an always contested and renegotiated group identity based on difference from the norm – in other words a postmodern version of identity politics (see Butler 1993a: 21). Essential to this post-structuralist deployment of opposition is the tenet that what is 'normative' is actually constructed through reference to deviance. Thus it is 'deviance' that is foundational and the 'normative' that is unstable (Butler 1993b).

This emphasis on 'opposition to the normative' and on the simultaneous destabilization of the normative are aspects of queer theory that allow great interdisciplinary mobility, as they permit theoretical concepts initially applied to issues of sexual identity and the oppression of sexual minorities to be deployed in studies of other social subgroups as well as in studies of the written and spoken word, the built environment, material objects, and other products of culture. It is, I argue below, precisely this emphasis on normativity and opposition that poses both opportunities and challenges for archaeologists engaging in studies of past sexualities.

Intersections: connections between archaeology and feminist theories of sexuality

These brief histories reveal that feminist archaeology and queer theory share certain temporal markers: both were founded on the political and academic feminisms of the late 1970s and early 1980s, emerged in opposition to the dominant political and academic climate of the early and mid-1980s, and, after a period of uncertain exploration, achieved a degree of academic legitimacy and popularity in the early 1990s. Of course this historical narrative may be unduly influenced by the archaeological tendency to interpret cultural developments through the 'formative/pre-classic/classic/post-classic' model. Nonetheless, I suggest that queer theory and feminist archaeology shared somewhat parallel chronological developments.

Despite their parallel trajectories, queer theory and feminist archaeology were rarely in dialogue with each other. Queer theory, grounded in grass-roots political activist movements such as Queer Nation (Berlant and Freeman 1993), arose to meet the particular challenges of sexual politics during the neo-conservative 1980s, while feminist archaeology emerged primarily within academia as a critique of androcentric archaeological practices and interpretations. However, many of the archaeologists involved in the genesis of feminist archaeology were (and still are) themselves feminist activists, concerned not only with representations of gender in the past but also with the politics of gender and sexuality in the present (Wylie 1991; Hanen and Kelley 1992). What, then, were the intersections between the growing feminist theorization of sexuality in the 1980s and the emergence of feminist archaeology? To what extent has queer theory informed feminist archaeologies in recent years?[2]

To consider these questions I reviewed bibliographies of feminist archaeological studies published throughout the 1980s and 1990s. Citational practices are one way in which scholars acknowledge their intellectual influences and position themselves within the larger field of academia, and thus bibliographies provide one imperfect measure of the extent to which particular schools of thought are being consulted and invoked by scholars in different sub-fields. My review focused primarily on nine edited volumes and proceedings which had been generated through conferences, conference symposia, and lecture series (Miller 1988; Gero and Conkey 1991; Walde and Willows 1991; Claassen 1992a; du Cros and Smith 1993; Balme and Beck 1995; Wright 1996; Claassen and Joyce 1997; Moore and Scott 1997). Because several of these volumes were limited to studies of prehistory, I also reviewed the 'gender' issue of *Historical Archaeology* (vol. 25 no. 4) and two monographs (Spector 1993; Wall 1994) to increase the representation of historical archaeology within the sample. Finally I included Conkey and Spector's 1984 article as well as three recently published syntheses of feminist archaeology (Conkey and Gero 1997; Nelson 1997; Gilchrist 1999). Together these sources represent 220 papers, articles, or monographs by authors who identify their work as feminist and/or gender archaeology. Although such a sample is not meant to be exhaustive or even statistically representative (for example few journal articles are included), it does include papers from a broad geographic and temporal distribution, spanning 1984 to 1999 and including authors from the United States, Australia, Canada, and Great Britain. In reviewing these works I noted citations belonging to three categories: first, early works about sexuality by feminist and gay and lesbian scholars dating to the 1970s and early 1980s; second, the literature surrounding the 'Sex Wars' of the mid-1980s; and, third, the emergent queer theory canon whose benchmarks include publications such as Sedgwick's *Epistemology of the Closet* (1990) and Butler's *Gender Trouble* (1990).[3]

Before beginning this exercise I expected to identify two trends: first, that feminist archaeologists have rarely, if at all, engaged with non-archaeological works on sexuality, and, second, that it is only in the last few years that queer theory has entered feminist archaeological discourse at all. My suppositions were wrong on both counts. I found that 18 per cent of the 220 works reviewed cited one or more works that fall into one of the three categories described above. This percentage did not increase or decrease markedly with time, but vacillated within a fairly stable range of 10 per cent to 35 per cent from year to year. This suggests that, while sexuality has not been a central topic of archaeological interpretation (Voss and Schmidt 2000), archaeologists have, over the last 15 years, consistently considered sexuality to be one important aspect of gender-focused research.

Second, I found that the relationship between queer theory and feminist archaeology is, while uneven, by no means absent. Although almost none of the works I reviewed referenced publications generated during the 'Sex Wars' of the mid-1980s, 'queer theory' publications by Foucault (especially *The History of Sexuality*, 1978), Butler (both *Gender Trouble*, 1990, and *Bodies That Matter*, 1993a) and Grosz (*Sexual Subversions*, 1989 and *Sexy Bodies*, 1995, with Probyn) were cited with regularity. Queer theory citations were especially common in introductions to edited volumes and conference proceedings and rare in archaeological case studies, suggesting that queer theory has been used predominantly to theorize the feminist archaeological project as a whole rather than to interpret archaeological evidence.

Finally the papers and monographs that I reviewed relied overwhelmingly on one source, Ortner and Whitehead's *Sexual Meanings* (1981), which accounted for over 30 per cent of all noted citations about sexuality. An edited volume of anthropological case studies generated in the mid-1970s, most (but not all) contributed papers in *Sexual Meanings* are focused on band, tribe, or chiefdom societies (ibid.: x), interpret gender and sexuality through a focus on symbolic constructs and the sex/gender system model (ibid.: 1–9), and emphasize 'considerations of hierarchical power and differential prestige between men and women' (Gilchrist 1999: 8). The prominence of *Sexual Meanings* as a source about sexuality for feminist-inspired archaeological research has not diminished with time, but appears to be as strong now as it was in the first decade of feminist archaeological enquiry. The persistent citations of *Sexual Meanings* may indicate a degree of theoretical conservatism in feminist archaeology with regard to conceptions of sexuality and its relationship to gender. As Roberts has noted, 'The paradox is that those interested in an archaeology of gender cannot afford to challenge the framework assumptions and paradigms of research practice' (1993: 18). In other words it is difficult for those feminist archaeologists who are occupied with legitimizing and developing gender studies simultaneously to embrace queer theories that deconstruct gender and sexuality. For example Butler's position that 'biological sex' is a discursive regulatory practice (Butler 1993a: 1) could be seen to challenge archaeological studies of gender that use physical indices to assign a 'sex' to human skeletal remains. Deconstructions of sex and gender destabilize precisely those categories (e.g. male, female, woman, man) that are necessarily invoked to model engendered social worlds of the past.[4] The fear of erasing or compromising 'gender' as a category of archaeological analysis may account for the apparent reluctance of many archaeological researchers consistently and critically to engage with queer theory.

At the same time there are also aspects of queer theory that resist its wholesale importation into archaeology. The feminist theories of sexuality that emerged during the particular sexual politics of the 1980s and 1990s addressed the conditions of modern, Western, and predominantly urban sexual subcultures. Rubin particularly notes that the organization of gender and sexuality 'as two distinct arenas of social practice' (1984: 308) may be specific to Western industrial societies. The enduring appeal of the sex/gender system model within feminist archaeology may be because it is sometimes a more appropriate, if imperfect, approach to considering sexuality and gender in pre-industrial and kinship-based cultures (Rubin 1975). Likewise, queer theorists tend to emphasize analyses of citational texts, cinema, and other representations at the expense of historical or social science research (Rubin 1994: 93) – what the historian Duggan has termed 'the discipline problem' (1995).[5] Broken pots, faunal remains, collapsed structures, burials, soil residues, and other evidentiary sources in archaeology rarely resemble the literary works or films that often form the basis of queer theory analyses (e.g. Butler 1993a). It is not always immediately apparent how to apply reading methodologies developed for modern cultural texts to the archaeological record.

Because of the temporal and geographic specificity of queer theory, archaeologists have important contributions to make in developing theories of gender and sexuality that can be applied to material evidence and that are appropriate for analysis of non-'Western' and non-'modern' cultures. Archaeology faces the unique challenge of stretching theories of sexuality in new chronological and cultural directions and in probing the cultural and representational limits of distinctions between gender and sexuality. While neither feminist nor queer theories should be applied unquestioningly to the past, together they provide powerful tools that can broaden archaeological interpretations of past sexualities.

Acknowledgements

This material is based upon work supported under a National Science Foundation Graduate Fellowship. My thanks to Meg Conkey, Alison Wylie, Liz Perry, Rob Schmidt, El Casella, Masha Raskolnikov, Deb Cohler, and Amy Ramsay, whose insightful comments and support greatly improved this essay.

Notes

1. These debates are perhaps best exemplified by two contradictory publications on lesbian sadomasochism, *Coming to Power* (SAMOIS 1982) and *Against Sadomasochism* (Linden *et al.* 1982), and by the controversies over the role of gay male bathhouses in safer-sex campaigns and AIDS transmission (e.g. Bayer 1989: Ch. 2; Berube 1996; Dangerous Bedfellows 1996). Excellent resources on this period include *Pleasure and Danger: Exploring Female Sexuality* (Vance 1984), *Powers of Desire: The Politics of Sexuality* (Snitow *et al.* 1983), and *Sex Wars: Sexual Dissent and Political Culture* (Duggan and Hunter 1995).

2. One could also, of course, ask the extent to which feminist archaeology affected the growing feminist theorizations of sexuality. However, my readings suggest that feminist scholars outside archaeology are not familiar with feminist archaeological projects, a point also noted by Conkey and Gero (1997: 424–5 – but see Rubin 2000 for a rare exception). In part this is because it is only recently that feminist archaeological work is becoming visible to cross-disciplinary audiences through topical monographs (e.g. Spector 1993; Gilchrist 1994; Wall 1994) and the appearance of archaeological case studies and reviews in multidisciplinary edited volumes and journals (e.g. Gero 1988; Conkey and Williams 1991; Bahn 1992; Conkey and Tringham 1995; Wright 2000).

3. Data and tabulations from this bibliographic review are on file with the author.

4. Note, however, that some feminist archaeologists (e.g. Joyce 1996, 2000) have found that models of gender performativity and other deconstructive approaches

to gender actually enhance the archaeological 'visibility' of prehistoric gendered identities and practices.

5. With this in mind it is not surprising that one of the most prominent uses of queer theory in archaeology at present is found in the interpretation of archaeologically recovered representational imagery, as in the works of Joyce (1996, 2000), Meskell (1996, 1998, 2000), and Vasey (1998) on imagery of the body in prehistoric Mesoamerica, Egypt, and Europe, respectively.

Bibliography

Bahn, P.G. 1992. Review of *Engendering Archaeology*. *Journal of Gender Studies* 1: 338–44.

Balme, J. and Beck, W. (eds). 1995. *Gendered Archaeology: The Second Australian Women in Archaeology Conference*. Canberra: ANU Press.

Bayer, R. 1989. *Private Acts, Social Consequences: AIDS and the Politics of Public Health*. New York: The Free Press.

Berlant, L. and Freeman, E. 1993. Queer Nationality. In Warner, M. (ed.), *Fear of a Queer Planet: Queer Politics and Social Theory*. Minneapolis: University of Minnesota Press, pp. 193–229.

Berube, A. 1996. The History of Gay Bathhouses. In Dangerous Bedfellows (eds), *Policing Public Sex*. Boston, MA: South End Press, pp. 187–221.

Bland, L. and Doan, L. (eds). 1998. *Sexology in Culture: Labeling Bodies and Desires*. Chicago: University of Chicago Press.

Brumfiel, E.M. 1991. Weaving and Cooking: Women's Production in Aztec Mexico. In Gero, J.M. and Conkey, M.W. (eds), *Engendering Archaeology: Women and Prehistory*. Cambridge, MA: Blackwell, pp. 224–54.

Brumfiel, E. 1992. Distinguished Lecture in Archaeology: Breaking and Entering the Ecosystem – Gender, Class, and Faction Steal the Show. *American Anthropologist* 91: 551–67.

Butler, J. 1990. *Gender Trouble: Feminism and the Subversion of Identity*. New York: Routledge.

Butler, J. 1993a. *Bodies That Matter: On the Discursive Limits of 'Sex'*. London: Routledge.

Butler, J. 1993b. Imitation and Gender Insubordination. In Abelove, H., Barale, M.A., and Halperin, D. (eds), *The Lesbian and Gay Studies Reader*. New York: Routledge, pp. 307–20.

Claassen, C.P. 1991. Gender, Shellfishing, and the Shell Mound Archaic. In Gero, J.M. and Conkey, M.W. (eds), *Engendering Archaeology: Women and Prehistory*. Cambridge, MA: Blackwell, pp. 276–300.

Claassen, C. (ed.). 1992a. *Exploring Gender through Archaeology: Selected Papers from the 1991 Boone Conference*. Madison, WI: Prehistory Press.

Claassen, C. 1992b. Questioning Gender: An Introduction. In Claassen, C. (ed.), *Exploring Gender through Archaeology: Selected Papers from the 1991 Boone Conference*. Madison, WI: Prehistory Press, pp. 1–10.

Claassen, C. and Joyce, R.A. (eds). 1997. *Women in Prehistory: North America and Mesoamerica*. Philadelphia: University of Pennsylvania Press.

Conkey, M.W. and Gero, J. 1991. Tensions, Pluralities, and Engendering Archaeology: An Introduction to Women and Prehistory. In Gero, J.M. and Conkey, M.W. (eds), *Engendering Archaeology: Women and Prehistory*. Cambridge, MA: Blackwell, pp. 3–30.

Conkey, M.W. and Gero, J. 1997. From Programme to Practice: Gender and Feminism in Archaeology. *Annual Review of Anthropology* 26: 411–37.

Conkey, M.W. and Spector, J.D. 1984. Archaeology and the Study of Gender. *Advances in Archaeological Method and Theory* 7: 1–32.

Conkey, M.W. and Tringham, R.E. 1995. Archaeology and the Goddess: Exploring the Contours of Feminist Archaeology. In Stanton, D.C. and Stewart, A.J. (eds), *Feminisms in the Academy*. Ann Arbor: University of Michigan Press, pp. 199–247.

Conkey, M.W. with Williams, S.H. 1991. Original Narratives: The Political Economy of Gender in Archaeology. In di Leonardo, M. (ed.), *Gender at the Crossroads of Knowledge: Feminist Anthropology in the Postmodern Era*. Berkeley: University of California Press, pp. 102–39.

Conkey, M.W. and Wylie, A. 1999. Summary of 'Doing Archaeology as a Feminist: Moving from Theory to Practice'. *Newsletter of the Women in Archaeology Interest Group, Society for American Archaeology* 1(2): 3–4.

Crimp, D. and Rolston, A. 1990. *AIDS Demo Graphics*. Seattle: Bay Press.

Dangerous Bedfellows (eds). 1996. *Policing Public Sex: Queer Politics and the Future of AIDS Activism*. Boston, MA: South End Press.

de Lauretis, T. 1991. Queer Theory: Lesbian and Gay Sexualities: An Introduction. *Differences* 3(2): iii–xviii.

Deagan, K. (ed.). 1983. *Spanish St. Augustine: The Archaeology of a Colonial Creole Community*. New York: Academic Press.

du Cros, H. and Smith, L. (eds). 1993. *Women in Archaeology: A Feminist Critique*. Canberra: Department of Prehistory, Australian National University.

Duggan, L. 1995. The Discipline Problem: Queer Theory Meets Lesbian and Gay History. *GLQ: A Journal of Lesbian and Gay Studies* 2(3): 179–92.

Duggan, L. and Hunter, N.D. (eds). 1995. *Sex Wars: Sexual Dissent and Political Culture*. New York: Routledge.

Ehrenberg, M. 1989. *Women in Prehistory*. London: British Museum Publications.

Foucault, M. (trans. Robert Hurley). 1978. *The History of Sexuality, Vol. I: An Introduction*. New York: Pantheon.

Gero, J.M. 1988. Gender Bias in Archaeology: Here, Then, and Now. In Rosser, S.V. (ed.), *Feminism within the Science and Health Care Professions: Overcoming Resistance*. New York: Pergamon Press, pp. 33–43.

Gero, J. 1991. Genderlithics: Women's Roles in Stone Tool Production. In Gero, J.M. and Conkey, M.W. (eds), *Engendering Archaeology: Women and Prehistory*. Cambridge, MA: Blackwell, pp. 163–93.

Gero, J.M. and Conkey, M.W. (eds). 1991. *Engendering Archaeology: Women and Prehistory*. Cambridge, MA: Blackwell.

Gibb, J.G. and King, J.A. 1991. Gender, Activity Areas, and Homelots in the 17th Century Chesapeake Region. *Historical Archaeology* 25(4): 109–31.

Gilchrist, R. 1994. *Gender and Material Culture: The Archaeology of Religious Women*. New York: Routledge.

Gilchrist, R. 1999. *Gender and Archaeology: Contesting the Past*. London: Routledge.

Grosz, E.A. 1989. *Sexual Subversions: Three French Feminists*. Sydney: Allen and Unwin.

Grosz, E.A. and Probyn, E. (eds). 1995. *Sexy Bodies: The Strange Carnalities of Feminism*. London: Routledge.

Hanen, M.P. and Kelley, J. 1992. Gender and Archaeological Knowledge. In Embree, L. (ed.), *Metaarchaeology*. Boston, MA: Reidel, pp. 195–227.

Harding, S. 1986. *The Science Question in Feminism*. Ithaca, NY: Cornell University Press.

Harding, S. 1987. Introduction: Is there a Feminist Method? In Harding, S. (ed.), *Feminism and Methodology: Social Science Issues*. Bloomington: Indiana University Press, pp. 1–14.

Hastorf, C.A. 1991. Gender, Space, and Food in Prehistory. In Gero, J.M. and Conkey, M.W. (eds), *Engendering Archaeology: Women and Prehistory*. Cambridge, MA: Blackwell, pp. 132–62.

Jackson, T.L. 1991. Pounding Acorn: Women's Production as Social and Economic Focus. In Gero, J.M. and Conkey, M.W. (eds), *Engendering Archaeology: Women and Prehistory*. Cambridge, MA: Blackwell, pp. 301–28.

Jagger, A.M. 1983. *Feminist Politics and Human Nature*. Sussex: Rowman and Allanheld.

Joyce, R.A. 1996. The Construction of Gender in Classic Maya Monuments. In Wright, R.P. (ed.), *Gender and Archaeology*. Philadelphia: University of Pennsylvania Press, pp. 167–98.

Joyce, R. 2000. A Precolumbian Gaze: Male Sexuality Among the Ancient Maya. In Schmidt, R.A. and Voss, B.L. (eds), *Archaeologies of Sexuality*. London: Routledge, pp. 263–86.

Joyce, R.A. and Claassen, C. 1997. Women in the Ancient Americas: Archaeologists, Gender, and the Making of Prehistory. In Claassen, C. and Joyce, R.A. (eds), *Women in Prehistory: North America and Mesoamerica*. Philadelphia: University of Pennsylvania Press, pp. 1–14.

Katz, J. 1976. *Gay American History: Lesbians and Gay Men in the U.S.A.* New York: Thomas Crowell.

Linden, R.R., Pagano, D.R., Russell, D.E.H., and Star, S.L. (eds). 1982. *Against Sadomasochism: A Radical Feminist Analysis*. East Palo Alto, CA: Frog In The Well Press.

Meskell, L. 1996. The Somatization of Archaeology: Institutions, Discourses, Corporeality. *Norwegian Archaeological Review* 29(1): 2–16.

Meskell, L. 1998. An Archaeology of Social Relations in an Egyptian Village. *Journal of Archaeological Method and Theory* 5(3): 209–43.

Meskell, L. 2000. Re-Em(bed)ing Sex: Domesticity, Sexuality, and Ritual in New Kingdom Egypt. In Schmidt, R.A. and Voss, B.L. (eds), *Archaeologies of Sexuality*. London: Routledge, pp. 253–62.

Miller, V.E. (ed.). 1988. *The Role of Gender in Precolumbian Art and Architecture*. Washington, DC: University Press of America.

Moore, J. and Scott, E. (eds). 1997. *Invisible People and Processes: Writing Gender and Childhood into European Archaeology*. London: Leicester University Press.

Nelson, S.M. 1997. *Gender In Archaeology: Analyzing Power and Prestige*. Walnut Creek, CA: AltaMira Press.

Ortner, S.B. and Whitehead, H. (eds). 1981. *Sexual Meanings: The Cultural Construction of Gender and Sexuality*. Cambridge: Cambridge University Press.

Reiter, R.R. (ed.). 1975. *Toward an Anthropology of Women*. New York: Monthly Review Press.

Roberts, C. 1993. A Critical Approach to Gender as a Category of Analysis in Archaeology. In du Cros, H. and Smith, L. (eds), *Women in Archaeology: A Feminist Critique*. Canberra: Department of Prehistory, Australian National University, pp. 16–21.

Rosaldo, M.Z. and Lamphere, L. (eds). 1974. *Women, Culture, and Society*. Stanford, CA: Stanford University Press.

Rowbotham, S. and Weeks, J. 1977. *Socialism and the New Life: The Personal and Sexual Politics of Edward Carpenter and Havelock Ellis*. London: Pluto Press.

Rubin, G. 1975. The Traffic in Women: Notes on the 'Political Economy' of Sex. In Reiter, R.R. (ed.), *Toward an Anthropology of Women*. New York: Monthly Review Press, pp. 157–210.

Rubin, G. 1984. Thinking Sex: Notes for a Radical Theory of the Politics of Sexuality. In Vance, C.S. (ed.), *Pleasure and Danger: Exploring Female Sexuality*. London: Pandora, pp. 267–319.

Rubin, G. 1994. Sexual Traffic: An Interview with Judith Butler. *differences: A Journal of Feminist Cultural Studies* 6(2+3): 62–99.

Rubin, G. 2000. Sites, Settlements, and Urban Sex: Archaeology and the Study of Gay Leathermen in San Francisco, 1955–1995. In Schmidt, R.A. and Voss, B.L. (eds), *Archaeologies of Sexuality*. London: Routledge, pp. 62–88.

SAMOIS (ed.). 1982. *Coming to Power: Writings and Graphics on Lesbian S/M*. Boston, MA: Alyson Publications.

Schmidt, R.A. and Voss, B.L. (eds). 2000. *Archaeologies of Sexuality*. London: Routledge.

Sedgwick, E.K. 1990. *Epistemology of the Closet*. Berkeley: University of California Press.

Seifert, D.J. (ed.). 1991. *Historical Archaeology: Gender in Historical Archaeology* 25(4).

Smith-Rosenberg, C. 1979. The Female World of Love and Ritual: Relations Between Women in Nineteenth-Century America. In Cott, N.F. and Pleck, E.H. (eds), *A Heritage of Her Own*. New York: Simon and Schuster, Touchstone, pp. 311–42.

Snitow, A., Stansell, C., and Thompson, S. (eds). 1983. *Powers of Desire: The Politics of Sexuality*. New York: Monthly Review Press.

Spector, J.D. 1991. What this Awl Means: Toward a Feminist Archaeology. In Gero, J.M. and Conkey, M.W. (eds), *Engendering Archaeology: Women and Prehistory*. Cambridge, MA: Blackwell, pp. 388–406.

Spector, J.D. 1993. *What This Awl Means: Feminist Archaeology at a Wahpeton Dakota Village*. St Paul, MN: Minnesota Historical Society Press.

Vance, C.S. (ed.). 1984. *Pleasure and Danger: Exploring Female Sexuality*. New York: Routledge and Kegan Paul.

Vasey, P.L. 1998. Intimate Sexual Relations in Prehistory: Lessons from the Japanese Macaques. *World Archaeology* 29(3): 407–25.

Voss, B.L. and Schmidt, R.A. 2000. Archaeologies of Sexuality: An Introduction. In Schmidt, R.A. and Voss, B.L. (eds), *Archaeologies of Sexuality*. London: Routledge, pp. 1–34.

Walde, D. and Willows, N.D. (eds). 1991. *The Archaeology of Gender: Proceedings of the Twenty-Second Annual Conference of the Archaeological Association of the University of Calgary*. Calgary: Archaeological Association of the University of Calgary.

Wall, D. di Zerega. 1994. *The Archaeology of Gender: Separating the Spheres in Urban America*. New York: Plenum.

Warner, M. (ed.). 1993. *Fear of a Queer Planet: Queer Politics and Social Theory*. Minneapolis: University of Minnesota Press.

Watson, P.J. and Kennedy, M.C. 1991. The Development of Horticulture in the Eastern Woodlands: Women's Role. In Gero, J.M. and Conkey, M.W. (eds), *Engendering Archaeology: Women and Prehistory*. Cambridge, MA: Blackwell, pp. 255–75.

Weeks, J. 1977. *Coming Out: Homosexual Politics in Britain from the Nineteenth Century to the Present*. London: Quartet.

Wright, R.P. 1991. Women's Labor and Pottery Production in Prehistory. In Gero, J.M. and Conkey, M.W. (eds), *Engendering Archaeology: Women and Prehistory*. Cambridge, MA: Blackwell, pp. 194–223.

Wright, R.P. (ed.). 1996. *Gender and Archaeology*. Philadelphia: University of Pennsylvania Press.

Wright, R.P. 2000. Digging Women: Feminism Comes to Archaeology. *The Women's Review of Books* 17(5): 18–19.

Wylie, A. 1991. Feminist Critiques and Archaeological Challenges. In Walde, D. and Willows, N.D. (eds), *The Archaeology of Gender: Proceedings of the Twenty-Second Annual Conference of the Archaeological Association of the University of Calgary*. Calgary: Archaeological Association of the University of Calgary, pp. 17–23.

Wylie, A. 1992. Reasoning About Ourselves: Feminist Methodology in the Social Sciences. In Harvey, E. and Okruhlik, K. (eds), *Women and Reason*. Ann Arbor: University of Michigan Press, pp. 225–44.

Wylie, A. 1996. The Constitution of Archaeological Evidence: Gender Politics and Science. In Galison, P. and Stump, D.J. (eds), *The Disunity of Science: Boundaries, Contexts, Power*. Stanford, CA: Stanford University Press, pp. 311–43.

Wylie, A. 1997a. Good Science, Bad Science, or Science as Usual? Feminist Critiques of Science. In Hager, L.D. (ed.), *Women and Human Evolution*. London: Routledge, pp. 29–55.

Wylie, A. 1997b. The Engendering of Archaeology: Refiguring Feminist Science Studies. *Osiris* 12: 80–99.

Wylie, A. 2001. Doing Social Science as a Feminist: The Engendering of Archaeology. In Creager, A.N.H., Lunbeck, E., and Schiebinger, L. (eds), *Feminism in Twentieth Century Science, Technology and Medicine*. Chicago: University of Chicago Press, pp. 23–45.

Chapter 9

Faience goddesses and ivory bull-leapers

The aesthetics of sexual difference at Late Bronze Age Knossos

Benjamin Alberti

Introduction

The artworks from Knossos, Crete, are traditionally interpreted as integral to a cultural visual aesthetic which embraced the greater part of the Aegean and endured for at least two millennia. Sophisticated studies include the search for schools of painters (Cameron 1975), individual styles and portraiture (Preziosi and Hitchcock 1999: 143), or the classification of iconographic groups (e.g. Younger 1993). The norms of the societies in question are understood to be produced in the imagery, among which the clear-cut distinction between men's and women's roles and male and female symbolism occupies a central position. Such studies are essential for any investigation of the art of the Aegean, but, as Coote and Shelton (1992a: 6) have remarked in the case of anthropology, stylistic analyses are a means to an end, not the end itself. There is an almost complete lack of critical discussions of art, aesthetics, and sexed differences within this literature. There is a need, therefore, to move beyond the classificatory or descriptive tendency in Bronze Age Aegean art studies to a consideration of recent developments in theory on art and aesthetics and, simultaneously, to begin a detailed engagement with the particularities of specific 'aesthetics' of sexual difference.

In this chapter I argue both against art as passively reflective of society's norms and against a binary organization to sex as a natural fact of the body which is a priori and central to representations of bodies. I present a general theoretical argument about the nature of human–object relations, especially in the context of human imagery, as well as a specific argument about the representation of sexual difference at Knossos. The latter serves to illustrate how a particular regime of sexual difference is both expressed by and generated through figurative imagery and, crucially, how that imagery articulates with particular instances of practice. Aesthetic and formal qualities of the imagery are understood to act as the channels for such connections. Rather than considering meaning as symbolically overlain or applied to static and arbitrary material (artefactual or corporeal), I take a relational view of 'art objects' (Gell 1998) and a processual view of the constitution of gendered identity. As such there is no atemporal, fixed 'core' to a person's identity – such as the peg of a natural, biological sex upon which culturally constituted gender is hung – outside the acts and gestures that constitute it (Butler 1990). Further, art objects are the objectification of, and the conduit for, agency and social relationships. The aesthetic and formal qualities of the objects in question constitute the crucial link between concepts of the body, their representation, and social practice.

Aesthetics is frequently treated as the response to visual stimuli and/or the appreciation of beauty. In its broader meaning, however, it encompasses sense perceptions in general (Firth 1992). The anthropology of aesthetics, as distinct from the anthropology of art, has emerged relatively recently (see Coote and Shelton 1992b) – a trend yet to be reflected in archaeology – and has generally concentrated on the visual as opposed to the more general sense of aesthetics. A possible reason for the avoidance of sense perception more generally could well be the analytical 'softness' or subjectivity that such an approach would appear to imply, reflecting the common (and possibly misplaced) critique of the universalizing tendencies of aesthetics in general (see Gell 1999a). Similar criticism of broadly phenomenological studies in archaeology (e.g. Tilley 1994), in which the particular 'embodied' experience of the archaeologist is apparently generalized to encompass the life world of past peoples, may reflect a suspicion that such an approach can create only the vaguest of (and therefore virtually meaningless) generalities about archaeological objects.

Gell (e.g. 1999a) has been particularly critical of the aesthetic turn in anthropology, arguing that an anthropological theory of art must make a complete break with aesthetics (1992: 42; 1999b: 210). However, Gell does not in fact advocate the abandonment of aesthetics altogether. His critique, rather, is centred on those who see in aesthetics a universalizing potential or those who tend to 'reify the aesthetic response' independently of social context (Gell 1998: 4). Part of the problem is the narrowness with which aesthetics has become defined. While I agree with Coote (1992: 246) that the category of 'visual art' has become so broad as to subsume many 'aesthetic' qualities within contemporary theory, I nonetheless concur with Gell (1998: 82) that the aesthetic response cannot be treated in isolation from the production of artworks and their social context. However, Gell's (1998: 81) claim that the pure aesthetic response is a myth is perhaps less contentious than he suspected. I believe the apparent dichotomy between artwork and aesthetic approaches can be largely transcended in analysis by recognizing the impact and potential of aesthetic responses within a particular social (or cultural) frame.

Within these discussions the status of the 'object' is of course of central importance for archaeology. There is a general consensus in certain archaeological and anthropological circles that a focus on the formal and active qualities of objects as objects is of importance if we are more fully to appreciate their roles in mediating, generating, and changing social relations (e.g. Gell 1998; Gosden and Marshall 1999). Art objects can be usefully thought of as exercising or referring to a particular type of agency, just as bodies can also act as art objects, blurring the theoretical distinction between the bodies of things and humans (Appadurai 1986; Gell 1998). Here, I believe, is where the aesthetic line taken by authors such as Coote (1992) can be reconciled with Gell's (1998) action-centred approach to art. Objects can be understood to have aesthetic effects that are conditioned by the conceptual regime of which they form part. Aesthetic response and effect – both visual and perceptual more generally – are the means through which ideas and social relations are objectified and experienced. Attention to the formal qualities of objects, advocated by both Gell and the 'aestheticians', within the general structuring context of a particular 'art production system', enables us to move towards a historically and culturally specific aesthetics (in its broadest sense) which is firmly anchored within the context of specific social relations and is not merely the elucidation of individual, subjective response.

The aspect of the 'art production system' which interacts most clearly with sexual difference in the figurative art of Late Bronze Age Knossos is the manifestation of a singular form to the human body which cuts across all other distinctions. Moreover in this system sexed differences are not marked in a clearly binary fashion (Alberti 2001). Treating this observation as the general context of figurative representation at the site, I analyse the relationship between two sets of figurines from the Palace at Knossos: the faience figurines (Figs 9.1, 9.2 and 9.3) from the so-called 'Temple Repositories', and the remains of the ivory bull-leaper figurines (Fig. 9.4) from the 'Stair Closet' and 'East Treasury' (see Fig. 9.5). I draw upon a series of structural oppositions and depositional symmetries as analytical resources to enable the general, material, and aesthetic similarities and their potential relationship to specific, practice-related differences in means of representing the human body at Knossos to emerge. From this evidence I argue that a general visual regime of sexual difference was mobilized and manipulated in varying contexts associated with the potential effects of particular, aesthetically distinct objects. Always within the greater structuring context of the Palace itself, social relations were mobilized and maintained through such material differences.

Art and gender in Minoan studies

The figurative imagery found at Bronze Age Aegean sites includes frescoes, seal-stones, sealings, large-scale relief sculpture, and ceramic, bronze, ivory, and faience figurines. There is an analytically hazardous familiarity about this artwork, above all the impressive frescoes from sites such as Knossos and Akrotiri. The formal similarities between the art and contemporary Western visual aesthetic standards have led to the development of easy analogies between two temporally distant cultural contexts. As a result the study of the art has moved from an original concern with the purely visual aesthetic impact of such work (e.g. Evans 1921, 1928, 1930, 1935) to the more recent trend of the painstaking yet relatively uncomplicated classification of the various elements that make up the imagery, especially the iconographic and symbolic aspects (e.g. Younger 1993). Gender has generally been considered an uncontroversial and key element of such classification, and almost exclusively interpreted as polarized in terms of iconography and hence actual activity, role, and status within Bronze Age Aegean society (see Preziosi and Hitchcock 1999: 18–20; Alberti 2001).

The varying interpretations of the artwork have been strongly influenced by the cultural milieu of their times (see Bintliff 1984; Lee 2000). Although establishing the origins and connections between the formal and stylistic contents of the art has always been a concern, the last few decades have seen an increased need to classify and order the material in a more systematic way. This work has mainly concentrated on, but is certainly not restricted to, studies of glyptic imagery (see Laffineur and Crowley 1992; Younger 1993; Kontorli-Papadopoulou 1996), and, although enormously useful for purposes of data collection, description, and stylistic comparison, it is based on the sorting of images by imposing, in a largely uncritical fashion, categories and classes which can obscure other ways in which the images are organized. A particular outgrowth of this classificatory urge has been the development of a loosely defined structuralist analysis of the imagery. Types are then accommodated into oppositional categories, in the case of the figurative imagery these categories are inevitably male versus female, and these images are then treated as evidence for a radical gender polarity throughout the Bronze Age Aegean (e.g. Marinatos 1987, 1995).

The various classes of figurines from the Bronze Age Aegean have been assigned gendered roles or functions based on the interpretive schema outlined above. They are functionally understood to be either offerings or actual venerated images of deities. The greatest numbers of figurines were found at so-called shrines, such as the peak sanctuaries, or at elite centres such as the palace sites. During the Late Bronze Age on Crete, bronze figurines are found most commonly at peak sanctuaries associated with major centres and are considered to be luxury goods (Hitchcock 1997; Preziosi and Hitchcock 1999: 132). There are a few examples of ivory (or chryselephantine) figurines or their manufacture, most notably at the palace site at Knossos, on the 'royal road' in the surrounding town, and a figure from Palaikastro (MacGillivray 1988). Faience figurines have been found only at Knossos.

Notwithstanding the contextual and numerical dissimilarities between the various types of figurines, they have generally all been used as comparable classes of evidence for the elucidation of gender. In the case of the faience figurines, their uniqueness as evidence is often ignored due to the clarity with which they display certain features such as clothing and patterning. Consequently, their material specificity has been underemphasized in favour of using them as the ideal type of Minoan woman, or as the basis for comparative studies of Minoan dress (e.g. Lee 2000). Similarly, the ivory figurines are taken as the quintessential male Minoan athlete – lithe and muscular – whose explicit lack of male genitalia is ignored.

Art objects and sexual difference

Previous approaches to the artworks from the Bronze Age Aegean have generally either studied the visual aesthetic norms of a culture or implicitly understood the iconography and imagery as symbolic of cultural meanings. However, rather than see the art as encoded symbolic messages, Gell urges that we think of art as 'a system of action' (1998: 6). To this end there is no distinction to be made among persons, bodies, and art objects, for each is subject to an 'abduction of agency' (ibid.: 13), and can therefore be perceived as acting like a social agent. Gell (ibid.: 15) argues that the understandings or interpretations we bring to bear on the aspects of art objects are similar or identical to how we interpret social others. In a discussion of the significance of fetishes (which can be generalized to other art objects), Gell argues:

> An instructed person, approaching such a fetish, does not see a mere thing, a form, to which…[he or she] may or may not respond aesthetically. Instead, what is seen is the visible knot which ties together an invisible skein of relations, fanning out into social space and social time. These relations are not referred to symbolically, as if they could exist independently of their manifestation in this particular form; for these relations have produced this thing in its concrete, factual, presence; and it is because these relations exist(ed) that the fetish can exercise its judicial role.
>
> (Gell 1998: 62)

Art objects therefore are 'indices' of the relationships which constitute them and which they objectify.

There is an obvious advantage for archaeologists in thinking of humans and objects as analytically similar, as we study their interrelation from the inanimate remains of their interactions (see the biographical approach to material culture, in Kopytoff 1986; Gosden and Marshall 1999). It also meshes well with recent feminist scholarship which emphasizes the constitutive power of performance, construed in its broadest sense (Butler 1990, 1993). Both approaches avoid intrinsic meanings and core, fixed identities; rather they emphasize the generative role of material culture, the relational aspects of identity, and the citational power of practice as precedent.

Butler's (1990) thesis of performativity involves a move away from the idea of an 'interior' space which contains a person's gender core. She argues that the body mobilizes psychic action in the first place: a gendered identity and a sexed body are produced by processes that occur on the surface of the body. The repeated stylizations of the body – everyday acts and gestures – produce the gendered identity of which they are thought to be the expressions. Because there is no transcendental inherent quality to gender, the stylization of the body must be continually repeated. Through that repetition the acts of gender congeal over time and give the appearance of a substance – of ontological integrity – to gendered identities. Consequently, there is no ahistorical corporeal core to gendered identities posited on the universal characteristics of sex. Gender is performative in that it constitutes the identity it is purporting to express (Butler 1990: 25).

Gell (1998) and Butler (1990, 1993) allow us to make the connection between the constitution of lived ideas of sexual difference through practice (or performance) via the medium of the aesthetic reception of art objects. Moving away from passive notions of art, gender and the relationship between practice and ideas allows us to reformulate a number of common understandings. First, art objects have real effects on practice and ideas, and do not merely reflect or simplistically transmit these ideas or social messages. Further, bodies, sex, and gender are not as distinct from objects (such as clothing, adornments, and painting) or from their representations as has been considered. In other words they are neither reflections of ideas nor cultural elaborations of an uncomplicated natural body. Finally and consequently, ideas of bodies and sex/gender emerge through material practices that are intimately related to the manipulation and sensory perception of particular forms. The culturally bound aesthetic effects of figurative imagery play an active role in producing specific conceptualizations and embodied experiences.

A particular area of convergence between these two theorists concerns their understanding of 'gestures' and performances as in some ways constitutive. In Butler's (1990) case they are constitutive of gendered identities, rather than expressions of such identities. Gell (1998: 191) argues that 'graphic gestures' can be constitutive rather than merely representational; they do not stand for something else which is absent, but are themselves an example of the supposedly absent thing. Nonetheless the means by which the legitimacy of that 'graphic gesture', and hence its efficacy, is guaranteed is through its stylistic coherence and hence resemblance to other imagery. Similarly, Butler (1993: 12–16) argues that the power of a particular act is through its citation of the network of prior, accepted practices. In other words objects are never just singular entities, but rather are members of categories of objects, artefacts, or artworks.

They have relationships with other objects which crucially affect their significance. The relations between art objects and other related art objects is akin to the relationship between other social agents (Gell 1998: 153). In the following discussion the relationship between the two sets of figurines is understood as a key to their significance and for understanding the corporeal aesthetic which they embodied and of which they formed a part. After Gell (1998: 153), and contra the idea of a universal aesthetic, I argue that the form and aesthetic particularity of objects gains meaning from their inclusion within a 'culturally and historically specific art production system'.

The material lives of the figurines

The remains of the ivory figurines (Fig. 9.4) were found in a closet under the so-called 'service staircase' in the 'Domestic Quarter' of the Palace (Fig. 9.5; Evans 1901–2: 70), alongside objects of gold, bronze, ivory, faience, and crystal. Evans (ibid.: 71) associated the finds in the closet with another deposit from the 'East Treasury' 6m to the south. The faience figurines (Figs 9.1, 9.2, and 9.3) and clothing were recovered from the 'Temple Repositories' (Fig. 9.5) in an area on the opposite side of the 'Central Court' to the ivory deposit, below two cists of a later date (Evans 1921: 464). The faience objects were predominantly found carefully laid out in the lowest layer of the eastern repository (Evans 1921: 498); other finds included further faience objects, gold foil, a large number of pots, bronze handles, a large number of faience and ivory inlays, and sealings. The faience figurines were found in a damaged condition and have been fairly heavily restored with plaster (Panagiotaki 1995: 146).

The ivory figurines were found in a 'very friable condition' (Evans 1901–2: 72). Gold-plated bronze hair attachments were also found, in one case still in place on the head. Evans (ibid.) suggested that the thin gold plate found in the deposit may have been loinclothing for the figurines, although none was found attached to the actual figurines. According to Evans (ibid.: 70), the ivory figurines were found immediately below a layer of 'transitional' (MM IIIB/LM IA) Minoan vessels. The faience figurines were dated by Evans (1921: 495–523) to the same period, but Panagiotaki (1993: 88) has argued on the basis of motifs on the sealings and faience objects from the deposit, as well as the pottery, that the deposit is more likely to have been from a LM I destruction context.

The 'Stair Closet' and 'East Treasury' where the ivories were found are very secluded areas. If Evans (1930: 401) is correct in assigning them to an upper-storey room, then the space would have been more secluded, with no windows or light-wells, and a solid floor of rough-hewn limestone blocks. The 'Treasury' room may have had a marine-style rock pattern flooring of red porphyry limestone (Koehl 1986: 407), creating an impressive visual effect, and lending strength to the idea that the room was of some importance. The existence of carbonized wood and bronze handles among the deposit led Evans (1901–2: 71–2; 1930: 401) to suggest that the items were originally kept in wooden chests. Access to the area would have involved following a circuitous route through a large part of the 'Domestic Quarter'.

In contrast the faience figurines were recovered from two specific storage units and were deliberately placed and arranged within them. All the remains of the figurines and associated objects were found laid out in the bottom context of the east repository, apart from the 'upper part' (Evans 1921: 495) of the larger figurine, which was

Fig. 9.1 The larger partially reconstructed faience figurine from the 'Temple Repositories'. Photo by the author.

Fig. 9.2 The smaller partially reconstructed faience figurine from the 'Temple Repositories' (after Evans 1921: Fig. 362).

found in the fill of the west repository. Panagiotaki (1993: 86) states that the objects must have been broken before they were introduced into the repositories, as no further fragments were found in the fill.

The room in which the 'Temple Repositories' are located is immediately north of a room where a large pithos was found embedded in the floor and which was apparently used for storage (Hallager 1987: 171). Both rooms form an adjunct off the 'Lobby of the Stone Seat', or 'Room of the Column Bases', which gives access to the 'Central Court' to the east, a confusion of possible halls to the south, and the 'Pillar Crypts' and 'West Magazines' to the west (see Fig. 9.5). The area underwent structural changes throughout the life of the Palace, but appears to have served as the principal access route to the 'West Magazines'. During the Minoan palatial periods a

Fig. 9.3 Back views of the faience figurines. After Evans (1921).

tripartite 'shrine' was constructed directly facing the 'Central Court' to the east of the room with the 'Temple Repositories' (although see Panagiotaki 1999).

It is clear that the material used in the manufacture of both sets of figurines involved a great deal of effort to obtain. Ivory is not found on Crete, possible Minoan sources of it being Egypt or Syria (Watrous 1994: 750). The faience includes natron, a mineral not locally obtainable (Foster 1987: 287), and manganese from Egypt was used in the black colouring on the figurines (Foster and Kaczmanczk 1982). The various parts of the faience figurines were moulded, each figure and body part from a separate mould, and then pinned together. The ivory pieces were carved and then

Fig. 9.4 The restored ivory 'bull-leaper' (from Evans 1930: Fig. 296).

pinned. Ivory allows for intricate carving which can better express an idea of movement and clean lines; faience is harder to work, but brighter colours can be produced on the objects. Furthermore the faience figurines include an extra layer of finely ground white quartz, applied as a paste (Panagiotaki 1995: 147); the result is an especially brilliant glaze which emphasizes the colours of the figurines.

The manner in which the materials were deposited and the condition in which they were found differ. Panagiotaki (1993: 86; see also Preziosi and Hitchcock 1999: 93) has suggested that the careful deposition of the faience figurines and the layer of red earth carefully laid over the deposit indicates that the broken figurines were given a 'ceremonial burial', a type of consecration for continuing use after reconstructions of the 'Temple Repositories' area. The idea that objects may be 'killed' (see Thomas 1996: 162) has been argued in the case of the Minoan bulls-head rhyton (Rehak 1995). Evans makes no reference to the condition in which the ivory figurines were found within the deposits, suggesting that such deposition was careless, or accidental, rather than deliberate.

The performative status of the Knossian sexed body

An analysis of the presentation of the bodies of the two sets of figurines within the context of the general template for Knossian imagery of the body reveals that the presentation of the body and sexed differences is distinct for the two sets of figurines. It is argued that the appearance of breasts on the faience figurines is a specific instance of departure from the Knossian body template, and that sexed differences appear only in conjunction with specific types of figurative imagery.

The details of the body of the restored ivory bull-leaper include: clear muscular definition on the surviving arms; open hands, long fingers, and protruding thumbs; long, flat feet; exaggerated ears; and gold-plated bronze hair attachments. Seen from the front, the restored figure gives an impression of great strength and movement; these traditional 'masculine' traits are not, however, backed up by an explicitly sexed body. The typical features – the broad shoulders, hand position, large ears, etc. – clearly place it within the Knossian template for representations of the body (see Alberti 1997, 2001).

Many of the same bodily details are emphasized on the faience figurines, including large ears, separately modelled hair, and particular hand positions. The musculature

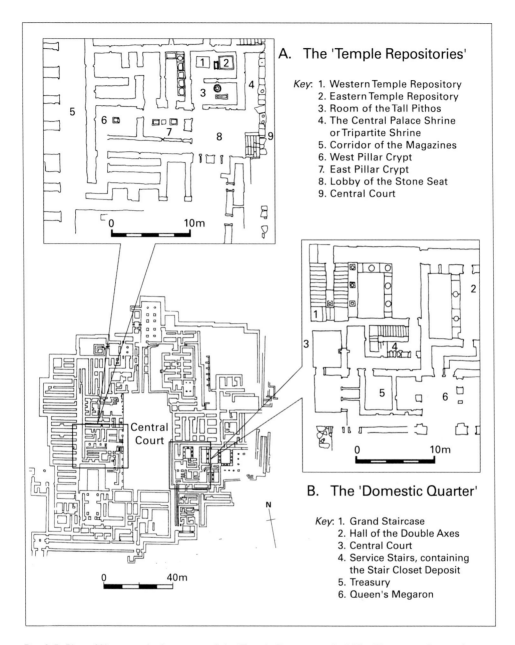

A. The 'Temple Repositories'

Key: 1. Western Temple Repository
2. Eastern Temple Repository
3. Room of the Tall Pithos
4. The Central Palace Shrine
or Tripartite Shrine
5. Corridor of the Magazines
6. West Pillar Crypt
7. East Pillar Crypt
8. Lobby of the Stone Seat
9. Central Court

B. The 'Domestic Quarter'

Key: 1. Grand Staircase
2. Hall of the Double Axes
3. Central Court
4. Service Stairs, containing
the Stair Closet Deposit
5. Treasury
6. Queen's Megaron

Fig. 9.5 Plan of Knossos. A. Area around the 'Temple Repositories'; B. The 'Domestic Quarter'.

of the arms of the faience figurines is not emphasized, although the breadth and musculature of their backs is (see Fig. 9.3). Furthermore the figurines do not have feet, but stand directly on the base of their skirts in an apparently more formal poise. The snakes emphasize the shape of the body of the larger figurine (Fig. 9.1), and appear to be an integral part of the figure.

The ivory figurines emphasize the musculature and activity of the body; the faience figurines are in a more rigid and 'fixed' position, and were clearly meant to stand up. Similarly, the faience figurines are more closely associated with the snakes they hold and the elaborateness of the clothing, as well as with a number of separate items of apparel, some of which may have formed part of a compositional arrangement. Perforations through the faience clothing found with the figurines, for example, indicate they could be hung or pinned up.

The opening in the bodices where the breasts are placed on the figurines is not indicated on the faience robes. If these objects were 'true' representations of the dress presented on the figurines, then a cut-away section at the neck of the robes would have been easily achieved to signify the absent breasts, and the shape of the female body around which the robes are supposed to open. Such a detail is not included; it would seem, rather, that breasts appear, or are indicated, only when the robes are combined with a body. Furthermore the use of different colour glazes for the breasts and faces of the figurines alludes to the status of the breasts as distinct or detachable from the rest of the body.

The sexed body, therefore, is brought into being – materializes (see Butler 1993) – when a particular type of garment is combined with a body within a specific context of representation. As such the breasts are an integral part of the costume of the figurines. A 'naked' body with breasts does not occur in the Knossian imagery. Rather the breasts combine with the dress and ornamentation of the figurines to produce a sexed body. As such a gendered body does not pre-exist its representation in Knossian imagery; rather the costumes, adornments, acts, body position, and medium of representation combine to produce gender performatively on the figurines.

Aesthetics and material practices

The two types of bodies appear to represent a dichotomy between a lithe, athletic, male body and a formal, religious female body. However, both groups of figurines adhere to and depart from the common body shape. The discrepancies between the two have more to do with the ways in which the general body template interacts with the aesthetic potentialities of the figurines within the context of the social practices of which they were a part than with a straightforward and atemporal male/female dichotomy. The task is to elucidate specific areas of practice in light of these arguments about the body in order to draw out the differences in the presentation of the human form and their relationship to the formal qualities of the art objects under consideration. The place of these objects within a number of overlapping contexts – material and social – enables their potential social effect to be elucidated. These consist of the actual material from which the figures were created, the process of their production, and their existence within the larger 'artefact' of the Palace itself.

The materials from which the figurines were produced indicate similarities and differences in their reception and aesthetic effects. The effect in a sense was double, or complementary. The materials from which they were made would have 'enchanted' through the difficulty with which they were obtained, referencing, as they would have, the ability of certain people at Knossos to attract trade and goods from far-off lands. However, the value of the objects, and their effect on social relations, did not merely accrue to these materials because they were difficult to obtain. Rather the individual aesthetic qualities and potential of their ingredients within the context of the Palace at Knossos gave them value. Although both essentially of foreign extraction, there are important formal and material differences between the sets of figures which reference distinct deployments of aesthetic qualities which are linked to the deviations from the general codes of Knossian sexed-body imagery.

Apart from their probable involvement in ritual, the efficacy of the faience figurines, and a probable reason for their careful deposition as still-potent 'agents' after their breakage, was guaranteed by the density of the relationships of which they were the objectification. The faience figurines were found in association with an area of the Palace explicitly devoted to storage. This function of the Palace was complemented by an equally explicit display of 'religious' or 'cultic' paraphernalia. Preziosi and Hitchcock (1999: 120, 132) argue for the recurring association of storage activities with certain cultic equipment or representations, such as the double axe and pillar rooms. Furthermore Hallager (1987) argues that the storage of goods at Knossos during the Minoan periods had a religious as well as secular significance. The images may well have served as vehicles for divinities, or have been considered divine themselves. Such an interpretation is supported by the large, hypnotic eyes on the faience figurines, often a sign of the animation of idols as divinities (Gell 1998). There were other faience objects found in the area, but not of the same scale as the figurines. It seems likely that the figures themselves embodied, quite literally, the various types of exchanges that defined the character of the Palace; the material not only manifested the ability of the Palace to continue successfully in such endeavours, but also reflected the efficacy of the social relations that surrounded them. The faience has often been quoted for its brilliance and the clarity of its polychrome decoration. In comparison to the unadorned and stark simplicity of both the metal figurines from other sites on Crete and to some extent the ivories, the faience figurines would have exerted a marked visual effect. Add to that the nature of their exposure to the 'public' – most certainly restricted and probably limited to a particular group – and one begins to get a sense of the potency of their involvement in the maintenance of asymmetrical social relations in and around Knossos.

Other formal qualities of the faience figurines will have had an effect on their reception. The figures are moulded and painted in three dimensions, indicating at the least, centralized display, and perhaps also a tactile role. Furthermore the detailed treatment of their clothing, apart from colluding in the aesthetic of sexual difference they present, ties them to both the practices associated with textile production and other imagery which displays a similar level of detail and/or similar patterns.

The ivory figurines share the exotic origins of the faience. However, their aesthetic effects on social relations are likely to have been quite different. They do not display such a rich layering of abducted meaning, nor a similar level of aesthetic effect. Against the singularity of the faience figurines, they are a more consistent, if not common, means of representing the human form. Furthermore they present the more common 'unsexed' body of Knossian art. Their depositional context was probably casual, not deliberate, and, although undoubtedly considered 'valuable', they were not nearly as effective as the faience figurines. Their active constituents consisted of imported raw materials, but their manufacture may have been more straightforward. As such the types of 'abductions of agency' (Gell 1998) they would have motivated may not have transgressed the realms of the natural. Moreover it is possible that they were commodities or valuables rather than actual iconic representations of divinities, which does not lessen their active participation in the world of cause and effect, but merely hints at their mortal status.

The most important material context for both sets of figurines is of course the Palace site itself. The areas in which the figurines were found contain multiple but controllable access points: evidence from Knossos (Evans 1930: 12; Shaw 1973: 149) indicates that doors could be barred and/or locked from either side. During the MM IIIB–LM IA transition period access points to the Palace and to areas within the Palace were extensively changed (see Evans 1928: 679–82; MacDonald 1990; Walberg 1992: 114–17). The changes in architecture did not occur at a single point in time, but were ongoing projects of construction and reconstruction. During the course of such reconstruction and construction various means of accessing and leaving the Palace and areas within it were blocked off and opened or reopened. It is becoming increasingly clear that a large part of Minoan architectural design was dedicated to transient areas, such as corridors, doorways, and stairs (Preziosi 1983; Polyvou 1987; Hitchcock 1994). Furthermore the Minoan system of pier-and-door partitions enabled particular areas to be closed off and opened, allowing control of multiple configurations of space (Hitchcock 1994). A general feature of the Palace in the Second Palace period was the increased number of corridors, leading to the greater possibility of privacy (Preziosi and Hitchcock 1999: 111–12).

There are two aspects of the Palace which will have played a role in the channelling of the aesthetic effect of the sets of figurines. The first is the simple result of an obvious aesthetic of display which was controlled, enabling the exhibition or closure of certain areas of the site. The figurines were in particularly isolated and controllable areas, lending support both to the idea of the figures as efficacious partly through limited access and also to the idea that the entire complex, in some sense, was designed for procession and display. As such an integral part of seeing and/or touching the images would have involved the sensory (haptic and motor) experience of manoeuvring through the spaces of the Palace, themselves richly adorned with static wall paintings and grand passageways.

This leads to the second aspect of the Palace layout. It may have been not only the effect of particular spaces and images that led to a final destination, and perhaps the small-scale but densely aesthetic figurines deep in the Palace, but also the overall effect of the layout which enhanced that effect. The labyrinthine plan of the Palace has often been noted. This was undoubtedly by design rather than accident, and has to do with the Palace itself constituting a kind of artefact, or even 'body', within which were housed other, potent artefacts. The experience of navigating these spaces – perhaps in the capacity of foreign emissary – and, of course, without the benefit of a floor plan, would have been extremely disorienting. Gell (1998: 83–95) has discussed the 'enchantment' that is a vital part of the aesthetic of certain complex designs such as mazes, the desired effect being to 'tantalize' and so 'capture' an opponent or malignant spirit. The Palace structure itself seems to have operated as a large 'trap' in this way, with the intention of perhaps 'capturing' a local populace (through seasonal embodied experience of the effects of the Palace) and/or 'dazzling' foreign emissaries or exchange partners through an ostentatious display of 'unfathomable' artistic skill and aesthetic effect.

Conclusions

The faience and ivory figurines represent two different deployments of Knossian bodily representation. The significance of different representations of the body is highly contextualized and dependent upon the aesthetic qualities of the medium of representations, the medium's embeddedness within a common style, the significance attached to particular spaces, and the mobility and potential visibility of the particular image. The sexed body emerges only in specific performative instances and in association with specific types of clothing and adornment. Furthermore the wider significance and distinctions between various representations of sexed differences can be understood as deployed in aesthetically distinct fashions. The particular aesthetic responses elicited by the material existence of the figurines within the cultural context of the Palace site at Knossos, itself a vehicle for a particular sensory experience, facilitated the social relations through which that idea of the sexed body was sustained.

Acknowledgements

I am grateful to Karen Alberti and Yvonne Marshall for their insights, help, and encouragement during the initial research for this chapter, and during its writing. Thank you also to Matt Leivers who drew the plans. I am extremely grateful to Dr Sue Sherratt of the Ashmolean Museum who was of invaluable assistance in providing me with figures and permission to reproduce them.

Bibliography

Alberti, B. 1997. Archaeology and Masculinity. Doctoral dissertation. Department of Archaeology, University of Southampton, Southampton.

Alberti, B. 2001. Gender and the Figurative Art of Late Bronze Age Knossos. In Hamilakis, Y. (ed.), *Labyrinth Revisited: Rethinking Minoan Archaeology*. Oxford: Blackwell, pp. 98–117.

Appadurai, A. (ed.). 1986. *The Social Life of Things: Commodities in Cultural Perspective*. Cambridge: Cambridge University Press.

Bintliff, J.L. 1984. Structuralism and Myth in Minoan Studies. *Antiquity* 58: 33–8.

Butler, J. 1990. *Gender Trouble: Feminism and the Subversion of Identity*. London: Routledge.

Butler, J. 1993. *Bodies That Matter: On the Discursive Limits of 'Sex'*. London: Routledge.

Cameron, M.A.S. 1975. A General Study of Minoan Frescoes with Particular Reference to Unpublished Wall Paintings from Knossos. Doctoral dissertation. Department of Archaeology, University of Newcastle-upon-Tyne.

Coote, J. 1992. 'Marvels of Everyday Vision': The Anthropology of Aesthetics and the Cattle-Keeping Nilotes. In Coote, J. and Shelton, A. (eds), *Anthropology, Art and Aesthetics*. Oxford: Clarendon Press, pp. 245–73.

Coote, J. and Shelton, A. 1992a. Introduction. In Coote, J. and Shelton, A. (eds), *Anthropology, Art and Aesthetics*. Oxford: Clarendon Press, pp. 1–11.

Coote, J. and Shelton, A. (eds). 1992b. *Anthropology, Art and Aesthetics*. Oxford: Clarendon Press.

Evans, A.J. 1901–2. The Palace of Knossos. *The Annual of the British School at Athens* 8: 1–124.

Evans, A.J. 1921. *The Palace of Minos at Knossos, Vol. 1*. London: Macmillan.

Evans, A.J. 1928. *The Palace of Minos at Knossos, Vol. 2*. London: Macmillan.

Evans, A.J. 1930. *The Palace of Minos at Knossos, Vol. 3*. London: Macmillan.

Evans, A.J. 1935. *The Palace of Minos at Knossos, Vol. 4*. London: Macmillan.

Firth, R. 1992. Art and Anthropology. In Coote, J. and Shelton, A. (eds), *Anthropology, Art and Aesthetics*. Oxford: Clarendon Press, pp. 15–39.

Foster, K.P. 1987. Reconstructing Minoan Palatial Faience Workshops. In Hägg, R. and Marinatos, N. (eds), *The Function of the Minoan Palaces*. Stockholm: Paul Åströms Förlag, pp. 287–92.

Foster, K.P. and Kaczmanczk, A. 1982. X-ray Fluorescence Analysis of Minoan Faience. *Archaeometry* 24: 143–57.

Gell, A. 1992. The Technology of Enchantment and the Enchantment of Technology. In Coote, J. and Shelton, A. (eds), *Anthropology, Art and Aesthetics*. Oxford: Clarendon Press, pp. 40–63.

Gell, A. 1998. *Art and Agency: Towards an Anthropological Theory*. Oxford: Oxford University Press.

Gell, A. 1999a [1995]. On Coote's 'Marvels of Everyday Vision'. In Hirsh, E. (ed.), *The Art of Anthropology: Essays and Diagrams*. London: Athlone Press, pp. 215–31.

Gell, A. 1999b [1996]. Vogel's Net: Traps as Artworks and Artworks as Traps. In Hirsh, E. (ed.), *The Art of Anthropology: Essays and Diagrams*. London: Athlone Press, pp. 187–214.

Gosden, C. and Marshall, Y. (eds). 1999. The Cultural Biography of Objects. *World Archaeology* 31 (2).

Hallager, E. 1987. A 'Harvest Festival' Room in the Palaces? An Architectural Study of the Pillar Crypt Area at Knossos. In Hägg, R. and Marinatos, N. (eds), *The Function of the Minoan Palaces*. Stockholm: Paul Åströms Förlag, pp. 169–87.

Hitchcock, L.A. 1994. The Minoan Hall System: Writing the Present out of the Past. In Locock, M. (ed.), *Meaningful Architecture*. London: Routledge, pp. 14–43.

Hitchcock, L.A. 1997. Engendering Domination: A Structural and Contextual Analysis of Minoan Neopalatial Bronze Figurines. In Moore, J. and Scott, E. (eds), *Invisible People and Processes: Writing Gender and Childhood into European Archaeology*. London: Leicester University Press, pp. 113–30.

Koehl, R.B. 1986. A Marinescape Floor from the Palace at Knossos. *American Journal of Archaeology* 90: 407–17.

Kontorli-Papadopoulou, L. 1996. *Aegean Frescoes of Religious Character*. Studies in Mediterranean Archaeology 117. Göteborg: Paul Åströms Förlag.

Kopytoff, L. 1986. The Cultural Biography of Things: Commoditization as Process. In Appadurai, A. (ed.), *The Social Life of Things: Commodities in Cultural Perspective*. Cambridge: Cambridge University Press, pp. 64–91.

Laffineur, R. and Crowley, J. (eds). 1992. *EIKΩN. Aegean Bronze Age Iconography: Shaping a Methodology*. Liège: Program in Aegean Scripts and Prehistory.

Lee, M.M. 2000. Deciphering Gender in Minoan Dress. In Rautman, A.E. (ed.), *Reading the Body: Representations and Remains in the Archaeological Record*. Philadelphia: University of Pennsylvania Press, pp. 111–23.

MacDonald, C. 1990. Destruction and Construction in the Palace at Knossos: LM IA–B. In Hardy, D.A., Doumas, C.G., Sakellarakis, J.A., and Warren, P.M. (eds), *Thera and the Aegean World, III*. London: The Thera Foundation, pp. 82–8.

MacGillivray, J.A. 1988. Excavations at Palaikastro, 1987. *The Annual of the British School at Athens* 83: 259–82.

Marinatos, N. 1987. Role and Sex Division in Ritual Scenes of Aegean Art. *Journal of Prehistoric Religion* 6: 23–4.

Marinatos, N. 1995. Formalism and Gender Roles: A Comparison of Minoan and Egyptian Art. In Laffineur, R. and Niemeier, W.-D. (eds), *Politeia: Society and State in the Aegean Bronze Age*. Liège: Program in Aegean Scripts and Prehistory, pp. 577–87.

Panagiotaki, M. 1993. The Temple Repositories of Knossos: New Information from the Unpublished Notes of Sir Arthur Evans. *The Annual of the British School at Athens* 88: 49–92.

Panagiotaki, M. 1995. Preliminary Technical Observations on Knossian Faience. *Oxford Journal of Archaeology* 14: 137–49.

Panagiotaki, M. 1999. *The Central Palace Sanctuary at Knossos*. London: British School at Athens.

Polyvou, C. 1987. Circularity Patterns in Minoan Architecture. In Hägg, R. and Marinatos, N. (eds), *The Function of the Minoan Palaces*. Stockholm: Paul Åströms Förlag, pp. 195–203.

Preziosi, D. 1983. *Minoan Architectural Design*. Berlin: Mouton.

Preziosi, D. and Hitchcock, L. 1999. *Aegean Art and Architecture*. Oxford: Oxford University Press.

Rehak, P. 1995. The Use and Destruction of Minoan Stone Bull's Head Rhyta. In Laffineur, R. and Niemeier, W.-D. (eds), *Politeia: Society and State in the Aegean Bronze Age*. Liège and Austin: Program in Aegean Scripts and Prehistory, pp. 435–65.

Sakellarakis, J.A. 1995. *Herakleion Museum Illustrated Guide*. Athens: Ekdotike Athenon SA.

Shaw, J.W. 1973. *Minoan Architecture*. Rome: Instituto Poligraphico dello Stato.

Thomas, J. 1996. *Time, Culture and Identity: An Interpretive Archaeology*. London: Routledge.

Tilley, C. 1994. *The Phenomenology of Landscape*. Oxford: Berg.

Walberg, G. 1992. *Middle Minoan III – A Time of Transition*. Studies in Mediterranean Archaeology 97. Stockholm: Paul Åströms Förlag.

Watrous, L.V. 1994. Review of Aegean Prehistory III: Crete from Earliest Prehistory Through the Protopalatial Period. *American Journal of Archaeology* 98: 695–753.

Younger, J.G. 1993. *Bronze Age Aegean Seals in Their Middle Phase (ca. 1700–1550 B.C.)*. Studies in Mediterranean Archaeology 102. Stockholm: Paul Åströms Förlag.

Chapter 10

Beyond Mother Earth and Father Sky

Sex and gender in Ancient Southwestern visual arts and ethnography

Kelley Hays-Gilpin

Traditional Navajo sandpaintings function in the context of healing ceremonies that focus on bringing the world into harmony. As originally given to the Navajo by the Holy people, sandpaintings should be made for no other purpose. Yet contemporary artists reproduce some sandpaintings in permanent form for sale. One of the most popular images shows Mother Earth and Father Sky (Fig. 10.1), who are benevolent, 'persuadable' beings (Parezo 1983: 93). Most sandpainting symbols are considered dangerous outside a ritual setting, but Mother Earth and Father Sky can be painted without causing harm to artists or their families. Buyers like them, too. Visitors to the southwestern United States find Native art and culture captivating for many reasons, among them 'The Indian's' reverence for Mother Earth. As Gaia or the Great Goddess, Mother Earth is also an ancient figure in European religious thought. She enjoys a revival in Europe and in North America in the women's spirituality movement (e.g. Sjoo 1975). Those who look to 'pre-patriarchal' European cultures for spiritual inspiration often say they feel kinship with Native American traditionalists in the causes of ecology, human rights, and non-violence, because members of both groups respect Mother Earth.

I will not deny the importance of Mother Earth in Native American traditions, nor in contemporary women's spirituality and 'New Age' movements, but I will explore the history of the concept of Mother Earth by examining a variety of depictions of female and male beings in ancient and historic Southwest art, together with ethnographic accounts of their use. I suggest that ethnographic evidence can be used to interpret prehistoric imagery and that prehistoric rock art and pottery provide a dated developmental sequence for some aspects of gender ideology in the Pueblo and Navajo cultures of the American Southwest.

Specifically, although the earth in prehistoric Southwest religion was probably both important and feminine, the Mother Earth figure was not approached as a single, unchanging deity. Additionally if one focuses on the roles of only female deities in the religions of Southwestern groups, leaving out male roles in fertility and reproduction, one will miss a central point of Pueblo and Navajo religions, that of gender complementarity.

Sam Gill, Professor of Religion at the University of Colorado, begins his book *Mother Earth, An American Story* (1987: 2) by noting that 'there has been uncontested agreement among Indians, scholars, and the general American populace that Mother Earth is a goddess widely known since antiquity, one central especially to the religions of native North American peoples'. Yet two things trouble Gill. First, refer-

a   b

Fig. 10.1 Mother Earth and Father Sky. (a) Navajo commercial sandpainting of Father Sky (left) and Mother Earth (right) purchased in Holbrook, Arizona, in 1999 (tracing by K. Hays-Gilpin); (b) petroglyph from the Lower Puerco River area, Arizona, probably Pueblo IV period (courtesy of Patricia McCreery).

ences to Mother Earth appeared to begin in only the past 100 years. Second, because virtually every other aspect of Native American life is regionally or tribally specific, Gill reasons that for all tribes to share any aspect of ideology would be very surprising. He compares female supernaturals in the oral traditions of many tribes (including several Southwestern ones) recorded around the turn of the twentieth century and earlier. He found that the nature and characteristics of female beings vary within and among tribes. No single female being corresponds very well to the present-day view of Mother Earth. Gill concludes that the widely shared view of Mother Earth is relatively recent in origin, having emerged over the last century or so during the process of conflicts over land and sovereignty in the American West. The rest of his book focuses on the historic process of developing this shared imagery.

Navajo and Pueblo traditions provide excellent examples of religions that have multiple female deities who are more or less identified with the earth and fertility. First Woman, together with First Man, is a central character in many Navajo stories. Although some aspects of her character concern fertility, First Woman has her home beneath the earth, and she ends up ambiguously associated with witchcraft. The central holy personage in Navajo tradition is Changing Woman, who created humans from her skin and cornmeal. She represents life cycles and the seasons. She lives not underground, but in the western sea; thus she is not the Mother Earth represented in the popular sandpainting. The horned-lizard forms of Mother Earth and Father Sky in the paintings recall 'the turtle or horned-toad sand-painting called Earth [that] is laid by a shaman at infant-naming' at Acoma Pueblo (Parsons 1939: 182); this or a similar image from one of the other pueblos is probably the source of the Navajo version (Navajo and Pueblo people have often intermarried and lived closely intermingled since at least the 1600s). But Acoma does not have a single 'Earth Mother' deity any more than Navajos do. The central personage in Acoma religion is Iatiku, a female creator who is identified with maize and earth. Parsons notes that she 'has the attributes of an earth mother, but Earth is referred to in prayer as a separable supernatural' (Parsons 1939: 182). Most of the pueblos (Hopi, Zuni, and others) have other female supernatural characters as well: Corn Maidens, Corn Mothers, Spider Grandmother, Dawn Woman, Dawn Girl, Clay Old Lady, Salt Old Lady. In addition, there is a Lady of turquoise, shell, and other 'hard substances', and a Mother of Game Animals, to name just a few. In contrast the Sun, Sky, Morning Star, Hero Twins, Coyote, and hunters are invariably male beings. The pueblos also have supernatural characters that are variably addressed as male or as female; the moon, for example, is female in some traditions and male in others.

Changes through time in rock art depictions

Is the widespread concept of Mother Earth a historic phenomenon, an instance of the converging and conflation of many female holy beings from many Old and New World traditions? Do prehistoric images of women provide any clues to her ancestresses? In this study I focus on two areas of the Colorado Plateau – the Four Corners, where Arizona, New Mexico, Utah, and Colorado meet, and the Lower Puerco and Little Colorado River drainages of Arizona. Data come from both published and unpublished sources, as well as original rock art fieldwork and research among extant rock art and artefacts collections.

Archaic period

Rock art that is dated to the Archaic, or pre-agricultural, period in the northern Southwest is widespread, distinctive, and relatively well recorded. During this time period (about 6500 to 1000 BC) rock art is characterized by geometric patterns such as grids and squiggly lines (Table 10.1). In some areas, such as southern Utah, both human and animal figures appear. The Barrier Canyon style emphasizes huge, ghostly anthropomorphic paintings (Schaafsma 1980: 61–72). Caves in the Grand Canyon and some sites in Utah yield split-twig figurines of animals, and, rarely, humans. Clay figurines appear before agriculture and ceramic containers in some areas of Utah (Coulam and Schroedl 1996). In virtually none of these figures is the subject's sex an obvious attribute. Most rock art scholars agree that Archaic rock art is 'about' spirit beings that help individual shamans (Schaafsma 1980; Cole 1989); the sex of such spirit beings was evidently not a particularly important or relevant feature.

Basketmaker II

Early agricultural populations of the Basketmaker II period (about 2000–1000 BC to AD 400) emphasized humans in their rock art, and to a lesser degree animals and geometric designs. Most of the rock art seems to depict shamans, their helpers, and their visions, but they may also function to mark band territories. Bill Hyder (1994) recorded numerous male–female pairs in the Cedar Mesa, Utah, area, and argues that they represent family ownership of arable lands. Michael Robins's (1997) research in

Table 10.1 Culture sequence for the ancestral Pueblo culture area of the northern US Southwest

Pecos Classification	Date Ranges	Characteristics
Archaic	6500 to 1000 BC (end dates vary by area and by researcher criteria)	Wild foods; temporary camps; low population density; baskets for gathering food; atlatls and darts for hunting; no pottery; geometric and non-sexed humans in rock art; animal and human figurines.
Basketmaker II	1000 BC to AD 400	Cultivated maize and squash; small pithouses and storage cists, sometimes in caves; atlatls and darts for hunting; some decorated baskets; no pottery; twined sandals; rock art emphasizes humans, often sexed.
Basketmaker III	AD 400 to 700	Cultivated maize, squash, and beans; larger, deeper pithouses, simple great kivas, some surface storage rooms; bow and arrow; pottery, but few decorated vessels; highly varied and often narrative rock art with lobed circles, crooks, staffs, processions, hair whorls, earrings, animals, and geometrics.
Pueblo I	AD 700 to 900	Pithouses with above-ground slab structures, simple great kivas, large villages in some areas such as Chaco Canyon; Black-on-white pottery; little use of caves – few perishables. Rock art not well understood.
Pueblo II	AD 900 to 1150	Small unit pueblos with kivas, large pueblos with multiple kivas and great kivas in some areas; little use of caves – few perishables preserved. Rock art loosely executed, mostly geometric, with lizard/men, animals.
Pueblo III	AD 1150 to 1300	Multi-storied masonry pueblos, sometimes in caves as at Mesa Verde; polychrome pottery in some areas; elaborate, fine rock art, with frequent humans (often sexed), ritual paraphernalia and narrative scenes, animals, and pottery/textile designs.
Pueblo IV	AD 1300 to c. 1540, Spanish entrada (dates of impact vary)	Large, aggregated communities in multi-storied masonry pueblos with plazas; polychrome pottery, depictions of katsinas and other supernaturals frequent in many media.

the Four Corners area shows that rows of sexed individuals are frequent in some areas and styles throughout the Basketmaker II period. Images may consist of males or females only, or mixed groups. Males are indicated by the presence of penises, and females are identified by triangular string aprons. Females are rarely identified by their genitalia. While all humans are depicted in a uniform frontal, static pose, details of adornment vary from place to place. Robins argues for a stylistic mosaic at this time, which, together with other data, suggests that seasonally mobile bands of Basketmakers were practising both farming *and* hunting and gathering. In contrast to the preceding Archaic styles, figures are frequently identifiable as male or female in Basketmaker rock art. Distinctive and male and female clothing styles also appear during this time, which may indicate increasing importance of gender identities.

Basketmaker III

Basketmaker III period (*c.* AD 400–700) rock art shows much continuity with its antecedents, but diversity increases over time, beginning perhaps sometime in the fifth century AD. The size and visibility of human figures are reduced. In addition to rigidly posed, frontal views of humans, a wider variety of subjects appears, including animal figures, geometric designs, and scenes of humans engaged in activities and manipulating a wide range of artefacts. Some of the most striking innovations include the lobed circle (Fig. 10.2), an icon that Steven Manning argues represents a womb and possibly a lactating breast at the same time (Manning 1992; see also Patterson and Patterson 1993). In rock art, lobed circles appear singly on the abdomens of female figures in fairly early styles, and, later, paired on the chests of male figures. They are also found paired in association with representations of great kivas, fluteplayers, plants, and male and female humans. Turquoise-encrusted mosaic pendants have been found on male burials in Canyon de Chelly, and similar items appeared in the fill of pithouses in Broken Flute Cave, also in northeastern Arizona (Hays 1992). Manning (1992) notes

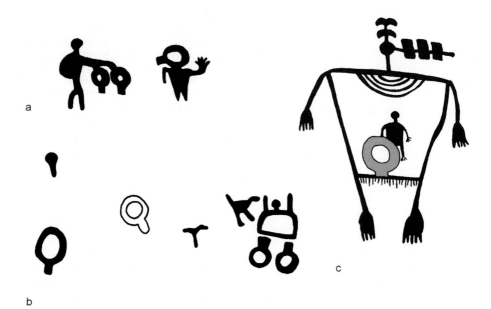

Fig. 10.2 The lobed circle in Late Basketmaker II to Basketmaker III rock art. (a) Petroglyphs from southeastern Utah (after Steven J. Manning); (b) lobed circles from Broken Flute Cave, northeastern Arizona (from Hays 1992); (c) lobed circle added later to the abdomen of the large Basketmaker II-style human figure, from southeastern Utah (after Steven J. Manning) (drawings by K. Hays-Gilpin).

that the lobed-circle shape is repeated later in the form of 'key-hole shaped' pithouses and kivas, ceremonial structures that contain a symbolic entranceway to the underworld, and that also represent wombs and birth or rebirth.

Processions become a popular rock art motif probably sometime in the AD 600s. Often the figures are phallic. They may depict group ritual activities undertaken primarily by males. I have argued elsewhere (Hays 1992; Robins and Hays-Gilpin 2000) that men may have developed ritual societies at this time, partly in resistance to the development of matrilocal extended family households. The previous emphasis on individual shamanic activity appears to yield to collective ritual activities that may have helped solidify cooperation among unrelated males. Male recruitment of feminine symbols would not be surprising in this context.

At this time, a number of icons emerge and proliferate; many of these icons are still important in Pueblo art and ritual today. Items such as flutes, crooks, atlatls, and staffs are depicted frequently; they are wielded by male and non-sexed individuals, but not by females (the atlatl or spearthrower seems to persist as a ritual icon long after it is replaced by a new weapon, the bow and arrow). Some female figures appear with their hair tied in two butterfly- or flower-shaped whorls. Called 'wearing a butterfly' in Hopi, these whorls mark a girl who has reached puberty but is not yet married. Sometimes figures with hair whorls have explicitly female genitalia, but sometimes they have no particular genitalia shown (Hays-Gilpin 2002, 2004). Very rarely, a figure with hair whorls has a possible penis depicted. Figure 10.3, for example, might represent a male person who has chosen a female gender role in life (*nadleeh* in Navajo, *llamana* in Zuni [see Roscoe 1991]).

Gender and sex do not always coincide in Pueblo and Navajo cultures. Zuni has at least three gender categories (male, female, and *llamana*), and Navajo traditions recognize five (male, female, male *nadleeh*, female *nadleeh*, and 'real' *nadleeh*, who are in fact genitally hermaphroditic). We do not yet know how long Puebloans have had more than two gender categories, and which gender attributes changed when. Representations in art may be helpful in resolving this issue, although we do not know which depictions represent humans and which represent spiritual beings. In any case it seems clear that during this time period, conventions for portraying males and females are extended to the representation of cross-gender individuals as well as to those whose sex corresponds with their gender identity.

Pueblo I–II

Pueblo I period rock art is difficult to identify in the study areas. It may be that little rock art was made during this period, or it may have been made too far from datable habitation sites to be conclusively associated. In the Pueblo II period (about AD 900 to 1150) human figures are few, and these are rarely sexed. The 'lizard/man' figure may be a male human, a lizard, or deliberately ambiguous. Zuni interpretation of these figures links them to the mythic story of human emergence, in which people in one of the lower worlds had tails and webbed feet, which they subsequently lost as they moved upwards to the next world. Note also that lizards, like snakes, are creatures that travel between the earth's surface and the underworld. Therefore these figures are not necessarily exclusively male. Depictions of female genitalia are rare or

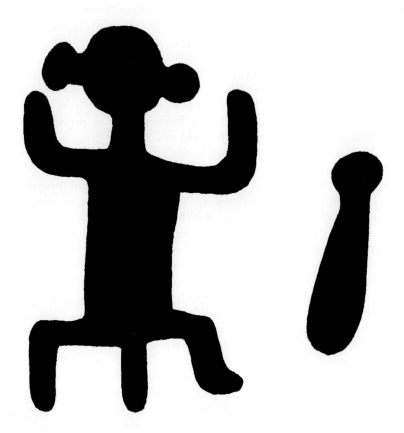

Fig. 10.3 Petroglyph figure with hair whorls and penis (?), from the Lower Puerco River area, Arizona, undated (drawing by K. Hays-Gilpin).

non-existent in Pueblo II rock art figures, but figures with hair whorls appear occasionally (e.g. Hays 1984: 530).

In the late Pueblo II or early Pueblo III period in the Puerco Valley, sets of carved and painted sandstone figurines usually include female beings, sometimes together with males, snakes, dogs, sandals, and unsexed humans (Lanford 1986: 35; Eaton 1991: 52; Fane 1991: 69; see also Martin 1961). The females do not appear to represent a single personage, but one of them appears to be a Hopi deity known as 'Child Sticking Out Woman' (see Fane 1991: 69, third figure from right). Pottery effigy vessels of seated males appear in Chaco Canyon, New Mexico, during the same era (Pepper 1906, 1920). Sexed beings appear in ritually important portable art more frequently than in rock art. This pattern suggests that depictions of such beings were 'private', that is, not meant to be visible to all members of a community. In fact Hopi elders consulted about the most recent find of a set of Puerco Valley figurines asked that they not be made public. They stated that these objects were not traditionally seen by people who were not initiated into one or another religious society. In accordance with their wishes, I will not replicate any of the images here.

Pueblo III–IV

Sometime after about AD 1150, the beginning of the Pueblo III period, human figures in rock art increase in frequency, many of the figures are sexed, and many are shown in active poses. Smaller figures appear to characterize the Pueblo III style, while very large figures appear near many Pueblo IV sites, together with depictions of katsinas, who are spirit beings that still appear in dances and other ceremonies among the pueblos today. Figures holding staffs, crooks, or bows and arrows usually do not show any indication of their sex, but are sometimes identifiable as males. Female figures rarely hold staffs, but their existence suggests that women sometimes performed ritual roles, much as they do today (McCreery and Malotki 1994: Fig. 9.11). A petroglyph in the Middle Little Colorado area strongly suggests Hopi Maraw society initiates (P. McCreery, pers. comm. 1996); Maraw is one of three Hopi women's societies that parallel male societies in having kivas, altars, and liturgies presided over by priestesses as well as priests.

During the Pueblo III and IV periods, sexed figures are frequently depicted in rock art, and females are especially common. Several depictions of females with hair whorls that date to this time period may indicate menstruation. A girl's first menstruation marks the transformation of a girl into a woman with life-giving powers; at this time a girl first 'wears a butterfly'. One especially graphic petroglyph in Catron County, New Mexico (Fig. 10.4a), shows a menstruating maiden with one hand on her belly, her womb indicated by a circle. An ithyphallic fluteplayer serenades her. A similar scene appears in an undated petroglyph on the San Juan River over 100 miles to the north in the Four Corners region (Fig. 10.4b).

Fluteplayers are apparently never depicted with female genitalia or hair whorls. Many are male, and many are ithyphallic. The Hopi Tribe has a Flute Clan and flute ceremony today, and the flute has traditionally been the young man's instrument of

a   b

Fig. 10.4 Maiden serenaded by fluteplayer. (a) Petroglyphs from Catron County, New Mexico (copyright J. Louis Argend-Farlow, reprinted by permission); (b) from Bluff, Utah area overlooking the San Juan River (drawing by K. Hays-Gilpin).

courtship. Pueblo oral traditions contain many references to fluteplayers (Parsons 1939: 41). The young male solar deity Paiyatamu at the pueblo of Zuni courts young women with his beautiful flute playing, for example. The Hopi Locust plays his flute to bring warm weather and help crops grow. As a side note, the depictions of fluteplayers in ancient art have captured the public imagination, and are invariably called 'Kokopellis'. Although the Hopi Kokopelli katsina is associated with fertility and lewd behaviour, he rarely carries a flute (when he does, he borrows one from another katsina).

Women giving birth appear in both rock art and pottery of this era. They do not appear to represent a single personage, a universal Earth Mother, but they do, certainly, suggest a central role for female fertility in Pueblo religion. Pueblo culture makes little distinction between procreation and creation. Pueblo artists often say that creation of anything is like giving birth to a baby. Making a pot, growing corn plants, weaving a blanket, carving a katsina doll, even killing an enemy – all these acts of creation are analogous to giving birth. Ethnographer Alice Schlegel demonstrates that pregnancy and birth are key metaphors in the Pueblo world view (Schlegel 1977; Young 1988). According to Will Roscoe (1991: 140), at Zuni 'all forms of making were homologized to the act of birth and the ability of women to create life'.

Supernatural female figures in rock art

Depiction of sexed beings in rock art can be linked with personages mentioned in historic Pueblo oral traditions. This association suggests that similar or identical oral traditions prevailed in the Pueblo III period, perhaps as early as the 1150s, in the Little Colorado River area of Arizona. Supernatural beings that can be tentatively identified in the rock art include the Mother of the Hero Twins, the Mother of Game Animals, and the Corn Maidens. Not all of these characters are benevolent and nurturing, at least not all the time, as befits our contemporary image of Mother Earth.

Maiden Mother of the Hero Twins

Cottonwood Ruin, one of the Homol'ovi Pueblos on the Middle Little Colorado River in Arizona, was inhabited by Hopi people during the early 1300s. Below the escarpment of the mesa on which the village perched, sandstone boulders form a rectangular chamber with one tunnel entrance and one long corridor entrance from the floodplain below. The corridor opening is guarded by a large phallic figure executed in the Pueblo IV period style (Fig. 10.5a), but marks apparently made by metal tools suggest he was modified more recently. His hands and feet have been deeply pecked into cupules. Standing on top of the mesa rim and looking into the chamber, one sees a large female figure on her back on the outermost boulder (Fig. 10.5b). Her arms, legs, and vagina are raised to the sky. She is flanked by depictions of frogs and concentric circles, which are probably symbols of water and sun. This female figure recalls Navajo and Pueblo stories about how the Hero Twins or Twin War Gods were conceived. In an Acoma story related by Matthew Stirling, the creator Iatiku's sister, Nautsiti, is lying on her back on a rock in the rain, and 'the rain streaming up from the ground enters her. She bears the Twins' (Parsons 1939: 245).

Fig. 10.5 Petroglyphs near Cottonwood Ruin, Middle Little Colorado River area. (a) Male figure, historic period; (b) female figure with sun and water symbols, probably Pueblo IV period, possibly later (drawings by K. Hays-Gilpin).

Although Navajo speakers may not have entered the Southwest until the 1400s, some Navajo clans trace their origins to Puebloan villages and some Navajo ceremonial narratives share a great deal with Puebloan ones. Some Navajo traditions, then, may provide additional evidence for earlier symbols that are found on the Colorado Plateau. Navajo ceremonial narratives, for example, involve numerous sets of twins. Most are the children of the Sun, an association that is also true at Hopi and Zuni (Parsons 1939: 204), as well as in Mesoamerica. In Navajo thought, the sun and water together can cause conception. Water, especially foam and mist, is sometimes considered the semen of the Sun. The Navajo Hero Twins (Monster Slayer and Born for Water) were conceived in this manner. Their mother is Changing Woman, an earth deity who is born in the spring, matures, and becomes an old lady in the winter. According to the traditional story, '[w]hen Changing Woman first became mature, she had not learned about sexual intercourse, but in trying to satisfy her desire, let the sun shine into her vagina; at noon when the Sun stopped to feed his horse, she went to a spring and let water drip into her' (Reichard 1950: 29) and so became pregnant with the twins. They matured rapidly after their birth, underwent an arduous journey to meet their father the Sun, who gave them magic weapons so they could destroy dangerous monsters and make this earth safe for people.

A similar story was told among the Chemehuevi of California, distant linguistic relatives of the Hopi: 'A woman was living alone in a cave on Wiyaatuwa, Whipple Mountain. Each morning it was her custom to go outside her cave and lie down with her legs spread wide apart, opening herself toward the rising Sun. On one of these mornings, Tavapitsi, the Sun, by a sudden concentration of his rays, caused her to conceive. She gave birth to twin sons' (Laird, cited in Gough 1987: 58).

At Zuni, the Twin War Gods are said to have been born to their Sun Father, from their mother, Laughing Water, at a particular canyon west of the Zuni reservation. Mathilda Coxe Stevenson (1904: 35) records that the Sun 'caused a heavy rain to fall until the cascade of the mountain side no longer glided placidly over the rocks to the basin below, but danced along; and in her joy, she [the cascade] was caught in the sun's embrace, and bore twin children, who issued from the foam'.

The place where the Zuni Twins emerged is a water-washed hollow near the top of a canyon filled with rock art. In the grotto itself, a petroglyph of a rayed circle probably represents the sun (Fig. 10.6a). The sun's rays penetrate this chamber on the summer solstice, a day also marked in the great kiva of Casa Rinconada in Chaco Canyon, and in numerous petroglyphs throughout the Pueblo region. The sun impregnates the earth mother on the first day of summer, ushering in a season of warmth and growth. In a rounded chimney-like formation just below the sun grotto, a petroglyph clearly represents a woman giving birth (Fig. 10.6b). She wears hair whorls, and the U-shaped element beside her probably represents the wooden tool that a young Hopi woman's mother uses today to hold the hair in place as she ties the butterfly-shaped whorls.

A petroglyph panel deep in Chevelon Creek near Winslow, Arizona, shows a woman giving birth (Fig. 10.7). Judging by the patina on the rock surface, the style of the rock art, and the ceramic dates of the nearby Homol'ovi Pueblos, the scene was probably made in the AD 1300s or early 1400s, during the early Pueblo IV period. Cupules have been pecked all around, and deeply into, this figure; moreover parts of her hands, torso, and legs have been repeatedly repecked. McCreery and Malotki (1994: Fig. 6.5) suggest this panel may have served as a fertility shrine.

Fig. 10.6 Petroglyphs at Hantlipinkya, Middle Puerco River area. (a) Sun symbol and (b) woman with hair whorls giving birth (drawings by K. Hays-Gilpin).

Fig. 10.7 Petroglyph depicting a woman giving birth from Baird's Chevelon Steps site, Middle Little Colorado River area, Pueblo IV period. Dotted circles show locations of deeply pecked cupules (drawing by K. Hays-Gilpin).

These pecked cupules resemble those described by Stevenson at Zuni fertility shrines where women who wanted to get pregnant would place offerings in natural or pecked rock (Stevenson 1904: 294–5 and Plate XII). Jane Young notes that Pueblo women's private pilgrimages to fertility shrines were 'a crucial focus of religion' (1987: 437), but she does not discuss the form and appearance of such shrines today; respecting the wishes of her Zuni hosts, she did not visit certain shrines (Young 1988: 177).

Was the Chevelon Creek figure used to help mortal women cure sterility, ease childbirth, or help offspring survive? Does she simply depict a fertile female? Or does she reference a particular personage? In all accounts of the birth of the Hero Twins, their mother is unmarried; the Chevelon, Cottonwood, and Zuni figures wear the hair whorls of unmarried women. These are not just any single mothers, however, but may represent the first woman giving birth, or a supernatural being, perhaps an earth deity like the Acoma creator, Iatiku, or the Mother of the Hero Twins.

In contrast several depictions of childbirth on Hopi pottery bowls show mothers without hair whorls, suggesting they are married women. The birth of infants is depicted on a Jeddito Black-on-yellow bowl found at Chevelon Ruin, another of the Homol'ovi ruins (Fig. 10.8a). One of these infants is clearly female. Two attendants flank the mother, holding branches of some sort of plant, perhaps sage or other herbs used today by Hopi midwives. A second bowl (Fig. 10.8b) depicts a mother, attendants, and one or more infants. The draftsmanship on this piece is rather loose, and the images somewhat ambiguous. This image may depict the birth of twins, or the bowls may be simply prayers for a successful marriage resulting in the birth of a certain number of children, including at least one female. Girls are especially desired in the matrilineal pueblos, because they inherit the clan house, lands, and important ritual responsibilities.

In summary not all depictions of childbirth necessarily have the same meaning. Whereas the rock art described above may depict supernatural or mythical events and serve as cures for sterility, the pottery depictions of childbirth may represent prayers of or for married women, perhaps newly wedded women. Today at Hopi, pottery is often exchanged at weddings, and Ruth Bunzel reported that at Zuni some pottery designs were considered to be a special form of prayer just for women (Bunzel 1972: 70).

Corn maidens and mothers

In addition to identifying the earth as a mother and the sun as a father, Pueblo people say, 'corn is life', and 'corn is our mother' (Ford 1994). At Hopi the word *poshumi* refers both to corn seeds saved for planting and to the young clan women of child-bearing age (Black 1984). Corn plants are called 'maidens' until they begin to produce ears. Then they are 'women', and the ears of corn are called their children. Some seeds are saved to become next year's 'maidens'. The rest of the crop becomes 'our mother', who will sustain the Hopi people through the year literally as food and metaphorically in the form of perfect ears of corn given to infants and initiates (Parsons 1939: 319–23; Black 1984; Ford 1994: 515).

There are seven Corn Maidens at Zuni, each with her own colour and direction (including up, down, and centre, as well as the four cardinal directions) (Young 1987: 440; see also Roscoe 1991: 140–1). The life cycle of the corn plantish identified with the life cycle of humans. Corn is born with the consent of the earth mother and grows due

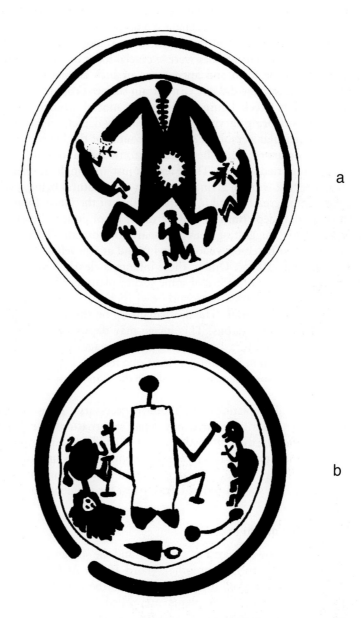

Fig. 10.8 Depictions on pottery of women giving birth, Pueblo IV period, Hopi. (a) Jeddito Black-on-yellow bowl (US National Museum, no catalogue number); (b) Jeddito Black-on-yellow bowl (Chicago Field Museum, catalogue number 75698) (drawings by K. Hays-Gilpin).

to the prayers and nurturing of mortal men. Richard Ford argues that when Pueblo people say, 'corn is our mother', they mean 'that corn creates culture, that it sustains life, and that it is the authority for social action' (1994: 513). He suggests that corn has been a key metaphor in Pueblo world view for at least 1,000 years, and exhorts archaeologists to look more closely at the contexts of corn in the archaeological record – particularly the perfect ears called 'corn mothers' or 'corn guardians'.

Corn Maidens also appear in prehistoric art. Several pottery bowls from the Mogollon Rim area (*c.* AD 1300 to 1450) depict figures (one with explicit female genitalia) that may represent the corn maidens (Fig. 10.9). A nearly identical figure appears in a petroglyph near Springerville in east-central Arizona and dates to the same era (Fig. 10.9c).

Fig. 10.9 Corn Maidens depicted on pottery and rock art. (a) Pinedale Black-on-white bowl (after Hammack 1974: 35); (b) Fourmile polychrome (Chicago Field Museum, number 73447) (drawings by Hays-Gilpin); (c) petroglyph near Springerville (copyright J. Louis Argend-Farlow, reprinted by permission).

Mother of Game Animals

Stories about mother(s) of game animals abound all over North America. A Hopi earth deity, Sand Altar Woman (also known as Child Sticking Out Woman) bestows infants and also guards game animals. She is the sister of the germination god, Muyingwa, and the wife (sometimes the sister) of the god of death and the earth surface, Maasaw (Stephen 1936: 261; Parsons 1939: 178, 964). She is not entirely benevolent: one story recounts that she seduced and murdered young men and, when discovered, left Orayvi village to live alone along the Little Colorado River. Hunters who saw her bloody countenance and survived intercourse with her came away covered in blood but were thereafter very lucky in the hunt.

The Mother of Game Animals herself appears in petroglyphs in the Little Colorado drainage in Arizona (Fig. 10.10; see also McCreery and McCreery 1986; McCreery and Malotki 1994: 139–42; Potter 2004). A variety of birds and animals accompany her, sometimes striking sexually receptive poses, with tails raised. Parsons notes (1939), however, that not all pueblos share this deity; at Acoma, for example, the female creator Iatiku creates a *Father* of Game Animals.

Pueblo hunters do not rely on luck to find game. Large game such as deer and antelope require respectful treatment and the performance of certain rituals. If the animals are pleased, their spirits will go back to their 'mother', they can be born again, and 'give themselves' again to the hunter. Human and animal sexuality and fertility are related. Hunters and their wives must abstain from sexual intercourse during the hunt

Fig. 10.10 The 'Mother of Game Animals', Lower Puerco River area, Arizona (photo by K. Hays-Gilpin).

(Parsons 1939: 81). Phallic symbols are also depicted in petroglyphs. Note for example that the 'phallic feet' located beside the female deity in the petroglyphs in Figure 10.10 not only have phallic middle toes, but they are also accompanied by penis prints, which appear between each pair of footprints, and by bows and arrows. These are probably meant to be emphatic statements that men made offerings or prayers at this place. Alice Schlegel writes that at Hopi: 'There is a subtle relationship between women and game animals, especially antelopes (the major type of hunted game), that crops up in various rituals and even in jokes about extramarital sexual adventures: men talk about hunting for "two-legged deer"' (1977: 259). Such a 'two-legged deer', the object of one's desire, may be represented in the depiction of an 'antelope maiden' on a polychrome bowl from Sikyatki Pueblo (Fig. 10.11). A similar association of animal as well as human fertility can be seen at Inscription Point, across the Little Colorado River from the Pueblo III period habitations at Crack-in-Rock Pueblo (Hays-Gilpin 2004: 38). Here an extensive but isolated rock art site depicts copulating humans and copulating animals.

Conclusion

Ancient art of the Puebloan region in the American Southwest shows male and female sexed individuals in a variety of activities and contexts, together with a variety of apparently supernatural personages of both sexes. Very often, artists did not indicate sex at all, suggesting it was not always an important attribute of the character depicted. This observation is particularly true for the pre-agricultural Archaic period. Imagery such as the lobed-circle complex suggests that female fertility was an important metaphor for

Fig. 10.11 Antelope Maiden, Sikyatki polychrome painted bowl from Sikyatki (Chicago Field Museum of Natural History, number 75246; drawing by K. Hays-Gilpin).

fertility and reproduction among humans as well as among plants and animals in the natural world. Female fertility may also be associated with some aspects of creation itself as early as the fifth century in the Four Corners area of the northern Southwest.

Female supernatural beings that are known from the historic Pueblo oral traditions are also found in rock art as early as the twelfth century (*c*. AD 1150) in the Little Colorado River area of Arizona. These include the Mother of the Hero Twins, the Mother of Game Animals, and Corn Maidens (or Corn Mothers). No single Mother Earth figure is identified in Pueblo oral traditions or in rock art, although female fertility and childbirth provide the central and enduring metaphors for many kinds of creativity, fertility, and well-being in the Puebloan Southwest.

Male figures depicted in rock art are more difficult to link to specific personages in the oral traditions, but again they are seen in a variety of roles and poses. Priests, hunters, and fluteplayers, although male, are also associated with fertility and increase among the historic pueblos. This association can also be seen in the rock art. The association of male figures with some aspects of fertility and reproduction suggests that, in Pueblo thought, the symbolic job of promoting fertility is not limited to women; the contribution of males is also important. It seems clear, however, as noted, that in the Puebloan Southwest female fertility and childbirth are central and enduring metaphors for many kinds of creativity, fertility, and well-being.

Pueblo ideology of gender complementarity (Schlegel 1977) is expressed in the placement of male and female rock art images relative to each other, and the placement of female images relative to solar events. The central complex of complementarity and diversity, then, ordered the Pueblo world since at least the twelfth century, long before the recent conflation of many holy beings into a Mother Earth figure who fills contemporary political and spiritual needs. This argument is not a rejection of a straw-man hypothesis (one might object that no good anthropologist believes that Native Americans venerated a single Mother Earth figure). Rather I intend to actively use archaeological and ethnographic evidence to resist popular American and European cultures' misrepresentation of Native American spirituality as an essentialist, unchanging, and unitary phenomenon.

Acknowledgements

Special thanks to Jerrold Levy for recommending Sam Gill's book and commenting on earlier versions of this research, and to Patricia McCreery, Steven Manning, and J. Louis Argend-Farlow for providing illustrations and insights into the rock art record. Claudette Piper and Dennis Gilpin commented on drafts of the chapter, Peter Pilles provided slides of the US National Museum pottery collections, and the Arizona Archaeological and Historical Society sponsored studies of the Field Museum of Natural History. Thanks also to the staff of these two museums and the Museum of Northern Arizona. Thanks to Alison Rautman, who organized the Gender and Archaeology Conference in East Lansing at which this chapter was presented, and to the University of Pennsylvania Press, who published the first version of this chapter in *Reading the Body: Representations and Remains in the Archaeological Record* (Rautman 2000).

Bibliography

Black, M. 1984. Maidens and Mothers: An Analysis of Hopi Corn Metaphors. *Ethnology* 23: 279–88.

Bunzel, R. 1972 [1929]. *The Pueblo Potter: A Study of Creative Imagination in Primitive Art.* New York: Dover.

Cole, S. 1989. Iconography and Symbolism in Basketmaker Rock Art. In *Rock Art of the Western Canyons.* Colorado Archaeological Society Memoir No. 3. Denver: Denver Museum of Natural History, pp. 59–85.

Coulam, N.J. and Schrocdl, A.R. 1996. Early Archaic Clay Figurines from Cowboy and Walters Caves in Southeastern Utah. *Kiva* 61: 401–12.

Cushing, F. 1896. *Outlines of Zuni Creation Myths; Zuni Ritual Poetry; Zuni Catkins: An Analytical Study.* Bureau of American Ethnology Annual Report, Vol. 13. Washington DC: Smithsonian Institution, pp. 321–447.

Eaton, L. 1991. The Heart of the Region: The Anthropology Collections of the Museum of Northern Arizona. *American Indian Art* 16: 46–53.

Fane, D. 1991. The Southwest. In Fane, D., Jacknis, I., and Breen, L.M. (eds), *Objects of Myth and Memory: American Indian Art at the Brooklyn Museum.* Brooklyn: The Brooklyn Museum in association with the University of Washington Press, pp. 45–159.

Ford, R.I. 1994. Corn is our Mother. In Johannesson, S. and Hastorf, C.A. (eds), *Corn and Culture in the Prehistoric New World.* Boulder: Westview Press, pp. 513–25.

Gill, S. 1987. *Mother Earth, An American Story.* Chicago: University of Chicago Press.

Gough, G.R. 1987. The Indian Hill Ceremonial Fertility Site Complex. In Hedges, K. (ed.), *Rock Art Papers*, Vol. 5. San Diego Museum Papers No. 23. San Diego: San Diego Museum, pp. 55–60.

Hammack, L.C. 1974. Effigy Vessels in the Prehistoric American Southwest. *Arizona Highways* 50: 33–5.

Hays, K.A. 1984. Rock Art of Northern Black Mesa. In Nichols, D.L. and Smiley, F.E. (eds), *Excavations on Black Mesa, 1982: A Descriptive Report.* Research Paper No. 39. Carbondale: Southern Illinois University at Carbondale Center for Archaeological Investigations, pp. 517–40 .

Hays, K.A. 1992. Anasazi Ceramics as Text and Tool: Toward a Theory of Ceramic Design 'Messaging'. Ph.D. thesis. Department of Anthropology, University of Arizona.

Hays-Gilpin, K.A. 2002. Wearing a Butterfly, Coming of Age: A 1,500 Year Old Puebloan Tradition. In Kamp, K.A. (ed.), *Children in the Prehistoric Southwest.* Salt Lake City: University of Utah Press, pp. 196–210.

Hays-Gilpin, K.A. 2004. *Ambiguous Images: Gender and Rock Art.* Walnut Creek, CA: AltaMira Press.

Hyder, W.D. 1994. Basketmaker Social Identity: Rock Art as Culture and Praxis. Paper presented at the 1994 International Rock Art Conference, American Rock Art Research Association, Flagstaff, Arizona.

Lanford, B.L. 1986. The Southwest Museum. *American Indian Art* 12: 30–7.

McCreery, P. and McCreery, J. 1986. A Petroglyph Site with Possible Hopi Ceremonial Association. In Snyder, E. (ed.), *American Indian Rock Art* II. El Toro, CA: American Rock Art Research Association, pp. 1–7.

McCreery, P. and Malotki, E. 1994. *Tapamveni: The Rock Art Galleries of Petrified Forest and Beyond.* Petrified Forest, AZ: Petrified Forest Museum Association.

Manning, S.J. 1992. The Lobed-Circle Image in the Basketmaker Petroglyphs of Southwestern Utah. *Utah Archaeology* 1992: 1–37.

Martin, P.S. 1961. A Human Effigy of Stone from a Great Kiva near Springerville, Arizona. *The Kiva* 26: 1–5.

Parezo, N.J. 1983. *Navajo Sandpainting: From Religious Act to Commercial Art*. Tucson: University of Arizona Press.

Parsons, E.C. 1939. *Pueblo Indian Religion*. Chicago: University of Chicago Press.

Patterson, A. and Patterson, M. 1993. The Rock Art of Bluff, Utah, and the Pendant Circle Complex. In Harris, F. (ed.), *Utah Rock Art*, Vol. 12. Green River, UT: Utah Rock Art Research Association, John Wesley Powell Museum, pp. 187–211.

Pepper, G.H. 1906. Human Effigy Vases from Chaco Canyon, New Mexico. In Anon (ed.), *Boas Anniversary Volume*. New York: American Museum of Natural History, pp. 320–34.

Pepper, G.H. 1920. *Pueblo Bonito*. New York: Anthropological Papers of the American Museum of Natural History 27.

Potter, J.M. 2004. The Creation of Person, The Creation of Place: Hunting Landscapes in the American Southwest. *American Antiquity* 69: 322–38.

Rautman, A. (ed.). 2000. *Reading the Body: Representations and Remains in the Archaeological Record*. Philadelphia: University of Pennsylvania Press.

Reichard, G.A. 1950. *Navajo Religion: A Study in Symbolism*. Princeton: Princeton University Press.

Robins, M.R. 1997. Modeling San Juan Basketmaker Socio-Economic Organization: A Preliminary Study in Rock Art and Social Dynamics. In Smiley, F.E. and Robins, M.R. (eds), *Early Farmers in the Northern Southwest: Papers on Chronometry, Social Dynamics, and Ecology*. Animas-La Plata Archaeological Project Research Paper No. 7, United States Department of the Interior, Bureau of Reclamation, Upper Colorado Region. Contract No. 1425-2-CS-40-11730, pp. 73–120.

Robins, M.R. and Hays-Gilpin, K. 2000. The Bird in the Basket: Basketmaker III Iconography. In Reed, P.F. (ed.), *Foundations of Anasazi Culture: The Basketmaker – Pueblo Transition*. Salt Lake City: University of Utah Press, pp. 231–47.

Roscoe, W. 1991. *The Zuni Man-Woman*. Albuquerque: University of New Mexico Press.

Schaafsma, P. 1980. *Indian Rock Art of the Southwest*. Albuquerque: University of New Mexico Press.

Schlegel, A. 1977. Male and Female in Hopi Thought and Action. In Schlegel, A. (ed.), *Sexual Stratification: A Cross-Cultural View*. New York: Columbia University Press, pp. 245–69.

Sjoo, M. 1975. *The Great Cosmic Mother: Rediscovering the Religion of the Earth*. San Francisco: Harper and Row.

Stephen, A. 1936. *Hopi Journal*. New York: Columbia University Press.

Stevenson, M.C. 1887. The Religious Life of the Zuni Child. In *Fifth Annual Report of the Bureau of American Ethnology for the Years 1883–1884*. Washington, DC: Smithsonian Institution, pp. 533–55.

Stevenson, M.C. 1904. The Zuni Indians: Their Mythology, Esoteric Fraternities, and Ceremonies. *Twenty-third Annual Report of the Bureau of American Ethnology*. Washington, DC: Smithsonian Institution, pp. 3–634.

Stirling, M. 1942. *Origin Myth of Acoma and Other Records*. Bureau of American Ethnology Bulletin 135. Washington, DC: Smithsonian Institution.

Young, M.J. 1987. Women, Reproduction, and Religion in Western Puebloan Society. *Journal of American Folklore* 100: 436–45.

Young, M.J. 1988. *Signs from the Ancestors: Zuni Cultural Symbolism and Perceptions of Rock Art*. Albuquerque: University of New Mexico Press.

Part IV

The body

An introduction

Timothy Insoll

The interconnections of the body with both gender and sexuality in the manifestation of identity are obvious, but the body 'perfect', either mentally or physically appears to be the primary focus of the limited archaeological attention accorded it as a component of identity. Deliberately then, this section starts with a consideration of the body and disability.

Morag Cross provides a thought-provoking examination of the interrelationship between disability and archaeology in multiple ways that have previously been neglected. Hence beyond considering the social and medical constructions of disability she also examines a variety of other subjects. These include the potentially positive role of archaeology in creating disability 'culture', the absence of 'disability' in archaeological parlance in favour of disease (see for example Roberts and Manchester 2005), and the need for change in archaeological attitudes to disability. 'Access' is a key word, at least in British society today, and Cross examines how we can make archaeology accessible to the disabled at a variety of levels – indicating, as should be obvious, that archaeologists are not immune from social responsibilities, nor is the archaeological record from which we interpret past identities somehow removed from contemporary concerns and issues.

Moreover Cross emphasizes, rightly, that disability or physical impairment has, or should have, as much importance as gender or ethnicity in examining past identities, and she makes the point that it is frequently omitted in relevant studies when it might be expected to be found, as in McGuire and Paynter's (1991) *The Archaeology of Inequality*. Again, conceptual complexity is stressed, in, for example, Cross raising the question that what might be regarded today as an impairment need not have been in the past, as with her example of how dyslexia is unlikely to have been a problem for a medieval peasant when literary culture was absent. Thus in this chapter Cross clearly presents her personal viewpoint primarily from a theoretical slant.

In contrast Tony Waldron's contribution places what he terms 'disadvantage', but also disability, within the framework of material indications of various conditions and their archaeological recognition. In so doing he focuses upon what Cross might define as the 'medical' model of disability and disadvantage, and the two chapters together present differing approaches to the archaeology of disability. The examples Waldron considers range from skeletal tuberculosis through to curvature of the spine (scoliosis), and perhaps more controversially, child abuse. However, what is provided is far from an ABC of archaeological recognition, but an empirically grounded insight into neglected aspects of the body which can impinge directly upon identity manifestations, and furthermore which do not neglect the relevant social implications either.

Waldron's chapter also clearly indicates the expertise which is required in recognizing the archaeological evidence attesting to 'disadvantage' and disability, and how both the medical and social elements of study need integrating in the successful consideration of these aspects of identities. Hence the practicalities of addressing the more idealistic position outlined by Cross are eloquently examined by Waldron.

The third chapter included in this section, by Julian Thomas, shifts the perspective to a more philosophical one in considering the dominance of humanism within modern understandings of the body. Thomas argues that such a standpoint has also influenced archaeological interpretations, and that this needs acknowledging in order to begin to liberate archaeology, where necessary, from the overriding concept of the autonomous individual. However, this is not an idealistic tract but rather a considered review of both humanist and anti-humanist perspectives in relation to the body. Thomas's chapter has resonance elsewhere in that the points he makes could easily be transposed to other identities as well. For example the frequent downplaying of the role of religion as a structuring identity (see Insoll 2004) has similarly been influenced by humanist perspectives.

The cultural construction of a dominant intellectual paradigm which has structured much archaeological thinking is exposed in questioning the notion of rationality, mind over body, and the other elements which constitute the humanist perspective and the correlates of modernity, as Thomas (2004) has elsewhere also more recently considered at greater length. Thomas's philosophical explorations also return us to the notion of 'difference' in relation to appreciating the past, and again the undercurrent, evident throughout the Reader, in questioning concept, category, and assumption is visible.

Bibliography

Insoll, T. 2004. *Archaeology, Ritual, Religion*. London: Routledge.
McGuire, R.H. and Paynter, R. 1991. *The Archaeology of Inequality*. Oxford: Blackwell.
Roberts, C. and Manchester, C. 2005. *The Archaeology of Disease*. Stroud: Sutton Publishing.
Thomas, J. 2004. *Archaeology and Modernity*. London: Routledge.

Chapter 11

Accessing the inaccessible

Disability and archaeology

Morag Cross

Introduction

It is very easy for an archaeological discussion of disability to consist of the bare bones of a history of the orthopaedic ward. However, disabled people are not all dead. I wish to raise some of the issues involved in disability politics, of which most archaeologists will be completely unaware. I outline the medical and social models of disability, and the adoption of the social model by the disabled people's movement in America, and then in Britain. The social model is currently undergoing refinement, as is discussion of the distinction between impairment and disability. Some of the meanings of 'access', a key concept in disability issues, are discussed, and some of the ways in which archaeology might become accessible to disabled people are explored. I mention a broad range of issues to put the discussion into a wider contemporary and political context. The social model of disability may have a contribution to make to the archaeological understanding of disability and vice versa, if archaeological considerations can be grounded in a theoretical context in which the past is relevant to the present and future of disabled people.

Why disability?

Why should archaeology matter to disabled people, and why should disabled people matter to archaeologists?

Archaeology is a means of accessing the activities of our predecessors, and it also serves a function once served by origin myths – the creation and explanation of identity. These issues are of special relevance to disabled people. A group excluded in the present can be included in the past, and, just as disability arts are being used to create a still-evolving disability 'culture' (e.g. Shape London/Disability Arts seminar on 'Disability Arts and Culture', references in Barnes 1992) so archaeology can show disabled people that their experiences are not uniquely contemporary. They have very ordinary disabled predecessors, and history can be used as another means of self-affirmation for disabled people, alongside arts and politics (Morrison and Finkelstein 1993). Indeed there is at least one instance of disabled people's contemporary existence being acknowledged in nineteenth-century archaeological writing (McCulloch 1868: 539). In that instance the brevity and uniqueness of the reference demonstrates that they truly are 'footnote people in...history' (Wallechinsky and Wallace 1978: 364).

Archaeology has engaged with other issues that are socially constructed and defined, such as race and gender, but disability is a neglected subject. Examination of the British Archaeological Bibliography (BAB) over the period from 1989 to 1996 reveals no entries under disability and numerous ones under 'disease' (e.g. BAB 1995: 276). Yet disability and disease are not the same thing. For archaeologists, disability is usually considered to be an orthopaedic condition experienced by someone in the past, but disabled people are not all dead. The existence of physical impairment is a historical constant, deserving consideration as much as race or gender, for it cuts across all boundaries. In dealing with identity, definitions, and the historical reconstruction of society, disability studies and archaeology have considered some of the same problems. 'In the history of the portrayal of disabled people is the history of oppressive and negative representation. This has meant that disabled people have been represented as socially flawed able bodied people, not as disabled people with their own identities' (Hevey 1993, quoted in Barnes 1992: 4). Disability politics is constructing an identity for disabled people in the present, and tentatively using history to extend that identity back in time. Working in chronological reverse, archaeology has sought to construct identities in the past, using material remains surviving into the present.

There is obviously a tension between a diversity of disabled identities today and in the past, and using the past to construct a present-day identity (Oliver 1991: 49). Anspach (1979: 768) states that 'the politicization of the disabled represents an attempt to wrest definitional control from "normals"'. Today among disability activists, although the debate over definitions is ongoing, people are considered to be disabled only if they identify themselves as disabled.

The social construction of disability, that is, the effect of personal attitudes and perceptions of what constitutes disability, has been illustrated by Finkelstein (1981). He describes a village where wheelchair use is the norm, all the architecture is adapted, and walking is literally a handicap. Walkers are seen as being uncommunicative and lacking eye contact because they are bent double, having poor social skills. The social criterion of disability, a problem created by the processes and institutions that structure society, is rather literally illustrated by Kurt Vonnegut in 'Harrison Bergeron'. To quote,

> The year was 2081 and everybody was finally equal....Nobody was smarter than anybody else....Nobody was stronger or quicker....All this equality was due to the 211th, 212th, and 213th Amendments to the Constitution and the unceasing vigilance of the Handicapper General.
>
> (1968: 19)

Here, to equalize ability, people are artificially impeded or handicapped by the state, and by this society's definition, impairment is 'normal'.

Disability itself is a neutral fact, and is only assigned positive or negative meanings in a social context (Hevey 1993: 119). It is unlikely, for instance, that dyslexia, a disadvantage today, would have been much of a problem for a medieval peasant. Extrapolation of the contemporary negative status and nature of disability back in time is a dangerous path. What may be regarded as an impairment and a personal disaster now may not have been so regarded in the past. This is a central tenet of the social model of disability – that injury and impairment do not necessarily equate with incapacity.

The medical model of disability

The two conventional views of disability, opposed like Scylla and Charybdis, are the medical and social models. According to the medical model, disability is viewed as a personal, individual medical tragedy amenable to either a medical intervention, cure, or control, or to incarceration in a segregated institution. Disabled people are stigmatized, but the interpretations as to why vary according to the commentator. Historical materials like Oliver (1990: 34–5) and Barnes (1991: 62) attribute stigma to economic and labour factors, because society and personal value are structured around the ability to work. They suggest that stigma is a learned response to the economic incapacity of disabled people (Abberley, 1987: 15–16 and 1993: 111; Oliver 1991: 51).

In the medical model of disability (see Brisenden 1986; Abberley 1987; Oliver 1993 for a fuller discussion), the medical condition, or impairment, is seen as being the disabled person's own 'problem' – the natural consequence of personal inadequacy. The solution is to make him or her conform to the physical norm as much as possible – e.g. prevent deaf schoolchildren from using sign language. The medical condition, illness, or disease is seen as being 'the disability' – the two concepts being regarded as synonymous. The medical model is beautifully summarized in the contents page of Barnes (1992: 5), 'The Disabled Person as Pitiable...Sinister...Atmosphere or Curio...Super Cripple...Their Own Worst and Only Enemy...Burden...Abominable...Incapable'. Disability status is attained by incapacity, failure, dependency, and passivity on the part of the individual, and strategies are written, researched, and administered to disabled people by able-bodied professionals, as it is socially created by these administrative procedures.

The social model of disability

The civil-rights movement in 1960s America, and the power of the Vietnam veterans lobby, transformed the self perception of disabled people in the United States (Fine and Asch 1988: 3–5; Hahn 1988). Because there was a written constitution, non-attainment of the rights enshrined therein was a civil-rights issue (Shakespeare 1993: 250–1). This led to the passing of the Americans with Disabilities Act in 1990, which is commonly viewed as the most significant civil-rights statute since the 1964 Civil Rights Act (Pfeiffer 1994: 534). In a situation of high-profile disabled activism quite unlike that in the UK, Pfeiffer suggests that '[judged] by the amount of attention it receives in the media, from the employer organizations...it may be the most visible piece of legislation passed during the Bush Administration' (ibid.).

Influenced by events in the United States, a radical reconceptualization of what it meant to be disabled began in Britain. In 1976, following unsatisfactory official definitions of 'disability', 'handicap', and 'impairment', the Union of the Physically Impaired Against Segregation defined disability as the loss or limitation of opportunities that prevents people who have impairments from taking part in the normal social life of the community on an equal level with others due to physical and social barriers (Pagel 1988: 3; Davis 1993: 289; Finkelstein and French 1993: 28). 'Impairment' was defined as 'the lack of part or all of a limb, or having a defective limb, organ or mechanism of the body'. In this definition the common use of the term 'disability' to mean a medical condition was rejected, along with the phrase, 'people with disabilities'. The focus was shifted from the functionally limiting impairment to the external physical environment, and the disabling society. This is termed the social model of disability.

People researching disability, such as Oliver, Barnes, Abberley and Finkelstein, began to examine how disability was socially constructed – other people's attitudes had to be challenged (e.g. Oliver and Barnes 1993). However, the main focus of their attention was disability as a social creation of industrialized societies, by institutionalized and economic discrimination, and an inaccessible physical environment. The 'problem' was external to the person – it was not the inability to climb steps that was the problem, but the lack of a ramp to make a public building accessible. This made 'disability' a civil-rights issue in a country with no civil-rights tradition (Barton 1993). Disabled people were able to perceive a commonality of experience for the first time, and to come together with similar goals, as an oppressed minority group (Pagel 1988; Hasler 1993: 280; Shakespeare 1993: 253).

This use of the social model made possible the creation of a disabled identity, a way to challenge stigma as a large group rather than as isolated individuals (see Fine and Asch 1988: 6–8 on disabled people's emerging minority-group consciousness). It also laid the foundations for political and self-help movements, and the creation of organizations of disabled people, such as local forums (Morris 1991: 176) as a substitute for the Victorian philanthropic charities for disabled people (Pagel 1988: Ch. 3; Barnes 1991: 222–5). The breakthrough of the social model was that social oppression and negative status were neither inherent nor inevitable. It broke the old reductionist equation that impairment necessarily led to limitation and incapacity. It provided a mechanism for social change and the removal of disability (Scotch 1988: 165–71). If environmental barriers like steps, inaccessible public transport, and segregated schools were changed, the disability would be removed. Since disability is socially constructed, disabled people's self-definition as members of an oppressed minority group, the social model of disability, enables them to engage in collective action to change and make accessible the social and physical world in which we live (Oliver 1993: 65).

Two social models: active and passive

In its early form, the social model was frequently uncritically promulgated with the fervour of revealed truth. It needed to be radicalized and expanded, to become more inclusive and self-critical. The disabled person exists in a tension with the disabling society. In the medical model they would be made to adapt and fit in with their environment. In the social model, which presupposes that the person is disabled almost entirely by external factors, one can modify one's surroundings to fit oneself, negotiating this relationship by political action, assertiveness training, the independent-living movement, etc. (Abberley 1987; Scotch 1988; Barton 1993).

There is, however, a paradoxical relation between the self and one's individual impairment or functional limitation (Oliver 1990: 65–77; Lenny 1993). Social-model theorists have placed less emphasis on this. Some strategies for dealing with impairment have been criticized on ideological grounds, for relocating the disabling problem within the individual, and making it a personal problem once again, what Finkelstein (1996) calls the passive social model.

The use of the term 'adjustment' for the process of grieving for lost abilities has been criticized (e.g. Oliver 1990: 63–5) because the process of dealing with impairment is one of constant renegotiation (Zola 1982, quoted in Oliver 1990: 64). Some counselling is seen as judgemental, and as reinforcing negative views of disabled people as psychologically inadequate or maladjusted to their situation (Lenny 1993: 235). It has been suggested that some negative or grieving responses to acquired impairment are learned behaviours due to the negative status of disabled people in society (Abberley 1993: 109, 111; Finkelstein and French 1993: 31–2). I would disagree – loss of abilities can cause real emotional pain because hearing, for example, is more than a purely utilitarian or optional means of communication.

On the other hand the attitude that if you have never had the use of them some faculties would not be missed (i.e. congenital impairment) seems especially common among deaf activists campaigning for minority-language status for sign language and a separate deaf culture. By neglecting the complexity of the experience, some statements about positive self-image can sound dangerously close to 'redemption through suffering'. By this I mean the numerous 'I wouldn't change/be without my impairment' testimonies, which can start to resemble just another way of dealing with the personal experience of disability and can walk a fine line between 'supercrip' hero stories. I am aware that there are differences in the experience of people who were born with, and those who have acquired, impairments, and therefore have some experience of an able-bodied existence against which to measure living with impairment. The difficulty, and sometimes impossibility, of comprehending another's experience does not diminish its validity, and can pose a challenge to its acceptance. The social model has largely neglected the individual's response to, and experience of, impairment, because it considers this to be divisive and subjective (French 1993: 24). However, we all have different experiences and can only make sense of them through the meanings available to us.

Recently some female writers have suggested that definitions of impairment need to be explored, and that the difference between impairments have been ignored (Crow 1992; Lloyd 1992; French 1993: Morris 1993). This is partly a gendered response, influenced by the feminist conviction that 'the personal is political'. Fine and Asch (1988: 5–6) summarize well the range of causes and effects of impairment which can be highly visible (e.g. wheelchair use), hidden (e.g. epilepsy), acquired (e.g. amputation), or congenital, mild, or progressive, and can vary over time. Many impairments themselves are disabling or restrictive, and are not amenable to remedy by societal or attitudinal change (French 1993). Although Liz Crow (1992) and Sally French (1993) have written about this, there is still an over-reaction against anything that even remotely links medical conditions, the individual, and restriction (Morris 1991: 70, 181; Lloyd 1993: 212). There has been a heated debate in the pages of *Disability Now* about attitudes to impairment and living with functional limitations, which can leave the individual feeling like a spectre at the feast, an onlooker ignored by those leading a 'normal' life (*Disability Now* 1996a; 1996b).

In some of its manifestations, the social model can fail to take account of multiple causation and simultaneous multiple meanings of disability and stigma and can be very prescriptive in an area full of shades of grey (Casling 1993: 203–4). Jenny Morris (1992: 159) calls for research that is not 'alienated knowledge', which allows space within the research for the absent subject, without treating disabled people as objects.

Jane Campbell and Mike Oliver published a history of the disability movement told through the experiences of disabled people using 'action research' strategies. It examined their own part in this history as 'collective, self-reflective inquiry', partly to circumvent disabled people's scepticism of much traditional research (Campbell and Oliver 1996: 24–6). Theoretical work on the social model is ongoing as it needs to be radically expanded to make room for those, albeit contentious, concepts with which it does not yet seem to deal with sufficient frequency (Crow 1992).

One such issue is impairment. The neglect of impairment is 'an obstacle' to the cohesion and expansion of the political movement 'if it is ignored by the theoreticians of the struggle' (Shakespeare 1993: 256–7). Work has been completed on such areas as the role of counselling and the social model (Terry Daly, Strathclyde University, UK) and the examination of women's perceptions of impairment (Carol Thomas, Lancaster University, UK). Finkelstein has suggested the social model has split into active and passive models, which have downplayed the practical struggle for social change (active), and overemphasized the psychological experience (passive). He suggests having a disabled point of view on mainstream issues and working with the majority community for the common good (Finkelstein 1996). Hopefully, rather than proving divisive, more structured analyses will allow a broader identification of ordinary disabled people with what can be abstruse, obscure, and jargon-laden debates.

The Greeks had a word for it – 'stigma' and prejudice

A word associated with disability is 'stigma' – which was originally a slave's brand in ancient Greece (Abberley 1993: 110). It is ironic that the plural, *stigmata*, has prestigiously divine associations that stigma does not. Although Oliver and others have rejected many psychological and cultural explanations (1990: 60–70) for the negative status of disabled people, Tom Shakespeare (1994: 283) has taken a broader view and examined the reasons for cultural prejudice against disabled people, as this prejudice can also be disabling.

Disabled people represent a variety of different things simultaneously, and are invested with multiple meanings. Shakespeare suggests that they are the 'other' (1994: 290–6) against whom we measure and define ourselves, and the transgressors of physical and social boundaries. They are reminders of mortality and physical frailty, as well as an economically and thus socially disadvantaged group. Popular culture is full of disabled villains and monsters (discussed at length in Barnes 1992; Casling 1993; Hevey 1993; Shakespeare 1994). Impairment in Western society is invested with negative cultural meanings, used to justify and normalize prejudice, as if it were the inevitable, natural outcome of difference. The Americans with Disabilities Act (1990) identified such prejudice as illegal (Pfeiffer 1994: 540).

Anthropological explanations of stigma (Murphy 1987, quoted in Oliver 1990: 20; Oliver 1990: 15, 17, 19, 61–3) acknowledge the overwhelmingly negative images of disabled people in Western culture, and the meanings attributed to them (e.g. Scheer and Groce 1988: 28–9, 32). However, recent research suggests that the status of disabled people in traditional societies can vary widely (ibid.). Impairment functions as the '*metaphor du jour*', standing in for the moral cause of the moment, as is revealed by any study of leprosy, epilepsy (Schneider 1988), or AIDS. Some disabled activists have even begun to reconstruct the disabled identity by 'reclaiming' stigma and disempowering language, and using it positively (Anspach 1979) and politically, after the models of the black and gay liberation movements.

Psychological explanations of the stigma attributed to disability (Oliver 1990: 65–8) consider what Harlan Hahn calls the aesthetic and existential anxiety engendered in the onlooker (1988: 42). Disabled people remind us of the frailty of the human body, of the threat posed to our self-image by the physically different or disfigured – aesthetic anxiety. Existential anxiety is the fear that 'it could happen to me', as indeed it can.

Fine and Asch examine the psychological assumptions made regarding disabled people by researchers who often root stigma in the individual's possession of the impairment itself, as if it were a 'natural' consequence (1988: 9, 11, 13), rather than in others' attitudes or in environmentally imposed restrictions. The reasons they suggest for these assumptions broadly parallel Hahn's definition of existential anxiety – the onlooker's perception of impairment as victimization, problems, and vulnerability, 'a reminder that we cannot control all life events' (Fine and Asch 1988: 15). As with Hahn, the impairment becomes a memento mori, a reminder of our own mortality like the medieval Dance of Death on a church wall.

As a direct consequence of the social model and its emphasis on disabling environments of all kinds (social, economic, institutional, and physical), the concept of 'access' has become prevalent and political. The stereotypical meaning of access is wheelchair ramps and lifts (English Heritage 1995). These things are very important in theory and practice, but there are more dimensions to 'access' than the width of doors. These include access to education and information.

However utopian the social model, in the short term it has been as revolutionary as Stonewall or the Alabama bus boycott. It has provided a point of identification for an emerging consciousness of disabled people as a minority group – defined by Dworkin as 'identifiability, differential and pejorative treatment, and group awareness' (Dworkin and Dworkin 1976: viii). It has identified issues of key concern to disabled people themselves – independence, access, choice, and identity. Independence is the choice to organize one's own life and personal care, not necessarily the ability to do everything physically unaided – hence the independent-living movement. The social model has challenged stereotypical assumptions that disabled people are victims, that they are always in need of help, that they identify only with others similarly disabled, and that impairment necessarily means inability and helplessness (Fine and Asch 1988). By being the motor for the mobilization and motivation of activism, the social model has simultaneously smashed and transcended any equation of impairment with concomitant powerlessness.

An arthritic approach: a need for change in archaeological attitudes to disability

So what of disability and archaeology? The medical model approach through the grouping of disease processes or deformity as manifest in skeletal remains is prevalent, for example in the *International Journal of Osteoarchaeology*. At the time of writing there were no entries under 'disability' in the British Archaeological Bibliography. Entries under 'disease' simply emphasize the lack of political or social context – 'disease – med, degenerative joint/prostatic; carcinoma' (BAB 1996: 253). Under osteoarchaeology we find 'med, chronic septic arthritis...bones (animal); bones (human)' (ibid.: 287). In Glasgow University, all books dealing with the archaeology of skeletal remains are classified under 'Medicine' next to 'History of Medicine', including *The Archaeology of Disease* (Roberts and Manchester 1995), suggesting that the mood is more that of epidemiology than social context. The disease, not the human being, has become the actor. The medical condition manifest in the skeletal or material record is the impairment, not the disability, although the impairment may prove disabling. The degree of disability or exclusion of an individual in the past may be hard to quantify or assess, but in the light of the growing differentiation between sex and gender in the past, it seems that the issues of 'impairment', and 'disability' in past societies should also be addressed.

To date very little theoretical work has been done on archaeology and the politics of disability – probably because disability is an isolated geographical and social event. There might be the practice of archaeology by disabled people, because there are disabled archaeologists. There might be an archaeology for disabled people, as some efforts have been made to improve site accessibility. There is, however, no archaeology of disabled people, probably because they have never been a homogeneous group in time, place, or type of impairment. Nevertheless some disabled activists have begun to make use of archaeology to construct a historical identity for themselves, such as John Hay, a deaf historian tracing the history of the deaf community in Scotland. He has 'reclaimed' the tomb of Princess Joanna, 'The Dumb Lady of Dalkeith', daughter of James I (of Scotland), in Dalkeith Collegiate Church, as a point of historical identification for the deaf community (*From the Edge*, BBC2, 16.10.1996). This raises various issues of identity and archaeological responsibility to which I will return in the conclusion.

In his discussion of how and why the medical model dominated capitalist views of disability, Oliver outlines the rather idealized theory that disabled people were integrated into pre-industrial society, when work was done at home and the individual could contribute according to his or her ability (1990: 25–32). Janssens says that 'the economy is also a decisive factor in fixing an attitude towards the sufferer' (1970: 145) – depending on the ability of the community to 'carry' unproductive members. Archaeologists have to rely heavily upon the medical model of disability (i.e. functional abnormality) because they excavate the material remains of people's bodies. However, the social model does privilege a material level of explanation as well, namely the contribution of the environment to the social creation of disability.

In the concluding chapter of *Archaeology of Disease*, Roberts and Manchester (1995: 196–202) concentrate on new technical and methodological aids to the analysis of data and specific disease processes. In some recognition of lacunae in the data, with which contemporary disability discourse is actively engaging, the need for consideration of human environmental adaptation (a concern of the social model) is suggested. To quote, 'Broad areas of investigation could provide useful information on past human adaptation to particular environments' (ibid.: 200), including urban and rural communities and environments, and health and gender. In an earlier and unusually inclusive book, P.A. Janssens (1970) seems to have taken a wider number of factors into account, including (brief) mentions of environments, climate, and religion.

It might be interesting to examine the physical environment of an excavated skeleton identified as mobility impaired, for example, using the social model's concept of environmental barriers as disabling. In a rural society with no wheelchairs or mobility aids, unimproved roads, and unmodified topography, is a person who may be economically unproductive necessarily going to be more integrated than someone today who is imprisoned at home by inaccessible public transport?

One study has examined the contemporary incorporation of the 'personal geographies of individuals with impaired mobility' (Vujakovic and Matthews 1994: 359), and how they 'read' the physical built environment of a city, into the design of graphic representations of accessible and inaccessible areas. The exclusion of individuals from the spaces between buildings is a form of political control (ibid.: 373), and the environmental perceptions of disabled people differed strongly from other users. Mapmakers, and possibly archaeologists planning ground surfaces, 'project with their own values' (ibid.: 375), while the mental (cognitive) maps of the environment, 3-D space, and hazard/barrier perception of the mobility impaired are often different (ibid.: 375–6). 'A person confined to a wheelchair cannot negotiate monumental stairs. Rather than having a sense of awe and respect, such a person is likely to feel angry at what is above' (Steinfield *et al.* 1977: 9). This is directly related to the basic precepts of the disabling environment in the social model of disability.

There is ongoing research into areas such as medieval attitudes to disability. Publication has begun to examine social attitudes to mental illness and leprosy, and coping strategies, one manifestation of which is leper houses and other forms of social provision and control (e.g. Cullum 1994). There have been studies of votive offerings (Radford 1949) and pilgrimage (Peter Yeoman pers. comm., Fife Council Archaeologist), an activity loaded with ambiguous moral messages about disabled people as ripe for divine intervention. This last area is a huge field of study, which is still ongoing, and seems to structure the discourse on disability in medical terms, as a catalogue of bodily defects.

There is a paradox here – in using the social model, it would be necessary not to equate a particular impairment in the past automatically with the experience of a similarly impaired person today – and there are still few cross-cultural studies of disability (Scheer and Groce 1988: 23; Oliver 1990). Since the meaning and effect of impairment is culturally constructed, what may be regarded as incapacitating today may not always have been so regarded, especially in economically marginal communities (Barnes 1991: 11; Finkelstein 1993: 12; mentioned briefly in Janssens 1970: 145). Interestingly, serious suggestions that some past religious figures may have suffered from epilepsy or other conditions can be greeted with anger by their modern followers, demonstrating a prejudice that reflects the contemporary stigma of psychiatric conditions.

'We see through a glass, darkly': museum presentation and representation

Unlike theoretical issues of disability and archaeology, the accessibility of museums to disabled people has been an issue for several decades. This has generated articles (the 'Open Doors' columns in the *Museums Journal*), case studies (Perth Museum entrance, Pickles 1996), committees (Pickles 1997), quangos, multimedia presentations, and lottery funding for enhanced accessibility (Stone 1997). Dr Margaret Faull of the National Coal Mining Museum for England has spoken in *Disability Now* of her experience as a disabled museum professional, words that are still too often an oxymoron. Trying to strike a balance between conservation and accessibility is difficult – what may be adequate lighting for one visually impaired person may be unsuitable for artefact preservation. Tactile access is hindered by traditional cases full of reflections. It is literally a case of seeing through a glass darkly.

Physical and intellectual access to collections are two separate but related issues. Able-bodied and disabled people are frequently ignorant of each others' limitations and perceptions. Consultation with access-panels of disabled people can challenge ways of looking at the environment. The new Royal Museum of Scotland has been designed with visitor accessibility as a primary consideration from the beginning. An access audit and consultation with local disabled groups has produced a guide to the original Victorian building (NMS 1996), and the content and degree of 'difficulty' of information labels and the museum's interactive catalogue and information system (MOSAICS) is also being carefully assessed (A. Watkins pers. comm.).

On intellectual access one approach is to address disabled people on their own terms and within their own cultural frame of reference, using tactile and audio aids where appropriate. Earlier curators like William McCulloch, born in 1815, were not entirely unaware of the tactile and voyeuristic attractions of some exhibits for a visitor population deprived of 'video nasties' and violence on television (although public executions provided a more-than-virtual reality alternative). In 1868 McCulloch wrote:

> Of the many objects of special interest to the student of Scottish history preserved in the Museum of Antiquities at Edinburgh, one of the most interesting is the old beheading machine, better known as The Maiden. It is an object that attracts the notice and awakens the sympathies of visitors from all climes and of every shade of colour. Mutes describe its action to each other with unmistakable significance; the blind handle it tenderly.
>
> (1868: 539)

It might be wondered whether the sympathies of disabled visitors were excited by thoughts of revenge against the patronizing Victorian perpetuators of the medical view of disability.

Professor John Hull, who is himself blind, uses scale models and tactile plans of cathedrals to attempt to 'reconstruct the cathedral' for visually impaired people 'through the use of their own senses...rather than the usual way of listening to descriptions by sighted people...not to attempt to convey to blind people a sighted person's experience' (*Innovations in Information* 1994b).

The archaeology museum at Nimes (*Innovations in Information* 1994b) has focused on visitor autonomy, to enable people to wander through the displays by themselves – with audio cassettes and relief maps. Another French museum has trained deaf people as conference guides using specialized art-history sign language. One aim is to provide deaf children with adult role models 'to feel confident about their future opportunities as professionals' (*Innovations in Information* 1994c). This approach (and McCulloch's, by default) uses already established elements of disability culture.

The appointment of access officers 'is a clear sign that the museums sector is starting to take ownership of the issues' (Pickles 1997). Disabled people themselves must take ownership of access and employment issues in the museum setting, so that they are represented not only by 'visitor figures' but also by disabled museum professionals, as Nimes has already envisaged.

The issue of the representation of disabled people has mainly been tackled with relation to visual representations in the media (e.g. Disability and the Media Project, by K. Ross at Cheltenham and Gloucester College). Less well-known is the issue of their representation in museums – that is, if and how they are incorporated into a model of the past. The closely analogous case of the (in)visibility of the lesbian and gay communities in museums was discussed by Gabrielle Bourn, 'despite museum rhetoric on recognising diversity, there is still one minority group which remains in the shadows' (Bourn 1996: 28–9). Letters on the subject of 'queer representation' in museums and the 'recognition of minorities of a perceived "controversial nature"', (Clayton 1997) apply equally or with even greater force to disabled people, who are the one minority group which anyone could join.

Making education accessible is a challenge to providers in all subjects, not just in archaeology. Bristol University has run a summer school in archaeology for visually impaired students since 1982. Toby Stone (1995) has written in the *Guardian* about the difficulties of being a student with undiagnosed dyslexia, and the misunderstandings that this caused. The assistance of a cooperative institution, the Institute of Archaeology at University College London enabled him to circumvent problems like drawing plans and sections (Stone, pers. comm.).

Conclusion

Mike Oliver suggested that 'the issue of disability and the experiences of disabled people have been given scant consideration in academic circles. Both the issue and the experience have been marginalised' (1990: xi). He states that only medicine has considered disability, and then only as a medical problem. 'Hence there is an urgent need for other disciplines such as sociology, anthropology, history…to take these matters seriously rather than to merely offer descriptive and atheoretical accounts which leave medical and psychological approaches unchallenged….On the experience of disability, history is largely silent' (ibid.).

Disabled people can only have a prehistory once they start writing their own history by actively participating in archaeology. The only archaeological article aimed specifically at disabled people that I have been able to find suffered because the disability journal editors were initially unable to find an archaeologist to assist them (*Perceptions* 1996). Archaeological data can be used to construct a past that does not merely replace 'negative' with 'positive' images, but attempts to structure the discourse to reflect the complexities of the experience of disablement, and consequent social estrangement or inclusion.

Deaf people have identified 'artefacts' such as the picture of Sir Joshua Reynolds at the Tate Gallery (*Self-Portrait As a Deaf Man*, 1736), which are produced by, if not for, disabled people. In this artefact, Reynolds fulfills Hevey's criteria of the disabled person producing and positioning his own representation, and how he (Reynolds) wished to be perceived.

Archaeology as a discipline does not have a static building or fixed location unless it is, itself, part of a museum display. Whom it serves, other than archaeologists, may not always be apparent. Archaeologists' attitudes are affected by lack of awareness of and interest in contemporary disability issues. This was demonstrated, for example, by the difficulty faced by the editors of the disability journal, *Perceptions*, when they attempted to find an archaeologist willing to write for them. This has resulted in archaeologists equating disability with illness and disease, rather than viewing disablement as a socially constructed phenomenon. On one side is the impairment, such as arthritis or osteoporosis, and on the other are the social and environmental limitations encountered/imposed. If there is to be a change, it should also be asked what the disabled community wants from archaeologists, if anything.

Beyond the aetiology of disease, epidemiology, and physical access to sites, there is a lack of literature from an archaeological perspective. Titles of archaeological books which conceivably cover the 'archaeology of people who were disabled' include *A Field Guide to Joint Disease in Archaeology* (Rogers and Waldron 1995) and *Identification of Pathological Conditions in Human Skeletal Remains* (Ortner and Putschar 1981), shelved in a library alongside 'History of Medicine'. Disability here is equated with an explicitly medical perspective.

Most writing on disability politics has been in the field of sociology. In contrast archaeology, which has been ready to embrace race and gender issues, has done little to incorporate disabled perspectives into models, beyond working from Hevey's ablist paradigm and treating disabled people as objects, a material resource like other archaeological remains. The failure to engage with disability politics suggests a lack of awareness of the disability movement. *The Archaeology of Inequality* (McGuire and Paynter 1991) looks at African American, Native American, colonial, and women's experiences, but does not consider disabled people, who continue to experience economic and physical inequality. Disabled people exist within every other group, and it could be argued that disability issues are relevant to everyone.

Kelley and Hanen consider the possibility of a 'sociology of archaeology' (1988: 100) since it is not 'a closed system unrelated to the societies in which it is embedded' (ibid.). Investigators' pre-existing biases influence approaches and degrees of 'objectivity', though 'the relationship of such factors to the actual practice of archaeology appears to be only dimly perceived by most archaeologists' (ibid.). Archaeologists, like society at large, have usually been unaware of disabled people among them, ignoring them for various reasons. Meanwhile the cohesive strategies enabled by the social model at grass-roots local level have coagulated into the collective and increasingly coherent voice(s) of disabled people. Excavated diseased joints, which were once disabled people, have modern equivalents, who have been functioning as cultural magnets for and aggregates of able-bodied people's analogies and values. They are one of Kelley and Hanen's 'variables'. To quote,

> On the whole, archaeologists have paid less attention to these variables than have anthropologists (especially ethnographers), probably in part because the latter, dealing as they do with living human beings who respond to the researchers, have been forced to a realisation that the cultural bias of investigators is a serious problem. The view gaining in popularity, however – that archaeology is making sense of the past in the present – is moving us toward a greater awareness of the effects of our own cultural backgrounds on archaeological questions.

(1988: 142–3)

Disabled people are a hidden group to whom archaeologists have some responsibility in terms of representation and incorporation. As mentioned previously, disabled people might require something from archaeologists in terms of their own history, but without dialogue it is hard to posit what this is, or whether there is an audience at all – disabled people have varying levels of political awareness and self-awareness as a minority group. Although 'the disabled' are considered as 'them' and 'over there', disability is a fluid category. Some archaeologists will become disabled; some disabled people are archaeologists. 'The disabled' are 'us', not 'them over there'.

In their concentration on 'fossilized disease' in the form of skeletal deformity, archaeologists dig up impairment, not disability. Joint disease is not a disability, it is an impairment. In archaeology there seems to be no concept of 'disability' according to the social model (as exemplified in the long list of books on the history of disease, not disability, classified as 'History of Medicine'). In the same way that the concepts of sex, sexuality, and gender are not the same things, so impairment, disease, and disability are not synonymous, and archaeology needs to develop its own, more social model of disability. In the wake of the implementation of the Disability Discrimination Act in 1996, now is the time to engage with disabled people and disability politics on their own terms. At present, although a means of accessing the past, archaeology itself is still an environment inaccessible to many disabled people.

Acknowledgements

I would like to thank Nyree Finlay, University of Reading; Dr Tom Shakespeare, University of Leeds; Dr Matthew Johnson, University of Durham; Professor John Hull, University of Birmingham; Mr Toby Stone, Cambridge University; Mrs L.E. Wilson; Mr Terry Daly, Strathclyde University; Dr Carol Thomas, Lancaster University; Mrs Antoinette Watkins, Royal Museum of Scotland; Mr Peter Bratvley, Strathclyde Equality Awareness Trainers in Disability; Ms Maureen McHugh, East Dunbartonshire Forum on Disability; Ms Judy Medrington, Institute of Archaeology, London; Mr B. Warner, Nasa Goddard Space Flight Center; Mr Bill Pickles, Disability Scotland; Mr Graeme Fairbrother, Disability Equality Officer, Edinburgh District Council; and especially Dr C.P. Graves, University of Durham, for her unfailing support, as ever.

Bibliography

Abberley, P. 1987. The Concept of Oppression and the Development of a Social Theory of Disability. *Disability, Handicap and Society* 2: 5–21.

Abberley, P. 1993. Disabled People and Normality. In Swain, J. *et al* (eds), *Disabling Barriers, Enabling Environments*. London: Open University, pp. 107–15

Anspach, R.R. 1979. From Stigma to Identity Politics: Political Activism among the Physically Disabled. *Social Science and Medicine* 134: 765–73.

Barnes, C. 1991. *Disabled People in Britain and Discrimination: A Case for Anti-Discrimination Legislation*. London: BCODP.

Barnes, C. 1992. *Disabling Imagery and the Media: An Exploration of the Principles for Media Representations of Disabled People*. Halifax: BCODP.

Barton, L. 1993. The Struggle for Citizenship: The Case of Disabled People. *Disability, Handicap and Society* 8: 235–48.

Bourn, G. 1996. The Last Taboo? *Museums Journal*. November: 28–9.

Brisenden, S. 1986. Independent Living and the Medical Model of Disability. *Disability, Handicap and Society* 1: 173-8.

Burton, N. 1995. Defusing the Disability Time Bomb. *British Archaeology* June: 11.

Campbell, J. and Oliver, M. 1996. *Disability Politics: Understanding our Past, Changing our Future*. Routledge: London.

Casling, D. 1993. Cobblers and Song Birds: The Language and Imagery of Disability. *Disability, Handicap and Society* 8: 203–11.

Clayton, N. 1997. Loud and Proud. *Museums Journal* January: 17.

Crow, L. 1992. Renewing the Social Model of Disability. *Coalition* July: 5–9.

Cullum, P.A. 1994. Leper Houses and Leprosy during the Medieval Period. *Interim* 19: 24–31.

Davis, K. 1993. On the Movement. In Swain, J. *et al.* (eds), *Disabling Barriers, Enabling Environments*. London: Open University, pp. 285–92.

Disability Now. 1996a. Radical Chic? *Disability Now* January: 32.

Disability Now. 1996b. Live and Let Live. *Disability Now* March: 28.

Doyle, B.J. 1996. *Disability Discrimination – The New Law*. Bristol: Jordan Publishing.

Dworkin, A. and Dworkin, R. (eds). 1976. *The Minority Report*. New York: Praeger.

English Heritage. 1995. Conference, 'Giving Access a Lift: the Policy and Practice of Improving Access to Historic Properties' held in Temple Anderson Hall, October, York.

Fine, M. and Asch, A. 1988. Disability Beyond Stigma: Social Interaction, Discrimination and Activism. *Journal of Social Issues* 44: 3–21.

Finkelstein, V. 1981. To Deny or Not to Deny Disability. In Brechin, A., Liddiard, P., and Swain, J. (eds), *Handicap in a Social World*. London: Hodder and Stoughton, pp. 34–6.

Finkelstein, V. 1993. The Commonality of Disability. In Swain, J. *et al.* (eds), *Disabling Barriers, Enabling Environments*. London: Open University, pp. 9–15.

Finkelstein, V. 1996. The Disability Movement has Run out of Steam. *Disability Now* February: 11.

Finkelstein, V. and French, S. 1993. Towards a Psychology of Disability. In Swain, J. *et al.* (eds), *Disabling Barriers, Enabling Environments*. London: Open University, pp. 26–33.

Foster, L. 1996. *Access to the Historic Environment, Meeting the Needs of Disabled People*. Shaftesbury: Donhead Publishing.

French, S. 1993. Disability, Impairment or Something in Between? In Swain, J. *et al.* (eds), *Disabling Barriers, Enabling Environments*. London: Open University, pp. 17–25.

French, S. and Anspach, R.R. 1993. Can you See the Rainbow: The Roots of Denial. In Swain, J. *et al.* (eds), *Disabling Barriers, Enabling Environments*. London: Open University, pp. 69–77.

From the Edge, BBC2, 1996. Article on Deaf Awareness Week in Edinburgh, 16 October.

Hahn, H. 1988. The Politics of Physical Difference: Disability and Discrimination. *Journal Social Issues* 44: 39–47.

Hasler, F. 1993. Developments in the Disabled People's Movement. In Swain, J. *et al.* (eds), *Disabling Barriers, Enabling Environments*. London: Open University, pp. 278–84.

Hevey, D. 1993. The Tragedy Principle: Strategies for Change in the Cultural Representation of Disabled People. In Swain, J. *et al.* (eds), *Disabling Barriers, Enabling Environments*. London: Open University, pp. 116–21.

Innovations in Information. 1994a. Sense this Space. *Innovations in Information* 3: 15.

Innovations in Information. 1994b. The Charta of Nimes. *Innovations in Information* 3: 3.

Innovations in Information. 1994c. A Little Knowledge. *Innovations in Information* 3: 13.

Janssens, P.A. 1970. *Palaeopathology: Diseases and Injuries of Prehistoric Man*. London: John Baker.

Kelley, J.H. and Hanen, M.P. 1988. *Archaeology and the Methodology of Science*. Albuquerque: University of New Mexico Press.

Lenny, J. 1993. Do Disabled People Need Counselling? In Swain, J. *et al.* (eds), *Disabling Barriers, Enabling Environments*. London: Open University, pp. 233–40.

Lloyd, M. 1992. Does She Boil Eggs: Towards a Feminist Model of Disability. *Disability, Handicap and Society* 7: 207–22.

McCulloch, W.T. 1868. History of the 'Maiden' or Scottish Beheading Machine, with Notices of the Criminals Who Suffered by it. *Proceedings of the Society of Antiquaries of Scotland.* 7: 535–45.

McGuire, R.H. and Paynter, R. (eds). 1991. *The Archaeology of Inequality*. Oxford: Blackwell.

MacIvor, I. 1963. The King's Chapel at Restalrig and St Triduana's Aisle: A Hexagonal Two-Storied Chapel of the Fifteenth Century. *Proceedings of the Society of Antiquaries of Scotland.* 96: 247–63.

Morris, J. 1991. *Pride Against Prejudice*. London: Women's Press.

Morris, J. 1992. Personal and Political: A Feminist Perspective on Researching Physical Disability. *Disability, Handicap and Society* 7: 157–66.

Morris, J. 1993. Gender and Disability. In Swain, J. *et al.* (eds), *Disabling Barriers, Enabling Environments*. London: Open University, pp. 85–92.

Morrison, E. and Finkelstein, V. 1993. Broken Arts and Cultural Repair: The Role of Culture in the Empowerment of Disabled People. In Swain, J. *et al.* (eds), *Disabling Barriers, Enabling Environments*. London: Open University, pp. 122–7.

Murphy, R. 1987. *The Body Silent*. Gloucester: Dent.

Museums Journal. 1996. British Museum First for Access. *Museums Journal* September: 10.

NMS (National Museums of Scotland). 1996. *The Royal Museum of Scotland Access Guide*. Edinburgh: National Museums of Scotland.

Oliver, M. 1990. *The Politics of Disablement*. London: Palgrave Macmillan.

Oliver, M. 1991. Disability and Dependency: A Creation of Industrial Societies? In Swain, J. *et al.* (eds), *Disabling Barriers, Enabling Environments*. London: Open University, pp. 49–59.

Oliver, M. 1993. Re-defining Disability: A Challenge to Research. In Swain, J. *et al.* (eds), *Disabling Barriers, Enabling Environments*. London: Open University, pp. 61–8.

Oliver, M. and Barnes, C. 1993. Discrimination Disability and Welfare: From Needs to Rights. In Swain, J. *et al.* (eds), *Disabling Barriers, Enabling Environments*. London: Open University, pp. 267–77.

Ortner, D.J. and Putschar, W.G.J. 1981. *Identification of Pathological Conditions in Human Skeletal Remains*. Washington: Smithsonian Institution Press.

Pagel, M. 1988. *An Introduction to the Self-Organisation of Disabled People*. Manchester: Greater Manchester Coalition of Disabled People.

Perceptions, first published March/April 1996, edited by Steve Cooper, Shaftesbury Centre, Percy Street, Swindon, SN2 2AZ.

Pfeiffer, D. 1994. The Americans with Disabilities Act: Costly Mandates or Civil Rights? *Disability and Society* 9: 533–42.

Pickles, R. 1996. Access...Revisited. *Scottish Museum News* 12: 34.

Pickles, R. 1997. MAGDA Scotland. *Disability Scotland News* March: 16.

Radford, U.M. 1949. The Wax Images Found in Exeter Cathedral. *Antiquaries Journal* 29: 165–7.

Roberts, C. and Manchester, K. 1995. *The Archaeology of Disease*. New York: Cornell University Press.

Rogers, J. and Waldron, T. 1995. *A Field Guide to Joint Diseases in Archaeology*. Chichester: John Wiley and Sons.

Scheer, J. and Groce, N. 1988. Impairment as a Human Constant: Cross-cultural and Historical Perspectives on Variation. *Journal of Social Issues* 44: 23–37.

Schneider, J.W. 1988. Disability as a Moral Experience: Epilepsy and Self in Routine Relationships. *Journal of Social Issues* 44: 63–78.

Scotch, R.K. 1988. Disability as the Basis for a Social Movement: Advocacy and the Politics of Definition. *Journal of Social Issues* 44: 159–72.

Shakespeare, T. 1993. Disabled People's Self-organisation: A New Social Movement? *Disability, Handicap and Society* 8: 249–64.

Shakespeare, T. 1994. Cultural Representation of Disabled People: Dustbins for Disavowal? *Disability and Society* 9: 283–300.

Steinfield, E., Duncan, J., and Cardell, P. 1977. Towards a Responsive Environment: The Psychological Effects of Inaccessibility. In Bednan, M.J. (ed.), *Barrier-Free Environments*. Stroundsbourg: Dowden, Hutchinson and Ross.

Stone, K. 1997. Heritage Cash Bonanza. *Museums Journal* March: 9.

Stone, T. 1995. A Torturous Route to Antiquity. *Guardian* 29 Aug., Education Section: 12–13.

Swain, J., Finkelstein, V., French, S., and Oliver, M. (eds). 1993. *Disabling Barriers, Enabling Environments*. London: Open University.

Vonnegut, K. 1968. *Welcome to the Monkey House*. London: Cape.

Vujakovic, P. and Matthews, M. 1994. Contorted, Folded, Torn: Environmental Values, Cartographic Representation and the Politics of Disability. *Disability and Society* 9: 359–74.

Wallechinsky, D. and Wallace, I. 1978. *The People's Almanac 2*. New York: Morrow.

Young, V. and Urquhart, D. 1996. *Access to the Built Heritage, Advice on the Provision of Access for People with Disabilities to Historic Sites Open to the Public. Technical Advice Note 7*. Edinburgh: Historic Scotland.

Zola, I. 1982. Social and Cultural Disincentives to Independent Living. *Archives of Physical Medicine and Rehabilitation* 63: 394–7.

Chapter 12

Hidden or overlooked? Where are the disadvantaged in the skeletal record?

Tony Waldron

So many vagabonds, so many beggars bold.
John Skelton

Introduction

In *The Beggars*, Pieter Breughel the Elder shows a group of five men with deformities of the legs and a variety of curious crutches and prostheses to help them get around. Three of the group face forwards, whereas the others have their backs to the group, one looking into the distance towards a stone arch. We can assume that he is similarly afflicted as his comrades, since the shaft of a crutch under his right arm can just be glimpsed emerging from under his cloak, adorned with what look like fox tails. Three of the remaining four have lost their feet and are all armed with crutches and all have wooden devices attached to their lower legs. Two of these devices (of the first and fifth beggars) look like elaborate shin guards, which were evidently used to shuffle along the ground: the beggar at the right of the group is on his knees indicating both how these rudimentary sledges were used and how they were attached to the leg. The shin guards of the third beggar have a long point projecting from the front which was used to support the knee, as he hobbled along with the aid of his crutches. The fifth beggar is standing with his right knee flexed as we may suppose the joint was fixed in this position, which would explain his need for crutches. His face has a rather vacuous expression and his eyes appear to be moving independently in the way those of a blind man move.

Breughel is by no means the only painter to include those with disabilities in his paintings, and other examples may be found, for instance in the works of Hieronymus Bosch. Bosch's paintings abound with bizarre figures and animals and while his depiction of the beggars may owe something to the idiosyncrasies of his style, they appear sufficiently frequently in his works to allow us to suppose that they were a common sight in the Low Countries in the late fifteenth and early sixteenth centuries. In his study *Beggars and Cripples*, Bosch depicts more than two dozen individuals with varying deformities and mechanical aids for getting around. Some of the devices are similar to those shown by Breughel, but some are novel. To the right of centre of the sketch is a portly man with bilateral, above-knee amputations, who seems to sit on a low stool. In fact the 'legs' of the stool are separate supports by which he may have been able to shuffle along slowly. Opposite this figure is another leaning heavily on two four-legged supports. It is difficult to see what is wrong with this man, but he may have lost his leg and he moves by advancing his supports and dragging his single leg forward. Just below the man on the stool and to the right is a man whose right leg is bandaged and swollen while his left is withered and twisted, perhaps as a result of poliomyelitis or cerebral palsy. There is of course no means of knowing how the individuals who featured in these paintings received these injuries, but it is likely that most of the amputations were traumatic in origin, although one cannot entirely rule out the possibility that some were surgical amputations for conditions such as compound fractures of the ankle or chronic osteomyelitis. Some trades would have been likely to carry a high risk of injury, particularly those engaged in building and maintaining the castles, monasteries, and collegiate churches of the period; for example during the reign of Edward I employment was found for 400 masons, 30 smiths and carpenters, 1,000 unskilled workers, and 200 carters at Beaumaris Castle (Knoop and Jones 1949: 3).

The methods of construction are well illustrated in medieval manuscripts of the period and leave little doubt of the potential for injury, but there are no actual accounts of this unless the victim was important. William of Sens, who was called to repair Canterbury Cathedral after the fire of 1174, was badly injured when the beams on which he was standing collapsed, and although he survived, he was not able to continue to supervise the work and had to return to France (Andrews 1974: 20).

There is no reason to suppose that William's injury was a unique or even an unusual occurrence, but evidence for such injuries in the archaeological record is scarce, as is evidence for other physical disabilities, and presents a considerable challenge to palaeopathologists to explain. Dwarfism seems to be an exception to this general rule, certainly so far as the written record is concerned. Dwarfs, especially those with achondroplasia, seem to have held a special place in some cultures, particularly that of ancient Egypt where there are several references to them in papyri and in tomb paintings (see Dasen 1988). Individuals with physical abnormalities were often the subjects of public curiosity; they were depicted on picture postcards in the early 1900s, the most common depictions being of pituitary dwarfism and achondroplasia, and it has been suggested that being put on show provided, at least in some cases, some social benefit (Enderle 1998).

Disability and disadvantage have a number of antecedents including injury, disease, and abuse. The apparent deficit of physical evidence for their presence in earlier times may be due to the fact that they occurred less frequently than now, that individuals with deformities may have been buried separately from the rest of the population, that they may have congregated in one place and have been buried in places which have not yet been excavated, or that skeletons of those with physical deformities survive less well than others. Alternatively the condition may have been missed or misdiagnosed by those examining assemblages of skeletons which have become available for study. These possibilities will be explored with reference to three conditions: child abuse, tuberculosis, and scoliosis. This chapter concentrates only on those with some kind of physical disability that would put them at a disadvantage compared with the general population. Disadvantage, however, is not to be found exclusively among the physically disabled; people who are deaf or blind, those with chronic heart or lung disease, those with brain damage, and those who have no disability other than poverty may be equally disabled, but their skeletons will provide no clues to their impairments or poverty.

Child abuse

> Child abuse is the difference between a hand on the bottom and a fist in the face.
>
> Henry Kempe

In modern Britain at least one child in 1,000 under the age of four years suffers severe physical abuse, including fractures, brain haemorrhage, severe internal injuries, or mutilation, and the mortality rate of such children is at least one in 10,000 children (Meadow 1997: 3). Child abuse is often spoken of as a modern phenomenon and many paediatricians and other medical people tend to feel that it all started with Kempe's famous paper (Kempe *et al.* 1962), in which he coined the term 'the battered baby syndrome' to provoke his colleagues and the general public into taking notice of what was happening to young children. In fact Caffey (1946, 1957) had pointed out some time before this that the combination of subdural haemorrhage and fractured bones might be the result of parental abuse, but this work seems largely forgotten. There is, however, plenty of documentary evidence that the phenomenon has a long and undistinguished history. Soanus of Ephasus, for example, writing in the early second century AD, was aware that infants might be neglected or abused. In his *Gynaecology* he gives advice on choosing a wet nurse and comments that she should be self-controlled, sympathetic, and affectionate and not ill-tempered. Angry women, he writes: 'are like maniacs and sometimes when the newborn cries from fear and they are unable to restrain it, they let it drop from their hands or overturn it dangerously' (Quoted in Temkin 1956: 156).

The Arab physician, Rhazes, who is the author of what is considered to be the earliest surviving treatise on paediatrics, was aware that some injuries in children may have been caused intentionally (Radbill 1971). The literary record is then silent on the matter until the seventeenth century, although Knight records a revealing oral tradition from the Shetland Islands (Knight 1986). For many years children sang what appears to be a meaningless jingle:

> Barn vil ikka teea, barn vil ikka teea,
> Tak an leggen, slog an veggen,
> Barn vil ikka teea.

The words were eventually recognized to be Old Norse and were translated as: 'The child will not be quiet, the child will not be quiet; take it by the leg and hit it against the wall: the child will not be quiet.' There is no doubt that this method would have been very effective at silencing the child – for good. It would be interesting to know how frequently it was resorted to.

References to child abuse appeared in the medical literature again in England during the sixteenth century (Lynch 1985) and increased in frequency during the eighteenth and nineteenth centuries. In France the condition came to be recognized and commented upon as the nineteenth century progressed (Knight 1986). Lynch suggests that it was the increasing awareness of child abuse which led to the foundation of Societies for the Prevention of Cruelty to Children first in Liverpool in 1883, and in London the following year. In its first three years the London society dealt with 762 cases of cruelty of which 333 were assaults, 81 starvations, 130 dangerous neglect,

30 desertions, 70 cruel exposures to excite sympathy, and 116 other wrongs: of the total 25 children died (Lynch 1985).

There seems no reason to suppose that human nature has altered in any important respect in the last 2,000 years or so, or that it is only in recent times that adults have treated children cruelly, yet in no skeletal assemblage which I have examined – and in which children account for up to a fifth of the total population – has a single case been found in which the death could be attributed to willful abuse.

The criteria by which child abuse may be recognized have been frequently described by paediatricians and radiologists. In addition to the soft tissue signs of trauma, which are not available to those who study human remains, there are some well-recognized radiological signs which can guide those who examine children's skeletons. The most revealing indication of deliberate abuse is the presence of multiple fractures at different stages of healing, indicating that they occurred over a length of time (Fig. 12.1). Fractures of the distal metaphysis – the so-called 'corner' fracture – in a child who has not started to walk should always raise the possibility of deliberate harm. Fractures of the ribs are common in abused children and they may also be found in the sternum, vertebrae, and skull (Resnik 1989).

The signs which may be found radiologically can also be easily recognized in the skeleton. Kerley (1978) has recorded the case of three infants who were killed by their parents and buried in the basement and backyard of the house. The case came to light when two children who were interviewed by their teacher as to the number of siblings they had, casually remarked that there had been three more of them but that their mother and father had killed them. Multiple fractures, some healed and some healing, were found in the skeletons of all three children. The sites affected included the mandible, ribs, clavicle, radius, and ulna; the left clavicle of one of the children had two separate fractures in it. In addition to these fractures Kerley noted some which he considered had been caused at or around the time of death, and there were also some breaks in the bone which had occurred during excavation. The latter could be distinguished by the fact that the broken ends of the bones were of a lighter colour than the surface.

All three skeletons that Kerley examined had unequivocal evidence of antemortem fractures in various stages of healing and which had certainly been caused at different periods of the children's lives, confirming that they had been subject to repeated trauma (the age of the fractures in the skeleton can be determined by physical or radiological appearances as shown in Table 12.1). Kerley stressed the impor-

Table 12.1 Peak times of morphological or radiological appearances of fractures in children

Morphological or radiological appearance	Time from occurrence of fracture
Periosteal new bone formation[1]	10–14 days
Loss of definition of fracture line	14–21 days
Soft callus formation	14–21 days
Hard callus formation	21–42 days
Remodelling	1 year

Notes
[1] Fracture without periosteal new bone is usually less than 7–10 days old and seldom more than 20 days. A fracture with only slight periosteal new bone formation could be only 4–7 days old.

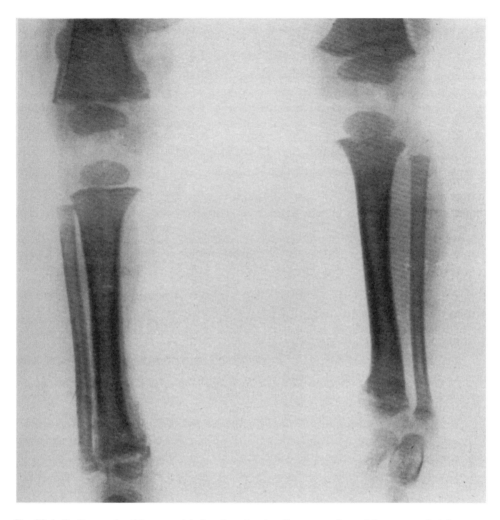

Fig. 12.1 Radiograph of battered baby showing healing metaphyseal fracture of right femur and both tibiae.

tance of X-raying suspected fractures as the increased density at the broken ends of the bones (indicating remodelling of the bone) is evidence that the fracture occurred before death; while this might be a requirement for forensic cases, it is doubtful that an experienced osteologist would fail to differentiate an ante-mortem or peri-mortem fracture from one which had occurred during excavation.

It is unlikely that the kind of injuries which would be sustained by an abused child would escape notice among a skeletal assemblage, but perhaps the children who died, as the result of abuse, were buried covertly, as happened with the infants in the modern case which Kerley described. The most satisfactory explanation for their non-appearance in the archaeological record, however, seems certainly to do with numbers. Modern data suggest that although approximately 0.4 per cent of children suffer abuse, the mortality rate is only about 1 in 10,000 and in those who survive into adulthood there will be no skeletal evidence to show they were harmed in child-hood. If the rates of child abuse in the past are at all comparable with those of the present day, the chances of finding an abused infant are remote indeed. Since the 95 per cent confidence intervals around the modern death rate are from $0.61–5.5/10^4$, approximately 2,000 infant skeletons would have to be examined in order to detect death from child abuse even at the upper limit. The apparent absence of battered babies in the past, then, is the result of chance effects due to the small numbers involved. Even were such children to be discovered, the true prevalence of child abuse would be a substantial underestimate, since the majority of children who suffer inten-tional harm nevertheless survive and the stigmata of their injuries vanish as their skeleton matures and remodels.

Tuberculosis

> I can get no remedy against this consumption ... the disease is incurable.
> William Shakespeare

Tuberculosis has some claims to be the oldest human bacterial infection. It is caused by *Mycobacterium tuberculosis*, one of a large group of related organisms widespread in the environment. The disease seems to be rare in wild animals which are not in contact with domesticated animals, although some strains of mycobacteria do cause epizootics in wild animals (Francis 1958). The disease does occur in a wide range of domesticated animals and in wild animals kept in captivity (Kovalev 1980) and it was probably only when animals were kept in close proximity that the acute form of the disease was able to develop. It is generally considered that man originally contracted the disease from domestic cattle. The supposition is that the form of the organism which affects cattle, *M bovis*, probably evolved from saprophytic soil bacteria and that the human form (*M tuberculosis*) then evolved from the bovine form (Stead 1997), being especially prevalent in the post-medieval period. The two forms are certainly very closely related – and to the mycobacterium which causes leprosy (*M leprae*) (Frothingham 1999). *M bovis* can infect an exceptionally wide range of hosts, including goats, cats, dogs, pigs, buffalo, badgers, deer, and bison (O'Reilly and Dabourn 1995). It is possible that the disease may have spread originally from other animals with which man came into contact rather than cattle, although the latter seem a more likely source.

Human infection with *M bovis* occurs through the ingestion of infected milk and milk products such as butter and cheese. The organism is absorbed from the gastro-intestinal tract and spreads to the abdominal lymphatic system and from there to other parts of the body, including the skeleton. Spread between infected animals occurs through droplet infection and this is also the mode of spread of the human organism. The target organ for *M tuberculosis* is the lung, and the natural history of the disease is different from that of the bovine form. Following primary lung infec-tion, the infection may then spread widely throughout the lung and to other organs; the predominant symptoms are those relating to the lung infection, resulting in the condition widely referred to as consumption in the nineteenth-century literature.

Bone infections are relatively uncommon in patients with pulmonary tuberculosis, occurring in between 3 and 5 per cent of cases; it is much more common in those with

Fig. 12.2 Cervical and upper thoracic spine of a young boy recovered from a Byzantine site in Turkey. The cervical spine is uppermost and points to the right. The spine has collapsed and the cervical thoracic spines have fused.

extra-pulmonary disease, affecting perhaps up to 35 per cent of cases (Resnick and Niwayama 1988). It is this characteristic of the disease which probably gave rise to the notion that skeletal tuberculosis was present *only* in bovine tuberculosis, but reference to the early literature on the disease, when it was very much more common than nowadays, suggests that anything between 40–97 per cent of cases of skeletal tuberculosis were *not* due to infection with the bovine bacterium (e.g. Fraser 1914: 6).

Spinal disease accounts for between 25 and 45 per cent of all cases of skeletal tuberculosis and the lower half of the spine is most frequently involved. Although a single vertebra may be involved, it is more common to find a number of adjacent vertebrae and their intervertebral discs affected (Revell 1986). The disease leads to erosion and destruction of bone tissue; in the spine, the vertebral bodies are especially prone to infection. The destruction which follows may cause the spine to collapse, leading to an acute angulation of the spine which is referred to as Pott's disease (see Fig.12.2); unusual forms of the disease may occur – it may be present in the cervical spine, for example (Slater *et al.* 1991), or affect the posterior parts of the vertebrae (Rahman *et al.* 1997), or there may be no disc involvement (Pertuist *et al.* 1999) – and the disease may also be found in any bone or joint. In dry bones, the disease appears as an erosive lesion with very little proliferation of new bone. There is nothing which is specific to these lesions, so with the absence of the classic Pott's spine, the diagnosis may represent considerable difficulty. Indeed more than 30 years ago, Morse *et al.* (1964) wrote that:

> If one were to attempt to make a diagnosis [of tuberculosis] from a dried bone specimen, the only chance of making even a good guess would be on the basis of involvement of the spine; bone tuberculosis in other locations would be indistinguishable from too many other diseases.

Kelly and El-Najir (1980) discussed the differential diagnosis of skeletal tuberculosis in considerable detail and suggested 19 different conditions with which it might be confused. Although, in practice, many of these other conditions would not be too difficult to exclude from the differential, some certainly would be easily confused and Ortner has recently noted that the differential diagnosis of tuberculosis 'can be challenging and in some cases, not possible at all' (1999: 257). The disease which would be most likely to cause most confusion is brucellosis. This is another disease contracted from animals – most likely cattle in the UK; in this case the disease is contracted by contact with infected blood, as may occur when helping a cow in labour, for example. There seems no reason to suppose that this disease was not present in adjacent herds or that those who tended them would not contract it themselves. The proportion of patients who develop skeletal brucellosis is variously reported and estimates range from 1 to 75 per cent but there is general agreement that the spine, particularly the lumbar spine, is commonly affected and the radiological and morphological appearance of spinal brucellosis and tuberculosis are similar (e.g. de Dios Colmonero *et al.* 1991).

Cases of Pott's disease have been reported in antiquity, indeed it was one of the first diseases to appear in the palaeopathological literature, being described in 1910 by Elliot Smith and Ruffer in a mummy from the 21st Dynasty (Elliot Smith and Ruffer 1921 [1910]) (Fig. 12.3). The number of cases, however, is relatively small, especially when one considers that the disease was likely to have been common in the past, in earlier times from the drinking of contaminated milk or eating infected butter or cheese, and in more recent times when pulmonary tuberculosis was common (for details of cases in the archaeological record see Ortner and Putschar 1981; Pálfi *et al.* 1999). The conclusion must be that the prevalence of tuberculosis in past populations will be greatly underestimated. There are two explanations for this, the first to do with the problems surrounding diagnosis referred to above, and the second to do with the small numbers of individuals who go on to develop skeletal tuberculosis. As noted above, probably no more than 5 per cent of those with pulmonary tuberculosis develop skeletal forms of the disease and not much more than 35 per cent of those with extra-pulmonary forms of the disease. It is not possible to know on morphological grounds whether individuals found with skeletal tuberculosis died from the pulmonary or the extra-pulmonary form of the disease, but even supposing that all those with skeletal lesions died from extra-pulmonary tuberculosis, then the prevalence of the disease would still be underestimated by up to 70 per cent. When one also considers that the only certain way of diagnosing the disease in skeletal remains depends upon the finding of the classic spinal changes and that these develop in no more than half the patients with skeletal tuberculosis, then it is obvious that the estimates of the prevalence of tuberculosis in the past will be substantially too low. An estimate of the order of magnitude of the number of expected cases of tuberculosis in the most badly affected countries is 100/100,000. If it is assumed that this figure applied in the past, and that between 5 and 30 per cent of cases develop bony lesions, then the number

Fig. 12.3 Sketch of a mummy from the 21st Dynasty from paper by Elliot Smith and Ruffer (1921). Note the angulation of the spine typical of spinal tuberculosis.

of cases detectable morphologically in the skeleton might be between 5–30/100,000. If only half develop spinal lesions, then Pott's disease of the spine would be found in between 2.5 and 15 cases per 100,000. It is perhaps not surprising that the number of reported cases remains small.

Recent advances in palaeopathology, however, do give some grounds for optimism and the hope that it may be possible, with adequate funding, to arrive at more reliable estimates of tuberculosis in the past, and also to test whether the human form derived from the bovine form or if the two have been coexisting from the earliest times.

The advances referred to depend on the observation that the organic component of bone survives much better in archaeological remains than had been previously supposed. Bone consists of a crystalline matrix (hydroxyapatite), an organic phase, comprising collagen, bone, other proteins, and DNA from various sources, and water. It has always been assumed that the organic component was broken down during the time that the bones were buried, leaving only the inorganic matrix behind, and that usually much altered by diagenesis. This supposition was overturned when various authors were able to extract blood and plasma proteins from bone and then ancient DNA (aDNA), both human and that derived from bacteria, using the polymerase chain reaction (PCR) technique. The first recovery of aDNA of *M tuberculosis* was reported by Spiegelman and Lemma (1993) from the spine of a young boy excavated from a Byzantine site in Turkey, followed shortly by the report of a similar extraction from the mummy of a 12-year-old girl from Peru, dating to about AD 1000 (Arriaza *et al.* 1995). It is possible now to differentiate *M tuberculosis* from *M bovis* and other strains of mycobacteria by using a technique referred to as spoligotyping (Kamerbeek *et al.* 1997), and using this method Taylor *et al.* (1999) were able to show that aDNA from three medieval bone samples was from the human rather than the bovine form.

The use of PCR seems to offer a valuable means whereby the diagnosis of tuberculosis can be confirmed in human remains and by which the form of the disease can be identified. There are, however, some caveats which need to be entered. First, although aDNA seems to preserve well in bone – and rather surprisingly, better in cremated than non-cremated bone (Brown *et al.* 1994), and apparently better in the bones of mummies than in the soft tissues, especially if the latter are degraded (Lassen *et al.* 1994) – the method is expensive and time-consuming and can only realistically be used in cases where tuberculosis is suspected on morphological grounds. Moreover the preservation of aDNA varies from place to place; it is preserved better in skeletons from the Mediterranean than from Romano-British sites, for example (Burger 1997), and only positive results of PCR analysis are informative. A negative result cannot be taken as evidence that the individual did not have the disease since the possibility that the aDNA has disappeared cannot be ruled out.

Mycobacteria have a waxy coat which contains a number of mycolic acids. Using gas chromatography it is possible to extract these compounds from the tissues of patients with tuberculosis and differentiate between different strains (Garza-Gonzalez *et al.* 1998). The technique is relatively straightforward and much more likely than PCR to be applicable on a large scale, and it is less susceptible to contamination than PCR. It has been used to demonstrate the presence of *M tuberculosis* in the fragment of calcified pleura some 1,400 years old (Donaghue *et al.* 1998) and it could be used to determine the prevalence of tuberculosis on a cemetery-wide basis. The application of the method to skeletons which do not have any morphological evidence of tuberculosis would provide a better indication of the frequency of the disease in the past, although even with this method, false negative results would be certain to occur, leading to an underestimate of the true prevalence.

Scoliosis

> Crookbacked he was, tooth-shaken, and blear eyed. Went on three feet, and sometimes crept on four.
>
> Thomas Sackville

Scoliosis is the term given to spinal deformities in which there is lateral curvature of the spine. The condition may be accompanied by a posterior curvature (kyphosis) or by an anterior curvature (lordosis) or both. It may be congenital, in which case it is associated with defects in the vertebrae, or idiopathic, by far the most common variety (Winter and Lonstein 1992). The idiopathic form is generally divided into an infant form, which appears before puberty, and an adolescent form, which appears after puberty, the latter being the more common. There is also a form which first appears in adulthood, and which is the consequence of other spinal disease such as osteoporosis, osteomalacia, or degenerative change. Idiopathic scoliosis is more common in females than in males and epidemiological studies suggest that the overall prevalence in the general population is up to 4.5 per cent (Rogala *et al.* 1996). The prevalence varies considerably, however, with the degree of curvature present. Where curves greater than 10° are considered, the prevalence is 2–3 per cent, for those over 20° it is 0.3–0.5 per cent and for those over 30°, it is 0.2–0.3 per cent (Winter and Lonstein 1992). Only the most severe degrees of curvature result in significant debility. The aetiology of the condition is not understood – as the name implies – although twin studies have shown that it has some genetic basis (Ponsetti *et al.* 1976).

The condition is likely to progress during adult life, especially in those with the more pronounced degrees of curvature. Although appearances may be alarming, the condition does not result in higher frequency of back pain than in the general population, but curves in the thoracic region interfere with pulmonary function and may lead to death from right-sided heart failure, secondary to raised pressure in the pulmonary vessels (Kolind-Sørensen 1973). The socio-economic effects of the condition may also be considerable; some studies have shown that those with scoliosis are likely to be unemployed or in receipt of disability pensions, and are self-conscious of, or embarrassed by, their condition (Fowles *et al.* 1978). Victor Hugo's hunchback of Notre Dame exemplifies the social distress which can be caused by the condition, and that it is inevitable that those with severe scoliosis would descend into vagrancy or beggary unless they enjoyed the support of their community, given that the condition would limit their opportunities for work.

There is no mistaking scoliosis in the skeleton (Fig. 12.4); the spine may show one or more curves of varying magnitude, wedging of the vertebrae on the concavity of the curves, and frequently osteoarthritis in the facet joints of the spine. It is not conceivable that the condition could be overlooked in a skeletal assemblage, no matter how inexperienced the examiner, but – again – the frequency with which it is reported appears low, compared with modern rates. From the crypt of Christ Church, Spitalfields, in London, for example, a total of 311 adult males and 312 adult females buried during the eighteenth and early nineteenth centuries were recovered. Two of the males and three of the females had appearances consistent with idiopathic scoliosis, giving crude prevalence rates for the condition of 0.64 and 0.96 per cent respectively, and an overall crude prevalence rate of 0.8 per cent. The estimates are considerably lower than expected, even though the sample is, by osteological standards, a large one.

By contrast Wells (1967) reported on a series of 50 burials which were recovered from the church of St Michael-at-Thorn in Norwich. Among this small group, of which only eight had well-preserved spines, Wells (ibid.: 41) found three cases with spinal deformities, two (both female) with scoliosis, and one (a male) with kyphosis. Finding two of eight spines with scoliosis is remarkable and prompted Wells to seek an explanation in the presumed occupation of the women by – as he put it – 'the integration of informed speculation based on a wide experience of bone pathology with information gleaned from the contemporary art of the period and ancient city records'. He noted that Norwich had for centuries been a centre of weaving and he supposed that the two women with scoliosis had been employed as weavers and that this had been the cause of their deformity. (The man with kyphosis Wells decided had not been a weaver but a tailor.) Even supposing that Wells was correct in his assumptions, and there is no hard evidence to support him, a much more likely explanation

Fig. 12.4 Spine with two very marked scoliotic curves. The upper curve is approximately 80° and the lower approximately 70°.

for this unusual cluster of cases suggests itself, that is, that those who are disadvantaged tend to gravitate towards large centres of population and that Wells's (ibid.) findings are an example of this. Certainly there can be no question of being able to determine an individual's occupation from skeletal pathology, even though a great many osteologists think that they can achieve this remarkable feat.

More recently Stirland (pers. comm.) has found another cluster of cases of scoliosis in a group of skeletons recovered from the church of St Margaret in Magdalen Street in Norwich (16 cases among 368 adults). The graveyard was used from about 1240 to 1468 and was the poorest medieval parish in the city. This finding lends support to the view that people who were disadvantaged in some way moved to the poorest parts of the city where there would be more opportunity to support themselves by begging or other means.

Conclusion

> And suppose we solve all the problems...? What happens? We end up with more problems than we started with...a problem left to itself dries up or goes rotten. But fertilise a problem with a solution – you'll hatch out dozens.
>
> N.F. Simpson

The problem as to whether those who were disadvantaged are hidden or overlooked in archaeology admits a number of possible solutions, although none may necessarily be correct. Unfortunately it is not possible to design the kind of epidemiological study which would be required to provide a definitive solution – or at least one as definitive as epidemiology can get – because of the nature of the material. All skeletal assemblages have been subject to processes which attenuate their numbers and degrade the bones which do remain. The resultant sample which is dug from the ground and presented to a bone specialist is far from random, and may not even be *representative* of the population of which it was originally a part, and a modern epidemiologist would certainly not be in a rush to deal with it.

Nevertheless using the examples discussed above, some solutions can be suggested, and at least some could be tested. It is clear that the number of some disadvantaged individuals is too small to be detected, given the small size of most skeletal assemblages. This is the case in child abuse, where very few of the children who are deliberately injured die from their injuries, and those who survive into adulthood will have no pathognomonic traces of childhood trauma on their skeletons. It would require the examination of many thousands of infant skeletons in order to be certain of finding even a single case of multiple fractures, and battered babies are likely to remain hidden from view, except through the medium of a chance finding.

The diagnosis of some conditions presents another problem to palaeopathologists, indeed it may be the most serious problem they face, as there are few diseases which leave pathognomonic signs on the skeleton. This is certainly the case with tuberculosis, except perhaps where there is a classic Pott's spine. An added difficulty with tuberculosis is that the skeleton is affected in only a minority of cases so that even where the disease is correctly diagnosed, the true prevalence in the population will be underestimated. The use of PCR to detect bacterial DNA or gas chromatography for the analysis of mycolic acids, however, offers an opportunity to confirm the diagnosis in cases where the spine is not affected, and even to estimate the prevalence of the disease in a group of skeletons which may show no signs of skeletal lesions at all. The detection of mycolic acids seems to offer the best prospect since it is a cheaper technique and not subject to contamination during the collection of samples or during analysis as is PCR.

There is no difficulty in detecting skeletons with severe physical deformities, such as scoliosis, although for the sake of comparison it would be necessary for different workers to agree on how to categorize the degree of disability. Minor degrees of scoliosis and kyphosis can be found commonly due to vertebral collapse following trauma or as a consequence of osteoporosis, for example, and these need to be differentiated from the gross changes resulting from idiopathic scoliosis. In orthopaedic practice, the magnitude of curvature of the spine is expressed in degrees, and it would be helpful if the same procedure were adopted when reporting scoliosis in the skeleton, as it is only the greater degrees of scoliosis which result in severe disability.

The suggestion has been made here that those with disabilities would be likely to migrate towards big towns or cities where they might better be able to support themselves. This could be tested by comparing the prevalence of scoliosis – or other conditions which might be of interest – in town and country settings and in poor and rich parishes with towns. The data required to carry out this analysis may already exist in published bone reports.

Finally, although it seems that the majority of individuals who were disadvantaged in life will remain hidden from archaeological gaze, diligent searching should reveal at least some to view.

Acknowledgements

I am grateful to those colleagues and students who have listened uncomplainingly to me discussing these matters over the years. I am also extremely grateful to Dr Anne Stirland for permission to quote data from her unpublished report on St Margaret's Church.

Bibliography

Andrews, F.B. 1974. *The Medieval Builder and His Methods*. East Ardley: EP Publishing.

Arriaza, B.T., Salo, W., Aufderheide, A.C., and Holcomb, T.A. 1995. Pre-Columbian Tuberculosis in Northern Chile: Molecular and Skeletal Evidence. *American Journal of Physical Anthropology* 98: 37–45.

Brown, K., O'Donoghue, K., and Brown, T. 1995. DNA in Cremated Bones from an Early Bronze Age Cemetery Cairn. *International Journal of Osteoarchaeology* 5: 181–7.

Burger, J. 1997. DNA Preservation Under Different Conditions. In Unpublished Conference Proceedings, Ancient DNA iv, Göttingen 5–7 June.

Caffey, J. 1946. Multiple Fractures of Long Bones in Infants Suffering from Subdural Haematoma. *American Journal of Roentgenology* 56: 163–9.

Caffey, J. 1957. Some Traumatic Lesions in Growing Bones Other than Fractures and Dislocations; Clinical and Radiological Fractures. *British Journal of Radiology* 30: 225–31.

Dasen, V. 1988. Dwarfism in Egypt and Classical Antiquity. *Medical History* 32: 253–76.

Dios Colmonero, J. de, Reguera, J.M., Fernandez-Nebro, A., and Cabrea-Franquelo, F. 1991. Osteoarticular Complications of Brucellosis. *Annals of Rheumatic Diseases* 50: 23–6.

Donaghue, H.D., Spiegelman, M., Zias, J., Gernaey-Child, A.M., and Minikin, D.E. 1998. *Mycobacterium Tuberculosis* Complex DNA in Calcified Pleura from Remains 1,400 Years Old. *Letters in Applied Microbiology* 27: 265–9.

Elliot Smith, G. and Ruffer, M.A. 1921 [1910]. Pott'sche Krankheit an einer Ägyptischen Mumie aus der Zeit der 21. Dynastie. In Moodie, R.L. (ed.), *Studies in the Palaeopathology of Egypt*. Chicago: University of Chicago Press, pp. 3–11.

Enderle, A. 1998. Dwarfism and Gigantism in Historical Picture Postcards. *Journal of the Royal Society of Medicine* 91: 273–8.

Fowles, J.V., Drummond, D.S., and L'Ecuyer, S. 1978. Untreated Scoliosis in the Adult. *Clinical Orthopaedics and Related Research* 134: 212–17.

Francis, J. 1958. *Tuberculosis in Animals and Man*. London: Cassell.

Fraser, J. 1914. *Tuberculosis of the Bones and Joints*. London: Adam and Charles Black.

Frothingham, R. 1999. Evolutionary Bottlenecks in the Agents of Tuberculosis, Leprosy and Paratuberculosis. *Medical Hypotheses* 52: 95–9.

Garza-Gonzales, E., Guerro-Olazaran, M., Tijerina-Menchaca, R., and Viader-Salvado, J.M. 1998. Identification of Mycobacteria by Mycolic Acid Pattern. *Archives of Medical Research* 29: 303–6.

Kamerbeek, J.L., Schouls, L., Kolk, A., Van Argterveld, M., *et al.* 1997. Simultaneous Detection and Strain Differentiation of *Mycobacterium Tuberculosis* for Diagnosis and Epidemiology. *Journal of Clinical Microbiology* 35: 907–14.

Kelly, M. and El-Najir, M.Y. 1980. Natural Variation and Differential Diagnosis of Skeletal Changes in Tuberculosis. *American Journal of Physical Anthropology* 52: 153–67.

Kempe, C.H., Silverman, F.N., Steele, B.F., Droegmueller, W., and Silver, H.K. 1962. The Battered Child Syndrome. *Journal of the American Medical Association* 181: 17–24.

Kerley, E.R. 1978. The Identification of Battered Infant Skeletons. *Journal of Forensic Science* 23: 163–8.

Knight, B. 1986. The History of Child Abuse. *Forensic Science International* 30: 135–41.

Knoop, D. and Jones, G.P. 1949. *The Medieval Mason*. Manchester: Manchester University Press.

Kolind-Sørensen, V. 1973. A Follow-Up Study of Patients with Idiopathic Scoliosis. *Acta Orthopedica Scandinavica* 44: 98–103.

Kovalev, C.K. 1980. Tuberculosis in Wildlife Reviewed. *Journal of Hygiene, Epidemiology, Microbiology and Immunology* 24: 495–504.

Lassen, C., Hummel, S., and Hermann, B. 1994. Comparison of DNA Extraction and Amplification from Ancient Human Bone and Mummified Soft Tissue. *International Journal of Legal Medicine* 107: 152–5.

Lynch, M.A. 1985. Child Abuse before Kempe: An Historical Literature Review. *Child Abuse and Neglect* 9: 7–15.

Meadow, R. 1997. Epidemiology. In *ABC of Child Abuse*. London: British Medical Association.

Morse, D., Brothwell, D.R., and Ucko, P. 1964. Tuberculosis in Ancient Egypt. *American Review of Respiratory Disease* 90: 524–41.

O'Reilly, L.M. and Daborn, C.J. 1995. The Epidemiology of *Mycobacterium Bovis* Infections in Animals and Man: A Review. *Tuberculosis and Lung Disease* 76, suppl.1: 1–46.

Ortner, D. 1999. Paleopathology: Implications for the History and Evolution of Tuberculosis. In Pálfi, G., Dutor, O., Deák, J., and Hutas, I. (eds), *Tuberculosis Past and Present*. Szeged: Golden Book Publisher, pp. 257–65.

Ortner, D. and Putschar, W.G.J. 1981. *Identification of Pathological Conditions in Human Skeletal Remains*. Washington: Smithsonian Institution Press.

Pálfi, G., Dutor, O., Deák, J., and Hutás, I. (eds). 1999. *Tuberculosis Past and Present*. Szeged: Golden Book Publisher.

Pertuist, E., Beudreuil, J., Liote, F., Horusitzky, A., *et al.* 1999. Spinal Tuberculosis in Adults. *Medicine (Baltimore)* 78: 309–20.

Ponsetti, I., Pedrini, V., Wynne-Davis, R., and Duval-Beaupere, G. 1976. Pathogenesis of Scoliosis. *Clinical Orthopaedics and Related Research* 120: 268–80.

Radbill, S.X. 1971. The First Treatise in Pediatrics. *Americal Journal of Diseases of Children* 122: 369–76.

Rahman, N.U., Jampoon, A., and Al-Tahan, A.M. 1997. Neural Arch Tuberculosis: Radiological Findings and their Correlation with Surgical Findings. *British Journal of Neurosurgery* 11: 32–8.

Resnik, C.S. 1989. Diagnostic Imaging in Pediatric Skeletal Trauma. *Radiologic Clinics of North America* 27: 1,013–22.

Resnick, D. and Niwayama, G. 1988. *Diagnosis of Bone and Joint Disorders*. Philadelphia: W.B. Saunders.

Revell, P. 1986. *Pathology of Bone*. Berlin: Springer Verlag, pp. 245–7.

Rogala, E., Drummond, D., and Gurr, J. 1996. Scoliosis: Incidence and Natural History. *Journal of Bone and Joint Surgery* 78: 314–17.

Slater, R.R., Beale, R.W., and Bullitt, E. 1991. Pott's Disease of the Cervical Spine. *Southern Medical Journal* 84: 521–3.

Spiegelman, M. and Lemma, E. 1993. The Use of the Polymerase Chain Reaction to Detect *Mycobacterium Tuberculosis* in Ancient Skeletons. *International Journal of Osteoarchaeology* 3: 137–43.

Stead, W.W. 1997. The Origin and Erratic Global Spread of Tuberculosis. How the Past Explains the Present and is the Key to the Future. *Clinical Chest Medicine* 18: 65–77.

Taylor, G.M., Goyal, M., Legge, A.J., Shaw, R.J., and Young, D. 1999. Genotypic Analysis of *Mycobacterium Tuberculosis* from Medieval Human Remains. *Microbiology* 145: 899–904.

Temkin, O. 1956. *Translation of Soranus'* Gynecology. Baltimore: Johns Hopkins Press.

Wells, C. 1967. Weaver, Tinker or Shoemaker? *Medical and Biological Illustration* 17: 39–47.

Winter, R.B. and Lonstein, L.E. 1992. Juvenile and Adolescent Scoliosis. In Herkowitz, H.N., Garfin, S.R., Balderson, R.A., Eismount, F.J., *et al.* (eds), *The Spine*. Philadelphia: W.B. Saunders, pp. 373–430.

Chapter 13

Archaeology's humanism and the materiality of the body

Julian Thomas

Introduction: humanism

In this chapter I intend to argue that throughout the modern era the dominant understanding of the body has been a humanist one, and that this remains influential within archaeology today. In particular I will suggest that the issue of the human body is one that troubles and polarizes the various approaches which are grouped under the term 'post-processual archaeology'. My assertion is that some interpretive archaeologies have been unable, or unwilling, to throw off the legacy of humanism, on the grounds that to do so is to do violence to the humanity of people in the past and the present.

Philosophical humanism is a view of the world which has involved the progressive replacement of Faith and God by Reason and Man (*sic*). In other words humanism replaced one set of certainties or moral universals with another. Renaissance humanism was grounded in the idea that we can become whatever we wish, and achieve whatever we desire, so long as we have a stable foundation (Carroll 1993: 25). This foundation was discovered in Man himself: a creature capable of exercising both reason and free will. Within this scheme of things history is perceived in terms of the gradual freeing of human will, accompanied by the more perfect application of reason. For the Enlightenment, a rational society was to be achieved by the erasure of tradition and superstition, the encumbrances on the deployment of free will. René Descartes argued that a person who acted freely and in a fully rational way would be incapable of sin: reason would lead to the best of all possible outcomes. This view finds an echo in the political economy of Adam Smith, who suggested that the 'invisible hand' of unrestricted free trade would inevitably secure the best possible distribution of goods and wealth (Carroll 1993: 122).

However, a cosmic order which places Man at the centre of the universe requires that the character of humanity must be both fixed and knowable. Indeed humanity has an *essence*, as a *rational animal*: a biological creature to which has been added a mind, a soul, and a particular self-understanding as a unique being (the *existentiell*) (Heidegger 1993: 226). Seeing humanity as 'built in layers' forces a distinction between mind and body, with the thinking self prioritized over its material vehicle (Cottingham 1992: 236). This conception of what it is to be human serves as a universal, and yet (as we shall see) it was established through a series of exclusions and repudiations. For Man to constitute a distinct entity, various forms of inhumanity needed to be cast out, and these have tended to proliferate through the modern era: blacks, Jews, perverts, the insane....These segregations of mind from body and human from inhuman can be seen as part of a more general process of intellectual hygiene, which was most marked in the scientific revolution, and which sought to establish the order of creation. Central to this conceptual 'purification' were the distinctions between the observing subject and the observed object, and between active culture and the passive nature upon which it operates (Jordanova 1989: 21).

The kind of human being that was celebrated by the humanist tradition was one which stood firmly on one side of each of these modernist oppositions: active rather than passive, rational rather than passionate, using the mind to transcend the body, achieving freedom by throwing off tradition. This sort of person is the rational individual, what Alasdair MacIntyre calls the 'unencumbered self, a self-contained centre of meaning and volition who operates in abstraction from social relations', (MacIntyre 1981; Lloyd 1986: 217). It needs to be emphasized that this identity is a cultural construct, and is quite specific to Western modernity. As well as being a free agent, the Western individual is perceived as being a centre, a point from which acts and meanings emerge and from which relationships are built (Strathern 1988: 269).

It is this model of the autonomous individual which forms the building block of the characteristic political philosophy of modernity – liberalism. Liberalism assumes a contract theory of society: human beings are in the first instance free and unrestricted agents, who then enter into relationships with others in order to promote their own interests. Relationships are only to be tolerated where they do not eclipse the freedom of the individual. It was with the formulation of liberalism that the humanist ideal of a society based upon Reason and Man crystallized (Mouffe 1993: 12). However, as we have already seen, such a move required the fixing of a 'human nature' as an unquestionable first principle. The legal codes of the modern West, for instance, have generally been constructed as means of regulating the rational behaviour of individuals. Indeed there is a continuing desire to ground ethical codes on a set of fundamental human needs and rights. In this connection Martha Nussbaum argues that these essential human characteristics can be identified by stripping away the layers of culturally specific attunements, leaving a kind of residuum (Nussbaum 1992: 205–8). What this implies is that culture is always an addition, something extra which has been spread over the surface of an essence which exists prior to and outside of culture, language, and signification.

Of course the specificity and partiality of the Western individual as a political subject has been devastatingly unmasked by recent feminist scholarship. For all of the denigrated categories of modernist thought are those which have been associated with women: passion, unreason, the domestic sphere, darkness, naturalness, physicality. The consequence has been the creation of an image of a supposedly gender-neutral Everyman with which men can freely identify, but which effectively excludes women from legitimate involvement in the public sphere (Caverero 1996: 191; Gatens 1996: 50). The notion of the autonomous individual serves to present as universal the actions and perspectives of one kind of person. Of course modernity and humanism have not been entirely negative phenomena. The late modern era with its scientific progress and liberal institutions has seen an unprecedented growth in material abundance, an improvement in standards of public health, and an expansion of political representation. The problem is that these have been bought at the cost of the sustained exclusion of those who least approximate to the humanist ideal: the autonomous (white, male, heterosexual) individual. Worse, because so many of the humanitarian enterprises of the past two centuries have been carried out from within the framework of humanism, it has tended to dictate the terms of any debate on human welfare.

Anti-humanism

Over the past century and more there has been a strong anti-humanist tradition in philosophy, which has gone hand-in-hand with the critique of modernity. Nietzsche, for instance, was immensely critical of triumphalist histories which portray the contemporary order as the outcome of a progressive development grounded in the civilizing virtues. In *The Genealogy of Morals* (1969) Nietzsche sought to demonstrate that reason and ethical values were not innate human qualities which founded civilization, but products of the historical process, which emerged as transformations of quite different sets of understandings. In explicitly attacking Sartre's humanism, Heidegger (1993) rejected the notion that humanity was an essential quality which could be added to an animal body. Humanity could not be isolated as a spark locked within a person, but lay in the way in which humans allowed things to 'show themselves'. Putting a contemporary gloss on this, humanness is not an attribute of the phenotype, and is to be located *outside* of the person, in the social relationships and the processes of signification in which they are engaged, and which render the world intelligible. The tragedy of humankind is that they constantly misrecognize themselves as *things*, yet are dimly aware that the solid ground of their self-contained status as entities is missing. With the emergence of post-structuralism these critiques of humanism were elaborated and extended. Lacan reworked Freud's conception of the unconscious to show that the human subject was produced rather than fixed by innate drives: the prior existence of language and signification was required for the assumption of identity. Foucault argued that the modern Western subject and its deepest hidden 'truth', sexuality, had a history. Finally Derrida 'de-centred the subject', or perhaps more properly investigated the processes by which subjects gain a centre (Deutscher 1997: 44), showing how humans were created by systems of signification, rather than vice versa.

These various approaches have tended to be critical of any attempt to place thought and language outside of the material world. For a start there is no separate metaphysical space outside of the world for these phenomena to occupy. Thought is not locked away in a separate mental realm, issuing forth when 'applied' as action. Similarly language does not merely describe things: it has effects, makes things happen, and renders material things intelligible (Butler 1997a: 10). In a real sense the material world is *articulated* by thought and language. In recent years similar arguments that developed within feminist philosophy have yielded a radical reconceptualization of the human body.

During the 1960s and 1970s, feminists made heuristic use of a distinction between 'sex' and 'gender', where the former was the biological distinction between bodies, and the latter the cultural distinction between social roles. This proved useful in demonstrating the arbitrary character in specific regimes of gender inequality. However, it nevertheless reiterated the culture/nature and mind/body dichotomies, leaving the body as something outside of history, upon which a cultural superstructure might be built under differing contingent conditions (Bailey 1993: 100; Gatens 1996: 51). Yet this surrenders the status of unquestionable truth to biological and medical knowledge of the body. This knowledge has been created in particular historical and social conditions, and is as much a set of interpretations as any other account. 'Sex' is just as much a cultural construct as 'gender', yet it serves to reassure us that *our* understanding of bodily difference is the truth, that other interpretations are fantasies, and that the human body has really been the same throughout history (Nordbladh and Yates 1990: 222; Deutscher 1997: 27).

Humanism still dominates our understanding of the body and its sexing. The body is presented as having an a priori nature, which can be defined by medical science. Culture is stamped on to its surface as a secondary matter. However, we can argue that culture and language do not take up and invest a pre-existing body whose capacities and limits are already known. Instead they reveal a body which is simply unintelligible prior to its signification. In a sense a body outside of culture and language has no materiality. The crux of the matter is this: *as long as we accept that the body's nature is fixed in biology, and that the character of its materiality is unquestionable, we have no option but to maintain the mind/body dualism.*

This line of argument has proven troubling to some, since to concede that the body's materiality is *constructed* seems to imply that it becomes no body at all (Bordo 1990: 145). However, no one is really suggesting that human bodies are immaterial, or made of discourse. As we have seen, anti-humanist perspectives deny any opposition between language and materiality. Language and culture create our understanding of the body: they form the body, but this is not the same thing as bringing the body into existence (Butler 1997b: 84). The point is that we can have no access to an understanding of the body which is not already an interpretation. We cannot know the thing-in-itself. It is only through the act of interpretation that we can gain a knowledge of the body at all. We do not first of all confront the material thing in its nakedness and then clothe it with meaning: it is revealed to us in its meaningfulness.

It is on this issue that Judith Butler's work has proven critical. Butler argues that Western thought has construed materiality as irreducible: the ultimate and unquestionable given. In place of this Butler suggests that materialization is something which happens, rather than something which simply *is*. Materialization is the process by which the world *reveals* itself to us in an intelligible form (Hull 1997: 23). In the case of the human body, materialization takes the form of a forcible reiteration of norms set within a heterosexual cultural matrix. Securing cultural intelligibility, avoiding the state of abjection, involves a constant gender performance which never achieves the closure of simply *being* male or female. The way in which the body becomes recognizable is both restricted and facilitated by discourse and power. In the absence of discourse and power there could be no human bodies, in the full sense (Butler 1993: 1).

Crucially the process by which the intelligibility of bodies is secured is lived, and is material. It is simply that the materiality of this embodiment would have no significance to human beings in abstraction from signification. Nonetheless Butler's argument that sex/gender is a performance on the body surface rather than a deep truth hidden inside the body has often been misconstrued as promising an 'end of gender' and an 'existence without limit' (Deutscher 1997: 13). As Butler herself complains (1993: x), this is to neglect the political character of embodiment, the imbrication of processes of bodily emergence with power relations.

For archaeology the greatest importance of an anti-humanist perspective is that once we recognize that no aspect of identity or embodiment is sufficiently knowable for their universality to be established, the potential difference of the past can be more fully appreciated. Casting aside the image of the autonomous individual immediately opens up a range of other possibilities for ways of being human. Even in the contemporary West it is arguable that people are not so much bounded and self-sufficient entities as 'ensembles of subject positions' (Mouffe 1993: 12), capable of operating in different ways in different contexts, and of generating antagonisms and struggles within themselves. Ethnography, of course, provides plentiful evidence of communities for whom the notion of 'individuality' is incomprehensible. In Melanesia, Strathern (1988: 192) has outlined the operation of processes of personification, in which personal identities emerge from a background of pre-existing relationships. Under these circumstances persons are conceptualized as amalgams or hybrids of relations and substances of different kinds (Strathern 1996: 526): they are 'partible' within themselves as much as they represent distinct entities. In the particular case of the 'Aré'Aré, different elements of human beings (body, breath, image, etc.) are exchangeable and substitutable for non-human entities (taro, pigs, ancestors) (Barraud *et al.* 1994). This presents a picture of persons linked and embedded in relationships and flows of substance which have a conceptual priority over the integrity of the subject or the body. Similarly in southern India, Busby (1997) describes a situation in which bodies are understood as bounded by flesh, and yet this boundary is permeable and persons are sustained by flows of substance and energy between human beings.

If Western modernity is characterized above all by generalized processes of alienation, it is reasonable to argue that the peculiar understanding of humanity which prevails in the West is an outcome of the 'stopping of flows', the creation of a closure around the person (Strathern 1996). Just as people have been severed from the social relations which might otherwise attend the flow of material goods, the notion of the autonomous individual is based upon a dissolution of the relationships implicit in sociality and language. The effect is to flatter us that our agency is absolute and unfettered, as if we operated outside of any set of power relations. Intriguingly in many non-Western societies agency is understood in relational terms: one always acts in relation to another, and they (rather than one's own interests) are seen as the cause of one's actions (Strathern 1988: 273). These examples culled from ethnography should not be seen as direct analogues for the past, but they do alert us to the possibilities of other humanities, and give us the option of asking different questions of our evidence.

Post-processual archaeology and humanism

I wish to suggest that the continued influence of humanist ideas is responsible for the ambiguous position occupied by the body within contemporary archaeological theory (see Yates 1993). In this respect it is instructive to consider Ian Hodder's introduction to the *Symbolic and Structural Archaeology* volume (1982), which can be regarded as of critical importance for the subsequent development of archaeological thought. Hodder's article was cast as a critique of the ecological functionalism which he considered to be dominant within archaeology. He argued that this critique was essential for the emergence of a mature discipline, and outlined a series of different failings which could be attributed to functionalism. Among these were the separation that the New Archaeology had introduced between function and culture, and the lack of emphasis on 'individual creativity and intentionality' in a functionalist perspective

(1982: 3). These two criticisms could potentially lead one in very different directions. Indeed the various contributions to *Symbolic and Structural Archaeology* are distinguished by a high degree of eclecticism. What was important about the book was that it signified a point at which archaeologists began to position their own debates within the social sciences, and particularly cultural studies, rather than finding their closest affinities with the natural sciences. Of course the human sciences contain an enormous variety of positions, and what has become known as 'post-processual archaeology' incorporates many of these, rather than representing a single point of view.

In Hodder's article and in his later publications, he strives to introduce 'the individual into social theory' (1982: 6). The New Archaeology had stressed the adaptive system and the long term, but it was now necessary 'to see how society affects the individual' (Hodder 1986: 6). Interestingly the authors to whom Hodder turned in the 1982 article were Bourdieu and Giddens, from whom he sought a *theory of practice*. In these terms practice is seen as intervening between the individual and society; yet both 'individual' and 'society' are taken as absolute and bounded entities. Moreover agency becomes conflated with the individual, and 'structure' with the social. What is missing from Hodder's account is a theory of the subject. This is curious, as Giddens had explicitly addressed this issue (1979: Ch. 1). While his 'stratified model of agency' (Giddens 1984: 7) is in some ways deeply problematic, it does begin to present persons as being in process, rather than as social atoms. Installing the active individual as one of the central planks of his form of a post-processual archaeology (1986: 6), Hodder is left in the position of arguing against cross-cultural laws and generalizations (1986: 148) while relying upon exactly such a thing. I suspect that this is because Hodder wishes to create an archaeology which is sensitive to the needs of human beings (e.g. Hodder 1984), and as a result is reluctant to relinquish the idea that humanity is something that can be fixed and defined. In this formulation personhood is something which one *is*, as opposed to something which one *does*.

In recent years this emphasis on the autonomous individual has been maintained. As Meskell suggests, it is widely held that 'accessing individuals in the past is an explicit aspect of a postprocessual archaeology' (1998: 363). Commenting on the problem of agency in archaeology, Johnson (1989: 206) suggests that social structure is extrinsic to agents, who draw upon it in everyday practice. However, he concedes that 'an unavoidable dualism remains between individual and society' (ibid.: 208). At times the problematic character of individuality has been recognized (Last 1998: 44), but much of archaeology seems unwilling to let go of the two perceived 'givens' of the body: the foundational character of its materiality, and its coincidence with a particular kind of being, the 'individual'. Indeed while employing insights derived from contemporary feminism, it seems that Knapp and Meskell (1997) wish to return to both of these foundations. Thus, they appeal to: 'a new desire for groundedness, whereby we regard the body as a material, physical and biological phenomenon irreducible to immediate social processes and classifications' (ibid.: 188). They go on: 'The body is not merely constrained by or invested with social relations, but also forms a basis for and contributes towards these relations' (ibid.: 188).

This suggests the humanist notion of an embodied subject who exists prior to his or her incorporation into the social field. It also hints at the image of the human being 'built in layers', which seems to be confirmed when they argue that:

Experiencing oneself as an individual entity is part of human nature....Layered upon this is a more culturally specific determination of what it is to be a person in a given time and place....Overlying this second stratum is a finer layer of interpretation, that of individually determined experience.

(ibid.: 198)

Two consequences flow from the continued emphasis on individuality and the notion of a pre-discursive body: a growing interest in an 'archaeology of emotion', and a denial of power. In the first case, Meskell (1998: 377) suggests that archaeology has failed to deal with emotion because of a sustained emphasis on objectivity. There is much to be said for this view, and for those archaeologists dealing with recent periods in the West there is little doubt that a consideration of the emotive content of experience can enrich interpretation (e.g. Tarlow 1992). However, there are also dangers. Replacing objectivity with a wholesale subjectivism (e.g. Carman and Meredith 1990) does nothing to displace the dichotomy between the two (Hekman 1990: 64). Moreover attributing emotional states to people in prehistory implies that particular emotions are transhistoric and fixed in 'human nature'. At worst this can mean that emotions can be reduced to biology, and construed as part of a hard-wired system of adaptation (Mithen 1991). This is not to say that emotions in the past lie beyond our investigation, simply that we cannot assume that we already know the moods and feelings that were experienced by past people. Approaching these will require that we recognize that emotions are culturally constructed, as well as lived and experienced.

Perhaps more serious is the attempt to reinstate the 'unencumbered self' in the guise of the knowledgeable agent. Meskell complains of archaeology's 'primary focus on power, at the expense of the embodied individual and agency....Ever popular models of dominance and resistance continue to posit issues of power and control as central' (1996: 1, 8). Again there is a defensible point here, in that archaeological discussions of power have tended to involve a binary image of societies composed of the powerful and the powerless. However, this is no reason to retreat into the dangerous utopianism of a society without power, the humanist dream of being free to be what we will. Rather it requires that we theorize power in more subtle ways: ways like those proposed by Foucault, which are seemingly more often parodied, decried, or given lip service than fully appreciated. For Foucault (1977, 1978, and elsewhere) power is a relational concept, a network of possibility immanent in the social field. The forms that power takes and the opportunities it creates are historically specific. Power cannot be held, only exercised; it produces and enables as much as it restricts. It has no centre, cannot be monopolized, and is operationalized as innumerable micro-powers. It is in these terms that Butler argues, when she says that: 'What constitutes the fixity of the body, its contours, its movements, will be fully material, but materiality must be rethought as the effect of power, as power's most productive effect' (1993: 2).

Without a consideration of power it is quite impossible to understand how bodies are materialized. Without power we return to the liberal view of the social as something that we can enter from outside, by free choice. Of course this does involve giving the social (rather than 'society') a priority over the subject. It is perhaps for this reason that Meskell suggests that: 'archaeology still tends to ignore the relationship of the individual to society in favour of treating individuals simply as micro versions of larger social entities' (1998: 363).

But rejecting the concept of the autonomous individual does not require that we resort to portraying past communities as being composed of faceless, identical automata. Instead it means that we recognize that people are different by virtue of their differential positioning within the networks of power and knowledge. We are not free to be what we will, but we realize our potentials differently because of our different opportunities, experiences, access to knowledge…and because we may have been excluded, dominated, or oppressed by others. The virtue of an anti-humanist approach in archaeology is that it does not simply accept that we are all different because of some primordial identity which is embedded in us from birth: it renders the sources of our difference accessible and open to investigation.

I have been anxious to point out what I see as the pitfalls of humanism in archaeology, above all because of its political implications. Humanism threatens to sever the personal from the political. It threatens to establish a depoliticized liberal archaeology, in which the political realm is always a supplement, arriving after the event of individual experience.

Neolithic bodies

This discussion has been theoretical, but it follows from what I have argued that different regimes of materialization will have existed in the past, resulting in bodies that were lived and experienced in ways which would be quite unfamiliar to us. How can we begin to unravel the cultural logic of materialization? In what follows I would like to make some suggestions concerning the character of embodiment in earlier Neolithic Britain.

In the absence of extensive information relating to everyday activities, much of what we know about Neolithic bodies comes from funerary contexts. In particular the earthen long barrows of eastern Britain, and the megalithic chambered tombs of the west often contain large assemblages of human remains, frequently in a state of disarticulation and apparent disorder. However, as Shanks and Tilley (1982) suggested, this seemingly random distribution of skeletal elements may mask a more ordered pattern. The processes of assemblage formation were both complex and highly variable. At chambered cairns like Ascott-under-Wychwood and Hazleton on the Cotswolds (Fig. 13.1), bodies appear to have been introduced to the chambers, cists, and passages both as fleshed corpses and as skeletal elements, possibly resulting from excarnation. Once soft body tissue had rotted away, bones were both reorganized and individually removed, and taken elsewhere. Skulls were sometimes clustered together at the feet of stone uprights, while a group of longbones at Ascott were placed in a cruciform arrangement (Benson and Clegg 1978; Saville 1990). Shanks and Tilley argued that the breaking down of bodies and their reconfiguration as a corporate mass served an ideological role in emphasizing the collective character of the community of ancestors, thereby drawing attention away from the inequalities which existed among the living. Unfortunately because in the later Neolithic and early Bronze Age the funerary record is dominated by single graves with bodies containing grave goods, it has proved possible for some archaeologists to imply that this horizon saw 'the birth of the individual' in the contemporary sense, and even that the

Fig. 13.1 The chambered tomb of Ascott-under-Wychwood, Oxfordshire (after Chesterman 1977).

'individuals' of the earlier Neolithic were merely hidden (Sherratt 1981; Shennan 1982). According to these arguments, these were 'people just like us'.

I would like to suggest that a quite different kind of personhood prevailed in Neolithic Britain. One place to begin such an argument would be the West Kennet long barrow, near Avebury (Piggott 1962; Thomas and Whittle 1986). At West Kennet, burial deposits in the five stone chambers seem to have built up over a lengthy period, through the deposition of fleshed and unfleshed remains, and their reordering, selection, and removal (Fig. 13.2).

Subsequently a series of secondary deposits composed of layers of clean chalk interspersed with burnt organic lenses were deposited in the chambers. The alternation of these layers suggests a series of repeated events. Within these layers considerable quantities of decorated pottery were located. Just as the spatial configuration of the chambers had been used to draw distinctions between different kinds of bodies (in particular the remains of young people were largely segregated in the southeast chamber), so pots bearing different decorative devices were concentrated in different chambers. Just as the bodies were 'broken' and their contents 'spilt', so the pottery vessels were smashed and their parts reorganized (sometimes fitted into the corners of the chambers, or in among the stones of the drystone walling, along with small bones of the hands and feet). What I am wishing to infer here is that in this case artefacts were in some way equivalent to or substitutable for human bodies: in repeatedly breaking and depositing pots in ways that recalled mortuary practice people brought the past back to mind.

Recently archaeologists have started to make use of the metaphor of the 'lives' of artefacts: crafted out of materials, circulated, used, broken, and disposed of (Kopytoff

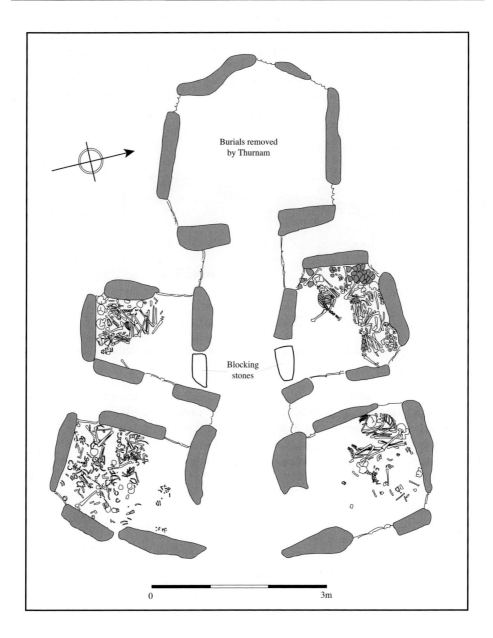

Burials removed
by Thurnam

Blocking
stones

0   3m

Fig. 13.2 Primary skeletal deposits in the chambers of the West Kennet long barrow (after Piggott 1962).

1986). But for many communities this metaphor has a deeper significance: objects passing from hand to hand in exchange may be recognized as being the equivalents of persons, or parts of persons, even as something of the substance of a person detached from them and entering circulation (Strathern 1988: 192). Like body parts, these things are inalienable.

Arguably the circulation of human bones in Neolithic Britain bore some similarity to the circulation of artefacts as gifts, in cycles of reciprocity. At Wor Barrow in Dorset, Pitt Rivers excavated what appears to have been a timber chamber beneath an earthen mound. Inside were three articulated skeletons, and three other bodies arranged as 'bundles' of longbones, each with a skull (Pitt Rivers 1898). Seemingly these bones had been brought to the place of burial from elsewhere, perhaps in some kind of container, and they might easily have been in circulation for some while before deposition. Moreover numerous other Neolithic contexts contain isolated human bones, particularly skulls and skull fragments: causewayed enclosure ditches, formal pit deposits, and so on. In these circumstances some of the funerary monuments are better seen as 'places of transformation' than as 'tombs', since many body parts appear to have moved between different kinds of sites. They were conduits through which human bodies and body parts flowed (Lucas 1996).

Elsewhere I have suggested that earlier Neolithic social life was characterized by a series of interconnected cycles: the seasonal movements of herders following cattle, the gathering of plant foods and herbs, the acquisition of materials like shed antler, potting clay, flint, and firewood, as well as periodic exchanges with other groups, and these protracted rites involving the remains of the dead and their movement from place to place (Thomas 1998). For this reason the similarities between bodies and artefacts are particularly revealing. The social life of a person is something culturally defined: it has often been pointed out that mortuary ritual is a means by which communities sanction the passing away of a person, and render them 'socially dead' (Parry 1982). We in the modern West distinguish death on biological grounds, but it is equally possible to construe the cease of biological function as a change to a different kind of life (Humphreys 1981). When we talk of the 'lives' of artefacts we do not imagine that objects always 'die' and become insignificant when they are broken. Indeed broken objects and waste materials are often deeply important (Moore 1982; Welbourn 1984). I suggest that in earlier Neolithic Britain, human bones continued to have a 'life' of sorts following their transformation in mortuary ritual. The dead were still an integral part of society.

Both artefacts and bodies were governed by the principles of partibility and circulation. Both formed elements in a more general 'economy of substances', which involved other materials. Both artefacts and bodies could be broken down into parts, and artefacts at least were made by putting different substances together. The strong inference is that human bodies were not understood as bounded and separate entities, but as temporary combinations of substances, tied in to encompassing flows and processes of circulation. The fleshed body of a living person might not have been perceived as the 'normal' state of affairs, or even as the only configuration of the body which had a social presence.

Acknowledgements

Thanks to Mary Baker, Chris Fowler, Matt Leivers, Sue Pitt, and Maggie Ronayne, who have discussed these matters with me at length.

Bibliography

Bailey, M.E. 1993. Foucauldian Feminism: Contesting Bodies, Sexuality and Identity. In Ramazanoglu, C. (ed.), *Up Against Foucault: Explorations of Some Tensions Between Foucault and Feminism*. London: Routledge, pp. 99–122.

Barraud, C., de Coppet, D., Iteanu, A., and Jamous, R. (eds). 1994. *Of Relations and the Dead: Four Societies Viewed From the Angle of their Exchanges*. Oxford: Berg.

Benson, D. and Clegg, I. 1978. Cotswold Burial Rites. *Man* 13: 134–7.

Bordo, S. 1990. Feminism, Post-Structuralism and Gender-Scepticism. In Nicholson, L.J. (ed.), *Feminism/Postmodernism*. London: Routledge, pp. 133–56.

Busby, C. 1997. Permeable and Partible Persons: A Comparative Analysis of Gender and Body in South India and Melanesia. *Journal of the Royal Anthropological Institute* 3: 261–78.

Butler, J. 1993. *Bodies That Matter: On the Discursive Limits of 'Sex'*. London: Routledge.

Butler, J. 1997a. *Excitable Speech: A Politics of the Performative*. London: Routledge.

Butler, J. 1997b. *The Psychic Life of Power: Theories in Subjection*. Stanford: Stanford University Press.

Carman, J. and Meredith, J. 1990. Affective Archaeology. *Archaeological Review from Cambridge* 9: 187–9.

Carroll, J. 1993. *Humanism: The Wreck of Western Culture*. London: Fontana.

Caverero, A. 1996. Towards a Theory of Sexual Difference. In Kemp, S. and Bono, P. (eds), *The Lonely Mirror Italian Perspectives on Feminist Theory*. London: Routledge, pp. 189–221.

Chesterman, J.T. 1977. Burial Rites in a Cotswold Long Barrow. *Man* 12: 22–32.

Cottingham, J. 1992. Cartesian Dualism: Theory, Metaphysics and Science. In Cottingham, J. (ed.), *The Cambridge Companion to Descartes*. Cambridge: Cambridge University Press, pp. 236–56.

Deutscher, P. 1997. *Yielding Gender: Feminism, Deconstruction, and the History of Philosophy*. London: Routledge.

Foucault, M. 1977. *Discipline and Punish: The Birth of the Prison*. New York: Vintage.

Foucault, M. 1978. *The History of Sexuality. Volume 1: An Introduction*. London: Peregrine.

Gatens, M. 1996. *Imaginary Bodies: Ethics, Power and Corporeality*. London: Routledge.

Giddens, A. 1979. *Central Problems in Social Theory: Action, Structure and Contradiction in Social Analysis*. London: Macmillan.

Giddens, A. 1984. *The Constitution of Society: Outline of the Theory of Structuration*. Cambridge: Polity.

Heidegger, M. 1993. Letter on Humanism. In Krell, D.F. (ed.), *Martin Heidegger: Basic Writings* (Second Edition). London: Routledge, pp. 213–65.

Hekman, S.J. 1990. *Gender and Knowledge: Elements of a Postmodern Feminism*. Cambridge: Polity.

Hodder, I.R. 1982. Theoretical Archaeology: A Reactionary View. In Hodder, I. (ed.), *Symbolic and Structural Archaeology*. Cambridge: Cambridge University Press, pp. 1–16.

Hodder, I.R. 1984. Archaeology in 1984. *Antiquity* 58: 25–32.

Hodder, I.R. 1986. *Reading the Past*. Cambridge: Cambridge University Press.

Hull, C.L. 1997. The Need in Thinking: Materiality. In Adorno, T.W. and Butler, J. *Radical Philosophy* 84: 22–35.

Humphreys, S.C. 1981. Death and Time. In Humphreys, S.C. and King, H. (eds), *Mortality and Immortality*. London: Academic Press, pp. 261–83.

Johnson, M.H. 1989. Conceptions of Agency in Archaeological Interpretation. *Journal of Anthropological Archaeology* 8: 189–211.

Jordanova, L. 1989. *Sexual Visions: Images of Gender in Science and Medicine Between the Eighteenth and Twentieth Centuries*. Brighton: Harvester Wheatsheaf.

Knapp, A.B. and Meskell, L.M. 1997. Bodies of Evidence in Prehistoric Cyprus. *Cambridge Archaeological Journal* 7(2): 183–204.

Kopytoff, I. 1986. The Cultural Biography of Things: Commodification as Process. In Appadurai, A. (ed.), *The Social Life of Things*. Cambridge: Cambridge University Press, pp. 64–91.

Last, J. 1998. Books of Life: Biography and Memory in a Bronze Age Barrow. *Oxford Journal of Archaeology* 17: 43–53.

Lloyd, C. 1986. *Explanation in Social History*. Oxford: Blackwell.

Lucas, G. 1996. Of Death and Debt: A History of the Body in Neolithic and Early Bronze Age Yorkshire. *Journal of European Archaeology* 4: 99–118.

MacIntyre, A. 1981. *After Virtue: A Study in Moral Theory*. London: Duckworth.

Meskell, L. 1996. The Somatisation of Archaeology: Institutions, Discourses, Corporeality. *Norwegian Archaeological Review* 29: 1–16.

Meskell, L. 1998. Intimate Archaeologies: The Case of Kha and Merit. *World Archaeology* 29: 363–79.

Mithen, S. 1991. A Cybernetic Wasteland? Rationality, Emotion and Mesolithic Foraging. *Proceedings of the Prehistoric Society* 57: 9 -14.

Moore, H. 1982. The Interpretation of Spatial Patterning in Settlement Residues. In Hodder, I. (ed.), *Symbolic and Structural Archaeology*. Cambridge: Cambridge University Press, pp. 74–9.

Mouffe, C. 1993. *The Return of the Political*. London: Verso.

Nietzsche, F. 1969. *On the Genealogy of Morals* and *Ecce Homo*. New York: Vintage.

Nordbladh, J. and Yates, T. 1990. This Perfect Body, This Virgin Text: Between Sex and Gender in Archaeology. In Bapty, I. and Yates, T. (eds), *Archaeology After Structuralism*. London: Routledge, pp. 222–37.

Nussbaum, M. 1992. Human Functioning and Social Justice: In Defense of Aristotelian Essentialism. *Political Theory* 20: 202–46.

Parry, J. 1982. Sacrificial Death and the Necrophagous Ascetic. In Bloch, M. and Parry, J. (eds), *Death and the Regeneration of Life*. Cambridge: Cambridge University Press, pp. 74–110.

Piggott, S. 1962. *The West Kennet Long Barrow*. London: HMSO.

Pitt Rivers, A.L.F. 1898. *Excavations in Cranborne Chase Near Rushmore, On the Borders of Dorset and Wilts. Vol. IV*. Privately Printed.

Saville, A. 1990. *Hazleton North: The Excavation of a Neolithic Long Cairn of the Cotswold-Severn Group*. London: English Heritage.

Shanks, M. and Tilley, C.Y. 1982. Ideology, Symbolic Power and Ritual Communication: A Reinterpretation of Neolithic Mortuary Practices. In Hodder, I. (ed.), *Symbolic and Structural Archaeology*. Cambridge: Cambridge University Press, pp. 129–54.

Shennan, S.J. 1982. Ideology, Change and the European Early Bronze Age. In Hodder, I. (ed.), *Symbolic and Structural Archaeology*. Cambridge: Cambridge University Press, pp. 155–61.

Sherratt, A.G. 1981. Plough and Pastoralism: Aspects of the Secondary Products Revolution. In Hodder, I., Hammond, N., and Isaac, G. (eds), *Pattern of the Past*. Cambridge: Cambridge University Press, pp. 261–306.

Strathern, M. 1988. *The Gender of the Gift*. Berkeley: University of California Press.

Strathern, M. 1996. Cutting the Network. *Journal of the Royal Anthropological Institute* 2: 517–35.

Tarlow, S. 1992. Each Slow Dawn a Drawing Down of Blinds. *Archaeological Review from Cambridge* 11: 125–40.

Thomas, J.S. 1998. An Economy of Substances in Earlier Neolithic Britain. In Robb, J. (ed.), *Material Symbols: Culture and Economy in Prehistory*. Carbondale: Southern Illinois University Press, pp. 70–89.

Thomas, J.S. and Whittle, A.W.R. 1986. Anatomy of a Tomb: West Kennet Revisited. *Oxford Journal of Archaeology* 5: 129–56.

Welbourn, D.A. 1984. Endo Ceramics and Power Strategies. In Miller, D. and Tilley, C. (eds), *Ideology, Power and Prehistory*. Cambridge: Cambridge University Press, pp. 17–24.

Yates, T. 1993. Frameworks for an Archaeology of the Body. In Tilley, C. (ed.), *Interpretative Archaeology*. London: Berg, pp. 31–72.

Part V

Class, caste, ideology, and religion

An introduction

Timothy Insoll

The final section draws together, perhaps what is at first impression, a seemingly disparate range of identities around the archaeology of class, caste, ideology, and religion. However, a recurrent theme throughout this volume has been the interconnections which exist between different identities and how, frequently, to treat them in the singular is to do them a disservice, both today and in relation to interpreting their former existence in the past. Hence the initial impression of dissimilarity dissolves and their inclusion together can be justified.

Class and caste, for example, are both similar and dissimilar and this is evident in the two chapters offered here which explore these subjects. The chapter by Susan Andrews and James Fenton considers the former, class, and indicates how this can be both constructed and maintained, in part, via material culture usage. Moreover it exposes how class image can be built upon the sufferings of others – an inadvertently Marxist viewpoint perhaps – but an image which utilized the capital gained from the dehumanizing commodification of fellow human beings via slavery, i.e. what they term 'distasteful' wealth converted into 'social' currency. Additionally this is a process not far removed in time but actually from very recent history – the mid-nineteenth century and in what is now defined as the 'First' World – the United States.

Andrews and Fenton's chapter is also useful in focusing upon, as they note, the white slave owner, who is usually abstracted in favour of the slaves themselves in terms of archaeological research. But to properly understand the true relations of slavery *both* need recognizing. The one identity functions with the other, for a slave is not a slave without a master, and a slave owner, obviously, needs to own slaves in order to qualify as such. This is stating a truism, but is something often neglected by archaeologists. Ultimately it is shown in their chapter how slaves were converted into capital which was in turn converted, for instance, into genteel table wares – markers of 'good breeding and civility'. The irony is painfully obvious. Andrews and Fenton are to be congratulated for reading the material culture in such a way as to expose the various tiers of meaning which existed and how these related specifically to the manifestation of class identity.

Robin Coningham and Ruth Young consider the archaeology of caste in South Asia. Caste like many of the other identities explored here has, surprisingly, been largely ignored by archaeologists even if it has been more exhaustively explored by anthropologists (see, for example, Quigley 1996). Furthermore what is apparent from the brief review of archaeological interpretations of 'caste' provided by Coningham and Young is that 'class' and 'caste' are sometimes seemingly used interchangeably by archaeologists, erroneously, when they in fact refer to different things.

Both historical and contemporary definitions of class are examined, but primary focus is given to a case study based around excavations in the major urban centre of Anuradhapura in Sri Lanka where both occupational debris and dietary remains are used convincingly to indicate that caste was not manifest spatially at this site. This in turn is interpreted as suggesting that the correlation between spatial differentiation and caste identity is largely symbolic and moreover a recent phenomenon. A divergence between what might be expected based upon readings of South Asian caste from ethnography and what can actually be interpreted from the archaeological record at Anuradhapura is thus evident.

Cutting across the lines between class, caste, and religion is ideology. 'Ideology' is defined in the *Oxford Handy Dictionary* as 'ideas characteristic of some class etc. or at basis of some economic or political theory or system' (Fowler and Fowler 1986: 428). Hence the relation to class is explicitly stated here. However, 'ideology' is often used in relation to religion as well, at least by archaeologists (Shanks and Tilley 1992: 130; Insoll 2004: 78–9).

Elizabeth Brumfiel in her chapter examines the role of ideology in the Aztec state within the context of power relations and in creating social inequality, and the overall relevance of 'ideology' within the archaeology of identities is clearly indicated. This is achieved through her discussion of how the Aztec state promoted an ideology linking warfare to the natural cycles sustaining human life: summer and winter, day and night, birth and death. However, complexity is again shown to be key because different ideologies were created aimed at different target groups – whether dominant or subordinate. Hence spectacles of pain and violence, and one might add, fear, were utilized in creating ideologies of power and control over subordinate groups whereas elites were addressed by an ideology of cosmological principles and moral hierarchies manifest through the interweaving of visual imagery with architecture and other aspects of material culture.

Ritual can also be used as a mechanism to reinforce and perpetuate ideology – as with the Aztec rituals of human sacrifice – or within the framework of religion as well. The blurring between ritual, religion, and ideology is often neglected by archaeologists, but definitions can potentially be sharpened up, if given adequate consideration, and, of course, evidence permitting (Insoll 2004).

Joanna Brück looks at the concept of ritual within archaeological parlance, with particular reference to the British middle Bronze Age but moves on to place this within the framework of belief, and emphasizes Enlightenment culpability in the creation of prehistoric rationality. In so doing she complements points made by Thomas in his chapter with reference to modernity, humanism, and the body. Brück is primarily concerned with ritual as understood in a religious, spiritual, or symbolic context, though she rightly critiques a simplistic ritual/secular or sacred/profane dichotomy. Yet ritual can extend beyond these domains and be utilized in the creation and maintenance of other identities as well. For example ritual can provide familiarity and continuity over time in the sustenance of national identities. Hence, as Brück indicates, ritual equates with much more than the oft-cited definition that it is 'non-functional action'.

Finally my contribution to this volume is concerned with world religions in contrast to Brück whose focus, as just described, is upon prehistoric ritual. Christianity, Islam, Judaism, and Zoroastrianism are considered within the framework of the

Arabian Gulf with particular reference to my recent archaeological research in Bahrain. What is evident is that their manifestations and material signatures are not clear-cut but vary according to complex patterns dependent on observer, observed, and degree of knowledge. Thus the patterns of 'internal' versus 'external' identity manifestation can be seen to differ, and this is in turn explored in relation to what Foucault (1977) has defined as the prevailing 'discourse', usually, but not exclusively, of power.

What is further highlighted in my chapter is how the different identities interlock, and, again in so doing, reinforces the point that a singular focus, on, for example, religion alone, is not necessarily useful. For although religion might form in some instances the 'structuring structure' into which other identities such as ethnicity or gender might be placed – obviously religion does not expunge these but rather co-exists beside them. Variability and complexity are again shown to be key words. Indeed two key words which apply to all the material considered throughout this reader.

Bibliography

Foucault, M. 1977. *Power/Knowledge*. London: The Harvester Press.
Fowler, F.G. and Fowler, H.W. 1986. *The Oxford Handy Dictionary*. Oxford: Oxford University Press.
Insoll, T. 2004. *Archaeology, Ritual, Religion*. London: Routledge.
Quigley, D. 1996. *The Interpretation of Caste*. New Delhi: Oxford University Press.
Shanks, M. and Tilley, C. 1992. *Re-Constructing Archaeology: Theory and Practice*. London: Routledge.

Chapter 14

Archaeology and the invisible man

The role of slavery in the production of wealth and social class in the Bluegrass region of Kentucky, 1820 to 1870

Susan C. Andrews and James P. Fenton

Introduction

In the last couple of decades, the archaeological study of slavery in the United States has tended to focus on the social and economic lives of enslaved people. Studies have been devoted to exploring the carry-overs of various Africanisms (Ferguson 1992; La Roche 1994; Stine *et al.* 1996; Young 1996), spatio-temporal variations in diet, health, and life expectancy (Gibbs *et al.* 1980; McKee 1987), resistance to the oppression of slavery (Young 1995), as well as studies of how slaves sought to improve their lives by alternative economic pursuits outside the demands made on them by their masters (Otto 1977, 1984; Wheaton *et al.* 1983; Singleton 1985; Wheaton and Garrow 1985; Brown 1994). These studies reveal the diversity of the institution of slavery as it was experienced by enslaved peoples, document the efforts that slaves made to survive, illuminate many aspects of their lives and living conditions, and demonstrate their efforts to preserve familial relationships in the face of slave owners' willingness to convert people to cash.

In an editorial in *African American Archaeology*, however, Epperson (1999) has argued that the current focus of African American archaeology on the lives of enslaved African Americans negates or obscures the real relations of slavery by omitting from the picture the actions of those individuals who held power over slaves and controlled the social and economic conditions of slavery; in other words white slave owners of the seventeenth, eighteenth, and nineteenth centuries. The absence of any significant reference to white slave owners, what Epperson has termed their invisibility, points up several problems with the study of slavery in America today. Three issues are at stake.

The first concerns the recognition that slavery was fully a part of the capitalist enterprise in the nineteenth century, and probably in earlier centuries, at least in southern North America. Slave owners invested in slaves both as a bonded labour force that generated wealth from agricultural and other labour, as well as in the production (breeding) of slaves for market. Slave breeding for market, particularly in the more northerly slave states such as Kentucky and Virginia, which were net exporters of slaves to the southern plantations of Mississippi and Louisiana, has been documented both in oral accounts given by ex-slaves in the 1930s to Works Progress Administration historians (Perdue *et al.* 1980) and by more recent historians (Sutch 1975). After real estate, slaves were one of the best long-term investments in terms of increased market value.

A second issue is that the study of slavery must encompass the analysis of the economic advantages that it gave to slave owners over those who used free labour. To do so requires that the archaeological analysis of slavery includes or develops models that incorporate the economic strategies of slave owners, as these affected the entire system of slavery. As slavery was part of the capitalist economy it follows that the history of capitalism in America has important consequences for the study of slavery. By failing to focus on the entire system of slavery, archaeologists risk misunderstanding its true nature and history. Without such a broad perspective, explanations of the slavery system that fail to integrate enslaved African Americans and slave-owning white Americans into a single economic and social system will be incomplete.

A third issue relates to the contribution of increased, slave-derived wealth to the social life of slave-owning society. We believe that individuals participated in slavery because it afforded them profitable returns which they could then invest in the kinds of social capital that could improve their social, as well as their economic, standing within their respective communities. To paraphrase a common statement, if all politics are to be understood at a local level, then economics are also to be studied locally. The social aspirations and motives of nineteenth-century slave owners must be addressed if we are to understand the social factors that promoted slave ownership and in effect structured the changing history of slave society. Slave owners could not have been insensible to the abhorrence with which many in the north, as well as internationally, viewed slavery. The irony that they were able to convert the 'distasteful' wealth produced by slavery into a social currency that attested to their good taste, good breeding, and higher civility cannot have been lost on commentators of the day.

Archaeological studies of a farmstead occupied by a white slave-owning family would appear, by the current definitions of historic archaeology, to fall outside the commonly defined notion of the archaeology of slavery, since we have no direct archaeological evidence of slaves, no slave cabins, no evidence of Africanisms. However, we believe that, by examining the economic and social conditions that promoted the slavery system, we can better understand slavery, and by extension the conditions under which African American slaves were forced to live. Without wishing to be polemical, and without demeaning the experience and history of enslaved African Americans, our starting premise is that the study of slavery as an economic and social system is first and foremost about white slave owners, since it was they who developed, promoted, and preserved it. It is a lot less about the African Americans who were forced to live under it.

We retain the terms 'slave', 'slave ownership', 'slavery', and related terms in this chapter, as we believe they more accurately portray how nineteenth-century slave-owning individuals viewed what they believed to be their property – no different for them than other kinds of property. We recognize that slavery is not an innate condition of people and that 'enslaved person' is a more accurate, humanizing description of a slave, but we wish to emphasize that slavery constituted a world radically different from our own. In mid-nineteenth-century southern states people were property, bought, sold, bred, and invested in like any other livestock. It is this world view, so abhorrent to our own, that demands the kinds of informed and expanded study that we feel Epperson (1999) is calling for in his evaluation of 'African American Archaeology'.

Founded around 1820 the Hardin farmstead in the Central Bluegrass region of Kentucky constituted a microcosm of nineteenth-century slavery. The home of Mr

Enos Hardin, his family, and the slaves that he owned, between 1820 and 1868, affords archaeologists and social historians an opportunity to examine the issues raised above, and to demonstrate that the kind of broad perspective we advocate is a powerful conceptual model for understanding the nineteenth-century cultural life ways of the world of slavery.

Relevant local, state, and federal documents reveal how completely Hardin's agricultural production in the antebellum era was oriented towards capitalism, with the production of cash crops for sale in local and national markets. The comparisons made for this study, using both historical documents and data from archaeologically documented farmsteads of the mid-nineteenth century, indicate that slaves contributed significantly to the greater economic output of farms where they were employed. Although some differences among these farms in terms of agricultural production may relate to the vagaries of the market in different states, or differences among census takers who assigned value to property, the overwhelmingly greater production of farms worked by slaves attests to the importance of slavery to capitalist production.

Investigation into available slave schedules of the mid-nineteenth century for Hardin's farmstead revealed a second arena in which slavery and capitalism were completely integrated: slave breeding. Mentioned in slave narratives from Works Progress Administration archives (Perdue *et al.* 1980) and documented by more recent researchers, analysis of the age and sex of slaves owned by Hardin and comparisons with several of his peers suggests that they were breeding slaves for market, which represented a long-term and highly profitable investment. As noted above many of the more northerly of the slave states were net exporters of slaves to markets further south (Lucas 1992). Enos Hardin, slave owner, was thus also a prudent capitalist, investing in a system of production that increased his monetary worth. As such the logic of his economic pursuits is no different from that of entrepreneurs in northern states who invested in factories or other enterprises. Slavery and capitalism in the American south were not discrete, but a single, integrated system of wealth creation and market exchange.

While historic documents can attest to the economic advantages of slavery for the slave owner, only rarely can they furnish information on the social conditions that motivated individuals to seek wealth or to examine what they sought to accomplish with it. These can be better addressed by examining the social, symbolic, and ritual aspects of the material culture that constituted and made real the social relations that existed among family members and with the broader community of which they were a part. Study of the Hardin household's material culture recovered as archaeological assemblages reveals the family's concerns to demonstrate its membership in a social class that was much higher in status and wealth than the one into which Hardin himself was most likely born. This window into the complex social world of slave owners seeking to convert what might be viewed (even by them) as tainted wealth into more socially acceptable means of wealth, display, and consumption is provided by analysis of the dining-related artefacts such as tea wares, dinner- and table wares used in the performance of the everyday rituals of etiquette, genteel dining, and representation of social-class affiliation. Studies of these artefacts demonstrate that he and his family participated in the socially complex dining rituals that developed during the course of the nineteenth century and which they believed marked them as individuals of good breeding and high civility.

We now examine the Hardin farmstead in relation to each of the three issues discussed above. Our goal is to demonstrate that the archaeology of slavery that we propose provides a better entrée into a past world, which, despite the familiarity of its material culture, espoused moral values very different from our own. The very familiarity of the Hardins' material culture has the potential to obscure the very different ways in which nineteenth-century people used these same objects to signal complex social statements about their lives to their peers and social inferiors. Without such analyses, we recognize only what is familiar about this material culture and not what it communicates to us about the very different world in which it played an essential role. The archaeology of the Hardin farmstead illustrates just how different was the world of slavery that Hardin and his peers promulgated in the era before the Civil War.

The Hardin farmstead

Archaeological study of the Hardin farmstead (site 150n55) was conducted for the Kentucky Department of Transportation as part of a mitigation effort of cultural resources located on US Highway 127 in Owen County, Kentucky (Andrews and Sandefur 2000; Fig. 14.1). Excavation focused on portions of the farmstead within the right of way of the proposed improvements. When studied the site had been returned to agricultural use, so that there were no surface indications that a home site had ever stood at this location. Documentary research identified this site as the homestead of Enos Hardin, who built a home there around 1820 and lived in it until his death in 1868. Approximately 500 acres of surrounding land constituted his farm. Archaeological evidence of the Hardin occupation was obtained by surface collection of artefacts from the ploughed soil, from hand-excavated test units, and from subsurface features revealed after plough-zone removal. Although no standing structures associated with the occupation were present when the site was investigated, archaeological excavation identified two chimney foundations, areas of midden in the yard around the house, and cellars that had been backfilled during the site occupation. Architectural evidence suggested that the house was built of logs with a rear ell or kitchen addition. As noted above no slave quarters were identified in the right of way, and no midden deposits or features could be assigned to slave-related activities or slave homes, although slaves probably comprised the bulk of the workforce at the home site as well as in the surrounding fields. Diagnostic artefacts, including kitchen ceramic types and measurements of window-glass thickness (Moir 1987), confirmed occupation from about 1820 to the 1870s.

In order to investigate Hardin's activities and place him in the context of nineteenth-century economic and social conditions, a survey of extant documents was conducted in local and state archives. These records allowed us to construct a picture of Hardin's activities over a period of some 40 years in which he accumulated land, wealth, and slaves. Comparisons with his neighbours, and with others in Owen County, afford an opportunity to rank Hardin's achievements in terms of his prosperity. Comparisons of his documented economic status with other farms studied archaeologically support the overall finding that Hardin was a significantly wealthy individual, and that slave ownership and possibly slave breeding played a role in his economic activities.

Fig. 14.1 The location of Kentucky in relation to the eastern United States.

A variety of documentary findings relating to Hardin, who was listed in the 1820 Federal census as an illiterate, are summarized in Table 14.1. They chart a remarkable increase in wealth, and attest to shrewd investments in land and slaves over a lifetime.

Appearing in the 1819 Owen County tax record as owning two slaves valued at $100, but no land in Owen County, Enos Hardin started with very little and quickly accumulated more than 500 acres and a total taxable wealth of $2,300 by 1825. These holdings constituted the farmstead on which Hardin built his homestead. Note that some of the blanks in Table 14.1 reflect variation in recording over the years. For example in some years, dollar values were assigned to livestock, and at other times head counts are given. In many slave schedules only the total number of slaves is given, not the number of children.

While these data show an impressive increase in his wealth, comparisons with neighbouring farmsteads for the two decades for which records are available attest even more powerfully to Hardin's involvement in production for surrounding markets. Compiled from agricultural schedules, slave censuses, and US population censuses between 1850 and 1860, Table 14.2 shows how Hardin's farming activities compared with those of several neighbours who owned farms close to his.

Hardin was clearly involved in a mixed farming enterprise typical for the region. His holdings were diversified, including fields in corn (i.e. maize), oats, and sometimes wheat, the ownership of horses, cattle, and sheep, as well as slaves. Most of his neighbours shown in Table 14.2 were involved in raising the same kinds of produce and livestock, although on a much smaller scale. Clearly Hardin was producing for market sale, as his household could not have consumed what his farm produced. The value of his holdings indicates that he was one of the wealthiest individuals in the region.

Comparisons were also made between Hardin and some of the wealthiest residents of Owen County, who would have constituted his social peers. Houchens (1977) has previously tabulated the wealth of some of these individuals. Combining her study with data from the US Slave Census Schedule of 1850, the three largest slave owners in Owen County owned between 21 and 24 slaves. The next three largest slave owners owned 16 slaves apiece. Hardin, with 12 slaves, fell within the top 10 per cent of slave owners in Owen County. Five of these six largest slave owners were farmers, the sixth, a speculator.

Table 14.1 Owen County tax records of Enos Hardin

Year	Acres	Horses	Cattle	Hogs	Slaves	Slave children	Personal items	Total value
1819					2			$100
1820		3						$300
1825	550	2			1			$2,300
1830		3			1			$550
1835	200	6	$100		2			$500
1840	378	6	15/$70		2/$2,300	4		$6,250
1845	425	5	12/$25		11/$3,000	4		$7,290
1851	500	14	$100		10/$4,000			$9,500
1855	400	12	8/$20	40	12/$4,200	4		$10,020
1858	388	12	7/$50	20	12/$6,000	2	$5	$12,835

While low compared to the larger slave plantations further to the south, these figures confirm the relative position of Hardin in his local community in terms of his investment in slaves. A review of the age and sex data for Hardin's slaves points to an additional investment that characterized Hardin's entrepreneurial activities: slave breeding. The US Slave Census Schedules for this era suggest, but do not confirm, that Hardin, like many of his wealthier neighbours, was involved in slave production. Slaves on Hardin's farmstead in the decade 1850–60 show a pattern similar to wealthier neighbours, as well as to patterns reported in regions where slave breeding was practised for sale to more southerly markets (Conrad and Meyer 1958; Phifer 1962; Sutch 1975). In 1850 Hardin owned 12 slaves: two women in their thirties, four individuals between the ages of 14 and 19, and six children aged between six months and 14 years of age. No adult male slaves are listed in the census. By 1860 at least four of the slaves listed in 1850 are unaccounted for, and may have died or been sold or given to family members as they married. Four previously unlisted children replaced them.

Comparisons with the ages of slaves owned by other Owen County residents are shown in Table 14.3. Like many of them, Hardin appeared to own many slave children, and few adults, which would have represented a long-term investment strategy either of breeding slaves using slave women he had purchased or of purchasing young children and raising them for sale. No records of slave sales were identified during the

Table 14.2 Hardin's wealth compared with his neighbours in Owen County

	1850					1860				
	Hardin	Ballard	Sanders	Karsner	Smith	Hardin	Ballard	Karsner	Smith	Spires
Acres	200	40	50	60		240	50		160	350
Acres improved	200	60	130	41		148	60		240	150
Corn (bushels)	2,500	200		1,250		500	500		1,000	2,000
Oats (bushels)	300	10		150			30		25	
Wheat				25		100			150	
Hogs (head)	30	40				6	40		80	30
Oxen (head)	9									
Horses (head)	18	1		1		6	2		4	7
Cattle (head)	14	7		3			34		22	9
Sheep (head)	8			43						
Slaves (persons)	12	2	1	1	1	12	2	1	4	8
Land value ($)	$6,500	$1,200	$1,200	$1,400		$6,208	$1,200		$3,600	$9,000
Slave value ($)						$6,000				

research on Hardin's farmstead, but these were not public documents, and are unlikely to have been preserved in county archives.

The documents provide profound insights into the economic pursuits that Hardin undertook over the course of his lifetime. He was clearly intent on investing in land and slaves, as records illustrate. He produced a variety of cash crops (corn and oats) and livestock (horses, hogs) over and above any needs for his home, and appears to have been involved in the sale of crops to local markets at Monterey, an important port and market a few kilometres away that provided access to the Ohio River boat traffic and associated regional markets. Using slave labour, Hardin was able to outstrip his near neighbours economically and align himself with his region's elite, successfully integrating himself into the top 10 per cent of property owners in Owen County. For an illiterate individual arriving in Owen County in 1819, he appears to have been an economic success.

Tables 14.1 and 14.2 attest to the importance of slaves and slave labour to Hardin's productivity. Undertaken to assess if the documents studied provide a true and fair indication of an individual's wealth, comparisons with archaeologically studied sites of the same era confirm these findings. Table 14.4 summarizes information on six archaeological sites for which comparable documentary data are available. These sites are divided among slave owners (Howells, Waters, Croghans, and Brabson) and farms worked by free labour (Stebbins and Colbert). Available data for these farmsteads/plantations are variable as reflected by blanks in the table columns.

Neither Stebbins nor Colbert owned slaves, and their overall wealth was much lower than Hardin's (although total wealth data are not available for Stebbins). Slave owners, on the other hand, such as Waters and the Croghans and Brabson families, were much wealthier in terms of landholdings and production than Hardin, and they owned many more slaves than him. Two of the farms constitute large plantations usually considered more typical of slavery production: the Brabsons owned twice the amount of land that Hardin owned; landholdings for the Croghans at Locust Grove for this decade are unknown. No values are available for the slaves but, even excluding these values, Hardin's wealth and productivity place him much closer to the large slave-owning planters of Arkansas and west-central Kentucky than to farms operated without slave labour. Howell, who owned 40 slaves, had almost twice as much acreage as Hardin, although it was valued at a lower rate, and he appears to have produced only as much corn as Hardin, although he may also have been producing cotton as a cash crop.

Table 14.3 Slaves by age group by top 10 per cent of Owen County slave owners

Slave owner	Children less than 14 yrs	Total persons	Percentage children
Hardin	6	12	50
Ford	8	16	50
English	8	18	44
Bainbridge	8	8	100
Herndon	9	24	37
McDowell	6	16	37
Yancey	14	21	66

These tables attest to Hardin's successful involvement in agricultural production for market and the contribution that slave labour made to his and others' success. The analyses presented so far suggest that Hardin's wealth derived from the slave labour employed on his farm, which allowed him to outproduce his neighbours, and possibly from his investment in slave breeding for export, as the census schedule reveals a population structure among his slaves that mirrors that of other slave-exporting regions.

Hardin's economic success furnished him with hard currency that he could use to purchase social capital. As noted earlier, Hardin is listed in the 1820 census as an illiterate and, although his background and origin are unknown, this fact suggests that he was not born into an elevated social class. Archaeological study of his material culture and related documents suggest that he was not only wealthy enough to afford expensive ceramics, own large land holdings, and purchase a private education for his children, but that he was also an active participant in the social differentiation of the upper and middle classes in the nineteenth century. By buying expensive goods he was also buying passage into a way of life that was more fluid in America than anywhere else in the world. He appears to have been engaged in the accumulation of capital so that he could participate in the consumption of material goods that constituted the correct props needed for membership in a social class to which he aspired and to which wealth alone did not guarantee access.

To participate in the forms of social interaction that marked class affiliation, mid-nineteenth-century custom called for prescribed behaviours, including participation in complex dining rituals that required expensive items of material culture (imported

Table 14.4 Documentary comparisons of the Hardin farm with archaeologically excavated farms and plantations, c. 1850 to 1860

	Hardin	Stebbin[1]	Colbert[2]	Howell[3]	Waters[4]	Croghans[5]	Brabson[6]
Acres	200		266	500	500	?	800
Acres improved	200		60	250	250	?	200
Corn (bushels)	2,500		150	2,000	2,000	?	1,500
Oats (bushels)	300						200
Wheat							
Hogs (head)	30	17		150	50	?	80
Oxen (head)	9						
Horses (head)	18	15					9
Cattle (head)	14	57		40	30		13
Sheep (head)	8	115					29
Slaves (persons)	12	0	0	40	36	41	49
Land value ($)	$6,500	$2,127	?	$3,000	$8,000	?	$10,000

Notes:
[1] Drake site (Phillippe 1990)
[2] Fair View Farm (McCorvie et al. 1989)
[3] Yell County, Arkansas (Otto 1980b)
[4] Yell County, Arkansas (Otto 1980b)
[5] Locust Grove (Andrews and Young 1992; Young et al. 1995)
[6] Brabson Ferry (Andrews 1988; Andrews and Young 1992)

ceramics) as well as the acquisition of esoteric knowledge pertaining to appropriate vessel form, function, contents, place settings, etc. To analyse the social processes involved in marking class affiliation, scholars have focused on related concepts of gentility and have analysed a variety of documents including probate records, etiquette literature, and even fiction (Kasson 1987; Fitts 1999; Wall 1999). Although this literature can be biased, it can and has been combined successfully with the study of material culture to provide compelling evidence for the ways in which social status and the negotiation of class affiliation among nineteenth-century Americans occurred. Here we use a contextual and symbolic approach to show how Enos Hardin used material culture to secure membership in the upper class, emphasizing the analysis of the ceramics recovered from the Hardin farmstead excavations. Before proceeding to an examination of these issues for the Hardin family, it is first necessary to show that the artefacts recovered from their homestead are a fair indicator of their wealth. If it can be shown that the ceramic wares recovered from the site place Hardin in a relatively high economic status, then it is reasonable to assume that other characteristics of the ceramic assemblage will be accurate indicators of class affiliation.

The documentary evidence above has established several parameters about the Hardin farmstead. First, we know that Hardin was among the wealthiest in his local community based on contemporary tax assessments. Second, we know that documentary evidence for six archaeological studies of farmsteads confirms that the documents relating to Hardin's economic status are on a par with documents studied for these other archaeological sites. It remains to demonstrate that the archaeological assemblage recovered from the Hardin farmstead is also a good indicator of wealth status. Table 14.5 presents a summary index, following Miller (1991), that shows Hardin's relative wealth, based on the relative value of the ceramic assemblage recovered from his homestead compared to others drawn from a number of regions across the United States. Note that the Warren and Allen households are included twice in the table, as separate ceramic indices were calculated for different years reflecting the changing economic fortunes of these two families (see McBride 1991). Miller's indices were conceived as a means of using archaeologically derived ceramics to assign relative wealth to households based on the relative costs of index ceramic types during what he terms the index year (Miller 1991). His indices assign a relative value to individual vessel forms, which can then be averaged for each index year represented in features or for the entire site. As the Hardin assemblage ranks high for what was essentially a luxury good (imported English ceramics), these findings suggest that the archaeological assemblage from Hardin's farmstead is a fair sample and can be usefully examined to assess his participation in the complex rituals of genteel dining that many commentators have implicated in the symbolic and social representation of class affiliation. Individuals at the lower end of the scale include a freed slave woman, a common labourer in a glass factory, and a tenant farmer, all of whom might be expected to rank lower on the economic scale than a gentleman farmer.

The Hardin assemblage thus appears to place Hardin in the upper echelon of middle-class society for nineteenth-century America. As this finding independently corroborates other evidence for Hardin's wealth, the ceramic assemblage may be further analysed to determine how he and his family structured the purchase and use of these vessels to signal aspects of class affiliation. As already noted, since Hardin was unlikely to have been born into the social class he wished to emulate, his family's use of ceramics as a

Table 14.5 Comparisons of Miller's mean ceramic indices

Site	Occupation	State	Mean ceramic index	Total vessels	Index year
Diaz	Merchant	California	2.69	74	1846
Cannon's Pt	Planter	Georgia	2.63	211	1824
Allen	Planter	Mississippi	2.59	132	1838
Hardin	**Farmer**	**Kentucky**	**2.40**	**125**	**1838**
Walker	Tavern	Michigan	2.37	35	1846
Green	Merchant	Vermont	2.29	94	1833
Warren	Merchant	Mississippi	2.16	225	1838
Allen	Merchant	Mississippi	2.12	21	1846
DeRossitt	Ferry	Kentucky	2.10	45	1826
Cannon's Pt	Overseer	Georgia	1.94	105	1824
Franklin Glass	Glass worker	Ohio	1.90	94	1824
Warren	Merchant	Mississippi	1.89	177	1846
Arnold	Farmer	Kentucky	1.85	69	1836
Drake	Farmer	Illinois	1.67	66	1846
Franklin Glass	Labourer	Ohio	1.67	62	1824
Blank Lucy	Freed slave	Massachusetts	1.53	58	1833
Tabbs	Tenant	Maryland	1.42	16	1846
Hale	Farmer	Ohio	1.34	45	1824

Source: after Spencer-Wood 1987a, 1987b *inter alia*

means of participating in the socially important tea ceremony and the complex, segmented dining rituals of the evening meal represents an opportunity to explore how social identities were constructed during this period of fluid social change.

Two lines of evidence can be followed to examine how Hardin created a new social identity of wealthy planter for himself and family. The tea-ware vessels (cups and saucers) were used in the socially prominent ritual of taking tea, a late-afternoon custom when families visited one another and exchanged gossip and social pleasantries. The elaborate decoration of these vessels reflects their expense. As vessel styles changed over the more than 40 years that Hardin lived at the site, his purchase and use of new tea wares as they became available indicates the extent to which he devoted financial resources to what he and his family believed to be important social occasions. Why he devoted financial resources to purchasing these items involves the degree to which he perceived genteel dining and taking tea as a prerequisite for being a respectable member of the upper middle class.

Nineteenth-century middle-class Americans believed that a person's table manners were a direct reflection of his or her moral character, and knowledge of genteel dining etiquette was an important marker of class affiliation (Grover 1987; Kasson 1987). To follow genteel dining properly, the table had to be set with certain ceramic- and glass-ware forms in a rigidly prescribed manner found in etiquette texts of the day. By the mid-nineteenth century a virtual explosion in the variety of patterns and vessel forms of table ware reflected this increased social focus on class and its representation at socially significant meals. Eating became a complicated affair and was no longer a one-pot meal of soup and bread as it might have been in earlier eighteenth-century American homes (Wall 1991, 1994b). It was highly desirable that each food type be separated from others and be served from its own vessel. As a result vessels with specific functions were required for genteel dining. Commentators of the day decried eating certain foods out of sequence or from improper vessels, as these were signs that one was ill-bred and low (Frost 1869).

Several researchers have shown that the frequency of certain vessel forms, generally serving vessels and particularly single-function vessels, is indicative of high economic or social status. For example at Cannon's Point Plantation, Otto (1980a, 1980b, 1984) found that bowls predominated at slave dwellings, while plates and other serving vessels dominated assemblages from the main house. McBride and Esarey (1995) report high frequencies of serving vessels and single-function vessels, including sauce boats, platters, and serving bowls/tureens at Ashland, home of a wealthy landowner and community leader in Lexington, Kentucky.

Dining vessels recovered from archaeological deposits at the Hardin farmstead offer additional insights into the extent to which the family believed itself to be middle-class. The proliferation of vessel forms and the associated etiquette involving knowledge of appropriate sequence and food contents is observable archaeologically in terms of variation in vessel forms and styles of decoration. The increased occurrence of covered vessels such as tureens also argues for increasing complexity of food service. Discussions of this aspect of nineteenth-century dining etiquette and its relationship to class affiliation can be found in Wall (1991, 1994a, 1994b, 1999) and Fitts (1999). The Hardin ceramic assemblage suggests that the family closely followed the prescriptive literature and middle-class norms of the time by taking tea with expensive wares, and by setting their table with matching, complex sets of ceramic vessels and glass ware. Multiple sets also suggest that the Hardins differentiated lunch from dinner or breakfast and between formal and family-oriented dining.

Analysis of the tea wares recovered from the Hardin site confirms his family's participation in this socially important ritual. A total of 67 vessels in the Hardin ceramic assemblage were assigned to tea wares and used to calculate Miller's ceramic index for tea-ware vessels (cups and saucers). Table 14.6 compares Miller's ceramic index for the Hardin site with other sites for which comparable indices were available. The table confirms that the tea wares from the Hardin site were expensive and comparable to tea sets used by a New York city physician, a California merchant, and a southern planter.

Typically, in the early to mid-nineteenth century, teacups, saucers, and teapots or other tea-service forms would not match in decoration or ware. Citing primary sources, Miller et al. (1994: 242–3) suggest that tea wares were usually sold in sets of six cups and saucers, whereas table wares sold by the piece, with consumers purchasing variable amounts at any given time. Only towards the end of the nineteenth century did prices for decorated wares decline to the extent that the purchase of sets (tea and table wares) that we would class as matched (i.e. identical patterns) became more common (Miller et al. 1994). Recent research suggests that the middle class in the 1860s considered groups of vessels sharing the same basic shape and motifs to be a matching set (Praetzellis and Praetzellis 1992; Fitts 1999; Wall 1999).

Archaeological and documentary research has identified chronological trends in the use of different styles of tea and table wares. This progression of tea and table ware characterizes the Hardin assemblage. In the 1820s tea wares used by the Hardin family comprised two distinct sets of porcelain; by 1825, during Hardin's initial settlement, his household already owned two Chinese Export porcelain (overglaze and undecorated) tea sets, as cups and complementary or matching saucers were recovered. Between 1830 and 1850, when Hardin was well-established financially, he purchased two different bone-china tea sets. One of these bone-china sets comprised the London-style shaped cups with the pronounced, rounded foot rings popular during the period. The second tea set included three overglaze painted bone-china cups with three matching or complementary saucers, and four plain/moulded bone-china cups with four matching saucers. There are additional vessels that suggest Hardin had more tea wares during this period than these two sets. Painted, printed (in four different colours), and sponged tea wares were also identified in the assemblage and date to this period (1830s to 1850s). It is likely that these sets were used contemporaneously with, or at least overlapped, the other sets, confirming that the Hardin household clearly used a number of different sets of tea wares. The less expensive painted and sponged tea sets of the 1830s to 1850s may have been used by the family in more private teas or perhaps by their house slaves. One printed pattern, Coral Border, was evident on tea ware (a cup and saucer) and one item of table ware, suggesting that the Hardins attempted to gather a matched set of tea and table ware, which would have been relatively rare before 1850 because of the expense in manufacturing (Miller *et al.*1994: 241). Complementary sets of printed tea and table ware in the same colour and general floral motif were also evident in the assemblage. The possession and use of many printed tea sets with complementary printed table ware indicates that the Hardin household could afford the expense of new styles of ceramics, and evidently thought it important to have matching and complementary sets of fashionable tea and table ware.

Table 14.6 Miller's ceramic index (tea wares) for Hardin and contemporaries

Site	Occupation	State	Cup and saucer index	No. of vessels	Index year
Diaz	Merchant	California	3.59	35	1846
Green	Merchant	Vermont	3.04	40	1833
Robson	Physician	New York	2.97	53	1836
Allen	Planter	Mississippi	2.86	132	1838
Hardin	**Farmer**	**Kentucky**	**2.77**	**67**	**1845/6**
Warren	Merchant	Mississippi	2.50	112	1838
Allen	Merchant	Mississippi	2.49	21	1846
Walker	Tavern	Michigan	2.31	35	1846
Warren	Merchant	Mississippi	2.26	83	1846
Cannon's Pt	Overseer	Georgia	2.24	35	1824
Franklin Glass	Glass Worker	Ohio	2.15	33	1824
Arnold	Farmer	Kentucky	1.90	47	1836/8
Black Lucy	Freed slave	Massachusetts	1.68	17	1833
Drake	Farmer	Illinois	1.62	42	1846
Hale	Farmer	Ohio	1.45	17	1824
Tabbs	Tenant	Maryland	1.44	16	1846

Source: after Spencer-Wood 1987a, 1987b *inter alia*

The remarkable diversity of the tea wares recovered from the Hardin farmstead indicates the extent to which Hardin and his family participated in the socially prominent ritual of taking tea. Expensive wares and later matched sets were purchased as they became available. Tea usually involved a social occasion when the best or most expensive set of matching or complementary cups and saucers was used. Private or family-oriented occasions when no outsiders were present might have involved the use of less-expensive wares. That several different sets were being used may also be an indication of distinctions in social standing: some guests may have merited the best china, whereas others merited only good china.

The recovered table wares also attest to the social prominence afforded to dining. Chronological analysis of different vessel types demonstrates a shift in the Hardin family dining etiquette that mirrors trends reported elsewhere in North America. During the early to mid-nineteenth century Hardin and his family owned several distinct sets of shell-edged and printed table wares. A count of vessels dating to the early nineteenth century includes 13 blue and green shell-edged table plates, three twifflers (8-inch diameter plates), three muffins (6-inch diameter plates), one platter, and a single serving dish. The predominance of plates, and the low count of platters and serving dishes, suggests that the Hardin household took their meals in a less elaborate dining style with few courses and little need for variously sized plates and soup plates during this period. In this regard they closely match norms documented by Wall (1987, 1994a, 1994b), who noted similar characteristics of assemblages from early nineteenth-century urban contexts; Miller *et al.* (1994) also suggest that this is typical for the period. The occurrence in the assemblage of printed wares (13 table plates, one twiffler, and two serving dishes) indicates that more highly decorated vessels of different patterns could have been used to differentiate breakfast and lunch from dinner, and that dining in general was becoming more elaborate. Dinner might have involved participation in genteel dining where outsiders would have been invited. The relatively low occurrence of serving-vessel forms in this early period reflects the dramatic price differential between plates and serving vessels (platters and tureens). Although pricing information on serving vessels is scarce, Miller (1980, 1991) suggests that platter forms were more than 50 per cent more expensive than regular-sized plates, with large-sized plates also being more expensive. The increased pricing likely reflects their larger size, increased decoration, and more ornate form. The occurrence of such vessels in an assemblage is a reasonably good indicator of wealth and genteel dining etiquette.

By the late 1850s a shift in the type of ware and decoration to plain/moulded whiteware and ironstone (white granite) occurred nationally. Fitts (1999) and others (Praetzellis and Praetzellis 1992; Wall 1999) have demonstrated that plain or simply moulded ironstone and porcelain were popular among middle-class urban households after 1850. Ironstone was an expensive ware in 1840 and would have been considered the latest in fashionable table ware. As it became more popular throughout the mid- to late nineteenth century, ironstone prices decreased. In the Hardin household undecorated and moulded ironstone in popular patterns of the 1860s was sought after and used in conjunction with complementary sets, along with transfer-printed whiteware tea and table wares.

Other late nineteenth-century table wares in the assemblage include one painted table plate, one painted muffin, and one appliqué bone-china table plate. These plates of various sizes suggest an elaboration in dining, such as multiple courses, which would have required specialized serving vessels. Also present in the assemblage were nine plain or simple geometric moulded whiteware table plates. These inexpensive, plain table wares may have been used in less formal, family-oriented dinners where status display was not important. On the other hand these plates strongly resemble the plain/simply moulded ironstone or white granite plates used by the Hardin family by the 1850s to 1870s. Although the whitewares would have been less expensive than ironstone, they may have been used as a complementary set with the more expensive ironstone/white granite set. For the most part, table ware in the Hardin assemblage dating after 1850 is dominated by ironstone or white granite specimens. Ironstone table ware includes three table plates, three twifflers, and three serving dishes, suggesting a continued desire to set an elaborate table.

By 1850 to 1870 the Hardin family was able to create large matching or complementary sets of plain/moulded tea and table wares. Moulded ironstone tea- and table-ware sets in matching moulded patterns are indicative of high status since matching sets were still an expensive proposition (Williams 1987; Miller *et al.* 1994). As a result the more complete a tea- or table-ware service in matching patterns, the higher the social status and wealth of the household. At the Hardin farmstead at least three distinct patterns of ironstone were identified: undecorated/plain, simple geometric or Gothic, and Moss Rose. These patterns occurred on both tea- and table-ware forms, implying that the Hardins were matching their tea and table wares. That they continued to emulate upper-middle-class ideals in dining etiquette is illustrated by Table 14.7, which documents the number of vessel forms of ironstone and table glass used by Hardin and contemporaries in late nineteenth-century America. Comparative data are derived from Fitts (1999).

Table 14.7 demonstrates that the affluence of the Hardin household extended to setting the same kind of genteel, segmented table that their peers in New York City were doing in the same period. Specialized vessels recovered from the Hardin site also attest to the specialized dining ritual. Plates were recovered in at least three sizes, and tea wares consisted of matching or complementary sets of cups, saucers, sugars, and creamers. Table glass shows a similar advice literature and similar elaboration in vessel forms for specialized uses.

Along with the specialized table-glass serving forms, a high percentage of the assemblage, 55 per cent or 11 vessels, consisted of tumblers. These would have been important in setting a complete table with individual place settings. The recovery of three stemmed glass-ware vessels also suggests that specialized forms were used for beverage consumption as well. Rather than the simple bowl-like forms of their earlier serving vessels, the mid- to late nineteenth-century vessels of ironstone consisted of moulded, lidded tureens, platters, and serving dishes. Clearly by 1850–70 the Hardins were setting a much more complex dining table than in earlier decades, both in numbers of serving vessels and in specialized forms that required diners to distinguish specific functions: for example the salt cellar, compote, and covered tureen all had specific functions and hidden contents. The evidence suggests that by the 1850s the Hardins were setting their table with covered dishes, and by the 1860s were following a new style of dining which emphasized table setting and decoration rather than food (Wall 1991, 1994b). This conformity between middle-class households in New York City and the Hardin family suggests that these families consciously adopted appropriate symbols and

Table 14.7 Number of ironstone vessel forms

Household	Ironstone vessel forms				Total forms
	Table ware	Tea ware	Serving	Serving	
Elmendorf (NYC)	2	3	4	0	12
Atwater (NYC)	5	5	6	0	17
Bates (NYC)	5	4	3	0	13
McGuire (NYC)	4	3	2	1	11
450 Carlton (NYC)	3	3	3	3	13
Hardin (NYC)	3	4	3	4	14

Source: after Fitts 1999

behaviours to mark themselves as middle-class. By adopting such material symbols of gentility and class affiliation, Hardin marked himself and his children as civilized, respectable members of their communities. Their adherence to prevailing notions of gentility communicated to their neighbours and social inferiors their elevated social status and economic success.

While it is evident from the above discussion that the social life of the Hardins mirrors that of other families of similar economic wealth, what has not been apparent until now is the extent to which families like the Hardins in the rural regions of the south actively pursued and achieved membership in a social class that was theirs by dint of wealth, but not of birth. From the relatively low social status of illiterate farmer, Enos Hardin improved his wealth and social standing by accruing capital, thereby gaining the ability to purchase expensive imported goods, which he and his family used to demonstrate their acquisition of appropriate etiquette behaviours and social knowledge to transform themselves into a social class that was appearing throughout America as individuals climbed the social ladder of success. Where Hardin differs from his peers elsewhere in America is that his wealth was founded directly on the exploitation and breeding of slaves.

Conclusion

We have shown in this study that slavery can be understood as an economic means for Americans in the south to increase their wealth dramatically, which enabled them to pursue and achieve a much higher social status than they could otherwise have done. Comparisons with farmers owning similar acreages to Enos Hardin, but who used free rather than slave labour, demonstrate the differences in wealth. Capital gains could be readily transformed into the same trappings of wealth and social class that citizens elsewhere in the United States could purchase. This pursuit of higher social status appears to have promoted slavery as much as any cultural tradition of the southern United States. Southern slave owners could avail themselves of markets to sell slaves where they could also spend their profits in purchasing expensive, and socially significant, items of material culture. That such trappings of social class are recognizable today only by careful comparison with archaeological assemblages from a wide range of sites attests to the characteristic of some aspects of material culture to become invisible with the passage of time. While it may seem that this study has moved far from an examination of slavery, the efforts, dreams, and intentions of the white slave-owning class must be understood within the context of the nineteenth-century class-formation process if we are to understand why slavery persisted in the United States until the end of the Civil War.

We have demonstrated that the unseen hand of the white slave owner was economic at its base, and entirely social in its intent, as slavery provided the means to a rapid increase in wealth and its transformation into a higher social status with all the respect and standing that wealth brought in one's community in the nineteenth-century American south. We have shown the ways in which this pursuit of such social capital appears to have underpinned and supported the institution of slavery and believe that we have demonstrated the need to create a more comprehensive archaeology of slavery, one in which the unseen hand of the slave owners, their social aspirations, and motives are addressed. Only by demonstrating the social significance of teacups and saucers can we begin to understand individuals such as Hardin, who sought to make themselves into civilized, well-bred, and prosperous members of their communities.

Acknowledgements

We would like to thank several people who aided in the research and editing of this manuscript. Archival research and general computer wizardry were ably completed by Tracey A. Sandefur. Dr W. Stephen McBride and Dr Kim McBride provided invaluable comments on earlier drafts of this chapter. The original study from which this chapter was prepared was conducted in compliance with Section 106 legislation for the Kentucky Transportation Cabinet.

Bibliography

Primary sources

Owen County, Kentucky (KY), Public Records

    1825. Deed Book B.
    1850. Deed Book K.
    1869. Deed Book T.
    1870. Deed Book U.
    1873. Deed Book W.
    1892. Deed Book 38.
    1907. Deed Book 51.
    1819. Order Book A.
    1825. Order Book B.
    1831. Order Book C.
    1870. Order Book U.
    1873. Order Book W.
    1892. Order Book 38.
    1907. Order Book 51.
    1875. Tax Books.
    1863. Owen County, KY, Will Book E. United States Agricultural Census.

1830. Henry County, KY, manuscript returns.

1850–70. Owen County manuscript returns.

United States Population Census

1820–1910. Published returns.

United States Slave Schedule

1850. Owen County, KY, manuscript return.

Secondary sources

Andrews, S.C. 1988. *The Brabson Slave House: The Brabson Ferry Plantation*. Unpublished paper prepared for Seminar in Historical Architecture, Charles H. Faulkner. Knoxville, TN, University of Tennessee.

Andrews, S.C. 1999. *Domesticity and Gentility in Nineteenth Century Owen County, Kentucky*. Unpublished paper presented at the Southeastern Archaeological Conference, Pensacola, Florida.

Andrews, S.C. and Sandefur, T.A. 2000. *Climbing the Social Ladder: Archaeology at the Enos Hardin Farmstead, Owen County, Kentucky, 1925–1870*. Lexington, KY: Wilbur Smith Associates. Submitted to the Division of Environmental Analysis, Kentucky Transportation Cabinet, Frankfort, KY.

Andrews, S.C. and Young, A.L. 1992. Plantations on the Periphery of the Old South: Modeling a New Approach. *Tennessee Anthropologist* 17(1): 1–2.

Brown, K. 1994. Material Culture and Community Structure: The Slave and Tenant Community at Levi Jordan's Plantation, 1848–1892. In Hudson Jr., L.E. (ed.), *Working towards Freedom: Slave Society and Domestic Economy in the American South*. Rochester, NY: University of Rochester Press, pp. 95–118.

Conrad, A.H. and Myer, J.R. 1958. The Economics of Slavery in the Antebellum South. *Journal of Political Economy* 66(2): 95–130.

Epperson, T.W. 1999. Beyond Biological Reductionism, Ethnicity, and Vulgar Anti-Essentialism: Critical Perspectives on Race and the Practice of African-American Archaeology. *African American Archaeology: Newsletter of the African American Archaeology Network* 24.

Ferguson, L. 1992. *Uncommon Ground: Archaeology and Early African America, 1650–1800*. Washington, DC: Smithsonian Institution Press.

Fitts, R.K. 1999. The Archaeology of Middle-Class Domesticity and Gentility in Victorian Brooklyn. *Historical Archaeology* 33(1): 39–62.

Frost, S.A. 1869. *Frost's Laws and By-Laws of American Society: A Condensed but Thorough Treatise on Etiquette and its Usages in America, Containing Plain and Reliable Directions for Deportment in Every Situation in Life*. New York: Dick and Fitzgerald.

Gibbs, T., Cargill, K., Lieberman, L.S., and Reitz, E. 1980. Nutrition in a Slave Population: An Anthropological Examination. *Medical Anthropology* 4: 175–262.

Grover, K. 1987. *Dining in America, 1850–1900*. Amherst: University of Massachusetts Press.

Houchens, M.S. 1977. *History of Owen County, Kentucky: Sweet Owen*. Louisville, KY: The Standard Printing.

Kasson, J.F. 1987. Rituals of Dining: Table Manners in Victorian America. In Grover, K. (ed.), *Dining in America, 1850–1900*. Amherst: University of Massachusetts Press, pp. 114–41.

Kolchin, P. 1993. *American Slavery, 1619–1877*. New York: Hill and Wang.

La Roche, C.J. 1994. Beads from the African American Burial Ground, New York City: A Preliminary Assessment. *Beads: Journal of the Society of Bead Researchers* 6: 3–20.

Lucas, M.B. 1992. *A History of Blacks in Kentucky, Volume 1: From Slavery to Segregation, 1760–1891*. Frankfort: The Kentucky Historical Society.

McBride, W.S. 1991. Flush Times on the Upper Tombigbee: Settlement and Economic Development in Lowndes County, Mississippi, 1833–1860. Ph.D. thesis. Department of Anthropology, Michigan State University.

McBride, W.S. and Esarey, M.E. 1995. The Archaeology of the Ashland Privy, Lexington, Kentucky. In McBride, K., McBride, W.S., and Pollack, D. (eds), *Historical Archaeology in Kentucky*. Frankfort: Kentucky Heritage Council, pp. 265–95.

McCorvie, M.R. 1987. *The Davis, Baldrige, and Huggins Sites: Three Nineteenth Century Upland South Farmsteads in Perry County, Illinois*. Carbondale, IL: American Resources Group.

McCorvie, M.R., Wagner, M.J., Johnston, J.K., Martin, T.J., and Parker, K.E. 1989. *Phase III Archaeological Investigations at the Fair View Farm Site (I1-Sa-336): A Historic Farmstead in the Shawnee Hills of Southern Illinois*. Carbondale, IL: American Resources Group.

McKee, L. 1987. Delineating Ethnicity from the Garbage of Early Virginians: Faunal Remains from the Kingsmill Plantation Slave Quarter. *American Archaeology* 6(1): 31–9.

Miller, G.L. 1980. Classification and Economic Scaling of 19th Century Ceramics. *Historical Archaeology* 14: 1–40.

Miller, G.L. 1991. A Revised Set of CC Index Values for Classification and Economic Scaling of English Ceramics from 1787 to 1880. *Historical Archaeology* 25(1): 1–25.

Miller, G.L., Martin, A.S., and Dickinson, N.S. 1994. Changing Consumption Patterns: English Ceramics and the American Market from 1770 to 1840. In Hutchins, C.E. (ed.), *Everyday Life in the Early Republic*. Delaware: Winterthur Museum, pp. 219–48.

Moir, R.W. 1987. Socioeconomic and Chronometric Patterning of Window Glass. In Jurney, D.H. and Moir, R.W. (eds), *Historic Buildings, Material Culture, and People of the Prairie Margin*. Dallas, TX: Southern Methodist University, pp. 83–96.

O'Malley, N. 1990. *The DeRossett-Johns Sites: Archaeological Exploration of Prestonsburg's Early History*. Department of Anthropology, University of Kentucky, Lexington.

O'Malley, N. 1995. Living the Good Life: Archaeological Explorations of Middle Class Life in Nineteenth Century Prestonburg, Floyd County, Kentucky. In McBride, K.A., McBride, W.S., and Pollack, D. (eds), *Historical Archaeology in Kentucky*. Frankfort: Kentucky Heritage Council, pp. 169–94.

Otto, J.S. 1977. Artifacts and Status Differences: A Comparison of Ceramics from Planter, Overseer, and Slave Sites on an Antebellum Plantation. In Schuyler, R. (ed.), *Research Strategies in Historical Perspectives on Ethnicity in America: Afro-American and Asian American Culture History*. Farmingdale, NY: Baywood, pp. 3–13.

Otto, J.S.O. 1980a. Race and Class on Antebellum Plantations. In Schuyler, R.L. (ed.), *Archaeological Perspectives on Ethnicity in America*. Farmingdale, NY: Baywood, pp. 3–13.

Otto, J.S.O. 1980b. Slavery in the Mountains: Yell County, Arkansas, 1840–1860. *Arkansas Historical Quarterly* 34(1).

Otto, J.S.O. 1984. *Canon's Point Plantation, 1794–1860: Living Conditions and Status Patterns in the Old South*. New York: Academic Press.

Otto, J.S.O. 1989. *The Southern Frontiers, 1607–1860: The Agricultural Evolution of the Colonial and Antebellum South*. New York: Greenwood Press.

Perdue, Jr., C.L., Barden, T.E., and Phillips, R.K. 1980. *Weevils in the Wheat: Interviews with Virginia Ex-Slaves*. Bloomington: Indiana University Press.

Phifer, E. 1962. Slavery in Microcosm; Burke County, North Carolina. *Journal of Southern History* 28: 137–9.

Phillippe, J.S. 1990. *The Drake Site: Subsistence and Status at a Rural Illinois Farmstead*. Normal: Illinois State University.

Praetzellis, A. and Praetzellis, M. 1992. Faces and Facades: Victorian Ideology in Early Sacramento. In Yentsch, A. and Beaudry, M. (eds), *The Art and Mystery of Historical Archaeology*. Boca Raton, FL: CRC Press, pp. 75–99.

Roth, R. 1961. Tea Drinking in 18th-Century America: Its Etiquette and Equipage. U.S. *Contributions from the Museum of History and Technology* 14: 61–91.

Schlotterbeck, J.T. 1982. The 'Social Economy' of an Upper South Community: Orange and Greene Counties, Virginia, 1815–1860. In Burton, O.V. and McMath, R.C. (eds), *Class, Conflict, and Consensus: Antebellum Southern Community Studies*. Westport, CT: Greenwood Press, pp. 3–28.

Singleton, T.A. (ed.). 1985. *The Archaeology of Slavery and Plantation Life*. New York: Academic Press.

Spencer-Wood, S. 1987a. *Consumer Choice in Historical Archaeology*. New York: Plenum.

Spencer-Wood, S. 1987b. Miller Indices and Consumer-Choice Profiles: Status-Related Behaviors and White Ceramics. In Spencer-Wood, S.M. (ed.), *Consumer Choice in Historical Archaeology*. New York: Plenum, pp. 321–58.

Spencer-Wood, S.M. and Heberling, S.D. 1987. Consumer Choice in White Ceramics: A Comparison of Eleven Early Nineteenth-Century Sites. In Spencer-Wood, S.M. (ed.), *Consumer Choice in Historical Archaeology*. New York: Plenum, pp. 55–84.

Stewart-Abernathy, L.C. 1986. *The Moser Farmstead: Independent but not Isolated: The Archaeology of a Late Nineteenth Century Ozark Farmstead*. Fayetteville: Arkansas Archaeological Survey.

Stine, L.F. 1990. Social Inequality and Turn-of-the-Century Farmsteads: Issues of Class, Status, Ethnicity, and Race. *Historical Archaeology* 24: 37–49.

Stine, L.F., Cabak, M.A., and Groover, M.D. 1996. Blue Beads as African-American Cultural Symbols. *Historical Archaeology* 30(3): 49–75.

Sutch, R. 1975. The Breeding of Slaves for Sale and the Westward Expansion of Slavery, 1850–1860. In Engerman, S. and Genovese, E. (eds), *Race and Slavery*. Princeton, NJ: Princeton University Press, pp. 179–80, 192–3, 207–10.

Wall, D. di Z. 1987. At Home in New York: The Redefinition of Gender Among the Middle Class and Elite, 1783–1840. Ph.D. thesis. Department of Anthropology, New York University.

Wall, D. di Z. 1991. Sacred Dinners and Secular Teas: Constructing Domesticity in Mid-19th Century New York. *Historical Archaeology* 25(4): 69–81.

Wall, D. di Z. 1994a. *The Archaeology of Gender: Separating the Spheres in Urban America*. New York: Plenum.

Wall, D. di Z. 1994b. Family Dinners and Social Teas: Ceramics and Domestic Rituals. In Hutchins, C.E. (ed.), *Everyday Life in the Early Republic*. Delaware: Winterthur Museum, pp. 249–84.

Wall, D. di Z. 1999. Examining Gender, Class, and Ethnicity in Nineteeth-Century New York City. *Historical Archaeology* 33(1): 102–17.

Wheaton, T. and Garrow, P. 1985. Acculturation and the Archaeological Record in the Carolina Lowcountry. In Singleton, T. (ed.), *The Archaeology of Slavery and Plantation Life*. New York: Academic Press, pp. 239–58.

Wheaton, T.R., Friedlander, A., and Garrow, P.W. 1983. *Yaughan and Curriboo Plantations: Studies in Afro-American Archaeology*. Marietta, GA: Soil Systems.

Williams, S. 1987. Introduction. In Grover, K. (ed.), *Dining in America 1850–1900*. Amherst, MA: University of Massachusetts Press, pp. 3–23.

Young, A.L. 1995. Risk and Material Conditions of African-American Slaves at Locust Grove: An Archaeological Perspective. Ph.D. thesis. Department of Anthropology, University of Tennessee, Knoxville.

Young, A.L. 1996. Archaeological Evidence of African-Styled Ritual and Healing Practices in the Upland South. *Tennessee Anthropologist* 21(2): 139–55.

Young, A.L., Andrews, S.C., and Carr, P.J. 1995. Ceramics and Slave Lifeways at Locust Grove Plantation. In McBride, K.A., McBride, W.S., and Pollack, D. (eds), *Historical Archaeology in Kentucky*. Frankfort, KY: Kentucky Heritage Council, pp. 253–64.

Chapter 15

The archaeological visibility of caste

An introduction

Robin Coningham and Ruth Young

Introduction

Caste is one of the most powerful dynamics ordering social space within settlements in South Asia. It is a dynamic which controls marriage partners, ritual purity, diet, occupation, and the location of habitation. Present in rural and urban settings, it is a dynamic which is found in Hindu, Buddhist, and Islamic communities throughout the subcontinent, from Sri Lanka to Nepal, and from Bangladesh to Pakistan. A recognizable modern phenomenon, attempts have been made to demonstrate that it forms a very real and pervasive link with the oral and written histories of South Asia. Such a powerful dynamic has not been ignored by archaeologists and historians; a number of such scholars have attempted to trace and identify it in architectural and artefactual distributions, ranging in date from the Early Historic to the Prehistoric (Auboyer 1965; Jarrige and Santoni 1979; Ratnagar 1991). This chapter will evaluate the success of these attempts, frame a methodology for testing two archaeological indicators – occupation and diet – and their application to archaeological evidence, and examine the archaeological visibility of caste.

Definitions

The very definition of caste is problematic as the word is derived from a sixteenth-century AD Portuguese term used to describe trading communities on the west coast of India. In this, its first application to South Asia, it meant nothing more than species or breeds among animals or plants; and tribes, races or lineages among humans. This simple meaning has become increasingly distorted and now is often used, as demonstrated by Quigley (1993), as an interchangeable translation of two, very different South Asian terms varna and jati. The former term, varna, refers to a fourfold division of society into Brahmana (priest), Ksatriya (warriors), Vaisya (merchants and craftsmen), and Sudra (labourers) which ensures social harmony and cosmic stability; the latter, jati, refers to a shared common origin through birth (ibid.). A clearly recognizable phenomenon in contemporary South Asian communities, a number of attempts have been made to demonstrate that caste forms a very real and pervasive link with the oral and written histories of the region. The earliest reference to this fourfold division is found in the Purusa-Sukta or 'Hymn of Man' of the *Rig Veda* (O'Flaherty 1981), which is traditionally dated to the first millennia BC: 'His mouth became the Brahman; his arms were made into the warrior; his thighs the people, and from his feet the servants were born' (*Rig Veda* 10.90.12).

However, the earliest evidence to suggest that this division was spatial as well as social is only found in the Arthasastra of Kautiliya (Kangle 1965). Traditionally accepted as a practical manual of information for a ruler written in the third century BC, it advocated the spatial separation of groups within cities (Fig. 15.1). Brahmans were to be in the north, Ksatriya in the east, Vaisya in the south, Sudra

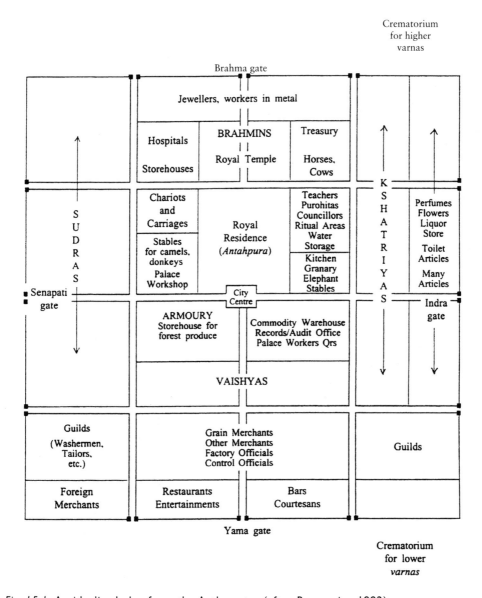

Fig. 15.1 An idealized plan from the Arthasastra (after Rangarajan 1992).

in the west, and outcastes outside the city (Arthasastra 2.4.7–23). Further codification of the regulations of access to dress, food, habitation, and social and sexual relationships for each group was recorded in the Manavadharmasastra or 'Laws of Manu', which was compiled between the second century BC and second century AD (Buhler 1886).

It is also noteworthy that while some scholars, such as Leach (1960), have argued for a definition of caste as a purely South Asian social phenomenon, others, most notably Barth (1960), have argued that it is merely a local term given to a universal form of social stratification. These problematic and well-discussed definitions aside, one of the most clearly presented working definitions of caste was produced by Hutton (1946: 49),

(i)   A caste is endogamous.
(ii) There are restrictions on commensality between members of different castes.
(iii) There is a hierarchical grading of castes, the best-recognized position being that of the Brahman at the top.
(iv) In various kinds of contexts, especially those connected with food, sex, and ritual, a member of a 'high' caste is liable to be 'polluted' by either direct or indirect contact with a member of a 'low' caste.
(v)   Castes are very commonly associated with traditional occupations.
(vi) An individual's caste status is finally determined by the circumstances of his birth, unless he comes to be expelled from his caste for some ritual offence.
(vii) The system as a whole is always focused around the prestige accorded to the Brahmans.

While such clear-cut attributions have been demonstrated to be more flexible in a number of cases (Banks 1960; Yalman 1960; Quigley 1993), archaeologists and historians still rely heavily upon such definitions, and we shall continue to use the term caste.

Caste in contemporary South Asian communities

Archaeologists are often tempted to use the present to make sense of the past, and this is certainly the case for the archaeology of caste. However, before presenting a number of archaeological attempts to identify caste in the past, it is useful to illustrate a 'classic' contemporary community in which, in Leach's words, caste 'defines the structural role of every sector in a total organic system' (1960: 10). The example is that of the village of Kumbapettai in Tanjore District of southern India as recorded by Kathleen Gough in the early 1950s (1960, 1981). This village of 962 people in 199 households was divided into three main groups:

(A) Brahmans
(B) Non-Brahmans
    (i)   Aristocratic managers and administrators, officer, and courtiers
    (ii) Tenant farmers and village labourers
    (iii) Craftsmen and traders
(C) Adi Dravida or 'Original Dravidian'

Gough also recorded seven main ways in which these three groups were differentiated:

(i)   Habitation location – Brahmans lived in the north of the village (1), non-Brahmans in the centre (2 and 3), and Adi Dravida on the western and southern outskirts separated by paddy land, streams, or cremation grounds (4 and 5) (Fig. 15.2).

(ii) Building materials – Brahmans lived in brick and tiled houses, non-Brahmans in large mud and thatch houses with door and windows, and Adi Dravida in small mud and thatch shacks with no windows.

(iii) Access to space – Adi Dravida were not allowed into the Brahman street, 'polluting' non-Brahmans were allowed into the Brahman street but not the houses, and 'clean' non-Brahmans were allowed into Brahman houses but not the kitchens. Adi Dravida may enter the streets of non-Brahmans but not the houses and vice versa.

(iv) Occupation – despite the appearance of the modern economy, Gough recorded that, 'The spatial organisation of castes corresponds in large measure to their occupational specialisation and mutual ritual rank' (1981: 18).

(v)   Diet – Brahmans were vegetarian, non-Brahmans and Avi Dravida were meat eaters, although only the Pallas ate beef. Inter-dining between these groups was impossible.

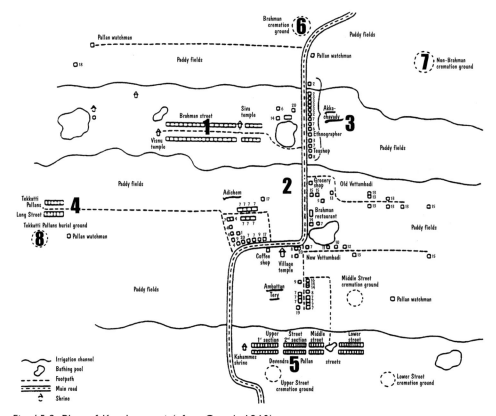

Fig. 15.2 Plan of Kumbapettai (after Gough 1960).

(vi) Intimate interaction – with the exception of Barbers and Midwives no group is allowed to touch persons of a higher category. Sex between Brahman men and Pallas women is strongly condemned, while a case of a non-Brahman man who had sex with a Brahman woman resulted in his castration and murder.

(vii) Cremation ground location – Brahmans are cremated at (6) and non-Brahmans at (7), while the Adi Dravida are buried at (8).

Similar social and spatial differentiation has been found within non-Hindu rural settlements elsewhere in South Asia as illustrated by Yalman among a Buddhist community in Sri Lanka (1960) and by Barth within an Islamic community in northern Pakistan (1960).

Caste and the past

Such a visible social structure has, of course, been used by archaeologists and historians as a model for the functioning of past societies as well as by social anthropologists and sociologists in attempts to explain present behaviour. As early as the 1920s the Bronze Age Harappan, or Indus, civilization was noted for the absence of royal palaces and tombs and the presence of an extremely strong conformity of material culture through time and space, which Wheeler referred to as 'disciplined and even regimented' (1953: 40) (Fig. 15.3). While he did not actually suggest that this was a result of the caste system, Kolenda asked the following question in 1978: 'There

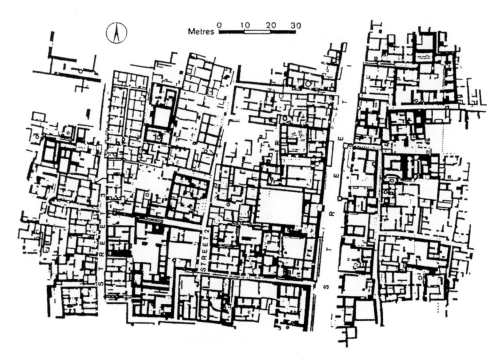

Fig. 15.3 Regimented grid-iron street pattern at Mohenjo-daro (after Marshall 1931).

were occupational specialists in Harappan society, but nothing is known of their social organisation...were they closed endogamous descent-groups like the later jatis?' This line of approach has also been followed by Malik (1968) and Gupta (1974), who have suggested that the stability and continuity of material culture within the Mature Harappan was a result of the presence of the caste system.

Jarrige and Santoni have made a further case for the presence of caste at the Chalcolithic/Iron Age site of Pirak in western Pakistan. Here the excavators identified a craft zone within the settlement dating to between the eleventh and ninth centuries BC. They stated that,

> the division into quarters, the existence of a block of buildings where craftsmen seem to have lived in a community, the stereotyped character of the layout of the houses...and the conservatism of the material culture throughout almost ten centuries are factors that suggest an organisation into social classes...just as in the present day villages.
>
> (Jarrige and Santoni 1979: 411)

They link this social organization, presumably caste, closely with the arrival of Indo-European languages and Vedic Hinduism.

> It is not due to chance that these important transformations which take us from the Chalcolithic cultures of the third millennium to the rural society of the historical periods are set against the spread of a language that was to remain the chief vehicle in India and a religion that was to serve as a framework for later religious developments.
>
> (ibid.)

The final archaeological example considered here is set in the Early Historic period of South Asia, which dates between the beginning of the first millennium BC and the fifth century AD. As the Arthasastra and Manavadharmasastra were compiled during this period, many historians and archaeologists have assumed that such social and spatial planning were physically realized, regardless of the absence of actual excavated evidence. Thus Rowe (1973) stated that: 'from the very earliest times, the Indian city has provided a symbolic representation of the social order, both in its spatial arrangement and in its social structure'. Gough provides a similar statement, 'from about the tenth century BC, the kingdoms of India all possessed five main orders....For three thousand years, these orders and their attached specialists formed the backbone of the caste system and underlay the basic principles of religious ranking. Only with the rise of capitalism are they being eroded' (1981: 26). The historian, Auboyer, writing in the 1960s, stated that, 'it does seem, though, that the capital was in fact divided into a certain number of well-defined districts....In such a scheme, each caste is supposed to have occupied a particular district' (1965: 120). More recently the archaeologist Erdosy, on the basis of a study of caste within modern village plans, has further suggested that, 'as the social organisation operated at both village and city levels and as the idealised plans of the ancient texts themselves were meant for both types of settlements, we may expect to find our hypothesis drawn on the basis of village plans to be confirmed in cities' (1986: 156).

The archaeological visibility of caste: towards a methodology

While many archaeologists, historians, sociologists, and anthropologists have thus argued for the presence of caste in the past, there have been very few suggestions of how one would actually identify it. Indeed most seem prepared to sidestep the issue as illustrated by Ratnagar who stated that 'there may have been a caste system in Harappan times....But even if this were detectable from archaeological remains, it would leave unanswered the question of political structure and economic system' (1991: 19). This is indeed a question of how one would identify caste from archaeological remains. Perhaps the solution is provided by Thapar, who suggested that 'material culture and cultural differences occurring consistently in distinctive sections of the town may suggest a variation of social groupings' (1978: 205). Surely such a varied urban community, if spatially and socially differentiated, should be archaeologically visible!

For the purposes of this chapter the spatial variability of two categories of material culture – craft waste and faunal remains – from a single Early Historic urban site will be examined. The former is interpreted as being indicative of occupation and the latter of diet, although clearly taboo and other symbolic pressures often distort the deposition of artefacts within the archaeological record (Moore 1982; Hodder 1986). Both selected categories are taken from a single site – the Citadel of Anuradhapura in Sri Lanka, which was excavated between 1969 and 1994 by a joint Sri Lankan–British project (Fig. 15.4).

One might query the selection of Anuradhapura as a test site as it is located at the southern periphery of the South Asian region, and, second, because the city was historically a centre of Theravada Buddhism. However, as noted elsewhere, there is clear evidence that the island was not peripheral as it played a pivotal role in trade networks during the Early Historic period (Coningham *et al.* 1996) and there is also evidence that caste has played an important role in the ancient and modern social organization of the island (Ryan 1953; Yalman 1960; Leach 1961; Coningham 1994). Finally Anuradhapura represents one of the most detailed archaeological samples from an Early Historic urban centre in South Asia. These samples are furthermore important as they are drawn from a total number of 14 trenches excavated at different locations throughout the walled site itself (Fig. 15.5). Trench ASW2 in particular, excavated close to the city's origin as a small Iron Age settlement at the beginning of the first millennium BC to its place as an imperial capital in the tenth and eleventh centuries AD, is of especial significance.

Occupation

As illustrated above, traditional occupations are often attributed to caste. Such occupations may be identified in contemporary communities through a combination of actual physical activities, specialist tools, specialist architectural elements, and waste products. For example a potter may make pottery using a wheel before firing it in a kiln and discarding wasters. While some occupations, such as potting, may thus be easy to identify in the past, others, such as leather-working or shaving, are more difficult due to differential survival within the archaeological record. Furthermore activities carried out 'off-site', such as washing, are even more difficult to find and identify.

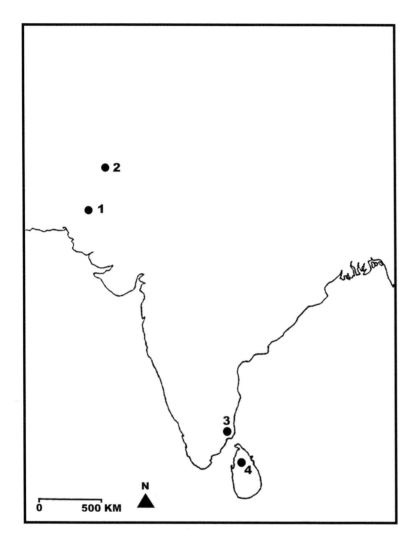

Fig. 15.4 The location of Anuradhapura and other sites mentioned in the text. 1. Mohenjo-daro. 2. Pirak. 3. Kumbapettai. 4. Anuradhapura.

For the purposes of the present chapter we shall limit our study to two main activities: metalworking – as represented by moulds, furnaces, crucibles, and slag; semi-precious, stone-working – as represented by blanks and debitage.

As discussed elsewhere (Coningham 1997), we share with Pracchia *et al.* (1985) the belief that while finds of these categories of material may not represent the precise boundaries of processing, certainly the waste products, such as slag, debitage, and cores, are unlikely to have been moved far. Traditional models of Early Historic urban planning (Auboyer 1965; Rowe 1973) indicate that activities were located within prescribed zones of the city, as described by the Arthasastra, or divided into less geographically prescriptive blocks in contemporary rural and

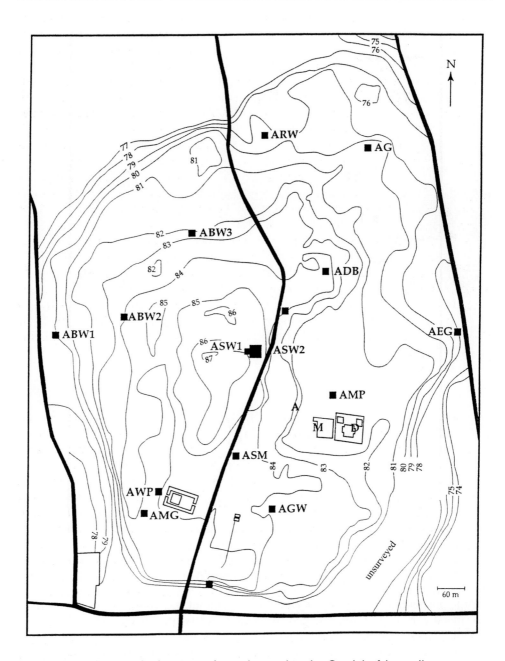

Fig. 15.5 Plan showing the location of trenches within the Citadel of Anuradhapura.

urban settlements. We would expect therefore either of two patterns within the distribution of evidence from the 14 trenches at Anuradhapura: workers of metal and jewels in the north (Arthasastra); a separate zone of craft activities within one area, not necessarily north.

The pattern of the archaeological evidence is, however, very different to either of the proposed models. While the sequence at Anuradhapura stretches from *c.* 900 BC to *c.* AD 1100, for the purposes of this chapter we shall only examine the data from two successive periods within the site, as they are well preserved.

Period I dates to between *c.* 350 and 275 BC and Period G/H to between *c.* 275 BC and AD 200. Of the 14 localities sampled at the first period, I, a total of seven trenches (ADB, ASW1, ABW3, AGW, ARW, AG, and AMP) had evidence of metalworking and semi-precious stone-working waste – giving a very diverse pattern for the distribution of similar crafts within the site. Our larger trench at ASW2, adjacent to ASW1, also showed evidence of metalworking waste, in addition to yielding evidence of bone, shell, and antler-working from its more detailed data base belonging to a single structure (Fig. 15.6). Both sets of data suggest a very diverse pattern of the location of craftworking activities within the city. During the succeeding period, G/H, a similarly diverse pattern was found with a total of seven trenches (ADB, ASW1, AG, ABW2, ABW3, AMP, and ABW1) providing evidence of metalworking and semi-precious stone-working waste. Again, the largest trench, ASW2, yielded waste products suggesting the presence of metalworking, semi-precious stone-working, glass-working, antler-, and even ivory-working in the same structure (Fig. 15.7). The patterns thus recovered from both periods are clearly at odds with the models forwarded for the Early Historic social organization of craft activities within urban forms (Coningham 1997) and are similarly at odds with the contemporary ethnographic examples cited above.

Diet

The faunal remains from Anuradhapura will also be examined as they are interpreted as being indicative of diet, although as has already been mentioned, taboo and other symbolic pressures often distort the deposition of artefacts within the archaeological record. Our data set is more limited than that for occupation, being reliant upon our own sample from ASW2 and that from a single trench, AG. We are fortunate, however, that while the former site is located within the centre of the city, the latter is located within the northeast of the city, thus spatial variation within diet should be clear. Although Deraniyagala interpreted all the bone recovered from trench AG as food waste on the basis of cut marks and the associated ash and charcoal (1972: 155), certain species were evidently also used for traction, haulage, general transport, milk, hides, horn, and breeding purposes. We hoped to identify spatial variation within diet between the two trenches, conforming to patterns of modern South Asian communities where selected diets are restricted to caste. Our sample consisted of 1,946 identified bones from trench ASW2 and a further 2,356 identified bones from trench AG (ibid.). As noted above further codification of the regulations of diet are recorded in the Manavadharmasastra or 'Laws of Manu', which was compiled between the second century BC and the second century AD (Buhler 1886).

Reference to the Laws will further assist us in understanding spatial variation within the archaeological faunal record. The Laws of Manu, for example, state that any twice-born man who knowingly eats village pig or cock will become an outcaste (ibid.: 172) and that any man who kills a horse, deer, elephant, fish, or snake will be degraded to a mixed caste (ibid.: 444). It also lists the following as forbidden:

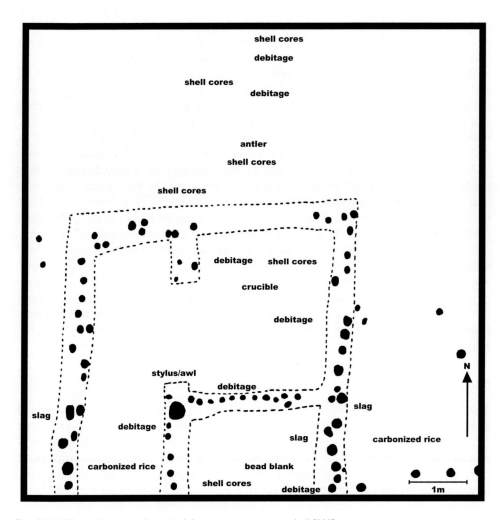

Fig. 15.6 Plan of exposed period I structure at trench ASW2.

(i)   All carnivorous and one-hoofed animals (ibid.: 170)
(ii) All solitary and unknown beasts (ibid.: 172)
(iii) All five-toed animals (ibid.)
(iv) Animals which eat fish (ibid.: 171)
(v)   Village pigs (ibid.)

In comparison with this list it is useful to record which species, permitted and forbidden, were recorded at trenches ASW2 and AG:

Trench ASW2

Forbidden	Permitted
cattle	*buffalo*
horse	*porcupine*

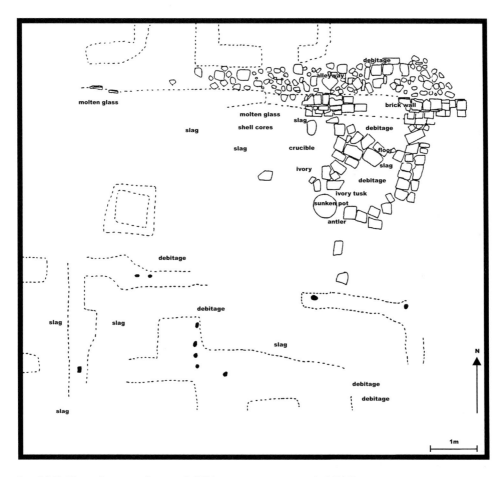

Fig. 15.7 Plan of exposed period G/H structure at trench ASW2.

pig	hare
deer	terrapin

Trench AG

Forbidden	Permitted
horse	terrapin
cattle	
deer	
pig	

While it should also be noted that certain forbidden animals can be made acceptable depending on the hunter and the rituals undergone, there is a clear pattern of the presence in both localities of species forbidden by the Laws of Manu – moreover many of those from trench AG are noted as having cut marks. The presence of cattle bones in both areas is particularly surprising considering the major beef-eating taboo on the island, which is thought to have occurred after AD 100 (ibid.: 157). In summary a comparison of the major identified faunal species from trenches ASW2 and AG shows the same general trends in both the species present and the periods in which they occur regardless of the fact that these mainly consist of forbidden species.

Conclusions

We may thus conclude that Thapar's suggestion that a study of the spatial variability of selected material culture within an urban form might confirm the presence of distinctive social groupings (1978: 205) has not been achieved. Indeed rather than finding clear patterns of spatial variation within the distribution of craft waste and faunal remains we have found broadly similar patterns in terms of the overall distribution of craft activities and the discarding of the remains of animal species within a single urban site. In effect this unexpected result suggests that the formal caste-based models proposed by the Laws of Manu and the Arthasastra were not realized physically. It is suggested therefore that the spatial differentiation which is observed today is a relatively recent phenomenon – the enforcement of a largely symbolic division.

Caste is, of course, a far more flexible system of social organization than suggested by the Arthasastra or the Laws of Manu, as illustrated by numerous modern examples of communities rising and falling within its rankings. Yalman (1960), for example, cited the example of a group of high-caste families moving into a locality within central Sri Lanka which had been recently vacated by lower-caste inhabitants. Through this spatial association alone their overall status was lowered among the surrounding high-caste families. Similarly there are a number of examples of lower-caste groups who underwent a process of Sanskritization as a strategy to legitimate a claim of higher caste. As Jayaram states, 'the flexible dimension of the caste system in the background of the open-endedness of Hinduism is reflected in the claims of higher caste status by the lower castes following their Sanskritization' (1996: 78). In contrast there have been a number of attempts to reverse this process of Sanskritization by backwards class movements in India as an active attempt to reach a lower grade in order to gain access to reserved government jobs (ibid.). In conclusion we may thus suggest that this first attempt to test the archaeological visibility of caste indicates that its artefactual manifestations may be more flexible and complex than traditionally assumed and that if we are to study it further we need to modify our methods and guiding assumptions.

Acknowledgements

As much of the primary data presented in this chapter were collected during the joint British–Sri Lankan excavations at Anuradhapura between 1989 and 1994, the first author would like to thank Dr Siran Deraniyagala, Director-General of the Department of Archaeology, Government of Sri Lanka, for his help and advice; and most especially for allowing access to his excavated data and site notes from Anuradhapura. The following bodies are also acknowledged for their financial sponsorship of the fieldwork: the Ancient India and Iran Trust, the Archaeological Survey Department of Sri Lanka, the British Academy, the McDonald Institute for Archaeological Research, the Society of Antiquaries and the Society for South Asian

Studies. This fieldwork was carried out while the first author consecutively held a King's College Research Studentship, an Ancient India and Iran Trust Junior Research Fellowship, and a Lectureship in South Asian Archaeology at the University of Bradford.

Bibliography

Auboyer, J. 1965. *Daily Life in Ancient India*. London: Weidenfeld and Nicolson.
Banks, M. 1960. Caste in Jaffna. In Leach, E.R. (ed.), *Aspects of Caste in South India, Ceylon and North-West Pakistan*. Cambridge: Cambridge University Press, pp. 61–77.
Barth, F. 1960. The System of Social Stratification in Swat, North Pakistan. In Leach, E.R. (ed.), *Aspects of Caste in South India, Ceylon and North-West Pakistan*. Cambridge: Cambridge University Press, pp. 113–46.
Buhler, G. 1886. *The Laws of Manu*. Oxford: Oxford University Press.
Coningham, R.A.E. 1994. 'Urban Texts': An Interpretation of the Architectural, Textual and Artefactual Records of a Sri Lankan Early Historic City. Ph.D. thesis. University of Cambridge.
Coningham, R.A.E. 1997. The Spatial Distribution of Craft Activities in Early Historic Cities and Their Social Implications. In Allchin, F.R. and Allchin, B. (eds), *South Asian Archaeology 1995*. Delhi: Oxford and IBH, pp. 351–64.
Coningham, R.A.E., Allchin, F.R., Batt, C.M., and Lucy, D. 1996. Passage to India? Anuradhapura and the Early Use of the Brahmi Script. *Cambridge Archaeological Journal* 6(1): 73–97.
Deraniyagala, P.E.P. 1972. Faunal Remains. *Ancient Ceylon* 2: 155–8.
Erdosy, G. 1986. Social Ranking and Spatial Structure: Examples from India. *Archaeological Review from Cambridge* 5(2): 154–66.
Gough, K. 1960. Caste in a Tanjore Village. In Leach, E.R. (ed.), *Aspects of Caste in South India, Ceylon and North-West Pakistan*. Cambridge: Cambridge University Press, pp. 11–60.
Gough, K. 1981. *Rural Society in Southeast India*. Cambridge: Cambridge University Press.
Gupta, S.P. 1974. Two Urbanisations in India. *Puratattva* 7: 53–60.
Hodder, I. 1986. *Reading the Past: Current Approaches to Interpretation in Archaeology*. Cambridge: Cambridge University Press.
Hutton, 1946. *Caste in India: Its Nature, Function and Origins*. Bombay: Oxford University Press.
Jarrige, J.F. and Santoni, M. 1979. *Fouilles de Pirak*. Paris: Commission des Fouilles Archéologiques.
Jayaram, N. 1996. Caste and Hinduism: Changing Protean Relationships. In Srinivas, M.N. (ed.), *Caste: Its Twentieth Century Avatar*. Delhi: Viking Penguin, pp. 69–86.
Kangle, R.P. 1965. *The Kautiliya Arthastastra*. Bombay: University of Bombay.
Kolenda, P. 1978. *Caste in Contemporary India*. Malo Park, CA: Benjamin and Cummings.
Leach, E.R. 1960. What Should We Mean By Caste? In Leach, E.R. (ed.), *Aspects of Caste in South India, Ceylon and North-West Pakistan*. Cambridge: Cambridge University Press, pp. 1–10.
Leach, E.R. 1961. *Pul Eliya: A Village in Ceylon*. Cambridge: Cambridge University Press.
Malik, S.C. 1968. *Indian Civilisation: The Formative Period*. Simla: Indian Institute of Advanced Study.
Marshall, J.H. 1931. *Mohenjo-Daro and the Indus Civilisation*. London: Arthur Probsthain.
Moore, H.L. 1982. The Interpretation of Spatial Patterning in Settlement Residues. In Hodder, I. (ed.), *Symbolic and Structural Archaeology*. Cambridge: Cambridge University Press, pp. 74–9.

O'Flaherty, W.D. 1981. *The Rig Veda*. Harmondsworth: Penguin Books.

Pracchia, S., Tosi, M., and Vidale, M. 1985. On the Type, Distribution and Extent of Craft Industries at Mohenjo-Daro. In Schotsman, J. and Taddei, M. (eds), *South Asian Archaeology, 1983*. Naples: Instituto Universitario Orientale, pp. 207–47.

Quigley, D. 1993. *The Interpretation of Caste*. Oxford: Oxford University Press.

Rangarajan, L.N. 1992. *Kautilya – The Arthasastra*. Delhi: Penguin Books.

Ratnagar, S. 1991. *Enquiries Into the Political Organisation of Harappan Society*. Pune: Ravish Publishers.

Rowe, W.L. 1973. Caste, Kinship and Association in Urban India. In Southall, A. (ed.), *Urban Anthropology*. Oxford: Oxford University Press, pp. 211–50.

Ryan, B. 1953. *Caste in Modern Ceylon*. New Brunswick: Rutgers University Press.

Thapar, R. 1978. *Ancient Indian Social History*. New Delhi: Orient Longman.

Wheeler, R.E.M. 1953. *The Indus Civilisation*. Cambridge: Cambridge University Press.

Yalman, N. 1960. The Flexibility of Caste Principles in a Kandyan Community. In Leach, E.R. (ed.), *Aspects of Caste in South India, Ceylon and North-West Pakistan*. Cambridge: Cambridge University Press, pp. 78–112.

Chapter 16

Huitzilopochtli's conquest

Aztec ideology in the archaeological record

Elizabeth M. Brumfiel

Introduction

This chapter examines the role of ideology in the Aztec state. It contributes to the debate over the ways in which systems of inequality are constructed and maintained. I have argued that dominant groups exercise power through coalitions of factions, that is, alliance groups that can use coercion to enforce their will on others (Brumfiel 1994a, 1994b). This position is challenged, however, by those that emphasize the ability of ideology to engineer consent without the use of coercive force. David Clarke never expressed a position regarding either power or ideology in prehistoric societies. But he did vigorously advocate asking new questions about prehistory and making explicit, experimental efforts to answer them. It is in David Clarke's honour, then, that I offer the following discussion. (Editor's note – this contribution was originally presented as the third David Clarke Memorial Lecture at Peterhouse College, Cambridge University, in 1997.)

For the purpose of this discussion, ideology can be defined as a system of values and ideas that promotes social behaviour benefiting some classes of interest groups more than others (Gilman 1989: 68; Thompson 1990: 73). Ideology has been regarded as a crucial factor in the persistence of social inequality. According to Shanks and Tilley (1982: 132), relations of inequality are frequently sustained by ideologies which deny, explain, or justify forms of social interaction that produce advantages for some and frustration for others. In the grip of such ideologies, subordinate groups may actively reproduce their own subordination. Subordinate groups may be so influenced by ideologies that they are unable to critique, resist, or reform their societies. Abercrombie *et al.* (1980) have labelled this the 'dominant ideology thesis'.

This proposal might explain the persistence of systems of inequality, but it is difficult to reconcile with numerous pieces of evidence indicating that subordinate groups can and do resist inequality. The numerous civil wars fuelled by popular discontent in non-Western states (Brumfiel 1983, 1994b), the recurrent outbreaks of peasant violence during the Middle Ages (Tuberville 1929), and peasant wars in the twentieth century (Wolf 1969) all bear witness to efforts by subordinates to alter the status quo. These incidents also underscore the importance of coercion in maintaining inequality. When subordinate groups do resist, dominant groups respond with force. The effectiveness of this repression is often determined by the unity and commitment of those who fight on behalf of the dominant group.

This suggests a second way in which ideology might act to perpetuate inequality. Ideology can bind together the coalitions that carry out the coercive policies of dominant groups (Hicks 1994). Ideology might enhance the unity of an elite coalition in three ways. First, it can prescribe the responsibilities and rewards that fall to its actors who assume membership in such groups. Second, it can establish the value of these rewards, making them prizes worthy of sacrifice. And third, it can place certain forms of behaviour in cosmological contexts that make them seem morally worthy (Kelly 1993: 13–17). In this way significant political challenges might occur whenever leaders construct new social coalitions based upon new concepts of cosmology, morality, and status (Lewis 1990; Fligstein 1994).

In this analysis I examine the role of ideology in sustaining the Aztec state. First, I explain how the Aztec state actively promoted an ideology that linked warfare, the engine of imperial expansion, to the natural cycles that sustained human life. Second, I ask whether this ideology operated as a dominant ideology, i.e. is there evidence that commoners believed that warfare was crucial in maintaining the cosmos? Third, I ask whether this ideology had a different target audience, namely the lower-ranking nobility that made up the core of the Aztec military. And finally, I suggest some general strategies for studying dominant ideologies in prehistoric societies.

Aztec ideology

The Aztec Triple Alliance was a military alliance among three city-states in the Basin of Mexico: Tenochtitlan (the dominant partner), Texococo, and Tlacopan. From the year of its formation in AD 1430, the Triple Alliance enjoyed great military success. In a short 90-year span prior to Spanish Conquest, the Triple Alliance created an empire that extended from the Gulf to Pacific coasts, from central Mexico to the Isthmus of Tehuantepec, encompassing an area of approximately 200,000 square kilometres and a population of 5 to 6 million people (Armillas 1964: 324) (Fig. 16.1).

Tribute collected from 31 imperial provinces formed the basis of the state economy. Tribute supplied the food staples that fed the ruler, his large household, and the several hundred lords and nobles who attended his person each day. Tribute also furnished feathered warrior's costumes and other sumptuary goods that were awarded to soldiers of outstanding accomplishment, and large quantities of cloth were distributed to servants of the state on a regular basis. Lower-ranking nobles and commoners probably used this cloth to purchase foodstuffs and other household necessities in the urban market.

Aztec state religion linked warfare to the natural cycles that sustained human life. The Aztecs recognized that human life depended upon the orderly alternation of cycles: day and night, summer and winter, birth and death. But while we see these cycles as natural and inevitable, the Aztecs asserted that they were the contingent outcomes of cosmic struggles where the strong prevailed over the weak. For example the sun rose victorious each morning, driving off the moon and stars to capture the daytime sky, but the sun's victory was only provisional, for each afternoon and evening the sun sank into weary defeat, and the moon and stars took back the heavens. The sun's success in this daily struggle depended upon its being nourished with the hearts and blood of sacrificial victims, preferably those taken in warfare.

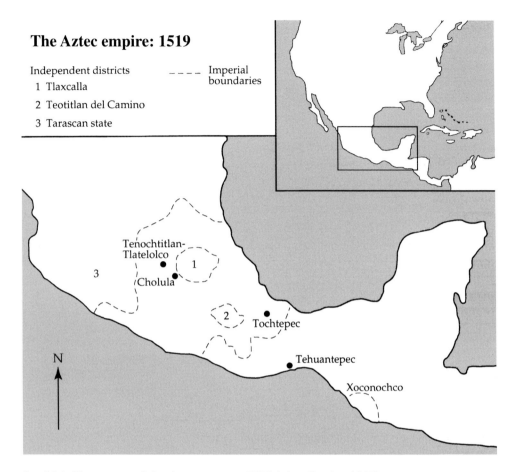

The Aztec empire: 1519

Independent districts
1 Tlaxcalla
2 Teotitlan del Camino
3 Tarascan state

---- Imperial boundaries

Fig. 16.1 The extent of the Aztec empire: 1519 (after Berdan 1982).

To underscore the contingency of human survival, the Aztecs embedded diurnal and seasonal cycles in longer cycles of orderly creation and destructive chaos. The Aztecs believed that four previous creations had come to an end: one destroyed by an invasion of Jaguars, one by Hurricane winds, one by a rain of fire, and the last by floods. The present creation was destined to be destroyed by earthquakes. It would persist only so long as it was strengthened by human sacrifice.

This view was vividly set forth in items of material culture commissioned by the Aztec state. For example the Aztec calendar stone (Fig. 16.2) is filled with symbols that refer to cosmic cycles: the four worlds that preceded the current one, the 20 days of the Aztec divinatory calendar, the solar and starry skies which alternate with day and night and which change together with seasons during the annual cycle. The need for human sacrifice is underscored at the centre of the calendar stone by the sacrificial knife which protrudes from the mouth of the central deity and by the talons on either side of the deity's face, which grasp human hearts (Townsend 1979: 63–70).

The importance of warfare and sacrifice was also communicated by monumental architecture. The Aztec Great Temple was a prominent, centrally placed building that

Fig. 16.2 The Aztec calendar stone, sacrificial stone of Montezuma II, *c.* 1512. Diameter 3.58m. Museo Nacional de Anthropología, Mexico City (Drawing after Umberger 1996).

represented Snake Mountain ('Coatepetl'). Snake Mountain was the place where the Aztecs' patron deity, Huitzilopochtli, was born in a primordial act of warfare and sacrifice (Matos 1988). According to Aztec texts, Huitzilopochtli was conceived in his earth-goddess mother as she performed religious duties at a shrine at the top of Snake Mountain. Because the earth-goddess's pregnancy shamed her daughter, the moon, and her other children, the stars, they decided to kill her. As they approached Snake Mountain, Huitzilopochtli, within his mother's womb spoke: 'Do not fear, Mother. I know what to do.' As Huitzilopochtli's sister and brothers neared the crest of Snake Mountain, Huitzilopochtli leapt from his mother fully armed. He attacked his sister and cut her to pieces; her dismembered body fell to the base of the mountain. Huitzilopochtli then attacked his brothers, and they scattered leaving Huitzilopochtli the Aztecs' solar deity, in uncontested possession of the celestial field (Sahagún 1950–82: Bk 2, Ch. 10).

Snake sculptures at the base of the Great Temple identified the structure as a representation of the mythical Snake Mountain. Atop the temple, Huitzilopochtli's statue stood within its shrine. At the base of the stairway leading to the shrine, a carved stone monument bore the dismembered body of Huitzilopochtli's unfortunate sister (Fig. 16.3). Clearly the layout of the Great Temple was meant to evoke the story of Huitzilopochtli's birth and to remind the viewers that warfare was a cosmic necessity upon which human life depended.

Some practices connected with the Great Temple suggest that it was intended to communicate with subordinate peoples. Aztec rulers made sure that the Great Temple would not be ignored. For example the Aztec state sponsored highly dramatic ceremonies of human sacrifice atop the Great Temple. Because of the temple's height, these ceremonies could be seen from all parts of the city. To draw attention to these sacrifices, they were announced by the beat of drums and the blare of trumpets. Díaz del Castillo, who fought with Cortés against the Aztecs, records:

> Again there was sounded the dismal drum of [Huitzilopochtli] and many other shells and horns and things like trumpets and the sound of them all was terrifying, and we looked toward the lofty [pyramid] where they were being sounded,

Fig. 16.3 Coyolxauhqui Relief depicting the dismembered body of Huitzilopochtli's sister. Diameter 3.25m. Great Temple, Mexico City (drawing: M. LaNoue).

and saw that our comrades whom they had captured...were being carried by force up the steps, and they were taking them to be sacrificed.

(1956: 436)

In addition Aztec rulers frequently rebuilt and expanded the Great Temple. The front stairs of the Great Temple were reconstructed 13 times in its 200-year history (Matos 1988: 30). When reconstructions were undertaken, commoners were brought to Tenochtitlan from numerous subject communities to labour upon the structure (Durán 1967 II: 133–7).

On the other hand some practices connected with the Great Temple suggest that communication with subordinate peoples was not an important goal. For example the Great Temple lay within a walled civic-ceremonial precinct to which commoners could not easily gain access. Excluded from this precinct, commoners would not have seen the snakes that lay at the base of the temple nor would they have seen the carving of Huitzilopochtli's sister that lay horizontally, like a large pavement stone at the base of Huitzilopochtli's shrine. Thus commoners would have missed much of the symbolism of the Great Temple that identified it with Snake Mountain and the story of Huitzilopochtli's birth.

Doubts about the dissemination of warfare-centred ideology to subordinate populations are deepened by archaeological evidence from hinterland sites. This evidence suggests that commoners were not impressed by the state's claim that its military activity was crucial for their existence.

Ideology and commoners

We might expect that the state's ideology of cosmic warfare and human sacrifice would be reflected in elements of commoner material culture. For example almost all Post-classical rural sites in the Basin of Mexico contain low frequencies of small, moulded ceramic figurines. These figurines were made by craft specialists (Cook 1950; Otis Charlton 1994), but they were used in household contexts – at least this is suggested by the invariable association of figurines with household debris. The figurines may have been used in ritual activity at the household level, or they should reflect popular priorities and concerns. The frequencies of different types of figurines in hinterland communities before and during the period of Aztec dominance should provide an indication of the extent to which popular consciousness was affected by state ideology.

The figurines from contexts that antedate the expansion of the Triple Alliance are most often anthropomorphic. Details of clothing and anatomy can be used to identify males and females, and in pre-Aztec contexts, males and females occur in approximately even ratio (Fig. 16.4). By contrast in collections dating to the period of Aztec dominance, female figurines become more frequent; they outnumber male figurines by a ratio of three to one. Moreover the male figurines recovered from Late Post-classic contexts are not often warriors. Male figurines sit rather than stand, and they hold drums rather than implements of war. This suggests that concern with male warriors and their work did not increase during the period of Aztec domination.

Female figurines, too, differ from the idealized images of women presented by the Aztec state. In state-sponsored media such as sculpture and painted manuscripts,

Fig. 16.4 Aztec period ceramic figurine of a woman holding two children. Height 19cm. Musée de l'Homme, Paris (drawing: M. LaNoue).

women are posed in a controlled kneeling position, perhaps in reference to their role as producers of cloth and food. In contrast female figurines more often stand than kneel, and they frequently hold one or two children, perhaps in reference to their reproductive roles. Again this suggests that commoners were not preoccupied with the state's definitions of social roles and status (Brumfiel 1996).

The period of Aztec domination did produce a new figurine type, the temple replica. Temple replicas are very small models of temple pyramids topped by temple structures or deity figures. The deities on the temples are usually male, and often hold weapons. Kaplan suggests that the temple replicas may have integrated peasant ritual with the cults of the urban elites (Pasztory 1983: 289–91). I accept Kaplan's suggestion, but I emphasize the rarity of these replicas in figurine assemblages. At Late Post-classic sites in the Basin of Mexico, temple replicas always constitute less than 5 per cent (Parsons 1972: 105–6; Brumfiel 1996: 155). In contrast in a collection of seven figurines from metro excavations at the centre of Tenochtitlan, two were temple replicas, and four were women presented in a kneeling pose (Arana and Cepeda 1967). This is what ideological domination would look like had it been present in hinterland sites.

The low frequency of warfare-centred images in the material culture of hinterland populations suggests that the ideology of cosmic warfare did not diffuse to rural regions of the empire. Comparing the well-documented expenditures of the Aztec state on architecture and monumental sculpture with its apparent lack of success in impressing commoners we might well question the state's competence as a purveyor of ideology.

Ideology and the nobility

But perhaps Aztec ideology was not aimed at subordinate groups. Perhaps Aztec ideology had a different target group: the younger sons of noble families. These men had been a source of endemic political instability during the pre-Aztec era. Before the formation of the Triple Alliance, the younger sons of rulers entered numerous conspiracies to seize control of local polities from their fathers and brothers (Brumfiel 1983: 268–70). Political stability under the Triple Alliance depended on deactivating this unstable element. Triple Alliance rulers offered these low-ranking nobles an ideology that weighed achievement in warfare over seniority of descent as determinate of status, and they established the worth of these achieved rankings with exclusive dress, special clubhouses, flashy rituals, and the promise of apotheosis as warriors of the sun.

Military achievement was recognized with numerous items of military attire and civilian dress, distributed according to a strict sumptuary code. Warriors were given different prizes according to their performance on the battlefield (Fig. 16.5). If a warrior distinguished himself by taking one, two, three, or five captives for sacrifice, he was entitled to wear military costumes and civilian cloaks of specific designs (Sahagún 1950–82: Bk 8, Ch. 21; Durán 1971: 197–8). These bold designs alluded to supernatural beings or powers. The iconography of the costumes ensured that the successful warrior would be associated with, and perhaps feel himself united with, supernatural powers of various sorts (Anawalt 1992). Outstanding warriors were also given titles with mythological and cosmological implications, adding to their exalted status (Brumfiel 1987).

Once a warrior had taken four captives, he gained entry into the Cuauhcalli, the Eagle House, a special hall associated with the ruler's palace (Sahagún 1950–82: Bk

Fig. 16.5 Military costumes worn by four high-ranking Aztec warriors. *Codex Mendoza* (1990: 67r).

8, Ch. 14; Durán 1971: 187–8). Here celebrated and titled warriors passed their days in the company of their fellows. The daily activities of the men in this exclusive club are not described, but the primary attraction seems to have been the heady enjoyment of their own exalted company.

Excavations on the north side of the Great Temple have revealed a structure commonly referred to as the Precinct of the Eagle Warriors (Matos 1988: 82–3).[1] It consists of two connecting rooms: an outer western room bordered by low benches, and an inner eastern room with a sunken patio or *impluvium*. Whether it was in fact the Eagle House, or another structure where Tenochtitlan's military elite gathered, this building reveals how such places contributed to a reified atmosphere that would have promoted the ideological indoctrination of elite warriors.

First, this site had limited access. Privacy was ensured by offset doors that shielded the inner patio from the eyes of passers-by (Molina 1987: 102). The limited access underscored the exclusiveness and prestige of the group inside, and within these private confines, the military elite could be subjected to intense ideological and emotional experiences.

Second, military elites were positively represented. The benches at the entrance to the structure and within the west room were decorated with processions of carved and painted warrior figures, richly attired in military dress. These figures were led by the Aztec ruler who is, himself, dressed as a warrior (Klein 1987: 314). The image implied a high status for the military, almost on a par with the ruler. Elite warriors were also depicted in large ceramic statues (Fig. 16.6). Statues of warriors dressed in

Fig. 16.6 Ceramic statue of an Eagle warrior, a man who had died in battle or on the sacrificial stone. Height 1.68m. Precinct of the Eagle Warriors, Mexico City (drawing: M. LaNoue).

eagle costumes flanked the door leading to the western room, and statues of skeleton figures stood on either side of the door leading to the interior patio. These statues evoked the fate of soldiers who died in battle or sacrifice. Transported to the sky, they accompanied the sun in its ascent from the eastern horizon to the zenith. They presided at the triumph of light over darkness (Sahagún 1950–82: Bk 6, Ch. 29).

These triumphal male images contrasted implicitly with two other sculptural forms in Aztec art. In the first, defeated foes were depicted as female sacrificial victims. Several of these statues have been recovered from locations in the civic-ceremonial precinct. These include the monumental rendering of Huitzilopochtli's dismembered sister, described above, and the 9-foot statue of the earth-goddess, Coatlicue. This sculpture celebrated the Aztec conquest of Xochimilco by rendering Coatlicue, Xochimilco's patron deity, as a beheaded sacrificial victim (Klein 1988). Thus the triumphal Eagle Warriors contrasted with the effeminate conquered enemies elsewhere in the city's central core.

The eagle warrior image also contrasted with the images of Aztec women who died in childbirth. In many ways women who died in childbirth were the female counterparts of warriors who died in battle or sacrifice. Like fallen warriors, women who died in childbirth rose to the sky to accompany the sun on its journey across the heavens. But whereas men who died in warfare accompanied the sun during its morning rise to the zenith, women who died in childbirth accompanied the sun during its afternoon descent (Sahagún 1950–82: Bk 6, Ch. 29). Moreover women who died in childbirth periodically returned to earth as violent spirits (the *cihuateteo*) who haunted crossroads at night, possessed and paralyzed adults, and stole children (Nicholson and Keber 1983: 67–8). The negative image of the disruptive and predatory *cihuateteo*, carved in stone and set by lonely crossroads, served to heighten the nobility of their male counterparts, the Eagle Warriors (Fig. 16.7).

This group of elite soldiers was, I would suggest, the real focus of the ideology of cosmic warfare. Through this ideology Aztec rulers transformed young nobles from a political problem to the core of an alliance network that could exercise coercion against any subordinate group.

Ideology, target audience, and political change

DeMarrais *et al.* (1996) discuss the ways in which ideology is given physical, material expression. They suggest that political elites use different media (ceremonial events, symbolic objects, monumental architecture, and written inscriptions) to direct ideological messages towards different segments of society. If elites can direct ideological messages to different audiences, they might also send different messages to different audiences.

The ideological message of cosmic warfare was conveyed to elite Aztec warriors in intimate interior spaces, filled with detailed, complex imagery that positively represented the target audience, warriors in idealized images; groups outside the target audience were objects of invidious comparison. Within this space, religious and social rituals repetitiously affirmed the dependence of all living things on human sacrifice and the high moral status of those who risked their lives to capture sacrificial victims.

Commoners also received a message, but it neither masked nor glorified their domination. The imposing Great Temple and the displays of human sacrifice, I suggest, were meant to impress upon commoners the overwhelming power wielded by the dominant class and its warrior allies, in Gilman's (1996: 57) words, 'to show who is boss'. Human sacrifice atop the Great Temple did not attempt to engage the commitment of the lower class; rather it was intended to confront commoners with the fact of their own subordination (see ibid.).

These two messages, the one directed towards elites in interior spaces and the other directed outwards towards commoners, were differently constructed. Ideologies aimed at recruiting and holding members to the dominant coalition attempt to engage potential allies in what Ortner (1984: 152) has called 'projects', that is, actions shaped by

Fig. 16.7 Stone statue of a Cihuateotl, a woman who had died in childbirth. Height 72cm. Museo Nacional de Antropología, Mexico City (drawing: M. LaNoue).

'images and ideas of what constitutes goodness – in people, in relationships, and in conditions of life'. These ideologies try to capture the commitment of potential allies by conferring on them a place of dignity within the new world view. They establish the moral worth of certain forms of behaviour by linking them to cosmological beliefs and then use this behaviour as the basis for social differentiation and esteem.

These ideologies are expensive. Their appeal is enhanced by costly objects, architecture, and ritual (DeMarrais *et al.* 1996). In the absence of modern communication technology, the ideology must be communicated at close range, over a prolonged period. Because ideology is expensive, and because its appeal derives directly from its exclusivity, most agrarian states target only a small portion of the total population for inclusion.

To the majority, dominant groups communicate ideologies of political terror (Foucault 1977: 49). The central message in these ideologies is the vulnerability of subordinate groups; dominant groups underscore their ability to punish disobedient subjects. This message is communicated through the size of state architecture and state-sponsored spectacles of human pain and death, both providing evidence of the state's power and the individual's lack of effective defence. Human sacrifice and other displays of power apparently did impress Aztec subjects, nobles and commoners alike. Gingerich (1988: 522) calls attention to the metaphors of danger which the Aztecs used to describe their world. Aztec elders advised their offspring:

> on earth we travel, we live along a mountain peak. Over here there is an abyss, over there is an abyss. Wherever thou art to deviate, wherever thou art to go astray, there wilt thou fall, there wilt thou plunge into the deep. That is to say, it is necessary that thou act with discretion in that which is done, which is said, which is seen, which is heard, which is thought, etc.
>
> (Sahagún 1950–82: Bk 6, Ch. 22)

Conclusions

This examination of Aztec ideology suggests, first of all, that the effectiveness of ideological domination can be, and should be, tested by comparing the material cultures of dominant and subordinate groups. This basic strategy can be used in many contexts. For example Leyland Ferguson (1991) recorded persistent differences in the ceramics of South Carolina slaves and their masters. Matthew Johnson (1997) noted the stylistic differences between seventeenth-century houses built on the green outside Leicester castle and the reconstructed castle itself. In both of these cases the archaeologists concluded that they were dealing with subordinate groups that had purposely rejected the conventions of the dominant group and the ideals which these conventions embodied. Archaeology provides perhaps the best means of examining popular resistance in cultures preceding the development of universal literacy and mass culture.

Second, the study of Aztec ideology suggests that political leaders may actively engage in constructing dominant ideologies. Althusser is disdainful of the idea that ideology is created by, 'a small number of cynical men who base their domination and explanation of the "people" on a falsified representation of the world which they have imagined in order to enslave other minds by dominating their imaginations' (1971: 163).

But indigenous narratives of Aztec political history portray Aztec rulers as active promoters of the state ideology. The Aztec ruler Itzcoatl introduced titles to honour his best warriors. Montezuma I created the Cuauhcalli within his palace, and Montezuma's chief advisor devised new and captivating forms of human sacrifice (Durán 1967 II: 99, 213, 171). Rulers frequently rationalized these acts as encouraging moral virtue and honouring the gods. But the ruler's definition of virtue happened to be those activities which most benefited the state.

In fact this study of Aztec ideology suggests that rulers manipulated not one but two ideological systems. The first was an ideology buttressed by moral hierarchies and cosmological principles. This ideology was addressed to a relatively small segment of society, namely the members of the elite coalition, to secure their loyalty. The second ideology was buttressed by displays of violence. Spectacles of pain emphasized, even overstated, the power of the dominant group and the powerlessness of the commoners. This ideology was addressed to the broader subordinate segment of society. Thus both dominant and subordinate groups were subjects of ideology, but with a difference. Elites accepted the legitimacy of the state and its activities, while subordinate groups did not. Commoners internalized the ideology of power while simultaneously waiting and hoping for deliverance from oppression. Thus their participation in a system of inequality was conditional, and given a number of different scenarios (e.g. factional conflicts within the dominant class, guerrilla warfare, attacks by foreign invaders) their compliance could have flared into active resistance.

I suggest, then, that dominant ideologies may be constructed in a number of different ways. Variation in the structures of dominant ideologies implies that an analytical approach to the subject might be taken. Such an approach would define the variation in the structure of ideologies, the ways in which each type is deployed, the limits which each type encounters, and the traces which each type leaves in the archaeological record (see Blanton *et al.* 1996). Ultimately a more analytical approach to dominant ideologies might help us to understand how systems of social inequality are constructed and how they can be altered.

Notes

1. Klein (1987: 305) suggests that this building was the Tlacochalco Quauhquiauc.

Acknowledgements

This chapter benefited greatly from the patient comments of Len Berkey and Molly Mullin. I appreciate their generous assistance.

Bibliography

Abercrombie, N., Hill, S., and Turner, B.S. 1980. *The Dominant Ideology Thesis*. London: George Allen and Unwin.

Althusser, L. 1971. Ideology and Ideological State Apparatuses. In Brewster, B. (trans.), *Lenin and Philosophy*. New York: Monthly Review Press, pp. 127–86.

Anawalt, P.R. 1992. A Comparative Analysis of the Costumes and Accoutrements of the *Codex Mendoza*. In Berdan, F.F. and Anawalt, P.R. (eds), *The Codex Mendoza*, Vol I. Berkeley, CA: University of California Press, pp. 103–50.

Arana, R.M. and Cepeda, G. 1967. Rescate Arqueológico en la Ciudad de México. *INAH Boletín* 30: 3–9.

Armillas, P. 1964. Northern Mesoamerica. In Jennings, J.D. and Norbeck, E. (eds), *Prehistoric Man in the New World*. Chicago: University of Chicago Press, pp. 291–329.

Berdan, F.F. 1982. *The Aztecs of Central Mexico*. New York: Holt, Rinehart, and Winston.

Blanton, R.E., Feinman, G.M., Kowalewski, S.A., and Peregrine, P.N. 1996. A Dual-Processual Theory for the Evolution of Mesoamerican Civilization. *Current Anthropology* 37: 1–14.

Boone, E.H. (ed.). 1987. *The Aztec Temple Mayor*. Washington, DC: Dumbarton Oaks.

Brumfiel, E.M. 1983. Aztec State Making: Ecology, Structure, and the Origin of the State. *American Anthropologist* 85: 261–84.

Brumfiel, E.M. 1987. Elite and Utilitarian Crafts in the Aztec State. In Brumfiel, E.M. and Earle, T.K. (eds), *Specialisation, Exchange and Complex Societies*. Cambridge: Cambridge University Press, pp. 102–18.

Brumfiel, E.M. 1994a. Factional Competition and Political Development in the New World: An Introduction. In Brumfiel, E.M. and Fox, J.W. (eds), *Factional Competition and Political Development in the New World*. Cambridge: Cambridge University Press, pp. 3–13.

Brumfiel, E.M. 1994b. Three Incidents of Resistance and Class Warfare in Aztec Ethnohistory. Paper presented at the 93rd Annual Meeting, American Anthropological Association, Atlanta.

Brumfiel, E.M. 1996. Figurines and the Aztec State: Testing the Effectiveness of Ideological Domination. In Wright, R.P. (ed.), *Gender and Archaeology: Research in Gender and Practice*. Philidelphia: University of Pennsylvania Press, pp. 143–66.

Caso, A. 1958. *The Aztecs: People of the Sun*. Norman: University of Oklahoma Press.

Codex Mendoza. 1990. *The Codex Mendoza*. Berdan, F.F. and Anawalt, P.R. (eds). Berkeley: University of California Press. 4 Vols.

Conrad, G.W. and Demarest, A.A. 1984. *Religion and Empire: The Dynamics of Aztec and Inca Expansionism*. Cambridge: Cambridge University Press.

Cook, C. 1950. Figurillas de Barro de Santiago Tlatelolco. *Memorias de la Academia Mexicana de la Historia* (Tlatelolco a Través de los Tiempos) 9: 93–100.

DeMarrais, E., Castillo, L.J., and Earle, T. 1996. Ideology, Materialization and Power Strategies. *Current Anthropology* 37: 15–31.

Díaz del Castillo, B. (A.P. Maudslay, trans.). 1956. *The Discovery and Conquest of Mexico*. New York: Noonday Press.

Durán, D. 1967. *Historia de las Indias de Nueva España*. Mexico City: Porrúa.

Durán, D. (F. Horcasitas and D. Hayden, trans.). 1971. *Book of the Gods and Rites and the Aztec Calender*. Norman: University of Oklahoma Press.

Ferguson, L. 1991. Struggling with Pots in Colonial South Carolina. In McGuire, R.H. and Paynter, R. (eds), *The Archaeology of Inequality*. Oxford: Blackwell, pp. 28–39.

Fligstein, N. 1994. The Cultural Construction of Political Action: The Case of the European Community's Single Market Program. Working paper. Harvard University Center for European Studies.

Foucault, M. (A. Sheridan, trans.) 1977. *Discipline and Punish*, New York: Pantheon.

Gilman, A. 1989. Marxism in American Archaeology. In Lamberg-Karlovsky, C.C. (ed.), *Archaeological Thought in America*. Cambridge: Cambridge University Press, pp. 63–73.

Gilman, A. 1996. Comments on 'Ideology, Materialization, and Power Strategies'. *Current Anthropology* 37: 56–7.

Gingerich, W. 1988. Chipahuacanemiliztli, 'The Purified Life', in the Discourse of Book VI, *Florentine Codex*. In Josserand, J.K. and Dakin, K. (eds), *Smoke and Mist: Mesoamerican Studies in Memory of Thelma D. Sullivan*. British Archaeological Reports, International Series 402. Oxford: BAR, pp. 517–44.

Hicks, F. 1994. The Middle Class of Ancient Mexico. Paper presented at the Annual Meeting, American Society for Ethnohistory, Tempe.

Johnson, M., 1997. The Medieval Castle and the Fashioning of Agency. Paper presented at the 62nd annual meeting, Society for American Archaeology, Nashville.

Josserand, J.K. and Dakin, K. (eds). 1988. *Smoke and Mist: Mesoamerican Studies in Memory of Thelma D. Sullivan*. British Archaeological Reports, International Series 402. Oxford: BAR.

Kelly, R.C. 1993. *Constructing Inequality: The Fabrication of a Heirarchy of Virtue Among the Etoro*. Ann Arbor: The University of Michigan Press.

Klein, C.F. 1987. The Ideology of Autosacrifice at the Templo Mayor. In Boone, E.H. (ed.), *The Aztec Temple Mayor*. Washington, DC: Dumbarton Oaks, pp. 293–370.

Klein, C.F. 1988. Rethinking Cihuacoatl: Aztec Political Imagery of the Conquered Woman. In Josserand, J.K. and Dakin, K. (eds), *Smoke and Mist: Mesoamerican Studies in Memory of Thelma D. Sullivan*. British Archaeological Reports, International Series 402. Oxford: BAR, pp. 237–77.

Lewis, M.E. 1990. *Sanctioned Violence in Early China*. Albany: State University Press of New York.

Matos, M.E. 1988. *The Great Temple of the Aztecs*. London: Thames and Hudson.

Miller, D. and Tilley, C. (eds). 1984. *Ideology, Power and Prehistory*. Cambridge: Cambridge University Press.

Molina Montes, A.F. 1987. Templo Mayor Architecture: So What's New? In Boone, E.H. (ed.), *The Aztec Temple Mayor*. Washington, DC: Dumbarton Oaks, pp. 97–107.

Nicholson, H.B. and Keber, E.Q. 1983. *Art of Aztec Mexico*. Washington, DC: National Gallery of Art.

Ortner, S.B. 1984. Theory in Anthropology Since the Sixties. *Comparative Studies in Society and History* 26: 126–66.

Otis Charlton, C.L. 1994. Plebians and Patricians: Contrasting Patterns of Production and Distribution in the Aztec Figurine and Lapidary Industries. In Hodge, M.G. and Smith, M.E. (eds), *Economies and Polities in the Aztec Realm*. Albany: State University of New York at Albany, Institute for Mesoamerican Studies, pp. 195–219.

Parsons, M.H. 1972. Aztec Figurines from Teotihuacán Valley, Mexico. In Spence, M.W., Parsons, J.R., and Parsons, M.H. (eds), *Miscellaneous Studies in Mexican Prehistory*. Anthropological Papers 45. Ann Arbor: Museum of Anthropology, University of Michigan, pp. 81–117.

Pasztory, E. 1983. *Aztec Art*. New York: Abrams.

Sahagún, B. de. (C.E. Dibble and A.J.O. Anderson, trans.). 1950–82. *Florentine Codex*. Santa Fe: The School of American Research and the University of Utah.

Shanks, M. and Tilley, C. 1982. Ideology, Symbolic Power and Ritual Communication: A Reinterpretation of Neolithic Mortuary Practices. In Hodder, I. (ed.), *Symbolic and Structural Archaeology*. Cambridge: Cambridge University Press, pp. 129–54.

Snow, D.A., Rochford Jr., E.B., Worden, S.K., and Benford, R.D. 1986. Frame Alignment Processes, Micromobilization, and Movement Participation. *American Sociological Review* 51: 464–81.

Thompson, J.B. 1990. *Ideology and Modern Culture*. Stanford: Stanford University Press.

Townsend, R.F. 1979. *State and Cosmos in the Art of Tenochtitlan*. Studies in Pre-Columbian Art and Cosmology 20. Washington, DC: Dumbarton Oaks.

Tuberville, A.S. 1929. Heresies and the Inquisition in the Middle Ages, c. 1000–1305. In Panner, J.R., Previté-Orton, C.W., and Brooke, Z.N. (eds), *Cambridge Medieval History*, Vol. 6. Cambridge: Cambridge University Press, pp. 699–726.

Umberger, E. 1996. Art and Imperial Strategy in Tenochtitlan. In Berdan, F.F., Blanton, R.E., Boone, E.H., Hodge, M.G., Smith, M.E., and Umberger, E. (eds), *Aztec Imperial Strategies*. Washington, DC: Dumbarton Oaks, pp. 85–106.

Wolf, E.R. 1969. *Peasant Wars of the Twentieth Century*. New York: Harper and Row.

Chapter 17

Ritual and rationality

Some problems of interpretation in European archaeology

Joanna Brück

Introduction

> Ritual: All-purpose explanation used where nothing else comes to mind
> Bahn, *Bluff Your Way in Archaeology*

In recent years there has been increasing interest in ritual practice in the past as archaeologists have sought to move away from narrowly functionalist interpretive frameworks. However, this has been accompanied by growing disquiet over archaeologists' ability to identify ritual in the archaeological record. Instinctively most archaeologists feel they know what ritual is but, on closer inspection, the picture becomes rather less clear. Not only has it been impossible to devise a satisfactory definition of ritual action in general terms but unambiguous archaeological correlates have also not been forthcoming. These problems are widely appreciated and have been debated in some detail in the archaeological literature (e.g. Levy 1982; Richards and Thomas 1984; Renfrew 1985; Hill 1995). Yet we have still failed to address some of the most fundamental problems raised by the application of the concept 'ritual'. The way in which ritual has been employed within archaeological discourse exemplifies the difficulties surrounding extreme positivist and idealist positions; as such, discussion of ritual continues to raise issues that must be resolved if a more subtle understanding of the past is to be reached.

In this chapter, the argument will be developed that the notion of ritual as a distinct category of practice is not common to all societies. Rather the identification and isolation of ritual is based on models of human practice and ways of knowing that are peculiar to contemporary society (Bell 1992: 13, 114–15). For archaeologists the imposition of the dichotomy ritual/secular on the past has resulted in particular interpretive dilemmas. As the anthropologist Catherine Bell has argued (1992: 16–17), these problems 'have less to do with the raw data and more to do with the manner in which we theoretically constitute ritual as the object of...interpretation'. In the following discussion a thorough critique of the concept of ritual will examine how the application of the dualism ritual/secular has had serious effects on our understanding of prehistoric rationality. A different approach will be proposed in which attention is shifted away from a concern to define archaeological correlates for ritual. Instead it will be argued that archaeologists need to explore how prehistoric conceptions of effective action may have differed from those enshrined in modern rationalist thought.

A discussion of an interesting group of finds from middle Bronze Age settlements in southern England will provide a working example of how one might begin to move towards this goal.

Anthropological definitions

In order to understand why the concept of ritual raises the problems it does for archaeologists, we need to trace the genealogy of the term and to understand the particular socio-cultural context within which it has its roots. As archaeological discussion of ritual has borrowed extensively from anthropology, let us begin with a review of anthropological approaches to the subject.

Anthropological definitions of ritual frequently stress its symbolic, non-technical, formal, prescribed, structured, and repetitive nature. Classic examples include: 'all actions exhibiting…conspicuous regularity not accounted for by the professed aim of the actions' (Nadel 1954: 99); 'a kind of patterned activity oriented towards the control of human affairs, primarily symbolic in character' (Firth 1951: 222); 'ritual acts differ, from technological acts in having in all instances some expressive or symbolic element in them' (Radcliffe-Brown 1952: 143); 'those aspects of prescribed formal behaviour which have no direct technological consequence' (Leach 1964: 607). Archaeologists have largely followed these definitions: Richards and Thomas (1984: 191), for example, describe ritual action as 'highly formalised or structured modes of behaviour', while Renfrew (1985) stresses its symbolic or expressive character.

The difficulties involved in attempting to mobilize these characteristics in the identification of ritual action have been discussed by Goody (1961: 156–7; 1977: 28), Fortes (1966: 410), Lewis (1980: 11, 1b–19), and other anthropologists. Similar problems have also been recognized by archaeologists such as Barrett (1988: 31) and Hill (1995: 95–6). These writers point out that many of the supposedly diagnostic properties of ritual practice are shared by secular action. For example baking a cake follows a structured sequence of rules while a committee meeting involves a high degree of formalization. Leach (1966, 1968: 523) attempted to deal with this problem by arguing that ritual is not a distinct category of behaviour but can be understood as the expressive, symbolic, or communicative aspect of all human behaviour. In other words he recognized that many objects and activities have both an expressive and a practical aspect: for example the cooking pots of one group of people may look very different from those of another, even though they perform the same task. As he puts it: 'almost every human action has a technical aspect which does something and an aesthetic aspect which says something: In those types of behaviour labelled ritual, the aesthetic, communicative aspect is particularly prominent' (Leach 1968: 523). However, Leach's redefinition does not solve the problem of why we recognize certain activities as ritual and others as non-ritual. As Fortes (1966: 41) has argued, many non-ritual activities, notably the act of speaking, are essentially expressive actions. He points out that 'if ritual is wholly subsumed within the category of "communication" then the policeman on point duty is performing a very explicit and efficacious ritual'.

Thus although anthropologists generally agree on a core group of ritual activities, such as Ndembu circumcision rites or a Catholic mass, the edges of the category are rather hazier, precisely because so many of the characteristics listed above are shared by both ritual and non-ritual practices. This problem, and Leach's contention that most human activities have a ritualized aspect, has encouraged a trend towards incorporating wider and wider groups of activities under the banner of ritual. Such mundane and secular activities as eating a meal, attending a board meeting, or going to a football match have been described as ritualized practices because they display several of the central characteristics of ritual, including formalization, repetition, and the deployment of symbols. Goody (1977: 26) has cogently criticized this standpoint, arguing that such an all-embracing definition of ritual strips the concept of its analytical value.

In anthropological discussion, then, the essential properties that differentiate ritual from other types of human action are still not agreed on. More effort has been expended on moving the definitional goalposts than on understanding how ritual has come to be constituted as a distinct analytical category within the social sciences. The latter question will therefore be the central concern here.

Identifying ritual in the archaeological record

Before tackling this issue let us consider how ritual is identified archaeologically. This is a question that has engaged archaeologists for some time. For example how can we distinguish hearth debris produced in the context of everyday domestic activities from material which represents the residue of a ritual meal? Should an animal figurine be interpreted as a votive object or simply a toy? First, we need to identify archaeologists' expectations. Let us begin with a simple example. The presence of sherds or knapping debris under a round barrow or in its surrounding ditch has often confounded British archaeologists.[1] These finds are generally explained in one of two ways. The first interprets them as evidence of preceding or succeeding domestic/economic activities, unconnected with the barrow itself (e.g. Smith 1965: 32–40). For example it is often argued that flint-knapping waste results from the expedient use of nodules accidentally unearthed during barrow digging activities (e.g. Barrett et al. 1991: 128). Alternatively such material is interpreted as votive deposits of an expressly ritual nature associated with the mortuary rites (e.g. Hughes 1996: 48; cf. Brown 1991: 105–7). In a similar vein the circular post-built structures found beneath certain round barrows have generally been interpreted either as domestic dwellings pre-dating the barrows in question (e.g. Piggott 1940; Gibson 1980) or as mortuary buildings, constructed specifically for the funeral rite (e.g. Fox 1941: 114; Ashbee 1960: 65). This suggests that archaeologists implicitly define ritual and non-ritual practices as mutually exclusive. One explanation is assumed to preclude the other.

There have been several concerted efforts to develop rigorous methodologies for the identification of ritual in the archaeological record, including work by Levy (1982: 21–4), Renfrew (1985), and Richards and Thomas (1984). However, these encounter the same problems as anthropological discussions in that they mobilize characteristics (e.g. repetition, structuring, expressive action) that are frequently shared by non-ritual activities. Contrary to the expectation that ritual and non-ritual activities are mutually exclusive and should thus be easily distinguishable, it has in fact proven impossible to propose watertight lists of criteria for the identification of ritual in the archaeological record. Certainly the archaeological evidence all too rarely fits the neat categories of ritual/secular constructed by archaeologists. For instance the material recovered from late Neolithic henge monuments provokes considerable interpretive dilemmas. Although henges are generally interpreted as ritual sites, it is difficult to accommodate all the evidence recovered from them within such a mono-thetic interpretive framework (see also Gibson 1982: 1–2; Lane 1986). For example bone awls, flint scrapers, and cooking vessels are frequently found in the enclosure ditches of sites such as Mount Pleasant, Dorset (Wainwright 1979: 35–47). Many archaeologists would interpret such finds as evidence for secular, domestic activities (e.g. Gibson 1982). Of course similar dilemmas are regularly encountered outside of British prehistory: the apparently contradictory interpretations proposed for a number of the buildings at Çatalhöyük (houses or shrines? See Hodder 1987: 44 for critical discussion) are a particularly well-known instance.

Because of, or perhaps in spite of, these difficulties, archaeologists have tended to fall back on a long-standing yet largely implicit way of identifying ritual archaeolog-ically. A recurrent yet unspoken theme underlying many archaeological discussions of ritual is the equation of ritual with non-functional action. For example artefacts such as the carved chalk axes, balls, and phalli found at certain late Neolithic and early Bronze Age sites are generally ascribed a ritual role because archaeologists have been unable to understand them in functional terms (e.g. Clarke *et al.* 1985: 80; Burl 1987: 127; Malone 1989: Fig. 37). In the same way Colt Hoare (1812: 18) noted the non-defensive nature of many late Neolithic enclosures, a feature that has recurrently been used as a means of substantiating the ritual significance of henge monuments. Thus artefacts or actions which cannot be ascribed a practical role often come to be inter-preted as evidence for ritual practices. What in fact happens is that ritual is identified by default: if sites or artefacts cannot be explained according to a contemporary func-tionalist rationale then they become relegated to a residual ritual category. As Richards and Thomas (1984: 189) have pointed out, 'it is common in the archaeo-logical literature for the term "ritual", to be used as a catch-all designation for any-thing which defies a crudely utilitarian explanation' (hence Bahn's playful definition at the beginning of this chapter). This equation of ritual with non-functional action is, I would argue, the single most important characteristic of both archaeological and anthropological approaches to ritual. A critique of this equation will reveal why ritual and non-ritual activities appear to be so difficult to distinguish on other grounds, as discussed earlier.

Ritual as the product of post-Enlightenment rationalism

In this section it will be argued that the characterization of ritual practice as non-functional or symbolic in contrast to practical and technological[2] activities is central to its constitution as a distinct social phenomenon within both anthropological and archaeological thought. Ritual is defined and distinguished through its opposition to a secular sphere of action (e.g. Turner 1967; Durkheim 1976; Bloch 1985). The isola-tion of ritual practice in contemporary conceptual frameworks is in part the legacy of the church/state divide evident throughout centuries of European history. More funda-mentally, however, this categorization of practice is a product of post-Enlightenment rationalism in which a scientific logic is prioritized as the only valid way of knowing the world (Goody 1961, 1977). Since the Enlightenment, dominant discourses within the sciences have postulated the existence of strict laws of causation in which prag-matic ends are attained by empirical means; in other words it is argued that there is a mechanical link between means and end (or cause and effect) and that this can be discerned through testing and observation (e.g. Popper 1963; Hempel 1965).

Let us examine this further. In both archaeology and anthropology certain processes of causation have tended to become prioritized because of the way in which objects of knowledge are constituted in the modern Western world. The development of the human and natural sciences during the eighteenth and nineteenth centuries cannot be understood without reference to the Cartesian model of the world. This constructed a series of analogous dualisms as a means of describing the universe (e.g. culture/nature, mind/body and subject/object). Foucault (1970, 1973, 1977) has traced the history of this process with particular reference to the human body. By drawing a distinction between mind and body, the latter became objectified as a focus of observation and examination. During the eighteenth and nineteenth centuries, human sciences such as anatomy, criminology, and psychology acquired knowledge by individuating, inspecting, dissecting, and recording the human body (Turner 1992). The emergence of the dualism culture/nature had a similar effect, constituting the natural world as an object for study (Thomas 1993; Pálsson 1996). Such developments enabled a very precise and manipulative kind of power to be held over objectified entities such as criminals, corpses, and animals (Foucault 1973, 1977). Direct action on a material object (that is, acts in which there is a mechanical link between means and end) became the primary means of intervening in the world, and processes such as experimentation and exploration became central to the acquisition of knowledge. Furthermore the radical individualism and liberal political theory that developed during this time also played an important role in constituting an autonomous subject who has an existence separate from the objectified natural world and who uses instrumental reason to act directly on that world (Morris 1994: 16).

Returning to our discussion of ritual, it is easy to see how the objective functionality espoused by post-Enlightenment science came to be contrasted with ritual practice in which no intrinsic means–end relationship can be recognized. Because it does not meet modern Western[3] criteria for practicality, ritual is frequently described as non-functional, irrational action. Furthermore as ritual acts do not appear to *do* anything, anthropologists have concluded that they must *stand* for something else: in other words ritual action is symbolic. Hence the practical and the symbolic are conceived of as opposed. 'What happens, then, is that symbolic acts are defined in opposition to rational acts and constitute a residual category to which meaning is assigned by the observer in order to make sense of otherwise irrational, pseudo-rational or non-rational behaviour' (Goody 1961: 157). One way of dealing with anything which does not make sense to the Western observer has therefore been to interpret it as ritual (cf. Sperber 1975: 1–4).

An extension of this argument situates the concept of ritual firmly within a colonialist discourse. Throughout the eighteenth and nineteenth centuries, a belief in the inevitability of progress from a state of savagery to a rational, moral, and technologically advanced way of life encouraged the view that rituals were survivals from a premodern age (e.g. Frazer 1890). The dichotomy ritual/secular therefore became conflated with the dualisms them/us, traditional/modern, irrational/rational (Goody 1977: 25; Bell 1992: 71). Thus the category ritual both exemplifies and reproduces a particular model of the world (Bell 1992: 13–14). As Bell argues (ibid.: 14), analytical categories such as ritual are not simply tools but are part of a specific discourse, a production of reality that serves political purposes.

Are the dualisms ritual/secular and practical/symbolic universal features of human thought and action?

Ritual practice has therefore been identified as something fundamentally different from (or even opposed to) other kinds of activities. As such it is frequently described as a distinct sphere of practice, separated spatially, temporally, and conceptually from more day-to-day activities. The first issue to consider is whether such dichotomies as ritual/secular or sacred/profane are universal categories of human thought. In the anthropological literature the notion of a universal distinction between the sacred and profane can be traced to Durkheim (1976). There is, however, a strong body of evidence to suggest that many societies do not articulate such a dichotomy (Goody 1961; Leach 1968: 523; Moore and Myerhoff 1977; Bell 1992: 123). Animistic peoples, for example, believe that the entire cosmos is infused with a pervasive 'life force' (e.g. Waterson 1990: 115–16). Both animate and inanimate things possess 'spirit' or 'soul'. Where such a conception of the universe is formulated, no sharp distinction is drawn between the sacred and profane, between organic and inorganic matter, or between nature and culture. For example the Atoni of Timor have no concept of a 'profane' category and have no word to express such an idea (Schulte Nordholt and Herman 1980: 247). Likewise the LoDagaa of Burkino Faso and Ghana do not differentiate the sacred from the profane (Goody 1961: 151).

When people do not draw such a categorical distinction between the sacred and the profane, ritual action may not be spatially or temporally distinguished from more 'mundane' or secular activities. For example each stage in the Berbers' agricultural cycle is accompanied by an appropriate ritual which acts to guarantee the success of the harvest (Bourdieu 1977: 100–6). In the Solomon Islands when heavy waves make it impossible to launch a canoe a group of elders will chant a spell and throw a knotted length of creeping beach plant into the waves (Hviding 1996: 173): here, again, ritual can be seen to be an integrated part of daily life. Descola and Pálsson (1996) have contrasted the modern Western world with a range of societies where such dichotomies as sacred/profane and ritual/secular are not as strongly drawn, if they are drawn at all. They describe such societies as having a 'monist' rather than a 'dualist' mode of thought; the world is not made up of a series of oppositions, but constitutes a unified whole.

However, although these examples appear to suggest that ritual permeates all aspects of day-to-day life, it would be a mistake to broad-brush all categories of human action as 'ritualized' to one extent or another (this would fall into the same trap as Leach [1966, 1968: 523] encountered). One way of avoiding this is to consider whether other cultures distinguish practical from symbolic action in the way that modern Western people do. There is much to suggest that many societies do not differentiate or prioritize the kind of means–end relationship characteristic of technological acts (Goody 1977: 28; Bell 1992: 72). Anthropologists have often found it difficult to decide whether an action observed in the field should be classed as a practical or a ritual act, and the actors themselves frequently do not make this distinction. Evans-Pritchard's classic ethnography of the Azande (1937) provides several examples. In order to encourage termites to come out of their mounds, a man will burn a piece of barkcloth and blow the smoke into the opening of the mound while holding a magical plant in one hand (ibid.: 464). Should an anthropologist interpret this as a ritual or a practical act? The Azande themselves do not perceive there to be a difference between the two types of means–end relationships. Hence they do not define causation in the same way as we do. For example between planting a seed and its germination there is an interval where nothing can be seen of what is happening. The Azande conceive of this gap as essentially similar to the lacuna between action and result in a ritual or magical act (ibid.: 464), for instance where magic is being worked to cure an illness. They say that the soul of the seed is the agency that produces crop growth. Nor are the Azande an exception: Fortune (1932: 97–8) argues that the Dobuans do not distinguish between the results of magical and technological action, while the Solomon Islanders consider their wave-calming technique as a pragmatic tool (Hviding 1996: 173). Closer to home the ancient Greeks did not distinguish between art and craft (Lewis 1980: 9).

Because the contemporary Western world prioritizes a mechanical relationship between means and end, archaeologists are in danger of ignoring the essentially practical nature of (what they would identify as) ritual action. Many 'rituals' aim to achieve a substantive change to material conditions while others provide people with a means of understanding how to get on in the world. The practitioners of curative cults and fertility rituals, for example, expect them to be effective (Goody 1977: 28); just as the well-being of a Malay house and its inhabitants is ensured by following the proper rituals during construction (Waterson 1990: 122), so too Ndembu boys will not flourish unless they undergo the Mukanda circumcision rite (Turner 1967). As Lewis (1980: 35) puts it, 'Ritual is not done solely to be interpreted, it is also done…to resolve, alter or demonstrate a situation!'

The question of rationality

It is clear that anthropologists and archaeologists distinguish ritual from other areas of human practice on the basis of a particular evaluation of what is rational action. However, the discussion that has just been presented calls this notion of rationality into question. The question of whether Western science provides context-independent truths that can be used as a yardstick whereby the rationality of 'pre-capitalist' peoples can be judged has been questioned by many philosophers and social scientists (e.g. Winch 1970; Tambiah 1990; Hviding 1996; cf. Habermas 1971; Foucault 1980; Harding and Hintikka 1983; Haraway 1991). The weight of these arguments favours the conclusion that Western science cannot be regarded as an independent reality and that it does not provide ultimate truths of universal applicability. As Habermas (1971) and Foucault (1970, 1977, 1980) have convincingly argued, knowledge of any sort (including scientific knowledge) is constituted within a nexus of power relations that defines 'suitable' questions and provides 'acceptable' standards for judging the validity of answers. Such standards are not untainted by socio-political interest but are the very instruments that enable the legitimation and reproduction of certain political institutions. Because the logical positivism of modern science is so deeply inscribed into Western epistemology through its diffusion into areas of life such as the economy, politics, and morality (Tambiah 1990: 150), it is often difficult to consider the possibility that other ways of understanding the world may be equally valid.

It therefore seems likely that ritual actions are perfectly logical[4] given a particular understanding of how the world works. They appear irrational only to those who cannot follow the historically specific logic which produced them (cf. Evans-Pritchard 1937; Winch 1970; Tambiah 1990; Hviding 1996). As we have seen causation is not conceptualized in the same way in other cultures as it is in modern Western society (Hviding 1996: 69). For example where there is a more holistic conception of the world, where subject/object and culture/nature are not differentiated, a direct mechanical relationship between means and end may not be prioritized. Rather powers of causation may be considered to reside in spirits, gods, and even inanimate objects. Thus the ways in which such things as 'magical' plants are understood to work and the properties that are ascribed to these by non-Western societies often differ substantially from our own scientifically based understanding of such materials. Clearly such ideas will influence what is judged to be effective action.

Schefold's account (1982: 126) of an incident that occurred during his anthropological fieldwork among the Sakuddei of Siberut, Indonesia, demonstrates this well. While conducting research on Sakuddei longhouses, he fell ill with malaria. The Sakuddei explained this in the following way: Schefold had examined the houses in such detail that he had effectively molested them. The houses had therefore become offended and had retaliated by making him fall ill. He would not recover unless a special ceremony was enacted whereby he would be reconciled with the longhouses. According to a modern, Western viewpoint this means of curing malaria would be considered entirely irrational. However, the Sakuddei have an animistic conception of the universe, in which all things, including houses, possess their own spirit or vital force. No division is made between nature and culture. Human beings must try to coexist in harmony with the world around them; only by doing so will they maintain the natural balance required to live a healthy and happy life. Given this understanding of how the world works, the notion that Schefold's malaria could be cured through a ritual of reconciliation does not appear illogical at all.

Brightman's work (1993) on Canadian Cree hunting practice provides similar insights. His research demonstrates that the subsistence practices of non-capitalist groups often include activities which would be labelled as irrational ritual action according to modern Western criteria. However, such activities make perfect sense given a particular rationalization of animal–human relationships. For example before setting out on a hunt Cree hunters often make offerings to the animals they will kill (ibid.: 116). To the Cree Indians, humans and animals form part of an undifferentiated universe; there is no absolute division of nature from culture. Within this framework animals are perceived as conscious beings with social attributes very similar to humans. Hunting is considered to be a formal reciprocal relationship into which both humans and animals willingly enter (ibid.: 188). Just as the animal surrenders its body, so must the hunter propitiate it with offerings and treat it with care and respect. Only in this way can the animals be expected to continue to give up their bodies for humans to eat.

However, it would of course be a mistake to polarize human rationality into the gross categories 'modern' and 'pre-modern'; the contrastive approach followed here is simply a means of underlining how deeply embedded certain expectations concerning human behaviour are within archaeological thinking. In the past, as in the present, there were many different ways of understanding how the world works and of conceptualizing humans' place within that world. The challenge for archaeologists will be to find ways of exploring the specificities of human rationality within different cultural contexts. These issues are just beginning to be explored in archaeology and ethno-archaeology, particularly in discussions of the symbolic and ideological dimensions of 'technological' processes such as metalworking and potting (e.g. Budd and Taylor 1995; Reid and MacLean 1995; Sillar 1996).

Problems caused by the use of the concept of ritual in archaeology

With these points in mind; let us return to the archaeological literature. Within archaeology the application of an inflexible theoretical framework which differentiates ritual from secular practice has resulted in several major problems. We have already seen in an earlier part of this chapter that the conception of ritual as a distinct category of action has caused considerable confusion when it comes to interpreting certain sites, structures, and artefacts. Within British prehistory the opposition of ritual and secular action has resulted in a conception of ritual as a distinct sphere of practice, differentiated spatially, temporally, and conceptually from the mundane activities of daily life. Thus ritual and non-ritual practices are assumed to be mutually exclusive. As we have discussed, however, much of the data does not appear to neatly fit the dualism ritual/secular. For example the structural and artefactual evidence recovered from sites such as henges and round barrows not only frequently confounds the attribution of these locations as ritual sites but such evidence is itself often difficult to label definitively as the result of either ritual or secular activities. In other words neither sites nor artefacts fit these preconceived categories. This suggests that societies in prehistoric Britain did not recognize or distinguish the categories 'sacred' and 'profane' (see Brück 1999; cf. Hodder 1987). The implications of this will be examined later.

An even more serious problem embedded within theories of human action that differentiate ritual activities from everyday practical tasks is that there is frequently a disparity in the kinds of interpretations applied to different types of data (a point which Hill [1995: 97] has also made). Those areas of ancient life about which scientifically provable inferences can be made become prioritized and ritual is relegated to an extraneous, non-utilitarian category about which nothing is truly knowable. The assumption is frequently made that such areas of life as subsistence are based on an accessible and universal logic that constitutes a means of dealing efficiently with an ahistorical, material environment. Irrational ritual acts, on the other hand, can never be understood because they refer to the historically specific belief systems of a particular people. Hawkes's 'ladder of inference' (1954: 161–2) is perhaps the best-known example of this approach, although it remains deeply embedded in contemporary interpretive schemes. The continued use of the concept of ritual therefore tacitly reinforces certain aspects of a positivist approach.

A good example of this trend is provided by the very different interpretive frameworks applied to early and middle Bronze Age sites in southern England. I have chosen this example deliberately because it sets the scene for the middle Bronze Age material discussed in detail in a later part of this chapter. The early Bronze Age is distinguished from later periods by a proliferation of what have widely been identified as ritual monuments, for example henges, round barrows, and stone circles. Settlement sites are rare and evidence for economic activities sparse. This contrasts with the middle Bronze Age, for which settlements and field systems dominate the archaeological record. Archaeologists have interpreted the development of such apparently familiar and domesticated landscapes during the middle Bronze Age as indicating the primacy of everyday, economic concerns. The practicalities of agricultural production, stock herding, grain storage, pottery production, and the like fill the literature (e.g. Drewett 1980; Darvill 1987: Ch. 5; Gingell 1992: 153–8). Terms such as 'farmstead' and 'homestead' are frequently employed in discussions of middle Bronze Age settlements and one site has even been described as 'almost a model farm' (Drewett 1980: 391). Fowler (1983: 40), for example, describes the middle Bronze Age landscape as demonstrating a 'concern with agrarian, practical and technological matters. [The middle Bronze Age] appears to be a functional period, with emphasis on the basics of food production.' Because the interpretation of middle Bronze Age sites appears relatively unproblematic in comparison with the ritual monuments of preceding centuries, they are discussed in largely functionalist terms (e.g. Burgess 1980: Chs V and VI).

The apparent familiarity of the middle Bronze Age landscape has had a major impact on explanatory frameworks for the early to middle Bronze Age transition. Because the dualism ritual/secular is transformed so easily into the dichotomy irrational/rational, it is assumed that the logic that lies behind middle Bronze Age action is somehow self-evident and accessible. In this way modern Western aims and rationales become imposed on the middle Bronze Age. In particular the supposed primacy of utilitarian concerns in the middle Bronze Age is often taken to indicate that economic requirements lie at the heart of changes in the archaeological record. For example the appearance of archaeologically identifiable fields and farmsteads at the beginning of the middle Bronze Age is widely understood to indicate a desire to intensify or maximize agricultural production (e.g. Barrett 1980: 90; 1994: 148; Whittle 1980: 373; Fowler 1981: 30, 44; Bradley 1984: 94).

In fact a closer examination of the middle Bronze Age settlement data indicates that there are serious problems with the application of such an interpretive framework. The fully worked example presented in a later part of this chapter will demonstrate that middle Bronze Age people did not always conform to our standards of functionalist behaviour. The notion that the appearance of farmsteads and field systems indicates the development of 'rational' aims and activities is belied by some of the more curious finds from settlement sites. These finds will be used to suggest an alternative interpretation of middle Bronze Age life.

Recent discussion of ritual within British archaeology

Over the last ten to 15 years there has been a resurgence of interest in ritual among British archaeologists. Many researchers have tried to move away from the traditional view of ritual as a non-functional epiphenomenon of daily life. They have stressed the social role of ritual practice, arguing that it enables the reproduction and renegotiation of the social order (e.g. Braithwaite 1984; Richards and Thomas 1984; Barrett 1991; 1994: 77–81; Garwood 1991; Mizoguchi 1993; Thomas 1996). However, because the renewal of interest in ritual has arisen as part of the postprocessual backlash against the more extreme forms of functionalism, many recent discussions have taken a strong idealist stance. In some cases (e.g. Parker Pearson

1982; Shanks and Tilly 1982) such approaches have been based on a Marxist formulation of society, in which the ideological beliefs expressed in ritual acts are conceptualized as part of the superstructure, itself a veil mystifying the reality of social inequality. This ideal/real dichotomy has a similar effect to approaches that oppose symbolic and practical action in that the materialities of day-to-day living seem divorced from the ideologies embedded within ritual practice. Barrett (1991: 6; 1994: 77) has criticized such work, arguing that 'ritual and religious knowledges are...built out of the same material conditions as everyday life' (1991: 6) and that 'the creation of ritual arises from the routine conditions of everyday life because people speak metaphorically about their conditions' (ibid.).

However, even where post-processual writers have attempted to break down the distinction between ritual action and daily life, certain aspects of the theoretical frameworks espoused continue to reproduce a disjunction between ritual and practical activities. Post-processual archaeology's interest in the social and ideological aspects of human existence, although timely, has meant that the symbolic aspects of human action have all too often been stressed at the expense of the practical. The material products of human action (artefacts, sites, etc.) are frequently interpreted as metaphorical representations of past social and cosmological orders. According to such a viewpoint, sites and artefacts (as repositories of cultural meaning) often appear to have been created through the application of abstract symbolic schemes; human action is seen as governed by belief systems rather than practical considerations. For example Parker Pearson and Richards (1994), Hill (1995), Brück (1995), and others have argued that many aspects of day-to-day life (for example refuse disposal or ways of moving in and out of a roundhouse) have a heavily ritualized character because cosmological principles are deeply embedded within the structure of habitual practice. Thus they attempt to break down the disjunction between ritual and secular practice by arguing that ritual becomes incorporated into all aspects of daily life. The danger of this approach is that everything becomes subsumed within the category of ritual. Although it is an attractive argument, ultimately it runs the risk of reducing human action to the irrational and symbolic, a curious collection of idiosyncratic practices aimed only at reproducing certain forms of social power. The practicalities of day-to-day living (for example such issues as the interaction between people and environment) become marginalized in these accounts. This is because although these researchers may have addressed the shortcomings of the dichotomy sacred/profane by questioning the universality of a spatially or temporally discrete sacred domain, they continue to implicitly apply the dualism symbolic/practical as a means of distinguishing and characterizing different spheres of activity. Clearly an alternative approach is required.

A logic for getting on in the world: should practical and symbolic action be differentiated?

The continued disjunction of ritual from secular action may be resolved through the realization that human action is always both practical and symbolic. If so then the existence of ritual as a distinct mode of practice is called into question at a very fundamental level. Contrary to Leach (1968: 523), however, this is not to suggest that action has both a symbolic and a practical aspect. Leach identifies the symbolic and the practical as quite distinct: two sides of the coin of human action. Rather I would argue that they are one and the same.

Let us explore this further. As discussed earlier, ritual is often considered an essentially practical activity by the actors themselves. Conversely, modern Western notions of 'practicality' are culturally constructed; they are part of a historically specific logic which itself forms an 'ideology', that is, a particular way of understanding the world. These different logics, which constitute a way of getting on in the world, become articulated as sets of cosmological beliefs and values. By acting practically upon the world in day-to-day life people play out the beliefs and values that constitute their particular way of understanding the world. In other words cosmologies are not abstract ideological/symbolic systems but enable people to understand the world and to get on in it by providing a logic for action and an explanation of the universe. Ideas about what constitutes an appropriate economic strategy, for example, are part and parcel of these systems of value and meaning (thus, for instance, modern Western notions of 'efficiency' or 'utility' are the product of a particular set of historical circumstances). In this sense, then, any practical action is also symbolic because it reproduces the sets of values and social relations which are embedded in cosmological schemes.

This suggests that the beliefs that lie behind what Western observers identify as ritual practices are in fact a particular manifestation of the values, aims, and rationales that shape practical action. In other words the notion that ritual is somehow special or different because it enables the reproduction of the social and cosmological order is problematic; in fact all human action draws on and reproduces the sets of cultural principles embedded within particular cosmologies or belief systems, as Barrett (1988: 31; 1991: 6; 1994: 77) and Hill (1995: 96–9) have also pointed out. An important conclusion that may be drawn from these observations is that 'practical' activities such as agricultural production cannot be expected to obey some kind of universal functionalist logic. Conversely, as has been argued above, what modern Western observers might label 'irrational' ritual activity in fact constitutes a perfectly logical and practical way of dealing with the world given a particular understanding of how the universe works.

From ritual to rationality

Up to this point we have discussed how the constitution of ritual practice as a distinct social phenomenon and as an object of anthropological study is the product of post-Enlightenment rationalism. Many other societies do not perceive a sharp distinction between ritual and secular action or between the symbolic and the practical. Hence it cannot be assumed that these categories were either identified or distinguished in the past. If this is the case we should not expect to be able to differentiate ritual from other types of activity in the archaeological record. The second important point is that adherence to the notion that there is a fundamental disjunction between ritual and secular action can result in a serious misapprehension of the nature of prehistoric rationality. The notion that certain aspects of daily life, notably subsistence production, are governed by a universally applicable, functionalist logic is clearly problematic.

Two main conclusions may be drawn.

(i)   The question 'how do we identify ritual practice archaeologically?' is redundant. In fact by pursuing this aim archaeologists have blinded themselves to a much more fundamental issue, namely:

(ii) What can past actions tell us about the nature of prehistoric rationality? If it is erroneous to differentiate the symbolic from the practical then it would seem unhelpful to apply a functionalist approach to certain aspects of prehistoric life (e.g. subsistence) while admitting that others (e.g. religious beliefs) cannot be explained in this way: rather, prehistoric people applied a historically specific logic to the world around them. This comprised a set of culturally specific values, aims, and rationales which shaped their practical interaction with the world. It is surely these that should form the focus of archaeological interest.

Importantly this is a very different approach from those that argue that ritual pervades all aspects of daily life. By rejecting the analytical value of the concept ritual we move from a vision of past society in which certain daily practices had esoteric ritualized aspects to one in which all the activities documented in the archaeological record represent people's practical engagement with material conditions, albeit based on a very different set of ideas about how the world works to that enshrined in modern Western thought. Those activities identified as 'ritual' by archaeologists and anthropologists are not categorized as qualitatively different (in terms of the means–end relationships implied) from other areas of practice by those carrying them out. Rather all activities, both 'ritual' and 'secular', are shaped by a very different sense of rationality and a different understanding of causation to those prevalent in our own cultural context.

Of course the reader may object that by abandoning the dualism ritual/secular we risk homogenizing human practice and suppressing the variability that forms the basis for archaeological interpretation. On the contrary I would argue that my approach does not presuppose a lack of difference. Rather it makes the nature of these differences the focus of archaeological enquiry instead of an a priori assumption. For example it is perfectly possible that middle Bronze Age people considered the kinds of depositional activities discussed later in this chapter as special or different in some way. If they did, however, it is inherently unlikely that they distinguished these activities from other types of practice using the criteria (i.e. 'oddness', 'impracticality', and 'irrationality') applied by archaeologists.

Following this line of thought, it is worth considering certain aspects of Barrett's work on ritual. Unlike many post-processual archaeologists who argue that the sacred permeates all aspects of life, Barrett (1991, 1994: 72–80) holds that ritual is a distinct 'field of discourse', bracketed off in time and space from other areas of human practice. He argues that the forms of knowledge created within this field are separate from and different to those created within the mundane world and that they provide a means of objectifying, commenting on, and challenging the accepted social order. In this he is following Bloch (1985). However, Bloch's argument depends on his separation of ideological from non-ideological cognition. He characterizes ideological cognition (a primary component of ritual practice) as 'a system of knowledge that legitimates the social order' (Bloch 1985: 33). Non-ideological cognition is 'a system of knowledge, which organises perceptions' (ibid.) and it is this that governs mundane activities. Thus Bloch's division of ritual from secular depends on maintaining the dichotomy between ideal and real that Barrett (1994: 77–8) so cogently criticizes for other reasons. Furthermore such an ideal/real dualism is clearly closely related to the set of intellectual structures that presuppose a difference between symbolic and practical action. In this sense Barrett does not adequately deal with the problems raised by the symbolic/practical dualism but still implicitly relies on it as a means of identifying ritual action in the archaeological record.

Barrett is right, however, to point out that different forms of knowledge exist within any one society and that these can be used as a source of comment and critique on other areas of social practice. However, to differentiate these into two broad forms – ritual and non-ritual knowledge – is not only to simplify human action but also to presuppose categorizations of practice that should remain a focus of discussion. 'Fields of discourse' are defined and bracketed in different ways according to cultural context and any one of these (not only that which archaeologists would label ritual) can form a platform from which to assess and question other areas of social practice. This is because culture is not a uniform entity; forms of knowledge vary from context to context within any one society and cannot simply be polarized into ritual and non-ritual categories. I do, however, agree with Barrett (1991, 1994) when he argues that in many societies there is a series of special activities that facilitate transformations between social categories. Following Turner (1967) he identifies these as ritual. However, I would maintain that when archaeologists discuss ritual they are referring to a wider range of practices than those characterized as rites of transition and, as such, the problems introduced by the application of the concept in archaeology deserve wider contextualization and appraisal. As argued earlier, it seems likely that where the practitioners of rites of transition identify these as categorically different from other areas of practice, this is on the basis of a quite different set of criteria to those used by anthropologists; clearly such criteria deserve discussion in their own right.

An archaeological example: 'odd' deposits on middle Bronze Age settlements

In recent decades, depositional practices which appear to defy functionalist explanations have become the focus of considerable archaeological attention (e.g. Richards and Thomas 1984; Thomas 1991; Cunliffe 1992; Pollard 1992; Hill 1995). Such deposits are usually described as 'special', 'votive', 'deliberate', or 'structured', with the implication that these are an archaeological manifestation of past ritual action.[5] Similar finds recovered from middle Bronze Age settlements have yet to be examined and will provide an interesting testing ground for the arguments developed in this chapter. In contrast to other studies of such deposits my aim in examining these is not to develop a methodology for the identification of ritual practice in the past, but to understand interpretive action in the present. When archaeologists single out these deposits as 'different' in some way, they usually assume that this sense of difference or specialness was appreciated and articulated by the ancient people who placed these objects in the ground. On the contrary I would argue that we cannot make this a priori assumption. In fact such finds are distinguished by archaeologists precisely because they look different or 'odd' to us. Two questions will be pursued in this section: first, why are these deposits singled out as 'odd' by archaeologists, and second, what can this sense of peculiarity or difference tell us about the nature of prehistoric rationality?

Let us begin by briefly contextualizing the data set to be examined here. Middle Bronze Age settlements consist of a recurrent package of structural/architectural elements. A typical site might comprise several roundhouses, accompanied by a few pits, a pond, and perhaps one or two four-post structures (the last are usually interpreted as raised granaries: Gent 1983: 245–50). These are often set within an enclosure and associated field system (e.g. Ellison 1975: 292–307; 1981: 417–21; Barrett *et al.* 1991: Fig. 5.42). The size and layout of such sites suggest that most were occupied by a single household, perhaps comprising a nuclear or small extended family group (Ellison 1975: 367; 1981: 432; Drewett 1982). We have already seen that the apparent cosy familiarity of these 'homesteads' has rendered them particularly open to functionalist interpretation. One result of this is that until recently some of the more curious finds recovered from these sites have been all but ignored (but see Barrett and Needham 1988: 136; Barrett 1989; Barrett *et al.* 1991: 144).

The finds that will be considered here are not a single group but comprise a variety of different kinds of objects within a range of archaeological contexts. For example at Itford Hill, East Sussex (Burstow and Holleyman 1957), the complete lower stone of a saddle quern had been placed on the base of a pit in roundhouse E. A number of the pits excavated at North Shoebury, Essex, contained whole pottery vessels, while a complete but smashed bucket urn had been carefully laid on the bottom of a further pit (Wymer and Brown 1995: 153). The left half of the carcass of a cow was found on the bottom of a pit in roundhouse 1 at South Lodge Camp, Dorset (Barrett *et al.* 1991). At Crab Farm, Dorset (Papworth 1992), the skeleton of a pregnant cow was found in the secondary filling of the inner enclosure ditch, while cut into the middle ditch was a pit containing the articulated remains of a pregnant sheep. 'Occupation deposits' on the floor of certain roundhouses occasionally yield bronze artefacts such as awls, knives, and razors. For example a tanged triangular blade and an awl were found on the floor of roundhouse 3, platform 4, Black Patch, East Sussex (Drewett 1982), while a layer of dark-grey soil covering the floor of roundhouse 1 at Chalton, Hampshire (Cunliffe 1970), produced a bronze knife, awl, and palstave.

The contexts of some of these finds is also interesting. 'Odd' deposits are sometimes located at angles, corners, or terminals of ditches. For example at South Lodge Camp, Dorset (Barrett *et al.* 1991), a number of bronze objects were deposited at or near three of the four corners of the rectilinear enclosure ditch. At Down Farm, Dorset (ibid.), a group of five dog skulls was deposited in the southeastern corner of the enclosure ditch. Artefacts buried in pits and ditches may also show signs of deliberate arrangement. Pit V in structure I at Cock Hill, West Sussex (Ratcliffe-Densham and Ratcliffe-Densham 1961), contained ten loomweights laid out in a straight line along the long axis of the base of the pit. At South Dumpton Down, Kent (D. Perkins, pers. comm.), a small pit had been cut into the side of the ditch. Four bronze palstaves had been placed in a fan shape on the bottom of this pit and a square piece of tabular flint laid on top of these. Further up in the silting of the pit was a further palstave; on top of this had been piled fragments of two bronze bangles.

Middle Bronze Age systems of logic and value

What unites this varied group of finds is that they do not satisfy modern Western criteria for rational action. In other words such deposits look 'odd' to archaeologists because they cannot be adequately explained in modern-day functionalist terms. In order to demonstrate this let us begin by considering the occurrence of intact and potentially reusable artefacts such as quern stones. These do not appear to have come to the end of their use-life and thus they do not fit our contemporary definition of rubbish. Those espousing a functionalist[6] approach might argue that such items were cached for future use. Perhaps the site was temporarily abandoned, but its inhabitants intended to return at a later date (cf. Deal 1985: 269; Joyce and Johannessen 1993). To begin with, such a suggestion can be challenged on theoretical grounds. Specifically, it is based on the notion that the principle of maximum utility and minimum wastage is universal. It is argued that people will remove as many items as possible when abandoning a site; the amount they take is supposed to relate to such practical considerations as how hurriedly they must leave the old site and how far it is to the new (Deal 1985: 268–70; Schiffer 1987: 90–1). However, we need to ask whether attempts to construct a universal index of practicality may be misleading. Customs such as the potlatch among North American Indians of the northwest coast (e.g. Druker and Heizer 1967) suggest that other societies see it as quite logical to 'waste' perfectly useable artefacts in certain circumstances. The obsession of the modern Western world with efficiency, utility, and savings is the product of a particular historical perspective. Value is socially constructed (Thompson 1979) and is not always conceived of in economic terms. Thus the way in which particular artefacts are treated and deposited in other cultures varies considerably. Indeed interpretations of bronzes recovered from watery places such as rivers and bogs underline the fact that it is already widely accepted that 'wasting' material goods was a socially acceptable strategy in certain contexts during the Bronze Age (e.g. Bradley 1990).

Returning to the data under consideration here, the caching model raises a number of substantive problems which need to be considered. For example this interpretation does not easily explain the presence of small personal artefacts such as bronze rings, razors, or knives in pits, in ditches, or on the floors of buildings. These small objects would not have been difficult to transport and many were still perfectly useable when they were deposited in the ground. Furthermore given the social significance of bronze during this period (e.g. Bradley 1990), they were probably also highly valued. One might therefore expect such small items to have accompanied their owners on the abandonment of a site so that they could either be reused or, if broken, recycled. That this did not occur in certain cases, however, suggests that middle Bronze Age people did not always obey the principle of least effort nor that of maximum economic gain. Similarly many of the other 'odd' deposits from middle Bronze Age settlements defy simple utilitarian explanations. The chalk phallus found standing upright at the bottom of a posthole in the entrance structure to roundhouse D, Itford Hill, East Sussex (Burstow and Holleyman 1957: 176), is one good example, as are the many animal burials documented in the literature. The argument that these animals may have been diseased beasts who died before their time seems difficult to uphold given the location of many such deposits, for example the cow burial beneath the floor of structure 1 at South Lodge Camp, Dorset (Barrett *et al.* 1991).

Indeed animal burials are often located at critical points in space, for example boundaries, corners, and entrances, suggesting that these deposits acted as a means of marking out or drawing attention to significant locations. At Boscombe Down East, Wiltshire (Stone 1936), for example, the skeleton of a sheep was buried on one side of the northern angle of the enclosure ditch and a goat on the other side. Finds such as the chalk phallus from Itford Hill, East Sussex (Burstow and Holleyman 1957: 176), can be interpreted in a similar way. This suggests that the act of deposition itself was important because it was a means of creating or adding to the significance of a particular place. If we apply this interpretive framework to certain finds then it is clearly contradictory to discount it in other cases. Items such as whole pots and quern stones have been found in similar contexts. Thus they can be seen to form part of a wider tradition of deposition and they may therefore have played a comparable role. If so then it becomes difficult to sustain the notion that these were simply cached for future use while deposits such as whole animal burials fulfilled more esoteric functions. That the act of deposition was important is also substantiated by evidence for the careful placing or arrangement of objects within features such as pits and ditches; the row of ten loomweights recovered from pit V at Cock Hill, West Sussex (Ratcliffe-Densham and Ratcliffe-Densham 1961), provides a good example. Certainly such careful arranging of finds is difficult to explain in modern functionalist terms.

When another strand of evidence is considered, further doubt is cast on the interpretation of whole, reuseable artefacts as cached items. Broken objects (which modern Western people would categorize as refuse) often seem to have been treated in a similar manner to the various types of finds documented above: for example a smashed pot was carefully laid on the base of one of the pits at North Shoebury, Essex (Wymer and Brown 1995: 153). It is obviously difficult to apply the caching explanation in this case. Similarly refuse deposits are frequently located at critical points in space, such as the butt-ends of ditches. The large dump of pot sherds, burnt flint, animal bone, and crop-processing waste in the eastern terminal of ditch 589 at Weir Bank Stud Farm, Berkshire (Barnes *et al.* 1995), is one example, suggesting that refuse may also have played an active role in marking out significant places. These examples indicate that it cannot be assumed that items which would be classed as 'rubbish' by modern Western people were perceived as useless, dirty, or worthless in the middle Bronze Age (for further discussion see Brück 1995).

Taking all these different lines of evidence into account it can be argued that what we are seeing here is a distinct tradition of deposition whereby things were placed in pits, ditches, and other features for reasons that modern Western people cannot immediately understand. Both the context and composition of certain groups of finds, for example the five dog skulls deposited in the southeastern corner of the enclosure ditch at Down Farm, Dorset (Barrett *et al.* 1991), defy explanations that satisfy a modern sense of rationality. Not only was it deemed appropriate in certain circumstances to 'waste' useable artefacts by burying them, but categories of 'refuse' were also sometimes treated carefully upon deposition. The fact that such deposits do not fit modern Western criteria for rational action suggests that the systems of logic and value that underlie middle Bronze Age social practice were substantially different from our own. This is hardly a surprising conclusion: however, its ramifications have as yet to be fully explored. We need to consider what such 'odd' deposits can actually tell us about the historically specific values, aims, and rationales of middle Bronze Age people.

The social context of middle Bronze Age depositional practices

For the reasons outlined in this chapter, archaeologists who interpret such deposits as a manifestation of ritual action run the risk of misinterpreting the nature of prehistoric rationality. How, then, can we construct alternative ways of understanding these deposits? Following the discussion set out in an earlier section, it may be proposed that such activities arose out of people's practical attempts to deal with the world around them. Given a particular way of understanding the world, these actions would have constituted a perfectly logical means of dealing with certain social/material circumstances. A consideration of their social context and objectives will clearly be an essential primary step in any attempt to interpret such finds.

One important hint is provided by the layout and structural components of middle Bronze Age settlements. At many of these sites, sequences of building can be identified. In other words the organization of space did not remain static throughout the lifetime of the site (e.g. Ellison 1987: Fig. 2; Barrett *et al.* 1991: Fig. 5.28; Russell 1996). Roundhouses fell out of use and were replaced, ponds became silted up with refuse, enclosures were constructed around previously unenclosed sites, and fences erected and dismantled to divide up a site in new ways. Such building sequences can best be understood within a framework that stresses how the demographic, social, and economic circumstances of a household change over the course of the human life cycle (cf. Goody 1958; Moore 1986: 91–102). Households expand and contract as children are born, young members marry and move away, or as elderly parents come to live with their adult offspring. Likewise the wealth and status of a household changes over time. These factors will affect the needs of a household for new facilities as well as its ability to construct these. It may therefore be surmised that the life cycle (or structural history) of a settlement was closely related at a practical level to the life cycle (or demographic, social, and economic history) of its inhabitants.

However, in many societies there is also a deep symbolic relationship between a particular settlement and the kinship group that inhabits it. The life cycle of the settlement is therefore not only related to that of its occupants in practical terms; each is also a metaphorical representation of the other. Waterson's work on southeast Asian houses (1990) provides a very good example. In many southeast Asian societies the house is considered to be an animate object with its own vital force (ibid.: 115). Houses are likened to human bodies and particular structural elements are described as the 'navel', 'bones', 'feet', and so on (ibid.: 129). They are 'brought to life' through a series of special rituals during house construction. In Malaysia, for example, offerings are placed into the hole that will receive the centre-post of the house (ibid.: 122). The 'death' of a house is an equally important event. Waterson describes how when a Torajan village was partly destroyed by fire, rites analogous to those enacted on the death of a person were carried out (ibid.: 135). As a metaphorical representation of a particular family or lineage group, the well-being of the house is intimately connected with that of its inhabitants (ibid.: 132). Rites of passage for its human occupants therefore draw on the symbolism of the 'living' house. For example among the Tetum of Timor, the placenta of a newborn child is placed on the altar at the 'navel' of the house, source of its vital energy (ibid.: 196).

Although the conceptualization of the house was undoubtedly very different during the middle Bronze Age, a close metaphorical relationship between the life cycle of the settlement and that of its inhabitants would convincingly explain the occurrence of the range of depositional practices described above. We have already seen that 'odd' deposits often seem to mark out significant points in space such as the butt-ends of enclosure ditches; a similar argument can perhaps be made with respect to the passage of time. Such acts as the deposition of small bronze objects in post-holes may have been carried out at critical points in the life cycle of the settlement, its structures, and its inhabitants. Birth, marriage, death, and other rites of passage may each have formed the context for particular acts of deposition, as may the equivalent points in the life of a structure: the concept of a foundation deposit is familiar to archaeologists but similar deposits may have been made when a structure was rebuilt, remodelled, or abandoned. Important points in the annual subsistence cycle may likewise have required the deposition of certain objects or materials. As such these acts would have had quite practical implications, for example to ensure the well-being of a building's inhabitants, to provide a safe place for the storage of seed-grain, or to placate the spirit of a newly deceased member of the household. The aim of each act of deposition may be impossible to pin down today, but the metonymic qualities of many of the items deposited (e.g. quern stones, deposits of barley, and animal burials) suggest that they were concerned to maintain the household's subsistence cycle and the social relations that sustained this.

To exemplify this argument let us consider what happened when certain round-houses were abandoned. The 'death' of a roundhouse seems to have been a significant event and may have been linked to the death of its owner(s). As argued earlier, finds such as the blade and awl on the floor of roundhouse 3, platform 4, Black Patch, East Sussex (Drewett 1982), are difficult to explain in modern-day functionalist terms. Certainly there is nothing to suggest hurried abandonment of this building in the face of some oncoming disaster: these artefacts can therefore be interpreted not as components of generalized de facto refuse but as evidence for culturally specific abandonment practices, in which special 'closing deposits' were made as a means of formally ending or transforming the relationship between the building, its dead inhabitant(s), and the rest of the kin group (cf. Barrett and Needham 1988: 136).

Site-maintenance practices

The range of depositional practices present on middle Bronze Age settlements makes it difficult to draw a sharp distinction between those that aimed to clear a site of refuse and those that had other purposes. We have seen, for example, how categories of rubbish often form part of 'odd' deposits. To us this crossing-over of categories may seem rather peculiar. In fact our confusion results from a problematic tendency to label refuse disposal as a purely 'functional' activity. As stressed above, 'functionality' is always culturally defined. Our own evaluation of what is refuse and what is not, and our understanding of the qualities of refuse and of the correct way to treat and dispose of this are all cultural products. Cross-culturally attitudes to refuse are extremely variable (Moore 1986: 102–6). For example the Mesakin Nuba of Sudan are not greatly concerned with the 'practicalities' of cleanliness but will cook and eat surrounded by refuse (Hodder 1982: 157–63). Gypsy groups, on the other hand, keep their caravans scrupulously clean even though their campsites may be littered with refuse (Okely 1983: 85–9); this is because rubbish (conceived of as a dirty, dangerous substance) is used to mark out the boundary between Gypsy and Gorgio society by highlighting the hazards and tensions inherent in relations between the two groups.

This discussion indicates that we cannot assume that middle Bronze Age refuse disposal practices will have obeyed some universally applicable notion of functionality. Because middle Bronze Age people understood and valued refuse differently to the way we do today, they treated it in ways that often seem difficult for us to understand. At the same time because their logic for dealing with the world was very different from our own, they sometimes appear to have 'thrown away' artefacts that remained perfectly useable. If we simply label the depositional practices discussed here as either refuse disposal or ritual activities we risk slipping into the trap of applying artificially polarized interpretive frameworks (i.e. functional versus symbolic) to data generated by a historically specific set of values, aims, and rationales. Of course this is not to imply that the various depositional activities documented in the preceding sections were not inherently practical – of course they were. However, they obeyed culturally specific notions of what was practical action; we need to investigate these rather than assume that we already know what constituted functional/logical action for middle Bronze Age people. I would therefore argue that it may be more helpful to describe all the depositional activities that were carried out at middle Bronze Age settlements as constituting a culturally specific group of *site-maintenance practices* that ensured the well-being of the settlement and its inhabitants.

Importantly these points indicate that the 'odd' deposits described here should not be studied in isolation. They have formed a primary focus of discussion here because the aim was to understand the mechanics of archaeological interpretation in the present rather than depositional activity in the past. Having questioned the criteria according to which these deposits are differentiated from others, the task will be to make detailed comparisons of different modes of deposition and to consider the modus operandi (Needham and Spence 1997: 86) that lies behind these. Several archaeologists have begun to do this, notably Needham (e.g. Needham and Sørensen 1988; Needham and Spence 1996, 1997).

Implications

This discussion has suggested that the apparent familiarity of middle Bronze Age settlements is deceptive. The kind of practical logic that middle Bronze Age people applied in their day-to-day dealings with the world appears to have been very different from our own. I have suggested that modern Western values and rationales are all too frequently imposed upon the middle Bronze Age because of this erroneous sense of familiarity. For example the appearance of settlements and field systems in the archaeological record from the beginning of the middle Bronze Age is often explained as the result of a drive (presumed to be a universal feature of human nature) to intensify or maximize agricultural production.

At this point it will be instructive to briefly relate our discussion to Pálsson's interesting anthropological study of human–environment relationships (1996). Pálsson identifies three different modes of interaction with the natural world: orientalism, paternalism, and communalism. Orientalism and paternalism both perceive a dichotomy between nature and society. Orientalism is exploitative, with negative reciprocity characterizing the relationship between humans and the natural world. This is very much a colonial regime, according to which the natural world is a neutral tabula rasa: exploring, conquering, domesticating, and exploiting are frequent metaphors (Pálsson 1996: 67–8). Paternalism also assumes a culture/nature dichotomy, but it protects rather than exploits; hence the idiom of balanced reciprocity is appropriate (ibid.: 69). Communalism, on the other hand, rejects the notion of a separation between humans and the natural world; rather, intimate and personalized relationships are realized between people and the environment. Here generalized reciprocity, contingency, participation, and dialogue characterize human–environment relations (ibid.: 66–7). Where societies do not distance and objectify the natural world, economic strategies such as exploitation, intensification, or maximization of subsistence production may have no place in the repertoire of human action. At present, archaeologists all too easily assume that the orientalist economic strategies of the modern Western world are applicable to the Bronze Age.

It is not stretching the evidence too far to suggest that some of the 'odd' deposits discussed above may have acted as a means of maintaining the productivity of land and livestock through the giving of offerings, perhaps to particular spirits, ancestors, or deities. This suggests a more mutualistic relationship between people and environment than is implied by the kinds of 'orientalist' economic strategies that have often been projected into the Bronze Age. This is not a novel argument; Childe (1949: 20) argued that animal burials such as those described earlier indicate the lack of a clear distinction between culture and nature (although he was discussing the European Neolithic rather than the southern English middle Bronze Age, the same conclusion can be drawn here). This suggests that the exploitative economic strategies that are so often attributed to middle Bronze Age people may be entirely inappropriate. Their evaluation of effective action appears to have been very different from our own.

Conclusion

Continued application of an interpretive framework that distinguishes ritual from secular action has given rise to a particular set of problems for archaeologists. This is because the concept of ritual is a product of post-Enlightenment rationalism and is not necessarily applicable to other cultural or historical contexts. Most importantly the use of the concept has resulted in a fundamental misapprehension of the nature of prehistoric rationality. Clearly these problems cannot be solved while human practice continues to be conceptualized in this way. By jettisoning the notion of ritual, archaeologists become free to explore the possibility that even those activities so often labelled as 'functional' or 'practical' (for example past subsistence practices) are likely to have been based on a logic for action and a model of the world very different from our own.

As well as developing a theoretical discussion of the concept of ritual, this chapter has examined a variety of 'odd' finds from middle Bronze Age settlements as a means of exploring the nature of prehistoric rationality. This has demonstrated that middle Bronze Age people did not always act in accordance with modern Western notions of rationality, a realization that casts into question the assumption that subsistence practices and other 'functional' activities were governed by universal laws of behaviour. Thus an approach that attempts to move beyond the identification of ritual practice in the past can open up a whole range of intriguing new issues. Only by appreciating the essential difference of the past in all aspects of life can we begin to write an anthropology of prehistory.

Acknowledgements

I am grateful to Stuart Needham, John Chapman, Ian Hodder, Mark Edmonds, Marie-Louise Sørensen, Willy Kitchen, Jo Sofaer, and an anonymous referee for commenting on early versions of this paper and to David Perkins (Trust for Thanet Archaeology) for unpublished excavation data.

Notes

1. My own research specialism is British prehistory: for this reason the majority of the archaeological examples discussed in the text are from the British literature. However, similar arguments can certainly be made concerning the use of the concept of ritual within European archaeology generally.
2. In describing previous approaches to ritual, the terms 'practical', 'functional', 'utilitarian', and 'technological' are frequently used interchangeably (this is the way in which they have generally been employed in the anthropological literature). However, these terms will themselves become a focus of enquiry over the course of the chapter.
3. I am aware here that the phrase 'modern Western' needs to be problematized more fully than the scope of this chapter allows. Although my use of the phrase can be criticized as totalizing what is in fact a fragmented phenomenon, for the purposes of this chapter, I am equating 'modern Western' ways of thinking with the hegemonic rationalism of post-Enlightenment science and economics.
4. Here the terms rational and logical are used interchangeably.
5. Such deposits form a distinctive historical tradition throughout British later prehistory (cf. Bradley 1990). Doubtless the significance and social context of the kinds of depositional activities in question changed over the centuries, a possibility that requires much further exploration. Comparing the middle Bronze Age with the late Neolithic and early Bronze Age, for example, it is clear that although the kinds of locations in which such deposits were placed remained similar at a certain level (with a notable emphasis on site boundaries and entranceways), important differences can also be discerned. In particular the depositional focus shifted from communal monuments such as henges (at which networks of kin or neighbouring communities may have gathered) to settlements inhabited by small-scale single-household groups, perhaps mirroring wider social fragmentation at this time. I hope to explore these issues in more detail in future work.
6. In this section, where I refer to 'functionalist' or 'utilitarian' interpretations, I mean those that would be judged functional or rational according to modern, Western standards.

Bibliography

Ashbee, P. 1960. *The Bronze Age Round Barrow in Britain: An Introduction to the Study of the Funerary Practice and Culture of the British and Irish Single-Grave People of the Second Millennium BC*. London: Phoenix House.

Bahn, P. 1989. *Bluff Your Way in Archaeology*. Horsham: Ravette Books.

Barnes, I., Botsimier, W.A., Cleal, R.M.J., Fitzpatrick, A.P., and Roberts, M.R. 1995. *Early Settlement in Berkshire: Mesolithic-Roman Occupation Sites in the Thames and Kennet Valleys*. Salisbury: Wessex Archaeological Report 6.

Barrett, J.C. 1980. The Evolution of Later Bronze Age Settlement. In Barrett, J.C. and Bradley, R.J. (eds), *Settlement and Society in the British Later Bronze Age*. British Archaeological Reports, British series 83. Oxford: BAR, pp. 77–100.

Barrett, J.C. 1988. The Living, the Dead and the Ancestors: Neolithic and Early Bronze Age Mortuary Practices. In Barrett, J.C. and Kinnes, I.A. (eds), *The Archaeology of Context in the Neolithic and Bronze Age: Recent Trends*. Sheffield: Sheffield University Department of Archaeology and Prehistory, pp. 30–41.

Barrett, J.C. 1989. Time and Tradition: The Rituals of Everyday Life. In Nordstrøm, H.-Å. and Knape, A. (eds), *Bronze Age Studies: Transactions of the British-Scandinavian Colloquium in Stockholm, May 10–11, 1985*. The National Museum of Antiquities Studies 6. Stockholm: Statens Historika Museum, pp. 113–26.

Barrett, J.C. 1991. Towards an Archaeology of Ritual. In Garwood, P., Jennings, D., Skeates, R., and Toms, J. (eds), *Sacred and Profane: Proceedings of a Conference on Archaeology, Ritual and Religion, Oxford; 1989*. Oxford University Committee for Archaeology Monograph 32. Oxford: Oxbow Books, pp. 1–9.

Barrett, J.C. 1994. *Fragments from Antiquity: An Archaeology of Social Life in Britain, 2900–1200 BC*. Oxford: Blackwell.

Barrett, J.C. and Needham, S.P. 1988. Production, Circulation and Exchange: Problems in the Interpretation of Bronze Age Bronzework. In Barrett, J.C. and Kinnes, I.A. (eds), *The Archaeology of Context in the Neolithic and Bronze Age: Recent Trends*. Sheffield: Sheffield University Department of Archaeology and Prehistory, pp. 127–40.

Barrett, J.C., Bradley, R.J., and Green, M. 1991. *Landscape, Monuments and Society: the Prehistory of Cranborne Chase*. Cambridge: Cambridge University Press.

Bell, C. 1992. *Ritual Theory, Ritual Practice*. Oxford: Oxford University Press.

Bloch, M. 1985. From Cognition to Ideology. In Fardon, R. (ed.), *Power and Knowledge: Anthropological and Sociological Approaches*. Edinburgh: Scottish Academic Press, pp. 21–48.

Bourdieu, P. 1977. *Outline of a Theory of Practice*. Cambridge: Cambridge University Press.

Bradley, R. 1984. *The Social Foundations of Prehistoric Britain: Themes and Variations in the Archaeology of Power*. Harlow: Longman.

Bradley, R. 1990. *The Passage of Arms: An Archaeological Analysis of Prehistoric Hoards and Votive Deposits*. Cambridge: Cambridge University Press.

Braithwaite, M. 1984. Ritual and Prestige in the Prehistory of Wessex, *c.* 2200–1400 BC: A New Dimension to the Archaeological Evidence. In Miller, D. and Tilley, C. (eds), *Ideology, Power and Prehistory*. Cambridge: Cambridge University Press, pp. 93–110.

Brightman, R. 1993. *Grateful Prey: Rock Cree Human–Animal Relationships*. Berkeley: University of California Press.

Brown, A. 1991. Structured Deposition and Technological Change Among the Flaked Stone Artefacts from Cranborne Chase. In Barrett, J., Bradley, R., and Hall, M. (eds), *Papers on the Prehistoric Archaeology of Cranborne Chase*. Oxbow Monograph 11. Oxford: Oxbow Books, pp. 102–33.

Brück, J. 1995. A Place for the Dead: The Role of Human Remains in the Late Bronze Age. *Proceedings of the Prehistoric Society* 61: 245–77.

Brück, J. 1999. What's in a Settlement? Domestic Practice and Residential Mobility in Early Bronze Age Southern England. In Brück, J. and Goodman, M. (eds), *Making Places in the Prehistoric World: Themes in Settlement Archaeology*. London: UCL Press, pp. 52–75.

Budd, P. and Taylor, T. 1995. The Faeirie Smith Meets the Bronze Industry: Magic Versus Science in the Interpretation of Prehistoric Metal-Making. *World Archaeology* 27: 133–43.

Burgess, C. 1980. *The Age of Stonehenge*. London: Dent.

Burl, A. 1987. *The Stonehenge People: Life and Death at the World's Greatest Stone Circle*. London: J.M. Dent.

Burstow, G.P. and Holleyman, G.A. 1957. Late Bronze Age Settlement on Itford Hill, Sussex. *Proceedings of the Prehistoric Society* 23: 167–212.

Childe, V.G. 1949. *Social Worlds of Knowledge*. L.T. Hobhouse Memorial Trust Lecture 19. London: Geoffrey Cumberledge/Oxford University Press.

Clarke, D.V., Cowie, T.G., and Foxon, A. 1985. *Symbols of Power at the Time of Stonehenge*. Edinburgh: National Museum of Antiquities of Scotland.

Colt Hoare, R. 1812. *The Ancient History of South Wiltshire*. London: William Millar.

Cunliffe, B. 1970. A Bronze Age Settlement at Chalton, Hampshire (site 78). *Antiquaries Journal* 50: 1–13.

Cunliffe, B. 1992. Pits, Preconceptions and Propitiation in the British Iron Age. *Oxford Journal of Archaeology* 11: 69–83.

Darvill, T. 1987. *Prehistoric Britain*. London: Batsford.

Deal, M. 1985. Household Pottery Disposal in the Maya Highlands: An Ethnoarchaeological Interpretation. *Journal of Anthropological Archaeology* 4: 243–91.

Descola, P. and Pálsson, G. (eds). 1996. *Nature and Society: Anthropological Perspectives*. London: Routledge.

Drewett, P. 1980. Black Patch and the Later Bronze Age in Sussex. In Barrett, J.C. and Bradley, R.J. (eds), *Settlement and Society in the British Later Bronze Age*. British Archaeological Reports, British Series 83. Oxford: BAR, pp. 377–96.

Drewett, P. 1982. Later Bronze Age Downland Economy and Excavations at Black Patch, East Sussex. *Proceedings of the Prehistoric Society* 48: 321–40.

Drucker, P. and Heizer, R.F. 1967. *To Make My Name Good: A Re-examination of the: Southern Kwakiutl Potlatch*. Berkeley: University of California Press.

Durkheim, E. 1976. *The Elementary Forms of the Religious Life* (Second Edition). London: Allen and Unwin.

Ellison, A. 1975. Pottery and Settlements of the Later Bronze Age in Southern England. Ph.D. thesis. University of Cambridge.

Ellison, A. 1981. Towards a Socioeconomic Model for the Middle Bronze Age in Southern England. In Hodder, I., Isaac, G., and Hammond, N. (eds), *Pattern of the Past: Studies in Honour of David Clarke*. Cambridge: Cambridge University Press, pp. 413–38.

Ellison, A. 1987. The Bronze Age Settlement at Thorny Down: Pots, Post-Holes and Patterning. *Proceedings of the Prehistoric Society* 53: 385–92.

Evans-Pritchard, E.E. 1937. *Witchcraft, Oracles and Magic Among the Azande*. Oxford: Clarendon Press.

Firth, R. 1951. *Elements of Social Organisation*. London: Watts.

Fortes, M. 1966. Religious Premises and the Logical Technique in Divinatory Ritual. In Huxley, J. (ed.), *Ritualization of Behaviour in Man and Animals*. Philosophical Transactions of the Royal Society of London, series B 251. London: Royal Society, pp. 409–22.

Fortune, R.F. 1932. *Sorcerers of Dobu*. London: Routledge.

Foucault, M. 1970. *The Order of Things: An Archaeology of the Human Sciences*. London: Tavistock.

Foucault, M. 1973. *The Birth of the Clinic*. London: Tavistock.

Foucault, M. 1977. *Discipline and Punish*. New York: Vantage.

Foucault, M. 1980. *Power/Knowledge: Selected Interviews and Other Writings. 1972–1977*. New York: Pantheon Books.

Fowler, P.J. 1981. Wildscape to Landscape: 'Enclosure' in Prehistoric Britain. In Mercer, R. (ed.), *Farming Practice in British Prehistory*. Edinburgh: Edinburgh University Press, pp. 9–54.

Fowler, P.J. 1983. *The Farming of Prehistoric Britain*. Cambridge: Cambridge University Press.

Fox, C. 1941. Stake-Circles in Turf Barrows: A Record of Excavation in Glamorgan 1939–40. *Antiquaries Journal* 21: 92–127.

Frazer, J.G. 1890. *The Golden Bough: A Study in Comparative Religion*. London: Macmillan.

Garwood, P. 1991. Ritual Tradition and the Reconstitution of Society. In Garwood, P., Jennings, D., Skeates, R., and Toms, J. (eds), *Sacred and Profane: Proceedings of a Conference on Archaeology, Ritual and Religion, Oxford, 1989*. Oxford University Committee for Archaeology Monograph 32. Oxford: Oxbow Books, pp. 10–32.

Gent, H. 1983. Centralised Storage in Later Prehistoric Britain. *Proceedings of the Prehistoric Society* 49: 243–67.

Gibson, A. 1980. A Re-Interpretation of Chippenham Barrow 5, with a Discussion of the Beaker-Associated Pottery. *Proceedings of the Cambridge Antiquarian Society* 70: 47–60.

Gibson, A. 1982. *Beaker Domestic Sites: A Study of the Domestic Pottery of the Late Third and Early Second Millennium BC in the British Isles.* British Archaeological Reports, British series 107. Oxford: BAR.

Gingell, C. 1992. *The Marlborough Downs: A Later Bronze Age Landscape and its Origins.* Wiltshire Archaeology and Natural History Society Monograph 1. Devizes: Wiltshire Archaeological and Natural History Society.

Goody, J. (ed.). 1958. *The Developmental Cycle in Domestic Groups.* Cambridge: Cambridge University Press.

Goody, J. 1961. Religion and Ritual: The Definitional Problem. *British Journal of Sociology* 12: 142–64.

Goody, J. 1977. Against 'Ritual': Loosely Structured Thoughts on a Loosely Defined Topic. In Moore, S.F. and Myerhoff, B.G. (eds), *Secular Ritual.* Assen, Netherlands: Van Gorcum, pp. 25–35.

Habermas, J. 1971. Technology and Science as Ideology. In Habermas, J. (ed.), *Toward a Rational Society: Student Protest, Science and Politics.* London: Heinemann, pp. 81–122.

Haraway, D. 1991. Situated Knowledges: The Science Question in Feminism and the Privilege of Partial Perspective. In Haraway, D. *Simians, Cyborgs and Women: The Reinvention of Nature.* New York: Routledge, pp. 183–202.

Harding, S. and Hintikka, M.B. (eds), 1983. *Discovering Reality: Feminist Perspectives on Epistemology, Metaphysics, Methodology and Philosophy of Science.* Dordrecht, Holland: D. Reidel.

Hawkes, C.F.C. 1954. Archaeological Method and Theory: Some Suggestions from the Old World. *American Anthropology* 56: 155–68.

Hempel, C. 1965. *Aspects of Scientific Explanation.* New York: Free Press.

Hill, J.D. 1995. *Ritual and Rubbish in the Iron Age of Wessex: A Study on the Formation of a Particular Archaeological Record.* British Archaeological Reports, British Series 242. Oxford: BAR.

Hodder, I. 1982. *Symbols in Action: Ethnoarchaeological Studies of Material Culture.* Cambridge: Cambridge University Press.

Hodder, I. 1987. Contextual Archaeology: An Interpretation of Çatal Höyük and a Discussion of the Origins of Agriculture. *Bulletin of the Institute of Archaeology* 24: 43–56.

Hughes, G. 1996. Lockington. *Current Archaeology* 146: 44–9.

Hviding, E. 1996. Nature, Culture, Magic, Science: On Meta-Languages for Comparison in Cultural Ecology. In Descola, P. and Pálsson, G. (eds), *Nature and Society: Anthropological Perspectives.* London: Routledge, pp. 165–84.

Joyce, A. and Johannessen, S. 1993. Abandonment and the Production of Archaeological Variability at Domestic Sites. In Cameron, C. and Tomka, S. (eds), *Abandonment of Settlements and Regions: Ethnoarchaeological and Archaeological Approaches.* Cambridge: Cambridge University Press, pp. 139–53.

Lane, P. 1986. Past Practices in the Ritual Present: Examples from the Welsh Bronze Age. *Archaeological Review from Cambridge* 5: 181–92.

Leach, E. 1964. Ritual. In Gould, J. and Kolb, W. (eds), *A Dictionary of the Social Sciences.* London: Tavistock, pp. 607–8.

Leach, E. 1966. Ritualization in Man in Relation to Conceptual and Social Development. In Huxley, J. (ed.), *Ritualization of Behaviour in Man and Animals.* Philosophical Transactions of the Royal Society of London, series B 251. London: Royal Society, pp. 403–8.

Leach, E. 1968. Ritual. In Sills, D.L. (ed.), *International Encyclopaedia of the Social Sciences.* New York: Macmillan and Free Press, pp. 520–6.

Levy, J.E. 1982. *Social and Religious Organisation in Bronze Age Denmark.* British Archaeological Reports, International Series S124. Oxford: BAR.

Lewis, G. 1980. *Day of Shining Red: An Essay on Understanding Ritual*. Cambridge: Cambridge University Press.

Malone, C. 1989. *Avebury*. London: Batsford.

Mizoguchi, K. 1993. Time in the Reproduction of Mortuary Practices. *World Archaeology* 25: 223–35.

Moore, H. 1986. *Space, Text and Gender: An Anthropological Study of the Marakwet of Kenya*. Cambridge: Cambridge University Press.

Moore, S.F. and Myerhoff, B.G. 1977. Introduction: Secular Ritual: Forms and Meaning. In Moore, S.F. and Myerhoff, B.G. (eds), *Secular Ritual*. Assen, Netherlands: Van Gorcum, pp. 324–41.

Morris, B. 1994. *Anthropology of the Self: The Individual in Cultural Perspective*. London: Pluto Press.

Nadel, S.F. 1954. *Nupe Religion*. London: Routledge and Kegan Paul.

Needham, S. and Sørensen, M.-L.S. 1988. Runnymede Refuse Tip: A Consideration of Midden Deposits and their Formation. In Barrett, J.C. and Kinnes, I.A. (eds), *The Archaeology of Context in the Neolithic and Bronze Age: Recent Trends*. Sheffield: Sheffield University Department of Archaeology and Prehistory, pp. 113–26.

Needham, S. and Spence, T. 1996. *Refuse and Disposal at Area 16 East, Runnymede*. London: British Museum Press.

Needham, S. and Spence, T. 1997. Refuse and the Formation of Middens. *Antiquity* 71: 77–90.

Okely, J. 1983. *The Traveller Gypsies*. Cambridge: Cambridge University Press.

Pálsson, G. 1996. Human–Environmental Relations: Orientalism, Paternalism and Communalism. In Descola, P. and Pálsson, G. (eds), *Nature and Society: Anthropological Perspectives*. London: Routledge, pp. 63–81.

Papworth, M. 1992. Excavation and Survey of Bronze Age Sites in the Badbury Area, Kingston Lacy Estate. *Dorset Natural History and Archaeological Society* 114: 47–76.

Parker Pearson, M. 1982. Mortuary Practices, Society and Ideology: An Ethnoarchaeological Study. In Hodder, I. (ed.), *Symbolic and Structural Archaeology*. Cambridge: Cambridge University Press, pp. 99–113.

Parker Pearson, M. and Richards, C. 1994. Architecture and Order: Spatial Representation and Archaeology. In Parker Pearson, M. and Richards, C. (eds), *Architecture and Order: Approaches to Social Space*. London: Routledge, pp. 38–72.

Piggott, S. 1940. Timber Circles: A Re-examination. *Archaeological Journal* 96: 192–222.

Pollard, J. 1992. The Sanctuary, Overton Hill, Wiltshire: a Re-examination. *Proceedings of the Prehistoric Society* 58: 213–26.

Popper, K. 1963. *Conjectures and Refutations*. London: Routledge and Kegan Paul.

Radcliffe-Brown, A.R. 1952. *Structure and Function in Primitive Society: Essays and Addresses*. London: Cohen and West.

Ratcliffe-Densham, H.B.A. and Ratcliffe-Densham, M.M. 1961. An Anomalous Earthwork of the Late Bronze Age on Cock Hill. *Sussex Archaeological Collections* 99: 78–101.

Reid, A. and Maclean, R. 1995. Symbolism and the Social Contexts of Iron Production in Karagwe. *World Archaeology* 27: 144–61.

Renfrew, A.C. 1985. *The Archaeology of Cult: The Sanctuary at Phylakopi*. London: British School of Archaeology at Athens.

Richards, C. and Thomas, J. 1984. Ritual Activity and Structured Deposition in Later Neolithic Wessex. In Bradley, R. and Gardiner, J. (eds), *Neolithic Studies: A Review of Some Recent Work*. British Archaeological Reports, British Series 133. Oxford: BAR, pp. 189–218.

Russell, M. 1996. Problems of Phasing: A Reconsideration of the Black Patch Middle Bronze Age 'Nucleated Village'. *Oxford Archaeological Journal* 15: 33–8.

Schefold, R. 1982. The Efficacious Symbol. In de Josselin de Jong, P.E. and Schwimmer, E. (eds), *Symbolic Anthropology in the Netherlands*. The Hague: Nijhoff, pp. 125–42.

Schiffer, M. 1987. *Formation Processes of the Archaeological Record*. Albuquerque: University of New Mexico Press.

Schulte Nordholt, H.G. and Herman, G. 1980. The Symbolic Classification of the Atoni of Timor. In Fox, J.J. (ed.), *The Flow of Life: Essays on Eastern Indonesia*. Cambridge, MA: Harvard University Press, pp. 231–47.

Shanks, M. and Tilley, C. 1982. Ideology, Symbolic Power and Ritual Communication – A Reinterpretation of Neolithic Mortuary Practices. In Hodder, I. (ed.), *Symbolic and Structural Archaeology*. Cambridge: Cambridge University Press, pp. 129–54.

Sillar, B. 1996. The Dead and the Drying: Techniques for Transforming People and Things in the Andes. *Journal of Material Culture* 1: 259–89.

Smith, I.F. 1965. Excavation of a Bell Barrow, Avebury G55. *Wiltshire Archaeological and Natural History Magazine* 60: 24–46.

Sperber, D. 1975. *Rethinking Symbolism*. Cambridge: Cambridge University Press.

Stone, J.F.S. 1936. An Enclosure on Boscombe Down East. *Wiltshire Archaeological and Natural History Magazine* 47: 466–89.

Tambiah, S.J. 1990. *Magic, Science, Religion and the Scope of Rationality*. Cambridge: Cambridge University Press.

Thomas, J. 1991. *Rethinking the Neolithic*. Cambridge: Cambridge University Press.

Thomas, J. 1993. The Politics of Vision and Archaeologies of Landscape. In Bender, B. (ed.), *Landscape: Politics and Perspectives*. Oxford: Berg, pp. 19–48.

Thomas, J. 1996. *Time, Culture and Identity: An Interpretive Archaeology*. London: Routledge.

Thompson, M. 1979. *Rubbish Theory: The Creation and Destruction of Value*. Oxford: Oxford University Press.

Turner, B.S. 1992. *Regulating Bodies: Essays in Medical Sociology*. London: Routledge.

Turner, V. 1967. *The Forest of Symbols: Aspects of Ndembu Ritual*. Ithaca, NY: Cornell University Press.

Wainwright, G.J. 1979. *Mount Pleasant, Dorset: Excavations 1970–1971*. Reports of the Research Committee of the Society of Antiquaries of London 37. London: Society of Antiquaries of London.

Waterson, R. 1990. *The Living House: An Anthropology of Architecture in Southeast Asia*. Oxford: Oxford University Press.

Whittle, A. 1980. Two Neolithics? Part 2. *Current Archaeology* 71: 371–3.

Winch, P. 1970. Understanding a Primitive Society. In Wilson, B.R. (ed.), *Rationality*. Oxford: Blackwell, pp. 78–111.

Wymer, J.J. and Brown, N.R. 1995. *Excavations at North Shoebury: Settlement and Economy in South-East Essex, 1500 BC–AD 1500*. East Anglian Archaeology Monograph 75. Chelmsford: Essex County Council Archaeology Section, Planning Department.

Chapter 18

Changing identities in the Arabian Gulf

Archaeology, religion, and ethnicity in context

Timothy Insoll

Introduction

The archaeological recognition of multiple and changing identities in the Gulf is difficult, perhaps more so than in many other parts of the world, as it was, and still is in many instances, fraught with political difficulties. Even the title of this chapter is not neutral because the use of the term 'Arabian Gulf' represents one of two options, the other being 'Persian Gulf'; both of which have ethnic, i.e. relating to Persians and Arabs, and by implication, political connotations, namely whose Gulf is being referred to: Persia (Iran) or Arabia? Here the term Arabian Gulf will be used, not because this author is privileging one claim over another, but merely because much of the evidence considered originates, and is viewed, so to speak, from the Arabian shore.

Such choices as 'Persian' or 'Arabian' Gulf, petty as they might seem, are a reflection of the ambivalent status of identity in the Gulf region, identities as expressed in religious, social, ethnic, or gender terms – depending from which perspective the construct of identity is viewed. The physical and ideological complexities of identity in the Gulf region are considered in some detail below, but it is also necessary to state that the study of multiple identities/diversity has also been used in itself for political purposes as well. For example Fuller and Francke (1999: 4) describe how a 'divide and rule' approach, built upon the pillars of diversity, was 'advocated by some Israeli strategists over past decades' in the Middle East. It is also certainly the case that older Orientalist approaches to the study of regions such as the Arabian Gulf created or amplified, again as Fuller and Francke (ibid.) note, differences within Muslim (the majority group) society for the sake of creating 'difference' and the 'other' (see also Said 1978 and Meskell 1998: 4–5 for a critique thereof).

Equally, from another perspective, the study of multiple identities and diversity from archaeological or other data has also been criticized by elements of the Muslim community. Specifically by what Denny (1985: 65) refers to as the guardians of 'normative' Islam who consider such studies, perhaps into unorthodox practices, syncretism, or 'heresy' as 'an attempt to undermine and discredit what Muslims hold to be sacred' (ibid.). These are issues which this author has had to contend with in writing about Islam (Insoll 1999a), for though there exist the immutable elements of being Muslim, what have been termed 'structuring principles' (ibid.: 13), myriad diversity and manifestations of different, changing, and multiple identities within the overall entity which is Islam also undeniably exist.

Theoretical and methodological frameworks

This in turn leads into a broader consideration of what constitutes identity. The 'rigidity of Western taxonomizing' has recently been critiqued from an archaeological perspective by Meskell (2001: 187; and see this volume) drawing upon similar criticisms made by Foucault (1977). This is a valid statement, but many of the identity categories/groups which exist today in the Arabian Gulf owe little or nothing to Western influence or process, especially the supra-categories, the relatively recent creations of national identity, subsuming, and it is often hoped by those that promote them, wiping away or homogenizing the greater diversity within under a national ethos. Thus issues of what Jenkins (1994: 198–9) refers to as 'internal' versus 'external' definition have to be considered as well.

Jenkins's (ibid.) definition relates, he argues, to two different 'labels': internally defined groups and externally defined categories. Both of these are entities which are of relevance within the Arabian Gulf, but the question can be asked as to whether such seemingly clear-cut labels are really so strictly defined in terms of internal versus external generation? This is an issue which will be returned to later with recourse to the archaeological data from Bahrain. Essentially the recognition of complexity and variability are key in looking at multiple identities, both within elements of identity, such as ethnicity, as Barth (1969: 14) has noted, but also between various elements as well. Hence in this respect to attempt to impose from the outside (the perspective of this author) one particular approach in interpreting identities based upon archaeological evidence is flawed. A variety of strategies are certainly employed today, and were probably similarly utilized in the past. Thus the subtleties which are inevitably manifest in the archaeological record preclude a singular theoretical approach. This is a point made with the proviso added that this situation could change as more archaeological research and indeed greater understanding of the processes of identity creation, sustenance, and manifestation in the Gulf in general is completed.

Yet besides acknowledging the existence of variability and complexity, it is also vital to reiterate that issues of who defines what – literally what comprises the essence of identity – are considered as well. The role of nationalism cannot be understated in the Arabian Gulf, an area where, following the withdrawal of colonial power/relationships (as for example by the British in the 1960s), newly independent states, not necessarily that differentiated from one another, had to redefine themselves along national lines. Equally, on the Arabian shore of the Gulf, 'pan-Arabism' (Fuller and Francke 1999: 38) was a further factor which had to be negotiated along with national identity. The latter is sometimes in conflict with the former, but the latter is also of significance in how history and the past, including past identities, were presented.

While academic works might adopt a neutral tone, one of non-recognition of identities, coffee-table books abound (see for example Vine 1993; Nowell 1999; Anon n.d.) which to greater or lesser degrees use archaeological and historical materials to reinforce, create, and in many instances project national identities far back into the past. Concerning Bahrain, for instance, one gets references to 'Bahraini' people in the third millennium BC (Nowell 1999: 12), rather than to the more factually correct 'inhabitants of Dilmun', the polity in existence on the island at the time. These might seem like minor concerns but as part of the overall national 'strategy' they make the recognition of the multiple ingredients of the national 'soup' difficult to achieve for a variety of reasons further outlined below. Indeed they form part of what Bernard Lewis (1973: 60) has termed, 'the twilight world of myth and fantasy' which surrounds the creation of national history and identity in much of the Middle East.

The relationship between national identity and the past has been well-investigated by archaeologists and historians (see for example Hobsbawm and Ranger 1983; Shennan 1989; Arnold 1990), though not to the same extent in the Arabian Gulf (for an exception see Potts 1998). Meanwhile the archaeology of facets of identity has also been well investigated (Meskell 2001), notably gender (Gero and Conkey 1991; Gilchrist 1999), or ethnicity (Jones 1997). However, that of religious identity has rarely at all been considered (Insoll 1999b, 2001, 2004). This is a critical omission within the Arabian Gulf where religion, especially, but not exclusively, Islam, is of critical importance, being what could be termed the structuring structure of identity within which categories such as ethnicity and gender are slotted. Certainly within Islamic philosophy the religion supersedes ethnicity, colour, and class in the creation and perpetuation of the *Ummah*, the ideal Islamic community (Waines 1995; Insoll 1999a: 10).

The predominance of ethnicity and gender within archaeological discourse on identities is probably more a reflection of the priorities of the scholars themselves rather than necessarily an approximation of past reality (Insoll 2004). Thus, for example, Jones (1997: 110), in reviewing scholarship pertaining to the changes of ethnic boundaries and identity which can take place, indicates that this has predominantly been assessed with regard to the 'strategic manipulation of identity with relation to economic and political relations'. The absence of religion within such mechanisms of identity change, certainly for the Arabian Gulf (and much else of the world), means that reconstructions of the past based on such limiting theoretical premises would be flawed.

Equally in archaeological investigations of identities in general, so-called 'single-issue questions' (Meskell 2001: 187) have tended to be the focus of research. The multiple strands of identity are rarely considered together, and thus here an attempt will be made to rectify this with reference to the Arabian Gulf. Consequently, once again, the cautionary point made above is valid, and can be reiterated, namely that a singular focus involving either the imposition of a particular theoretical approach in the pursuit of interpreting identity, or a focus upon one identity 'strand' within the Arabian Gulf is not yet valid. This is primarily because the research completed thus far (archaeological and otherwise) on identity in this region has still to fully explore the dimensions of variability and complexity which exist, and without this being better delimited such an exercise is largely futile.

Hence this chapter provides a broad overview of the archaeology of identities in the Arabian Gulf and a range of examples are thus considered, which in terms of geographical range are drawn from various parts of the Gulf region as a whole. Though this said, special attention will be paid to Bahrain. The reasons for this being that, first, Bahrain has been the focus of one of the author's recently completed research projects (Insoll 2005), and, second, as it is one of the most open states in the Gulf region, it is thus amenable to such research.

Chronologically the Early and Middle Islamic periods will be the primary focus of attention, correlating approximately with the medieval period in European terms.

However, as well as archaeological and historical perspectives on identities, contemporary ones must also be considered, for as already noted present concerns have greatly influenced reconstructions of past identities, and, to a lesser degree, vice versa. Finally the issue of why identity – let alone multiple identities – has been ignored by archaeologists in the Gulf, even where the evidence might well allow such an investigation (see for example Sasaki 1990; Kennet 1997; King 1998), will be returned to, and a brief consideration provided of why the initiative now lies with archaeologists working in the Gulf region to adequately theorize their own material in relation to identities.

Contemporary perspectives on identities

Numerous permutations of identity are possible in the Arabian Gulf today based upon region, nationality, tribe, clan, religion, gender, profession, class, ethnicity, language, and other variables (Fuller and Francke 1999: 9). Examples of labels include: Arab, Arab Muslim, Arab Shi'ah, Ibadi, Omani, Arab Sunni, Bahraini, Iranian, Wahabi, Saudi, Kuwaiti, Shi'ah, Muslim, Christian, Hindu, male, female, foreign archaeologist, indigenous archaeologist. Indeed these are all labels which apply within the present, and are far from exhaustive. Syncretic identities might also be created (Shaw and Stewart 1994), blended from heterogeneous elements and crosscutting categories. The fusing of Muslim and traditional African religious practices evident in sub-Saharan Africa, but also exported to the Gulf by the slave trade, and seemingly manifest in aspects of Sufi practice, provides a case in point (Insoll 2003a). Contemporary observations indicate that a variety of identities can be, and are, manifest at the same time depending on the context of the individual in the Gulf.

Yet these multiple identities need not all be on simultaneous display either. Elements might be suppressed for political or other reasons, or more effort might be put into maintaining one aspect of identity depending upon who the individual or community expressing and reading the identities is: in other words what Barth (1969: 14) refers to in the context of ethnicity as the 'varying amounts and forms of content (given) in different socio-cultural systems'. A hypothetical illustration of this is provided by considering how in the Gulf some individuals will actively strive to enforce their Muslim identity as a way of (as it ideally should be within Islam as mentioned) cancelling out or lessening their ethnic identity – someone of Bangladeshi or Indian origin perhaps. An Arab, however, might take his or her Muslim identity as given, and instead put effort into maintaining their Arab identity.

The element of choice in what to suppress and what to give prominence to in terms of identity might not be there either. In Saudi Arabia, for instance, religious freedom does not exist, and it is difficult to be other than what everyone else is – a Muslim, preferably of the Sunni, Wahabi sect. Here identity, though multiple identities obviously exist as everywhere else, is actively controlled. In fact what occurs in Saudi Arabia is what Jenkins (1994: 217) describes as 'the capacity of one group of people to define effectively or to constitute the conditions of experience experienced by another'. Even Shi'ah Muslims report repression in Saudi Arabia. Hansen (1968: 27) refers to the Wahabis as the 'antagonists of the Shi'ites'; while more recently Fuller and Francke (1999: 184) have described the Saudi Shi'ah as suffering from what they term 'cultural discrimination'. The 'manifold relations of power' described so eloquently by Foucault

(1977: 93) are in operation – relations of power which accompany and are structured by the prevailing 'discourse'.

This discourse can, obviously, have archaeological repercussions. Bibby (1996: 154) describes how the Shi'ah shrine of al-Khidr on Failaka Island off Kuwait had been repeatedly pulled down by the Kuwaiti authorities as they 'could hardly tolerate a practice which smacked strongly of idolatry' – the objection being to the Shi'ah practice of sacrificing to the saint at this shrine. Bibby (ibid.) describes the interior as full of chicken and sheep bones, and the central stone pillar 'smeared with a dark stickiness which can hardly have been anything other than blood'. Bibby's account refers to the 1950s, yet today the 25–30 per cent of the Kuwaiti population who are Shi'ah are described as encountering little persecution, integrated into economic life, and free to practise their religion (Fuller and Francke 1999: 155). The prevailing discourse has altered, assisted perhaps by the invasion of Kuwait by Iraq and the ensuing Gulf War.

Thus in other areas of the Arabian Gulf, outside Saudi Arabia, the expression of multiple identities or identities contrary to the majority is easier – in Bahrain for example. A Bahraini has a gender, a nationality, but can also be an Arab, or claim, or be assigned, other ethnic origins, be of noble or other descent, be Muslim, of Sunni or Shi'ah affiliation, or more rarely be a Christian or a Hindu. Can Bahrain then be said to be closer to the Islamic ideal as regards the recognition or rather non-suppression of identity?

The ideal has already been described: an Islamic community devoid of distinction, and within Islam the existence of other religious minorities, 'peoples of the book', such as Christians and Jews, upon payment of a tax, should, theoretically, be tolerated. Lewis (1973: 135) remarks upon the absence of persecution of other faiths in Classical Islam, but not the absence of discrimination – for Islam 'insisted on the privileged superiority of the true believer in this world as well as in the next'. Similarly there is, ideally, an absence of colour consciousness within Islam, and certainly a lack of 'institutionalized racism' (Segal 2001: 61) in comparison to parts of predominantly Christian North America for example. A person of African descent can be, unquestionably, an Arab.

The fluidity of identity labels with reference to ethnicity can certainly be seen within Bahrain if gazetteers and census data from the last 100 years or so are consulted. Under the British-compiled 'Gazetteer of the Persian Gulf' (Lorimer 1908: 241) of the early twentieth century, one sees a preoccupation with colour, 'negroes' (sic) are described as numerous, composed of both free and enslaved; while within the 1991 census data reported by Seikaly (1994: 418) any colour reference has disappeared. A point also made by Seikaly (ibid.: 417) helps to explain this change, though her explanation relates to the equal preponderance given to tribal groups in earlier census data, namely that such classification was a result of British policies of control and dominance. To classify was (is) to control; thus providing, once again, a return to Foucault's (1977) notion of discourses of power.

Similar short-term identity change is seen in the categorization of the majority Shi'ah population of Bahrain (c. 65–70 per cent of the population in 1991 [Seikaly 1994: 419]). Lorimer (1908: 248) refers to the 'Bahranis' or 'Baharinah' as the village-dwelling population whose situation is 'little better than one of serfdom'. Whereas James Belgrave (1954: 29), the son of the then-long-standing British advisor to the ruler of Bahrain, also refers to the 'Baharna' as the 'original' inhabitants of the islands who were formerly 'second class citizens' but who 'today [the 1950s] take an active part in all walks of life in Bahrain'. While Hansen (1968: 22) in her anthropological study of the predominantly Shi'ah village of Saar in 1960 refers to two strata of population, Persian and Arab, or Shi'ah and Sunni, with the villagers she studied not then describing themselves as Arab. Finally Seikaly (1994: 419) describes the same group as Shi'ah Arabs. Thus over the span of 100 years we have what are first an indigenous named group become Persians and finally Arabs.

In this latter example identity change is less easy to ascribe to British policy, but rather to local issues of subordination and domination. These include regional power struggles pivoting around former Iranian claims to control of Bahrain (Hansen 1968: 19), as well as relations between the ruling family and the Shi'ah elements of the population. The ruling family, the Al-Khalifa, who conquered the islands in the late eighteenth century are Sunni Arabs of impeccable pure Bedu origin from Najd in Central Arabia and related also to the ruling families of Saudi Arabia and Kuwait (Scarce 1985: 21). Therefore here there was evidently something of a collision between Sunni and Shi'ah, and the settled and the sown.

In the examples just discussed, ethnicity, and religion and ethnicity combined, were factors of importance. Thus far gender has been neglected. The importance of gender studies in archaeology in general has already been noted as an identity which has merited much research recently. Within the Arabian Gulf, and within Islamic studies, the study of contemporary gender, largely concerned with women, has also become increasingly important (Beck and Keddie 1978; L. Ahmed 1992; Seikaly 1994). The exception, unfortunately, is provided by archaeology, which serves up largely undifferentiated fare as regards gender. Its recognition, where achieved, has been accidental rather than intentional, whereas research concerned with the archaeology of sexual identity in the Arabian Gulf has yet to be pursued. There is only one recognized sexual orientation in the region, and other avenues of research into this aspect of identity have yet to be explored.

The point of the contemporary examples just considered is to indicate that even within a relatively short space of time identity categorization can shift immensely. Equally recent changes in identity ascription and the policies behind them, as will be considered, can have fundamental implications for what may or may not be researched. As archaeologists we have this, and all the other factors already discussed, to contend with in the pursuit of the recognition of past complex and variable identity.

Historical and archaeological dimensions of identities

Yet the situation is not one of despair, even if to the already mentioned contemporary labels of identity we must add extra categories with a solely historical and archaeological dimension, thereby further complicating the task. Examples of these could include Jew, Carmathian, Sasanian/Zoroastrian, Nestorian Christian, Zanj/slave, and to examine these it is required to turn to the archaeological evidence from Bahrain. However, owing to the paucity of relevant comparative interpretation and/or published data it is also necessary to choose examples from elsewhere around the Gulf. It should also further be noted that owing to the nature of the data, the examples discussed favour, predominantly, the dimensions of religious and ethnic identity.

Christian identity

The archaeology of Christianity within the Arabian Gulf is in its infancy. This is due to various reasons including the overall lack of interpretation of any form within relevant archaeology (see for example the Saudi journal *Atlal*). Other reasons include an absence of relevant research, and as Potts (1998: 196) notes, a general lack of comprehension among inhabitants of the Gulf as to how 'extensively Nestorian Christianity was practiced in the area even after the Islamic conquest'. But Christian communities there were, including Nestorian bishoprics, recorded for Bahrain, Tarut (Saudi Arabia), and possibly Qatar in the fifth century AD (Larsen 1983: 59–60). Otherwise, to provide a historical outline of Christianity in the Arabian Gulf here is unnecessary as it is a subject which has already been more than adequately summarized by Potts (1990: 241–7).

This said, archaeological indication of the presence of these former Nestorian Christian communities is variable and within Bahrain has not yet been conclusively found (see Potts 1985: 705). For example the identification of three tombstones from Bahrain as probably Christian has been seriously questioned (Beaucamp and Robin 1983: 187), while other traces of a Christian presence, '*auraient disparu aujourd'hui*' (ibid.). However, these communities have left an archaeological legacy elsewhere in the Gulf. Survey on the islands off the coast of Abu Dhabi in the United Arab Emirates, for example, has found remains of buildings including courtyard houses and fragments of carved and moulded plaster dated to the sixth to seventh centuries on Sir Bani Yas Island which might be linked with a Nestorian diocese based in this area in the same period (King 1998: 18–27). Although this identification as yet remains unproven, more definite indications of these Christian communities have been reported from Saudi Arabia (Langfeldt 1994). These include the remains of a church complete with four cross impressions set into its western wall, and associated monastic cells and Christian burials at Jubail in the Eastern Province. Not an isolated instance either, for a further church has also been described as found at Thaj, as well as a Christian cemetery at al-Hinnah, both also within the Eastern Province.

Langfeldt (1994: 52) describes the controversy generated over these finds, attesting as they did to an unwelcome facet of identity in Saudi Arabia, for reasons already alluded to above. He mentions how access to the monuments was restricted, and how the church in Jubail supposedly had its impressed crosses obliterated. Besides vandalism, the presence of these Christian remains caused a debate over what exactly they signified. Langfeldt (ibid.: 52, 57) outlines how the Saudi Department of Antiquities stated, 'that the church was nothing but a foreign seafarer's chapel of short chronological duration, ending with the arrival of the Islamic faith in AD 634'. This was an interpretation at odds with his own, namely that it represented, 'either a typical parish or monastic structure situated within a stable Christian community and existing for a considerable period of time both before and after AD 630, not unlikely to have been a couple of centuries in either direction'. Even allowing for the limited available data, Langfeldt's interpretation is far more convincing within the historical framework for Christianity within the region (see Potts 1990), but the issue as to the extent and duration of Christian occupation on the eastern coast of Saudi Arabia will only be settled by further research, and thus awaits Saudi permission.

Yet should the continuation of Christian communities in the Arabian Gulf after the arrival of Islam really be so surprising? The answer is negative. Here some aspect of continuity in religious identity is indicated, but one which remains little understood and investigated for various reasons. In this respect Talal Asad's (1986: 3) relevant statement that 'Christianity and Judaism are also indigenous to the region' (the Middle East) is being ignored, but not because, as he continues, 'it is only Muslim belief and practice that western anthropologists appear to be interested in' – rather than lack of interest, it is because in certain instances the archaeological and historical investigation of other elements of identity is not currently possible.

Other identities

The notion of exploring Jewish identity within the archaeological record of the Arabian Gulf might also prove politically controversial. As far as this author is aware this has not yet been undertaken, but equally the existence of Jewish communities is historically attested; for example Potts (1990: 262) describes how Jewish-run taverns serving Christian clientele were still in existence in Eastern Arabia in the 670s, i.e. as has been described, after the acceptance of Islam in the region. While Lorimer (1915: 2, 381) refers to there being, 1,200 years later, approximately 200 Jews in Kuwait, others on the Persian coast, and about 50 in Bahrain. It is reasonable to suggest that some archaeological legacy of this small community might have survived.

The same suggestion can be made for archaeological evidence attesting to Sasanian identity. This, however, is a more ambivalent category for it defines an empire of Persian origin, a polity which appeared in the third century AD when the first Sasanian king, Ardashir I, 'overthrew the remaining Parthians in AD 224 and began a four hundred year dynasty' (Larsen 1983: 58). Thus Sasanian is not a specific religious, ethnic, or other identity, but is a label subsuming multiple identities (see for example Simpson 2000: 58). However, this statement can be qualified by possibly isolating Persian (Iranian) associations and links between the Sasanian elite and the Zoroastrian religion as a 'state religion' (Boyce 1991: 172), as more specific defining criteria linked with a specific 'Sasanian' identity.

Aspects of research into Sasanian archaeology have been undertaken to varying degrees in different areas of the Arabian Gulf (see for example Kennet 1997; King 1998), but in general Potts (1990: 263) is quite correct in noting that periods earlier than the Sasanian have been the primary focus of archaeological attention. To this must be added the factor of a lack of relevant archaeological evidence in many areas attesting to a Sasanian presence. On Bahrain for example although Salles might note that historical sources appear to 'highlight the logical integration of the archipelago in the Sasanian empire' (1999: 146), no trace of a Sasanian presence was found during the recent excavations completed in the early Islamic capital, Bilad al-Qadim (Insoll 2005). This is an area where such indications might be expected, but these were absent, other than a couple of sherds of possible Hellenistic or Partho-Sasanian date – the latter hardly providing a conclusive basis from which to conjecture the presence of Sasanian occupation in Bilad al-Qadim.

Sasanian material is rare from other sites in Bahrain as well (see Potts 1990: 124–5), but includes some sherds of pottery recovered, for example, from Qala'at al-Bahrain (S.F. Andersen, pers. comm.; Højlund 1994), and from Barbar Temple (Andersen and Kennet 2003). The latter is a site which also yielded nine 'Parthian-Sasanian' sculptural fragments and one piece of inscription similarly ascribed a 'late pre-Islamic' attribution (Anon 2003: 311). A possible fire temple has also been reported as being identified at Saar according to a display panel and photograph in the Bahrain National Museum. The caption of this panel relates that

> a building excavated at Sar [*sic*] may, from its plan, be a Zoroastrian temple. The chief ceremony was the sacrifice before the holy fire in a central room surrounded by narrow passageways. The finds include a silver coin with a fire altar on the reverse, and on its obverse the king – probably Kavad I (488–531 AD) known for his religious zeal.
>
> (personal observation 29/3/04)

However, other details of this 'fire temple' are, as yet, unpublished.

But in general the Sasanians provide something of a historical and archaeological conundrum in Bahrain at least, an issue compounded by the fact that on Bahrain their history, identity, and archaeology are sometimes subsumed under the label 'Tylos'. This is described as 'Greek' (Nowell 1999: 14) or 'Hellenistic' (Cabana 1999: 15) in origin and is usually defined as encompassing the period between *c.* 330 BC to AD 622–30 (Nowell 1999: 14): therefore from the era of Alexander the Great's passage to the north through the Persian empire to the coming of Islam. In this respect it could be suggested that it is a wholly inappropriate and pointless label to apply to such a diverse range of archaeological and historical material.

Similarly, even if subdivided, as it often is into Early, Middle, and Late Tylos, it could also be seen to be ineffectual, with Hellenistic, Parthian, and Sasanian perhaps being more viable alternatives. However, it has to be recognized that the lack of sources (Salles 1999: 149) frustrates our understanding of Sasanian history, archaeology, and identity, making its attribution also problematic, but does this excuse this cultural misnomer of 'Tylos', equivalent, it could be suggested, to extending the Roman period in Britain by some 500 years. It could be asked, then, why does the label 'Tylos' exist? Various suggestions could be made: lack of interest, absence of relevant research, habit, echoes of fears over labelling the past as 'Persian', all could be suggested as possible contributing factors. Yet it is correct that 'Tylos' is to a degree neutral (S.F. Andersen, pers. comm.; F. Højlund, pers. comm.), and alternatives such as 'Parthian' or 'Sasanian' might be an overstatement with regard to the available evidence. Although this is reasonable, it can be further suggested that a search for alternatives might be useful, even if it means using statements such as 'Bahrain in the fourth to seventh centuries AD or CE', rather than 'Late Tylos' or 'Sasanian'.

Sasanian might be an ambiguous label, as described, with regard to the elements of identity which it includes; Indian as another identity category might be less so. Or is it? All the identities considered contain elements of ambiguity and overlap, with 'Indian', for instance, covering a wide range of ethnic, religious, and cultural domains. These identity categories can have, as this volume explores, multiple dimensions, and interestingly Potts (1998: 196) describes how the ascription of 'Indian' to archaeological contexts in the Gulf can again engender concern. He relates how the evidence for Harappan (*c.* 2500–2000 BC) contacts found in Oman has led to fears by contemporary Omanis that this could lead to claims by expatriate Indian/Pakistani inhabitants that the original pre-Arab population was 'Hindi'.

In the much later Islamic era evidence for Indian contacts with, and more importantly presence in, the Gulf is found. This usually comprises fragments of cooking vessels of Indian origin interpreted as being an unlikely item of trade, but rather the residue of cooking activities by Indian seafarers, merchants, or workers using vessels they were familar with (Kervran 1996; Insoll 2005). At the group of sites known as Julfar in Ras al-Khaimah (United Arab Emirates), Hansman (1985: 48) suggests that the presence of sherds from such wares in levels dated to the fourteenth to eighteenth centuries attests to the 'presence of Indian workers or seafarers at Julfar in earlier centuries'. Similarly in the excavations in Bilad al-Qadim in Bahrain, a few sherds of Indian coarse wares were found (Insoll 2005). These might provide a handle on possible ethnic identity, if this is what in fact they indicate, but little more. We cannot say if they were used by Indian Muslims or Hindus for example, or by male or female. However, they might seemingly attest, as today, to the presence of expatriate workers from the Indian subcontinent in Bahrain and elsewhere in the Arabian Gulf, though this remains unproven. The presence of the Chinese and other Far Eastern ceramics also found, however, are unlikely to be interpreted in the same way: for these were prestige trade items shipped by Arab and other merchants (Tampoe 1989), not everyday unglazed ceramics which might have been brought by the communities who used them.

The closer one looks at the archaeology of the Gulf, the more it seems to have been a 'melting-pot' (Potts 1990: 151) of identities. Yet, as noted, some are much more difficult than others to identify and that of the African presence provides a case in point. This would have been largely, but not exclusively, composed of slaves. The numbers of African slaves employed in the Gulf, certainly in Mesopotamia, were vast. The Zanj (a generic term for slaves from East Africa) were employed in large gangs of between 500 and 5,000 workers to prepare the ground for cultivation in the salt flats of southern Mesopotamia (Freeman-Grenville 1975: 117); this was an occupation which exposed them to extreme privations and harsh conditions. As a reaction they revolted several times, possibly in 694, in 765, and again in 869–883. The last revolt is generally regarded as the most serious and involved between 100,000 and 300,000 slaves, and required 50,000 soldiers to suppress it (Afolayan 1998: 713). To this earlier historical dimension of African identity within the Gulf could be added Segal's (2001: 146) statement that in Oman in 1840 an estimated one in three of the population of 800,000 was black. Colour classification is not at all useful as an identity criteria as already noted, but some of this sizeable figure must have been of African origin, an interpretation lent support by Oman's strong links with Zanzibar for example.

These are vast numbers of people, possibly with their own cultural traditions and material culture, albeit perhaps in a syncretic or creolized form (Insoll 2003a). However, their presence within the reported archaeological record is negative. Slavery, for instance, is one of the great archaeological invisibles of the trade of the Islamic world (Insoll 1996), but equally any archaeological manifestations, enslaved or otherwise, of an African identity, in itself another category encompassing great diversity and multiple forms, are lacking in the Arabian Gulf. Yet ethnographic and anthropological sources tell us about communities of African origin on Bahrain. Al-Khan (1991: 8), for example, describes the performers of the *leewah* collective dances as coming to Bahrain from East Africa, 'not directly, but rather through the Omanis who settled in Bahrain to make a living'. Regardless of whether they reached Bahrain directly, indirectly, free or enslaved, the African origin of the *leewah* groups is seemingly indisputable, and they are considered (and consider themselves) as ethnically closed groups. Hence we have various 'clues' indicating African contacts and identity, but archaeologically further research is needed on investigating this as-yet little understood aspect of identity.

Muslim identity

It could be assumed that Muslim identity must present an easier facet of identity to investigate through archaeological evidence in the Arabian Gulf. But, needless to say, it does not: first, because it can subsume many of the identity categories already considered – African or Indian for example, and second because it has been poorly served by archaeologists and those concerned with heritage presentation. Islam is frequently presented as devoid of agency, people, life, identity, variety, or complexity. It is moulded in archaeology and museums in the Gulf (and elsewhere) largely in a sterile and idealistic way that bears little resemblance to the true complexities of Islamic history. The past is presented as non-challenging, as if there is potentially nothing foreign or different about it (personal observation).

Other than a rapid transit through a series of dynasties reduced to chronological labels, the presentation of Islam is frequently achieved as almost devoid of time. This is surprising, as most religions are explicitly concerned with time, controlled, for instance, through the ritual cycle (Bell 1997). While in Islam there is of course the imposition of a new calendar, 'arranged, without intercalation, to be independent not only of the old Arabian lunar year but especially of all solar reckoning which was traditionally linked to the structures of agricultural society and religion' (Denny 1985: 71). Thus Muslim identity is structured through time, both individual and community time, and manifest in prayer times, pilgrimage, fasting, and festival time (Insoll 1999a).

Another failing within Islamic archaeology is that Muslim identity is often presented as 'mono-religious'; complexity is not acknowledged (see Fuller and Francke 1999). One might get a link between Islamic practice and material culture – mosques + Muslim burials = Islam (Insoll 1999a) – but the net result is an archaeology devoid of sects, gender, heresy, complexity, or difference. These are, however, aspects of identity approachable through archaeology in the Arabian Gulf. The existence of the Shi'ah, for instance, once the evidence is sifted, can be acknowledged archaeologically. Porter (2001: 202) describes prayer stones, compressed blocks of earth from the Shi'ah shrine of Najaf, which were recovered from the excavations at Bahrain Fort, as well as a seal stone cut with the names of the 12 Shi'ah Imams. A similar prayer stone is reported by Salles (1983: 99) as found at Barbar South, also on Bahrain, the latter bearing an inscription; *'une invocation religieuse à Ali'*. The reference to Ali being of importance in relating to one of the central figures of Shi'ah theology, considered by Shi'ites 'to be the only rightful successor to the Prophet' (Halm 1997: 7).

Space precludes a presentation of the origins and doctrines of Shi'ism (but see Halm 1997; Daftary 1998; Insoll 1999a: 20–1), but one key point needs to be made: that the origins of Shi'ism were firmly, according to Halm (1997: 684), within an Arab environment, in Iraq in the late seventh century, not as many stereotypes hold within a Persian one. In fact, as Lewis (1973: 219) notes, Shi'ah Islam was 'first carried to Persia by the Arabs themselves'. Hence it is as much part of the Arab cultural milieu as Sunni Islam, and not a foreign imposition.

Yet the differences between Sunni and Shi'ah Islam, besides that of the Imamate, or religious leadership, are in the end minimal. The Qur'an is central, the Five Pillars are the same, 'the Sunni ideal also holds for the Shi'ah' (A. Ahmed 1988: 57). The material differences denoting Sunni versus Shi'ah identity are not profound (see Insoll 2005). However, this said, the term 'Shi'ism' as an identity category in itself covers a range of movements. The comments just made refer to the majority 'Twelver' Shi'ism, a reference to belief in the 12 Imams, whereas 'Severner' Shi'ah movements, those that stop the line at the seventh Imam, Ismail, differ (see Daftary 1998); the schism in the overall Shi'ah community occurred over succession in the Imamate in the mid-eighth century (Petrushevsky 1985: 236).

Related to the reason just cited for the development of Severner or Isma'ili Shi'ism are further political factors: what Petrushevsky (1985: 235), admittedly writing from a Marxist perspective, describes as the result of a reaction to the 'class contradictions evident in the Caliphate', with inequality and feudalism on the increase. This occurred in the ninth to tenth centuries during the period of hegemony of the Abbasid Caliphate. The Abbasids initially arose as a social and political movement of seemingly inclusive persuasion (Ahsan 1979), promoting 'the universal religion (Islam) of a universal empire' (Lewis 1973: 222), but over time became more orthodox, Sunni orthodox, and were, according to Rippin (1990: 109), persecutors of the Shi'ah. Therefore a combination of social and religious reasons gave rise to new religious movements.

One of these was the Carmathians, an Isma'ili Shi'ah movement which controlled Bahrain (including, as the term Bahrain then referred to, a large part of the Eastern Province of Saudi Arabia as well), from circa the end of the first quarter of the tenth through to the late eleventh centuries (Van Donzel 1994: 63). This, along with various other non-Sunni Muslim communities, was a movement which was branded as heretical by Sunni Muslims (see Daftary 1998: 22), and which does have, in comparison to majority Twelver Shi'ism, greater archaeological implications as regards the recognition of their specific identity. Historical sources, for example, describe their religious and social practices. Nasir-i-Khusraw, a Tajik Persian poet who visited part of the Carmathian state in the mid-eleventh century, refers to an absence of mosques in their domains, exceptional for Muslim communities, as well as their retailing and eating 'the flesh of every animal including cats and dogs' (Petrushevsky 1985: 247). Undoubtedly there is an aspect of exaggeration here in creating a demon out of a popularly perceived heretical movement; a movement that went so far as to carry off the Black Stone of the Ka'ba until a ransom was paid by the Abbasids for its return in the mid-tenth century (De Goeje 1862; Daftary 1988: 48). Yet other more prosaic information exists: Khusraw also describes how transactions were completed with baskets or sacks of lead tokens (Petrushevsky 1985; Insoll 2005).

At this point it could be asked what is the reason for this lengthy excursion into the historical particularities of the Arabian Gulf? The answer is that the struggles over religious, social, and political identities manifest in movements such as the Carmathians are evident archaeologically. On Bahrain various lead coins and weights were found which might have been linked, in part, as Khusraw relates, with Carmathian commerce (Insoll 2003b). These on their own are not necessarily convincing indicators of the former presence of this heretical movement, but are also contextualized by a Fatimid gold dinar which was found.

This coin along with two Abbasid gold issues also recovered could be read solely as signifiers of trade perhaps, and ascribed to a particular ruler and mint (for details see Insoll 2003b – they were issues of Abbasid Caliph Abu al-Abbas Saffah, AD 750–751; Abbasid Caliph Harun al-Rashid, AD 786–809; and Fatimid Caliph Nezar al-Azaiz, AD 989). However, they too are signifiers of identity, shifting affiliations, power, and control. The Fatimids were an Isma'ili Shi'ah dynasty, but much more powerful than the Carmathians, with whom they had a 'more or less constant, although often secret' alliance (Kervran 1982: 62) until the Carmathians were defeated by the Abd al-Qays in 1076. This coin would appear to be an indicator of such links – of Shi'ah identity and alliances manifest across large parts of the Muslim world – with the source of the dinar; it having been minted at Mansuriya near Kairouan in Tunisia thus indicating the extent of these connections.

Khusraw's aforementioned comment regarding Carmathian diet is also pertinent. Too often within the relevant archaeology of the Arabian Gulf and indeed in Islamic archaeology in general (Insoll 1999a: 94–9) the evidence for diet is either ignored, given short shrift, or treated as solely the residue of economic decisions. Within Bahrain it is possible, again, using the dietary evidence to suggest a possible link with the Carmathians. The presence of a male mandibular canine from a pig (Insoll 2005) in a context interpreted as associated with the period of Carmathian control (eleventh century) is interesting, as perhaps reflecting the Carmathians' eclectic diet. Yet the bulk of unorthodox dietary evidence – cat, dog, pig – does not date from the period of Carmathian control, contrary, perhaps, to expectations. Rather something more complex is indicated by the faunal remains recovered, possibly signifying a pragmatic position by a Muslim community towards obtaining sustenance in the face of impoverishment as seemingly indicated towards the end of the sequence, or alternatively a manifestation of more diverse, multiple identities as yet otherwise not understood.

These are just brief examples which have been provided drawn from this author's own archaeological research on Bahrain. Yet they serve to indicate that a complex Islamic archaeology is achievable which begins to show the multiple identities which can be manifest. However, no attention has been paid to gender or ethnicity. Both these elements of identity are also represented in the excavated sequences from Bahrain and the question can be asked as to who used the ovens found? The status and identity of a group producing pottery towards the end of the occupation sequence in the late twelfth to thirteenth centuries is also a perplexing one, as is the meaning and possible identity associations represented by an egg found buried beneath a floor (Insoll 2005). Issues revolving around the role of parody and emulation between and even within different identity groups, and the role of material culture therein, could also be considered. Essentially many questions remain and in the end it has to be admitted that at present we only reach an ambivalent position indicating multiple possibilities rather than final answers.

Yet equally the Bahraini evidence indicates that these categories are not necessarily bounded entities either. Many of these are identities which can overlap or which could be changed. All the seemingly clear-cut identity categories are in fact anything but, and modern labels are not necessarily useful for past populations. Risso (1989: 385) for instance describes how 'many eighteenth century inhabitants of the Iranian coast were of Arab background' but most had adopted the Persian language and Twelver Shi'ism. Would these people today call themselves Arabs or Persians? How does one define their past identities on the basis of archaeological evidence? Identity has thus to be considered within its wider regional and historical context. Unfortunately this has rarely, if at all, been examined within the Arabian Gulf region, where the practice of archaeology could be said, until recently, to resemble that of the bulk of Soviet and post-Soviet archaeology, described by Antony (2001: 627) as concerned with chronology and descriptive culture history, rather than the variable meanings of material culture, the nature of identity, and the dynamics of cultural change.

Conclusions

Again a question can be posed as to why such a situation has persisted. The practice of archaeology within the Arabian Gulf has been considered by Potts (1990, 1998) and he describes a range of reasons which could be adapted to answer this question. Issues such as who is funding archaeological research are of relevance, as is the existence of contract work in the Gulf. Both these could mean that fears over securing repeat funding/contracts might lead to self-censorship for real or imagined reasons. Equally even where external funding is in place similar fears over the issuing of research permits might also impinge upon how, if at all, issues of identity are approached via the archaeological data; to this can be added the simple factor of neglect. Other issues have already been described: national and political concerns for example. But here the Arabian Gulf can hardly be said to be unique; though perhaps the violent subjugation of some identities, the Shi'ah Marsh Arabs of Iraq after the first Gulf War, for instance, means that sensitivities in this region are greater.

From an external perspective, the obvious position of the author of this chapter, the situation as regards the archaeological examination of identity is improving. The recent reforms initiated by the ruler of Bahrain provide a case in point. New freedoms and democratic reforms can (and are) having an effect upon other areas, including archaeological practice and interpretation in the country. The completion of the recent archaeological project whose results have been alluded to above, funded in part by the Court of the Crown Prince as well as various companies on Bahrain, is an indication of this. The recording and interpretation of the archaeological data in their entirety has been actively encouraged, allied with, for example, the examination of other facets of identity. A survey of Shi'ah shrines was also completed, an urgent priority in the face of the rapid development Bahrain is undergoing – shrines which indicate facets of religious continuity, the results of which are only just beginning to be assimilated (Insoll 2005).

The initiative is now with the archaeologists and others who interpret the past to examine the multiple, sometimes complementary, sometimes conflicting identities which certainly exist today and have previously existed in the Arabian Gulf. An approach is needed which is both holistic yet at the same time does not deny the role of the individual in negotiating and ascribing identities – 'the dialectic of both structure and agency' (Dobres and Robb 2000: 8). We need to include all the actors in writing the past, in attempting to achieve, as much as possible, an end result resembling what Asad (1986: 11) describes as 'along the lines of an action play'.

However, as was stated earlier, there is no particular theoretical approach to identity which archaeologists can currently privilege in its application within the Gulf. Rather each specific context needs examining and the relevant possibilities considering from a broad perspective, a situation which will persist until the body of comparative data expands. But this said, a useful recurring notion which can be isolated is related to Jenkins's (1994: 198–9) definition of two different identity 'labels': those of internally defined groups and externally defined categories. However, this is most usefully adapted to a broader perspective invoking the concept of dualism – the simultaneous creation of identity within the individual and its simultaneous imposition from outside as well. This was seen, for example, in the consideration of the colonial gazetteers and census data, with the external categorization of identity labels; though the individuals therein would have undoubtedly ascribed their identities in a different manner. Similarly in relation to the archaeological data from Bahrain, the Carmathians were ascribed a heretical identity externally, but internally they would have considered themselves Muslims, and individually identity labels could, as has been described, have been much more diverse and variable.

In conclusion this chapter has indicated something of the complexities of identity evident in the Arabian Gulf, where much of the material is from historically supported contexts, or sometimes allied with extant identity groups. The practice of interpretation is difficult enough here, but in prehistoric contexts devoid of such supporting evidence such a task is even more challenging. Finally it is hoped that archaeologists working in the Gulf will begin to rise to the challenge of acknowledging both the 'human' element within their material, and that it reflects identity in all its complex and variable forms. In so doing this should allow the debate on identity manifestations and their archaeological recognition to become more focused, and for archaeologists working in the Gulf to become contributors to the development of relevant theoretical approaches rather than being either merely passive recipients or avoiding them altogether.

Acknowledgements

Thanks are extended to the Crown Prince Court of Bahrain, BAPCO, and the AHRC as major sponsors of the Early Islamic Bahrain Project. The authorities in the Bahrain National Museum (Abdurahman Musameh and Khaled al-Sindi) and the Department of Heritage (Dr Yateem) are also gratefully acknowledged for permission to complete the research. The author would also like to thank all the team in Bahrain for their assistance, but especially Mustafa Salman without whom the day-to-day practicalities could not have been achieved.

Bibliography

Afolayan, F. 1998. Zanj Slave Revolts (c. 689–883). In Rodriguez, J.P. (ed.), *The Historical Encyclopedia of World Slavery*. Santa Barbara: ABC Clio, p. 713.
Ahmed, A.S. 1988. *Discovering Islam: Making Sense of Muslim History and Society*. London: Routledge.
Ahmed, L. 1992. *Women and Gender in Islam*. New Haven: Yale University Press.
Ahsan, M. 1979. *Social Life Under the Abbasids*. London: Longman.

Al-Khan, W. 1991. The *Leewah* in Bahrain as an Art Form. *Al-Ma'thurat Al-Sha'biyyah* 21: 7–29.

Andersen, S.F. and Kennet, D. 2003. Sasanian and Islamic Pottery. In Hellmuth Andersen, H. and Højlund, F. *The Barbar Temples*. Moesgaard: Jutland Archaeological Society, pp. 307–10.

Anon. No Date. *Oman: The Modern State*. Muscat: Ministry of Information.

Anon. 2003. Parthian–Sasanian Sculpture. In Hellmuth Andersen, H. and Højlund, F. *The Barbar Temples*. Moesgaard: Jutland Archaeological Society, pp. 311–13.

Antony, D. 2001. Review of 'The Tarim Mummies' by J.P. Mallory and V. Mair. *Antiquity* 75: 627.

Arnold, B. 1990. The Past as Propaganda. Totalitarian Archaeology in Nazi Germany. *Antiquity* 64: 464–78.

Asad, T. 1986. *The Idea of an Anthropology of Islam*. Washington: Center for Contemporary Arab Studies.

Barth, F. 1969. Introduction. In Barth, F. (ed.), *Ethnic Groups and Boundaries: The Social Organisation of Cultural Difference*. Bergen: Universitets Forlaget, pp. 9–38.

Beaucamp, J. and Robin, C. 1983. L'Evêché Nestorien de Mâsèmâhîg dans L'Archipel d'Al-Bahrayn (Ve–IXe Siècle). In Potts, D.T. (ed.), *Dilmun: New Studies in the Archaeology and Early History of Bahrain*. Berlin: Dietrich Reimer Verlag, pp. 171–96.

Beck, L. and Keddie, N. (eds). 1978. *Women in the Muslim World*. Cambridge: Harvard University Press.

Belgrave, J.H.D. 1954. *Welcome to Bahrain*. Manama: J.H.D. Belgrave.

Bell, C. 1997. *Ritual Perspectives and Dimensions*. Oxford: Oxford University Press.

Bibby, G. 1996. *Looking for Dilmun*. London: Stacey International.

Boyce, M. 1991. Zoroastrianism. In Hinnells, J.R. (ed.), *A Handbook of Living Religions*. London: Penguin, pp. 171–90.

Cabana, C. 1999. Preface and Foreword. In Lombard, P. (ed.), *Bahrain: The Civilisation of the Two Seas*. Paris: Institut du Monde Arabe, pp. 14–15.

Daftary, F. 1998. *A Short History of the Ismailis*. Edinburgh: Edinburgh University Press.

De Goeje, M.J. 1862. *Mémoire sur les Carmathes du Bahrain*. Leiden: Brill.

Denny, F. 1985. Islamic Ritual: Perspectives and Theories. In Martin, R.C. (ed.), *Approaches to Islam in Religious Studies*. Tucson: University of Arizona Press, pp. 63–77.

Dobres, M.-A., and Robb, J. 2000. Agency in Archaeology: Paradigm or Platitude. In Dobres, M.-A. and Robb, J. (eds), *Agency in Archaeology*. London: Routledge, pp. 3–17.

Foucault, M. 1977. *Power/Knowledge*. London: The Harvester Press.

Freeman-Grenville, G.S.P. 1975. The Arab Geographers and the East African Coast. In Chittick, N. and Rotberg, R.I. (eds), *East Africa and the Orient*. New York: Africana Publishing Company, pp. 115–46.

Fuller, G.E. and Francke, R.R. 1999. *The Arab Shi'a*. New York: Palgrave.

Gero, J. and Conkey, M. 1991. *Engendering Archaeology*. Oxford: Blackwell.

Gilchrist, R. 1999. *Gender and Archaeology*. London: Routledge.

Halm, H. 1997. *Shi'a Islam: From Religion to Revolution*. Princeton: Markus Wiener.

Hansen, H.H. 1968. *Investigations in a Shi'a Village in Bahrain*. Copenhagen: National Museum of Denmark.

Hansman, J. 1985. *Julfar, An Arabian Port*. London: Royal Asiatic Society.

Hobsbawm, E. and Ranger, T. 1983. *The Invention of Tradition*. Cambridge: Cambridge University Press.

Højlund, F. 1994. Tylos. In Højlund, F. and Hellmuth Andersen, H. (eds), *Qala'at al-Bahrain: The Central Monumental Buildings*. Moesgaard: Jutland Archaeological Society, pp. 213–15.

Insoll, T. 1996. *Islam, Archaeology and History: Gao Region (Mali) Ca.AD 900–1250*. BAR S647. Oxford: Tempus Reparatum.

Insoll, T. 1999a. *The Archaeology of Islam*. Oxford: Blackwell.

Insoll, T. 1999b. *Case Studies in Archaeology and World Religion: The Proceedings of the Cambridge Conference*. BAR S755. Oxford: Archaeopress.

Insoll, T. 2001. *Archaeology and World Religion*. London: Routledge.

Insoll, T. 2003a. *The Archaeology of Islam in Sub-Saharan Africa*. Cambridge: Cambridge University Press.

Insoll, T. 2003b. Three Gold Dinars from Bahrain. *Numismatic Chronicle* (Un-numbered): 395–8.

Insoll, T. 2004. *Archaeology, Ritual, Religion*. London: Routledge.

Insoll, T. 2005. *The Land of Enki in the Islamic Era: Pearls, Palms, and Religious Identity in Bahrain*. London: Kegan Paul.

Jenkins, R. 1994. Rethinking Ethnicity: Identity, Categorization and Power. *Ethnic and Racial Studies* 17: 197–223.

Jones, S. 1997. *The Archaeology of Ethnicity*. London: Routledge.

Kennet, D. 1997. Kush: A Sasanian and Islamic-Period Archaeological Tell in Ras al-Khaimah (U.A.E.). *Arabian Archaeology and Epigraphy* 8: 284–302.

Kervran, M. 1982. *Excavation of Qal'at al-Bahrain*. Manama: Ministry of Information.

Kervran, M. 1996. Indian Ceramics in Southern Iran and Eastern Arabia: Repertory, Classification, Chronology. In Ray, H.P. and Salles, J.-F. (eds), *Tradition and Archaeology: Early Maritime Contacts in the Indian Ocean*. New Delhi: Manshar, pp. 37–58.

King, G. 1998. *Abu Dhabi Islands Archaeological Survey*. London: Trident Press.

Langfeldt, J.A. 1994. Recently Discovered Early Christian Monuments in North Eastern Arabia. *Arabian Archaeology and Epigraphy* 5: 32–60.

Larsen, C.E. 1983. *Life and Land Use on the Bahrain Islands*. Chicago: University of Chicago Press.

Lewis, B. 1973. *Islam in History*. London: Alcove Press.

Lorimer, J.G. 1908. *Gazetteer of the Persian Gulf, Oman, and Central Arabia. Volume 2. Geographical and Statistical*. Calcutta: Superintendent Government Printing India.

Lorimer, J.G. 1915. *Gazetteer of the Persian Gulf, Oman, and Central Arabia. Volume 1. Historical*. Calcutta: Superintendent Government Printing India.

Meskell, L. 1998. Introduction: Archaeology Matters. In Meskell, L. (ed.), *Archaeology Under Fire*. London: Routledge, pp. 1–12.

Meskell, L. 2001. Archaeologies of Identity. In Hodder, I. (ed.), *Archaeological Theory Today*. Cambridge: Polity, pp. 187–213.

Nowell, J. 1999. *Now and then Bahrain*. Dubai: Zodiac Publishing.

Petrushevsky, I.P. 1985. *Islam in Iran*. London: Athlone Press.

Porter, V. 2001. Arabic Inscriptions from Qala'at al-Bahrain Excavations. In Frifelt, K. 2001. *Islamic Remains in Bahrain*. Moesgaard: Jutland Archaeological Society, pp. 201–7.

Potts, D.T. 1985. Reflections on the History and Archaeology of Bahrain. *Journal of the American Oriental Society* 105: 675–710.

Potts, D.T. 1990. *The Arabian Gulf in Antiquity*. Oxford: Clarendon Press.

Potts, D.T. 1998. The Gulf Arab States and their Archaeology. In Meskell, L. (ed.), *Archaeology Under Fire*. London: Routledge, pp. 189–99.

Rippin, A. 1990. *Muslims: Their Religious Beliefs and Practices*. London: Routledge.

Risso, P. 1989. Muslim Identity in Maritime Trade: General Observations and Some Evidence from the Eighteenth Century Persian Gulf/Indian Ocean Region. *International Journal of Middle Eastern Studies* 21: 381–92.

Said, E. 1978. *Orientalism*. London: Routledge.

Salles, J.-F. 1983. *Barbar-Sud 1982*. Unpublished Report. Lyon: Maison de l'Orient Méditerranéen.

Salles, J.-F. 1999. Bahrain, from Alexander the Great to the Sasanians. In Lombard, P. (ed.), *Bahrain: The Civilisation of the Two Seas*. Paris: Institut du Monde Arabe, pp. 146–9.

Sasaki, T. 1990. Excavations at A'Ali – 1988/89. *Proceedings of the 23rd Seminar for Arabian Studies*. London: Society for Arabian Studies, pp. 111–29.

Scarce, J. 1985. *The Evolving Culture of Kuwait*. Edinburgh: Royal Scottish Museum.

Segal, R. 2001. *Islam's Black Slaves*. London: Atlantic Books.

Seikaly, M. 1994. Women and Social Change in Bahrain. *International Journal of Middle Eastern Studies* 26: 415–26.

Shaw, R. and Stewart, C. 1994. Introduction: Problematizing Syncretism. In Stewart, C. and Shaw, S. (eds), *Syncretism/Anti-Syncretism: The Politics of Religious Synthesis*. London: Routledge, pp. 1–26.

Shennan, S. 1989. Introduction: Archaeological Approaches to Cultural Identity. In Shennan, S. (ed.), *Archaeological Approaches to Cultural Identity*. London: Unwin Hyman, pp. 1–32.

Simpson, St J. 2000. Mesopotamia in the Sasanian Period: Settlement Patterns, Arts and Crafts. In Curtis, J. (ed.), *Mesopotamia and Iran in the Parthian and Sasanian Periods: Rejection and Revival c.238 BC–AD 642*. London: British Museum Press.

Tampoe, M. 1989. *Maritime Trade between China and the West*. British Archaeological Reports S555. Oxford: BAR.

Van Donzel, E. 1994. *Islamic Desk Reference*. Leiden: Brill.

Vine, P. 1993. *Bahrain National Museum*. London: Immel.

Waines, D. 1995. *An Introduction to Islam*. Cambridge: Cambridge University Press.

Index

Related titles from Routledge

Archaeology Coursebook, 2nd Edition
An Introduction to Study Skills, Topics and Methods

Jim Grant, Sam Gorin and Neil Fleming

This fully updated and revised new edition of the bestselling title *The Archaeology Coursebook*, is a guide for students studying archaeology for the first time. Including new methods and case studies in this second edition, it provides pre-university students and teachers, as well as undergraduates and enthusiasts, with the skills and technical concepts necessary to grasp the subject.

Specially designed to assist learning it:

- introduces the most commonly examined archaeological methods, concepts, and themes, and provides the necessary skills to understand them

- explains how to interpret the material students may meet in examinations and how to succeed with different types of assignments and exam questions

- supports study with case studies, key sites, key terms, tasks and skills development

- illustrates concepts and commentary with over 200 photos and drawings of excavation sites, methodology and processes, tools and equipment

- contains new material on British pre-history and the Roman Empire; new case studies, methods, examples, boxes, photographs and diagrams; as well as updates on examination changes for pre-university students.

A book no archaeology student should be without.

Hb: 0-415-36076-5
Pb: 0-415-36077-3

Available at all good bookshops
For ordering and further information please visit:
www.routledge.com

Related titles from Routledge

Archaeology: An Introduction
Fourth Edition

Kevin Greene

> 'The best one-stop introduction to archaeology.'
> Mick Aston, University of Bristol, Time Team

This substantially updated fourth edition of the highly popular, and comprehensive *Archaeology: An Introduction* is aimed at all beginners in the subject. In a lucid and accessible style Kevin Greene takes the reader on a journey which covers history, techniques and the latest theories. He explains the discovery and excavation of sites, outlines major dating methods, gives clear explanations of scientific techniques, and examines current theories and controversies.

This fourth edition constitutes the most extensive reshaping of the text to date. New features include:

- A completely new user-friendly text design with initial chapter overviews and final conclusions, key references for each chapter section, an annotated guide to further reading, a glossary, refreshed illustrations, case studies and examples, bibliography and full index

- A new companion website built for this edition providing hyperlinks from contents list to individual chapter summaries which in turn link to key websites and other material

- An important new chapter on current theory emphasizing the richness of sources of analogy or interpretation available today.

Archaeology: An Introduction will interest students and teachers at pre-university and undergraduate level as well as enthusiastic general readers of archaeology. The stimulating coverage of the history, methods, science and theory of archaeology make this a book which has a life both within and beyond the academy.

Hb: 0-415-23354-2
Pb: 0-415-23355-0

Available at all good bookshops
For ordering and further information please visit:
www.routledge.com